THE BROKEN SEAL

"*Operation Magic*"
and the Secret Road
to Pearl Harbor

by **Ladislas Farago**

Westholme Publishing / Yardley

Westholme Publishing, LLC
904 Edgewood Road
Yardley, Pennsylvania 19067
Visit our Web site at www.westholmepublishing.com

ISBN: 978-1-59416-171-1
Also available as an eBook.

Printed in the United States of America.

FOR MY WIFE

If you at last must have a word to say
Say neither, in their way,
"It is a deadly magic and accursed,"
Nor "It is blest," but only "It is here."

—Stephen Vincent Benét,
John Brown's Body, Book 8

This book does not presume to present anything like a comprehensive prehistory of the Pacific War; it is rather the story of a widely discussed and yet still very little known activity—the role of cryptological espionage in the gradual erosion and eventual break of Japanese-American relations over a period of two decades.

It is no secret, of course, that the United States had succeeded in breaking the Japanese diplomatic codes, first in 1920 and then in 1940, and was thus privy to Japan's innermost confidences up to the hour of the commencement of hostilities. The fact that we could read their secret dispatches raises a festering question: Since we possessed this fantastic source of intelligence about an enemy who was poised to make, as Mr. Churchill phrased it, the most fearful plunge in its long romantic history, why did we fail to anticipate the blow?

The question was answered but only tentatively and in a partisan spirit, despite seven grand inquisitions, including the mammoth inquest of the Joint Congressional Committee.

Our failure—deliberate or otherwise—to resolve the historic question left doubts in many minds about the sagacity and honesty of President Roosevelt and his Administration. While it raised the crucial issue of responsibility, it failed—to the detriment of the nation's conscience—to settle it.

This book attempts to answer the question, as definitively as possible, by presenting all facts, including many which have been omitted by the previous probes.

Contents

THE BROKEN SEAL

"This Means War!"

December 6, 1941, was a tranquil, ordinary Saturday in Washington. The United States was complacently at peace, confident that no mad rush of events could possibly mar the pleasant routine of the balmy weekend, with its full schedule of football games and early Christmas shopping. From what they were told, Americans had every reason to be smugly confident.

Colonel Frank Knox chose this day to issue his annual report as Secretary of the Navy to the President of the United States. A robust document, reflecting the Secretary's innate optimism and journalistic flair, and studded with glittering claims, it was calculated to give the American people the reassurance they wanted, and the Japanese the warning they apparently needed.

"I am proud to report," Mr. Knox wrote, "that the American people may feel fully confident in their Navy. In my opinion, the loyalty, the morale and technical ability of the personnel are without superior. On any comparable basis, the United States Navy is second to none."

At this moment the Navy was indeed what the Secretary claimed—a mighty force deployed in two oceans, capable of supporting the policy Mr. Knox had spelled out in his report. "Our aim must always be," he wrote, "to have forces sufficient to enable us to have complete freedom of action in either ocean while retaining forces in the other ocean for effective defense of our vital security. Anything less than this strength is hazardous to the security of the nation."

A pleasant late-fall day was drawing to its close—an *ordinary* day, for, after all, this was not yet "the day before Pearl Harbor." The government offices had slowed down for the weekend. Only skeleton crews had reported for work during the day, even in the State, War and Navy departments, which were most closely involved in the acute crisis in Japanese-American relations. By four-thirty the last of the Saturday shifts had left for home. The avenues and the bridges crowded up quickly, then emptied again just as fast.

Never a city to roar or fume, and ostentatious only in its inert external splendor, the capital became very quiet by nightfall. It was quietest in the vast circle around the monolithic stone shaft of the Washington Monument, where the massive government buildings stood.

The baroque contours of the Old State Building seemed faintly etched against the darkness of Pennsylvania Avenue. The huge new Pentagon loomed dark beyond the Potomac. In the Munitions Building on Constitution Avenue, where the War Department and the General Staff were housed, only a few scattered watches remained on duty in the handful of branches that worked around the clock. Next door the rambling low wooden structure of the Navy Department was eerily ablaze. But there was no fuss and flutter at the center of Mr. Knox's mighty Navy, no unusual activity to reflect the preparedness of which the Secretary spoke in his report—the lights were kept on for the char force. Downstairs four young Marines lounged in the Provost Marshal's guard room off the main entrance.

Of the dozen men who grappled with the crisis in the top echelons, not one was at his desk. Secretaries Cordell Hull, Henry L. Stimson and Frank Knox, old men no longer bound by the obligations of Washington's social life, were at home. So was General George C. Marshall, the Army Chief of Staff, spending the evening with his bed-ridden wife, who had broken a few ribs in a fall a few weeks before. Admiral Harold R. Stark, the Chief of Naval Operations, was at the National Theater with Captain Harold D. Krick, an old friend, watching a performance of Sigmund Romberg's operetta *The Student Prince*.

Stark's chief of War Plans, Rear Admiral Richard Kelly Turner, was alone at home with his pet Lhasa terriers, taking them for long walks in Chevy Chase. Rear Admiral Leigh Noyes, the Director of Naval Communications, was at a neighborhood movie with Mrs. Noyes.

Captain Theodore S. Wilkinson, the Director of Naval Intelligence, had also gone home at half past four. Walking out of the Navy Building toward his car in a rear lot along Potomac Park, he chatted with Turner and a group of younger officers.

"You're mistaken, Kelly," Wilkinson had said to Turner.

"Mistaken in what?" Turner asked a bit gruffly.

"Mistaken that the Japs would attack the United States."

Now Wilkinson was at his home in suburban Arlington, at a dinner party he was giving for Brigadier General Sherman Miles, the chief of Military Intelligence. Other guests around the table were Captain John R. Beardall, the President's naval aide, Captain Roscoe E. Schuirmann, the Navy's liaison officer at the State Department, and their wives.

It was a pleasant party. All talk about Japan was avoided in front of the ladies.

The White House, too, seemed quiet, only a cluster of big bulbs illuminating the pillared portico off Pennsylvania Avenue, and the dimmed lamps of the inner corridors shimmering in the window-panes.

But there was faint light upstairs, behind a row of curtained windows. President Franklin D. Roosevelt was at his desk in his oval-shaped private office on the second floor of the Executive Mansion. There was a miasmic tension in the White House air, caused by the uncertainties of the situation rather than by any premonitions of an acute emergency.

At half past nine Lieutenant Robert Lester Schulz, a young naval officer standing the late watch in the White House mailroom, reported to the President with a locked dispatch box that had just come over from the Office of Naval Intelligence. When Mr. Roosevelt opened the pouch with a key he had, dangling on a chain, he found the transcript of a long telegram from the Foreign Ministry in Tokyo to the Japanese ambassador in Washington, with the text of what appeared to be a meticulously worded diplomatic note designed for presentation to the American government.

The President spent the next twenty minutes studying the

document, then said to Harry L. Hopkins, who was keeping him company at this late hour:

"This means war!"

He uttered the words—somberly but without even a trace of apprehension—almost exactly fifteen hours before the bombs began to fall on Pearl Harbor.

Why, then, did he not act upon this recognition?

Why did he sit back, go to bed and spend half of the next fateful day idling in the White House, in the face of this ominous document whose hidden message he apparently understood?

Why did Pearl Harbor happen?

PART I

The Code Crackers

Herbert O. Yardley and the "American Black Chamber"

It is possible that the United States would not have gone in for code-breaking when it did if a probationary clerk in the State Department's Code Room had not become bored on the night shift. To relieve the monotony of his nocturnal watch, the young man—whose job it was to send and receive the diplomatic dispatches but not to encode or decode them—began to play with encrypted telegrams passing through his hands.

It proved a fascinating game. By and by the supposedly safe codes and ciphers * of the United States crumbled under his

---

* Since secret writing is an inexact science, its terminology is imprecise and often confusing. The term *cryptology* covers both *cryptography*, the process of rendering plain text incomprehensible, and *cryptanalysis*, the methodical study of crypto-systems and the reconversion of crypts into plain text. The two basic crypto-systems are *codes* and *ciphers*. Code is a system of letters, numbers, words and symbols with certain specific meanings attributed to them. A cipher may use any letter of the alphabet as a substitute for another (*substitution cipher*) or it may transpose them (*transposition cipher*); it may spell words backward, make arbitrary divisions between words, or substitute numerals or symbols for letters. Ciphers are made increasingly complicated by the multiple use of transpositions or substitutions or the scrambling of numerals or symbols, or by the insertion of dummy letters.

Coding, encoding, enciphering or *encrypting* is the conversion of plain or clear text into *cryptograms* or *crypts*. *Decoding, deciphering* or *decrypting* is the reverse process. In the vernacular of cryptology, the word "code" is used as a generic term. It may mean either a code *per se* or a pure cipher or both, or

attack. He tried his hand at a few foreign dispatches and succeeded in cracking their codes as well. All this was highly irregular,
of course. But the young man overcame his qualms by convincing
himself that he was performing a patriotic service. He hoped to
demonstrate that the American system of codes was vulnerable.
Then, as a reward for his important contribution to the security of
the nation, he expected to move up on the ladder in the government's tight little cryptographic establishment. This enterprising
junior telegraphist was Herbert Osborne Yardley, one of the truly
remarkable figures in the twilight world of cryptology.

In the earliest days of the Republic, the primitive first office of
this kind was both the nerve center and symbol of revolutionary
diplomacy, as the original name of the State Department—Committee of Secret Correspondence—illustrated.

The first code clerk, in fact even if not yet in name, was Richard
Forrest, hired when John Quincy Adams was Secretary of State.
But it was only in 1867 that the first regular code room was set up,
with Thomas Morrison in charge.

In 1873 the Code Room was placed in the newly established
Bureau of Archives and Indexes in the Old State Building at 17th
Street on Pennsylvania Avenue. By 1910 it had 29 clerks and
telegraphists out of a total of 135 in the entire Department,
handling ten thousand documents and some one thousand telegrams each month, under David A. Salmon, hired from the War
Department.

The Code Room was the clearing house of America's diplomatic
correspondence, to be sure. But it had none of the conspiratorial
air of similar establishments in other countries. It was on the
ground floor of the hideous granite structure, a high-ceilinged and
airy office set back from the street by a pillared alcove overlooking
the tennis courts on the White House grounds. It smelled sweet of
aromatic coffee and was always shrouded in a haze of pale blue
cigarette smoke.

In the center of the Code Room stood two huge flat-top desks,
over which the code clerks huddled, encrypting or decrypting
telegrams. Scattered about were several specially constructed type-

---

an encoded cipher or enciphered code in which both code elements and cipher
systems are combined. Codes and ciphers are solved, broken, compromised,
"taken out," "cracked" or "recovered."

writers, capable of making fifteen copies of a dispatch in a single operation. There was an enormous safe in one corner to "secure" the code books when not in use, and a battery of steel cabinets in which file copies of old telegrams were stored.

Along the western wall was the long table of the telegraphists, cluttered with their paraphernalia—resonators, sounders and other gadgets going clickety-clack all day and part of the night. Though the area was supposedly restricted—the doors had to be locked at all times—the State Department's Code Room was a favorite meeting place, where the diplomatic crowd could talk shop or barter gossip in a congenial atmosphere during their coffee breaks.

This, then, was the office which Herb Yardley joined the morning after New Year's Day in 1913, as a junior telegraphist at $17.50 a week. He moved in boldly, with a sophisticated air about him that belied his Midwest origin and modest background. Born on April 13, 1889, in Worthington, Indiana, Yardley was the son of a Pennsylvania Railroad agent, and a graduate of the public schools of Worthington and Eaton Rapids, Michigan, the last word in his formal education.

But he was a wizard with the Morse key. When he was a boy he had learned telegraphy in his father's office at the Pennsy station and worked at it all his free time, even while his friends were playing baseball. After graduation he became a telegrapher at the Western Union office at Vincennes, the county seat some forty miles from his home town, then moved to Washington with a pocketful of dreams. After a year or so with one of the telegraph companies, he was appointed a "clerk in the $900 class, on probation, under Civil Service rules" in the State Department.

A tall, handsome young man, always impeccably groomed and having a penchant for bow ties, Yardley was suave, glib, alert, intelligent and ambitious. He was not at all awed by the mysteries of the Code Room or the pseudo-Continental air of the Department. Nor was it long before he was convinced that he was at least as smart as any of the veteran code clerks, and as polished and wise in the ways of the world as the "smartly dressed pygmies," as he called the younger set of career men he watched strutting about with affected mannerisms.

He had come to the Code Room with great expectations and

was raring to assert himself. But he found nothing but drudgery in this inner sanctum, tedious work performed by plodding, unaspiring, overworked nonentities. "Daily," Yardley wrote, "history passed through their hands in one long stream and they thought less of it than of the baseball scores. The murder of Madero, the shelling of Veracruz, the rumblings of threatening World War—these merely meant telegrams, longer hours—nothing else."

Yardley cultivated the friendship of the one high-ranking diplomat in the department who was not a regular Foreign Service officer. He was William T. S. Doyle, a New York lawyer "little interested in drawing rooms and amorous intrigues." Doyle had been brought into the Department in 1907, to aid in the "implementation" of what became known as "dollar diplomacy." It was a brash effort to utilize the dollar in support of the expansion of American interests in the world.

Yardley found in Doyle what he vainly sought in others. He admired his buccaneering approach to the conduct of America's diplomacy. Eager to learn the confidential background of events in South America in which his idol had played an important but inconspicuous part, he took from the shelves the old telegrams which contained the record of Doyle's machinations. By then his interest in diplomacy was all-consuming.

In his eagerness to climb out of the doldrums of his technical job, he sought out, with Doyle's help, an area nobody in this sleepy cryptographic bureau seemed to be interested in. As he read the telegrams about the Venezuelan incident, when German and British warships laid siege to La Guaira, the seaport of Caracas, to force the bankrupt regime of President Cipriano Castro to pay the overdue installments on the country's foreign debts, he became fascinated by the inside story the telegrams revealed. What, he thought, if the British had succeeded in breaking through to the secret of these coded telegrams from Doyle to Washington? Yardley assumed that foreign countries, long experienced in procuring vital intelligence by breaking codes, were continuing the practice.

Why, he asked himself, did the American government not have a bureau of its own for interpreting secret diplomatic telegrams of other governments? Suddenly he had found what he was seeking— a purpose in his profession, a mission in his life.

Without taking any of his colleagues into his confidence or bothering to get permission from his superiors, Yardley began, in the methodic manner that was one of his great assets, to train himself as a cryptographer and as a code breaker. He read everything he could find in the Department and the Library of Congress about the subject; from Edgar Allan Poe's elementary writings to the United States Army's manuals about military ciphers.

He began by testing his new skill on a few telegrams a friend at one of the telegraph offices in Washington had "borrowed" for him from the diplomatic pile. He was amazed how simple it was to break their codes.

By then it was 1915 and Europe was at war. But in the United States, business continued as usual despite the country's involvement in a comic-opera "war" with Pancho Villa in Mexico. Yardley himself had been transferred to the night shift in the Code Room, where he now whiled away his idle hours by working on his hobby.

On one of those nights he was roused from his tedium by a call from New York on the wire, alerting the White House to a five-hundred-word message from Colonel Edward M. House, Woodrow Wilson's confidant. House was in Europe, trying to persuade the belligerents to make peace. Yardley was electrified. This was his opportunity to test the most important and supposedly safest American code, the one used by the President himself.

He took down the telegram, started working on the code—and had it cracked in two hours. The message that emerged from the crypt made him angry. It contained highly confidential information from inside Germany of great value to the British, who, as Yardley knew, were monitoring all such traffic. And what about the Germans; were they also intercepting such messages? Was House an unwitting tool of British and German intelligence? And how could the White House be so reckless as to entrust such vital messages to a cipher even a schoolboy could break?

During the following months Yardley avidly read all that was passing on the wire from and to the White House. He became privy to his country's highest confidences, much of which Wilson was withholding even from the State Department. It was the most frustrating period of his life. There he was, informed beyond compare, yet unable to flaunt his knowledge. And he was aware of the woeful deficiency of the White House cipher, yet could not let "them" know that it was so easy to crack.

He had also succeeded in breaking the whole set of ciphers the State Department was using, but was reluctant to warn his superior, David A. Salmon. Salmon was responsible for the preparation of these codes and ciphers, and was smug in his belief that they were safe. Yardley thought it might be a blow to the old man's professional pride, and maybe even a threat to his own job, if he revealed what he knew.

But finally he decided to take the matter up with Salmon. He wrote a hundred-page memorandum entitled "Solution of American Diplomatic Codes," and, prepared for the worst, presented it to his superior. But Salmon was too big a man to take this as a personal rebuff. He called Yardley's opus "a masterly analysis" and set to work at once to devise new codes he hoped this young wizard could not break.

In early May 1917 Yardley told Salmon that he was entering the Army, where he hoped to be commissioned in the Signal Corps. He left shortly afterward, with the best wishes of Assistant Secretary of State William Phillips, and with word from Salmon to Major General George O. Squier, the Chief Signal Officer, that the Army was getting "a magician with codes and ciphers" and that he had better keep an eye on the young man.

General Squier was interested in Yardley's suggestion that the Signal Corps set up a special cipher bureau, but in the chaotic first months of the war, when he was struggling with the infinite technical problems of the Signal Corps, he was not especially eager to add such a potential headache to his other woes. He shunted Yardley to Colonel George S. Gibbs with instructions to find a billet for him.

Colonel Gibbs called a major at the War College, told him that he was sending "somebody" to see him—and the Signal Corps was rid of Yardley. The major at the War College was Ralph H. Van Deman (remembered as the "Father of American Military Intelligence"). Just then the diminutive major was working around the clock in a tiny office at the War College to revamp the intelligence organization of the General Staff.

Yardley poured out his heart to Van Deman. He told him his grandiose ideas about a supersecret cipher-bureau operation under cover in the Intelligence Division, and outlined, without any false modesty, the contribution he thought he could make to it.

At this very first meeting a new section was added to Military Intelligence—M.I.8, as it came to be called—to handle "the cryptographic needs of the Intelligence Division." Major Van Deman, thoroughly impressed with his visitor's qualifications, named Yardley to head it, with the rank of lieutenant, and established him, amidst elaborate secrecy, first in a makeshift office on the balcony of the War College Library, then in an apartment at 15th and M streets, and finally on the top floor of a house on F Street in downtown Washington, next door to where the National Press Club Building now stands.

Yardley organized M.I.8 in five subsections: (1) Code and Cipher Compilation (to "build" some of the Army's own codes and ciphers); (2) Communications; (3) Shorthand (to "recover" the text of intercepted documents written in one or another of about thirty different stenographic systems); (4) Secret Ink Laboratory; and (5) Code and Cipher Solution (also called "Code Instruction," presumably to camouflage its true functions), the cryptanalytical subsection.

Among Yardley's aides in M.I.8 were some of the true pioneers of cryptology in the United States. The staff included Major Arthur Newgarden of G-2; Dr. (Captain) John M. Manly, an expert on Chaucer who headed the English Department at the University of Chicago; Miss Edith Rickert, a philologist and coauthor of the monumental *Text of the Canterbury Tales*; Charles J. Mendelsohn, a historian and linguist; a mysterious German-American stamp dealer named Victor Weiskopf; Thomas A. Knott, an associate professor of English; Frederick Bliss Luquiens, who taught Spanish at Yale; David H. Stevens, an English instructor; and Charles H. Beeson, a Latin scholar. It was a relatively young crowd. At fifty-two, Manly was the patriarch of the group. Yardley, who was then twenty-eight years old, was its youngest member.

Also serving in M.I.8 as Major Newgarden's successor as executive officer was (Captain) George Waldo Bicknell, who was to gain prominence later in American counterintelligence in Hawaii on the eve of Pearl Harbor. Yardley himself was chiefly interested in Subsection 5. Its assignment was to crack the codes and ciphers of the country's enemies, and was the first American organization of this kind to be made a firm fixture anywhere within the government of the United States.

Yardley performed brilliantly during the war, mostly catching spies by compromising their codes. In the final analysis, however, his wartime service was useful to him mainly because it enabled him to complete his cryptographic education. It was only toward the end of the war, in August 1918, that he managed to get overseas, and then merely to study the cryptographic establishments of the Allies.

Yardley's tour of duty in Europe—first as a sightseer and then as the cryptographer of the American delegation at the peace conference in Paris—had a profound influence on him. What he saw in Versailles of European diplomacy, with its polished hypocrisy and elegant by-play of plots and counterplots, baffled this man, whose own cunning was of a coarser make. What especially rankled him was that he had been snubbed by his British and French colleagues, to whom he was but an upstart at the old game. And he, who was pampered and praised in Military Intelligence, was ignored even by his own delegation, whose members—the "smartly dressed pygmies" he loathed during his years with the State Department—felt deeply embarrassed by his adventurous approach to cryptography.

Forever producing breathless scoops from his flotsam of broken codes, Yardley once claimed that, in a telegram he had decoded, he had discovered a plot to poison President Wilson. He traced the plot, not to the Germans, bitter in defeat, but to the French and British secret services. When he took his discovery to his diplomatic liaison man, he was admonished to be careful with such reckless charges. Yardley never forgot or forgave the rebuff, and was convinced to the end of his days that Wilson's debilitating illness, which was to make him a shadow President during his second term, had had its origin in the Allied poison plot no one but he was willing to take seriously.

Yardley returned from abroad a bitter and cynical man, consumed by hatreds—of President Wilson (who, to him, was a "tyrant schoolmaster"); of Walter H. Page, the American ambassador in London (because Page touted Admiral Sir Reginald Hall, Yardley's chief British "competitor"); and of all "goddam foreigners."

In Washington an even greater disappointment awaited him. The Intelligence Division was in an advanced stage of decomposition. The war was over. There was a rush back to normalcy. The military establishment was being cut down to size, left to subsist on a niggardly budget. There remained, it seemed, no place in the American system for the kind of activity Yardley had been allowed to practice during the war.

He tried frantically to save his section, but it seemed hopeless. M.I.8 was slated to be eradicated, with not even a trace left of its past to betray that it had ever existed.

Yardley was not alone in his efforts to save the cipher bureau. Every war produces men whose dormant penchant for machinations is given wide scope during hostilities, and who then find it difficult to return to the normalcy of peace. The Intelligence Division was full of them. And they had a vigorous sponsor in Brigadier General Marlborough Churchill, director of Military Intelligence toward the end of the war, who was also chafing under the limitations peace threatened to place upon his craft.

Churchill decided to save at least one of its branches that could by itself assure to the United States "an intimate knowledge of the true sentiments and intentions of other nations." He let M.I.8 go down the drain; there was nothing he could do about that. But he was determined to preserve Subsection 5, the Code and Cipher Solution subsection, as intact as possible.

It was not an easy undertaking to keep alive such a sensitive agency and tuck it away deep underground in the government. General Churchill had still another problem to solve. He could scrape up only $60,000 from his unvouchered funds for the new agency. But Yardley estimated he would need a minimum of $100,000 annually to run an efficient code-breaking bureau.

The Navy Department, where communications security was a fetish, refused to join Churchill's venture. But then a solution was suggested. Who would benefit most from code-cracking in peace time? The State Department, of course! Why not invite State to buy into the business, at a bargain price of only $40,000 a year?

The State Department also had its quota of little Machiavellis

—Acting Secretary of State (former Counselor) Frank Lyon Polk among them, and a career officer named William Hurley who headed the Foreign Intelligence Division. They both knew Yardley and regarded him highly; Polk from his State Department days, and Hurley from the peace conference, where he alone thought that the euphoric code master had something on the ball.

A deal was quickly made, but then a peculiar problem arose. It was precisely in order to prevent the State Department from engaging in this kind of secret diplomacy that the rules by which its special funds were set up prohibited their expenditure within the District of Columbia.

"How about New York?" Yardley asked.

"There is nothing in the law to prevent us from spending special-funds money there," Hurley said.

"Well," Yardley shot back, "why don't we put up the bureau in New York?"

The project was approved, and Yardley was sent to New York to find "a suitable place where the famous American Black Chamber * could bury itself from the prying eyes of foreign governments."

In New York, "Bozo"—Yardley's code name in the new operation—established himself first in the former town house of T. Suffern Taylor at 3 East 38th Street, and then in a four-story brownstone at 141 East 37th Street, between Park and Lexington avenues in a quiet residential section. He used the top floor as his

* Yardley's clandestine organization in New York had no official name, and when reference was made to it at all, it was discretely called "the Yardley bureau." Yardley's choice of the name "black chamber" was a misnomer. His bureau was not the old *chambre noire* of European absolutism but a much older institution, the *camera decrittazione* or *camera decifratoria*, as it was called in fourteenth-century Florence. They were secret agencies of expert cryptanalysts employed to unravel the secret correspondence of the princes. The "black chamber"—*cabinet noir* or *schwarzes Kabinett*—was a censorship bureau run by the secret-police organization in countries like Czarist Russia and the France of Joseph Fouché. They were *domestic* agencies set up to stem revolutionary tides or antimonarchist movements by steaming open the envelopes of suspicious letters and gaining clues to activities threatening the states through the exalted person of the sovereigns. Yardley's adoption of the name for his bureau was an affront to Americans. Never in peacetime was the privacy of the mail violated in the United States, not even between 1919 and 1929, when Yardley indulged in his indiscriminate cryptanalysis.

living quarters. He moved in with all the paraphernalia inherited from M.I.8—a library of dictionaries, maps, reference books, mathematical and statistical texts, reconstructed codes and a huge morgue of newspaper clippings with a bearing on foreign affairs.

Working with Yardley in New York were some of his old associates from M.I.8 and a number of new recruits—Manly, Mendelsohn, Weiskopf, Miss Rickert, also a young Harvard-bred businessman named Frederick Livesey, John Meeth, and two young ladies, Ruth Willson and Edna Ramsaier. Meeth served as Yardley's chief clerk; Livesey moved up rapidly in the secret hierarchy, and with a salary of $3000 a year, eventually became the deputy chief of the "black chamber." Miss Ramsaier, in a different process of advancement, became the second Mrs. Yardley.

At last Yardley was his own boss, doing as he pleased. He was comfortably off. His new job was paying him $7500 a year, considerably more than his first salary of $900 at the State Department or his major's pay during the war. Money was an important consideration with Yardley. He was a man of expensive tastes, as well as an inveterate gambler and a heavy drinker.

In July 1919 General Dennis E. Nolan, Churchill's successor in Military Intelligence, sent for Yardley. His friends in the State Department had something in mind they wanted to discuss with him. At the meeting in Washington, John Van Antverp McMurray, chief of the Division of Far Eastern Affairs, put the question bluntly to Yardley:

"Could you do something about the Japanese codes?"

McMurray explained that Japan had risen to a place in the postwar world where it had to be regarded as one of the great powers. With a navy growing by leaps and bounds, she was confronting the United States with a direct challenge. "It is imperative for us," he continued, "that we have a pretty good idea of just what the Japanese are up to. We believe we could get the guidance we need from their diplomatic dispatches."

This was Yardley's great moment of triumph in the State Department. As he himself put it later: "They begged me to turn all my efforts to the unraveling of Japanese secrets." He assured McMurray that he would either crack the Japanese diplomatic codes within a year or hand in his resignation.

Japan had indeed become the foremost adversary of the United

States. The Japanese of the Meiji era (1867–1912), groping their way out of the *shogunate* (feudatory government) toward modern imperialism, watched uneasily as America was getting one foothold after another in the Pacific—pushing on to the Samoan islands, to Hawaii, and collecting, somewhat haphazardly, scattered islands including Midway, Wake and Guam. In 1898 the Philippines were taken over. Then, in 1905, after her stunning victory over the Russians in the Far East, Japan emerged as a first-rate power.

Uncertainties and frictions multiplied. Just how solid a basis in the facts of international life there actually was for these frictions is difficult to say. But it is as much a truism in diplomacy as in psychology that if men define situations as real, they become real in their consequences.

The United States made two major moves—one overt, the other covert—to counter Japan's increasingly boisterous maneuvers. As an open and unmistakable gesture, elements of the American fleet were moved into the Pacific. And in strict secrecy the decision was now made to place Japan under surveillance by reading her confidential correspondence with the help of Herbert O. Yardley.*

Back in New York, Yardley went to work at once on the Japanese code system. The task was formidable. All he had to begin with were about a hundred Japanese telegrams. From each of them, columns of ten-letter code groups—like *yotomatoma, upuggeyity* and *pyokoemiso*, for example—stared at him. These mumbo-jumbo consonant-vowel or vowel-consonant combinations concealed words Yardley would not have understood even if they had been spelled out in plain text. He could read or speak no Japanese.

But he broke down the barriers one by one, pursuing doggedly the basic methodology of analytical cryptology. He collected elaborate statistics of the manner in which the letters, syllables and words were formed, then indexed the clues he thus gained. He

---

* This sensitive operation was not initiated in the highest echelons of the government. The President was not told of its existence. Neither was Newton D. Baker, Mr. Wilson's Secretary of War and Generals Churchill's and Nolan's civilian superior, whose intelligence department was in charge of the operation. Nobody in Congress was admitted to the secret.

recorded separately the beginnings and endings of the different telegrams. In due course this yielded dividends. The data led Yardley to believe that the Japanese were using two-letter elements in their codes, such as *py* or *ok* or *mo*, and so on.

Early in his effort Yardley had compiled an arbitrary table of *kana*, the Japanese syllabic writing system of phonetic symbols, and added their Romanized forms.*

The idea of a solution occurred to him one dawn while he was trying to catch some sleep after an uninterrupted twenty-hour session at work. Why not relate the contents of the telegrams to current topics in the news? He was sure that certain names of people and places would show up and recur in the encrypted text. This, he hoped, would provide points at which he could break into the crypt.

He jumped out of bed, ran downstairs to his office, removed his work sheets from the safe—and found what he sought. At that time the Sinn Fein movement was suppressed and the war between the Irish rebels and the British forces flared up. Yardley assumed that some of the telegrams he had under scrutiny might have in them the encoded forms of *A-i-ru-ra-n-do*, the Japanese spelling of Ireland. And he expected that occasionally *Airurando* would be followed by *do-ku-ri-tsu*, Japanese for "independence."

There, in several of the telegrams he was working on, he now found two code groups recurring at intervals—WIUBPOMOIL and REREOSOKBO, each consisting of five two-letter code elements.

Working on his hunch, Yardley assumed that WI stood for "a," UB for "i," PO for "ru," MO for "ra," IL for "n." With RE borrowed from the next group and standing for "do," he had WIUBPOMOILRE, which could add up to *Airurando*, or Ireland. It then followed that RE of the rest of the second group stood for

* In the eighth century the Japanese developed a method of writing by adapting Chinese characters to Japanese phonetics. During the Heian period a phonetic script called *katakana* came to be used, made up of abbreviated Chinese ideographs. *Kana* is of two varieties—*katakana* and *hiragana* (running script). *Katakana* is composed of forty-five basic syllables and twenty sonants (*ga, za, da, ba*, etc.). There are also half-sonant sounds (*pa, pi, pu, pe, po*). In addition there are the contracted sounds, or *yo-on*, which are a combination of two *kana* symbols (as in *ka* + *tsu* or *ho* + *shi*). Dr. James C. Hepburn (1815–1911), an American Presbyterian medical missionary and educator, established the so-called Hepburn system of Romanization of the Japanese language by transcribing the *kana* into Roman letters.

"do," the first syllable in *dokuritsu,* and he took for granted that os stood for "ku," ok for "ri," and bo for "tsu," Japanese for "independence."

He had broken into the code! He had isolated nine syllables of the basic *kana.* It was an excellent beginning, and more than that. It was the first crack in the code which would ensure the eventual collapse of the entire system. He had penetrated to the principle of the Japanese system's structure, and at that stage of cryptology, the finding of the principle was tantamount to solution.*

On January 12, 1920, Yardley was able to send to Washington the first translation of a decrypted Japanese diplomatic dispatch. It was merely a sample. It still had gaping holes and far too many garbled passages. However, he gradually perfected the system. From the middle of 1920 on, the translations he forwarded to the State Department were complete and practically free of garbles.

The triumph could not have been better timed.

Interest in Japan had sharpened in Washington. A simmering dispute over Yap, one of the former German islands in Micronesia the Japanese had occupied in 1914, flared into a violent controversy at the International Communications Conference held in Washington in the fall of 1920. The United States objected to permanent occupation of the island group by the Japanese. One of the submarine cables linking North America with eastern Asia ran through Yap, and the American government found it intolerable to leave such a vital line of cummunications to China, the Dutch East Indies, and especially to the Philippines, at the mercy of the Japanese.

During the dispute, Yardley's intercepts proved helpful in guiding the State Department in the controversy. Decoded telegrams revealed that the Japanese were indeed tampering with American

* The Japanese are convinced to this day that Yardley did not solve their codes by the analytical method but by gaining access to their code books, instructions and keys. In 1919 they discovered that crypto-material kept at their consulates in several South American countries had been tampered with. In early 1920 a code clerk named Yatanube absconded with the codes used by the Japanese delegation to the international maritime conference in Genoa, Italy, and sold them. The Japanese believe that Yardley was the buyer. Subsequently other Japanese codes were lost through the indiscretion of a Japanese guard named Sakawa, attached to the consulate at Manchouli, and the carelessness of an interpreter named Nakamura in Switzerland.

diplomatic and military messages passing through Yap. But even more important developments were in the making. An international conference on naval disarmament was to meet in Washington in November 1921. It was essential to have access to the Japanese telegrams that would be exchanged between the Foreign Ministry in Tokyo and its delegation in Washington.

2   **Diplomatic Stud Poker**

November 1921 was unseasonably warm in Washington, but there was something in the air that made the climate invigorating—the spectacle of a major international conference.

The hotels were filled to overflowing. Up and down the streets swept limousines with flags of nine countries on their fenders. Assembled in the auditorium of the dainty Pan-American Building were many of the world's leading statesmen—Arthur Balfour and Lord Leed of the British Empire, Alfred Sze and Wellington Koo of China, Aristide Briand of France, and Navy Minister Tomosaburo Kato, Prince Tokugawa and Admiral Hiroharu Kato of Japan. The American delegation was headed by the formidable Charles Evans Hughes, Secretary of State in the new Harding Administration, and included former Secretary of State Elihu Root and Senator Henry Cabot Lodge.

This was the halcyon period of diplomacy by conference. The great powers tried frantically to liquidate the troublesome legacy of World War I in meetings at San Remo, Hythe, Boulogne and Spa, in London, Paris and Geneva. Now it was Washington's turn. Mark Sullivan, the eminent correspondent of the Baltimore *Sun*, called the Washington Conference on Limitation of Armaments "the great adventure." It certainly was. But just how great the purely adventurous aspects of the conference would turn out to be, only a handful of men could know, and Sullivan was not one of them.

The conference met at the invitation of the United States government to consider problems of the Far East and naval armaments. It opened on November 12, with a prayer whose piety was surpassed by President Harding's opening speech. It bore no relation to what was to come in its immediate wake.

Secretary of State Hughes then rose and shocked the delegates by declaring: "The way to disarm is to disarm." He continued in the same vein to offer a series of blunt suggestions.

The American delegation proposed that the conference declare a ten-year naval holiday. During this period, a 5:5:3 ratio was to be maintained in capital ships by the United States, Britain and Japan, and no vessel of more than 10,000 tons with guns larger than 8-in. bores would be added to the fleets. Total tonnage of aircraft carriers was to be restricted, and a maximum size for capital ships, aircraft carriers and cruisers would be established.

The audacious plan created consternation among the delegates. Colonel Repington, military editor of the London *Times*, cabled to his paper: "Secretary Hughes sank in 35 minutes more ships than all the admirals in the world have sunk in a cycle of centuries." *

The American proposal forced the Japanese government into a strange quandary. Although it secretly favored a limitation of armaments on pressing economic grounds, it could not adhere to it without offering at least a token resistance, to placate the vociferous navalists at home. The Japanese delegation was instructed to oppose the American proposal and gain as a minimum concession an increase in the Japanese ratio.

That pushed the conference into a cul-de-sac. The remarkable feature of the deadlock was not Japan's objection. It was rather the uncompromising stand of the United States. By November 24 the newspapers gloomily predicted that the conference would adjourn without reaching an agreement. In London and Paris, Rome and Tokyo, the Americans were criticized for their inexplicable unwillingness to make any concessions. Their seemingly

---

* If the proposition stunned the other delegates who had no warning of the American plan, it scandalized the United States Navy. In the corridors of the conference during these days, American naval officers could be heard saying in a paraphrase of the gladiators' greeting: "We who are about to be abolished salute you."

unreasonable stand was attributed to the naïveté of American diplomats and the inexperience of the new Secretary of State. But on December 11, just when it seemed that the conference would collapse, the Japanese suddenly capitulated. Reading scribbled notes on a scrap of rice paper, Prince Tokugawa, president of the House of Peers and head of the Japanese delegation, announced Tokyo's unconditional surrender.

The agreement was formalized in the Five-Power Treaty of 1922. Ex-Secretary Elihu Root said with deep satisfaction at its signing on February 6: "I doubt if any formal treaty ever accomplished so much by doing so little."

Japan was the loser. "This humiliation," wrote Robert H. Ferrell in his history of American diplomacy, "preceded by refusal of the Paris Conference to grant the principle of racial equality, followed in 1924 by the United States's complete barring of Japanese immigration, badly hurt Japanese pride, serving to create a situation where not too many years later Japan would use mercilessly a deteriorating political situation in Europe to expand her power in Asia."

The United States was not usually noted for any special astuteness in diplomacy. Rather it was wont, as George F. Kennan expressed it, to excuse its recurrent failures with the "sacred untouchableness of its lofty habits."

Yet now it had scored a triumph so complete that it astounded the world and filled it with admiration for America's unsuspected diplomatic skill. How was it possible for Mr. Hughes, a newcomer to diplomacy, to emerge victorious in a head-on clash with the seasoned diplomatists of Britain, France and Japan? The American triumph was produced by a fortuitous combination of assets the State Department happened to possess at this time. In Secretary Hughes the State Department had a statesman of extraordinary stature, iron nerves and consummate forensic skill. And in Herbert O. Yardley's New York "black chamber" it had a source of first-hand intelligence, enabling the American negotiators to penetrate to the innermost confidences of the Japanese delegation.

Each day during the conference a courier had arrived from New York with a locked diplomatic pouch which he delivered into the

hands of John McMurray, chief of the State Department's Far
Eastern Division and also a member of the American delegation's
technical staff. The courier was Tracy Lay, a young Foreign Service officer on special duty at the Department for the conference.
He had been recalled from his consular post abroad to act as
confidential messenger, conveying to the Department the diplomatic telegrams Yardley's "black chamber" was decoding in a
steady flow.*

The first pertinent telegram he had decoded was dated July 10,
1921. It was from Baron Shidehara, the Japanese ambassador in
Washington, reporting to Tokyo an interview he had had with
Secretary Hughes the day before, during which he had learned
that the Harding Administration was planning to convene the
conference.

Several more messages were decoded and translated in the next
few days, including one on July 13 that indicated how invaluable
this intelligence would be for Hughes in planning and running the
conference. Tokyo was advising Shidehara to show no haste in
accepting the American initiative, because it seemed to be directed
mainly against Japan.

"What course the discussion might take is unknown," Tsuneo
Matsudaira, director of the Foreign Ministry's European and
American Department, told Shidehara, "but it would open the
possibility of our policy toward China and toward Siberia receiving
a check from the Powers."

Yardley's ability to procure this kind of intelligence assured the

---

* The "black chamber" was not confined to the decrypting of Japanese
telegrams. It had also broken the British diplomatic code and was reading
many of the telegrams of the London Foreign Office. It was, in fact, on the
impetus of certain British dispatches Yardley had decoded in the summer of
1921 that the Harding Administration conceived the idea of holding the
conference in Washington. The telegrams revealed that the Lloyd George
government was seriously concerned about an arms race between Britain, the
United States and Japan. They decided that a conference would be convenient
to forestall the costly competition, and prepared to convene it in London in
the fall. Determined to head off the British (and also to steal a march on
Senator William E. Borah of Idaho, who was making political hay by
"trumpeting for a conference"), President Harding had startled the world, on
July 11, with the offer to organize the conference in Washington. At the same
time invitations were issued to Britain, France, Italy, Japan, China, Portugal,
Belgium and The Netherlands.

State Department that it could learn in advance the plans and intentions of the adversary, and get an insight into his strengths and weaknesses, hopes and fears.

At this point, however, and even before Yardley's contribution could be of any real value, the operation suffered a setback that threatened to deprive State of its advantage. The Japanese suddenly decided to tighten the security of their communications. On July 15 they introduced a complicated new system they called the YU code.

Yardley had not only expected something like this—for it is customary in all chancelleries to change codes in preparation for important events—but had actually been trying to solve in advance the kind of code he assumed the Japanese would introduce. But all efforts to break the YU code failed. Yardley's bureau worked feverishly to find the key, but the new system defied solution throughout August and September.

Then the State Department received help from an unexpected quarter. The Office of Naval Intelligence succeeded in obtaining the advance information Mr. Hughes needed but could no longer obtain from Yardley.

When it had been decided to hold the conference in Washington, the high command of the United States Navy became keenly interested in finding out the attitude of the Japanese naval high command toward limitations of naval armaments. Captain Andrew T. Long, the Director of Naval Intelligence, instructed Captain Edward Howe Watson, the American naval attaché in Tokyo, to "explore the extent to which the Japanese [would be] willing to go in accepting a compromise solution."

Watson was an exceptionally astute and resourceful intelligence officer, ideal for the job in a country whose navy was considered the primary potential adversary of the United States Navy. He had a sounding board that enabled him to procure much of the firsthand information he needed. Once a week he would meet with influential members of the Japanese Naval General Staff in convivial, presumably off-duty celebrations at one of the elegant geisha houses of the Shimbashi district. The Japanese guests at these parties included Captain (later Admiral and Ambassador) Kichisaburo Nomura, who was then director of the *joho kyoku*, or Naval Intelligence; Captain (later Admiral and Chief of the

Naval Staff) Osami Nagano; and Commander (later Admiral, Premier and Navy Minister) Mitsumasa Yonai. It was a formidable little group, representing the powerful inner core of the Naval General Staff.

Watson enjoyed the confidence of these men, for he believed in giving information in exchange for what he was getting. He had devised a technique (by a judicious mixing of sensitive topics and powerful cocktails) to make his Japanese friends talk. Now it was to this sounding board he turned to gain conclusive answers to Washington's inquiries.

In order to give the impression that no important topics would be discussed and thus relax the guarded discretion of his friends, Watson decided to absent himself from a special series of seemingly routine celebrations. He sent two of his younger aides— Lieutenant Commander Ellis Mark Zacharias and Lieutenant Commander John Waller McClaran. "The information we were permitted to dole out [was] carefully apportioned and weighed," Zacharias recalled, "leading questions [were] rehearsed in advance, even the tone of our conversation, feigned surprises [were] practiced ahead of time so as to play our role as perfectly as possible when the performance came."

It came on the evening of September 21, 1921, at one of the meetings at a geisha house. It was still seven weeks before the scheduled opening of the Washington Conference, but Vice-Admiral Kato had already been chosen as the chief technical advisor to the Japanese delegation. The Japanese Cabinet had by now decided upon the policy line Navy Minister Kato and Prince Tokugawa were to follow.

The meeting produced the information Watson wanted. Through leading questions, Zacharias and McClaran lured Captains Nomura and Nagano into revealing that a conciliatory attitude was shaping up in the highest Japanese councils, and that a "compromise" was a distinct possibility "even on America's terms."

When Watson sent in his long report to ONI on October 17, he could advise the Navy Department with certainty that "Japan would eventually accede to the ratio to be proposed by Secretary Hughes." The information, obtained five weeks before the conference opened, was fully borne out by subsequent events.

Captain Watson and his young aides secured this critical intelligence in a shrewd but casual "intelligence operation." Moreover, it was dirt-cheap. Captain Nomura had insisted upon picking up the bill at the meeting in the geisha house where the information was elicited.

Working day and night on the solution of the YU code, Yardley found himself confronted with an intricate puzzle. The text sent in the new code appeared to be similar in crypt to those encoded in the compromised systems—represented, that is, by ten-letter groups like *efaxenafho* and *okinetupbe*—and apparently made up of two-letter or four-letter elements. But while the code words in all other ciphers had been divisible by two, the YU defied such division. This so confused Yardley and his aides that, as he put it, they "could not even set about solving the code."

Early in August, Yardley discovered that the Japanese had interspersed three-letter code groups throughout the messages, to make the code more difficult to break, and then he began to dissolve the ten-letter groups into two-letter and three-letter ingredients. Soon after he had established the presence of the three-letter elements in the code, everything began to make sense, and by October he had the YU completely solved.*

The "black chamber" was again reading the Japanese telegrams, supplying the clues Mr. Hughes needed to prepare his strategy for the conference scheduled to open in a few weeks. The Secretary already knew from the ONI report that Japan was prepared to accede to the American proposals at the psychological moment. It was left for Yardley to provide the tactical information on a day-by-day and cable-by-cable basis, exposing both the manipulations and the tribulations of the Japanese.

The crisis was reached in late November. It began with the arrival of a telegram on the 28th. Signed "Uchida"—Foreign Minister Yasuya Uchida, who was relaying Tokyo's instructions to the delegation in Washington—and addressed to Ambassador Shi-

---

* YU was the Japanese name for the new code. Yardley called it by the letters JP—J standing for "Japan" (to distinguish the series from his B, or British, system, for example). P—the sixteenth letter in the English alphabet —indicated that YU was the sixteenth Japanese code he had broken since January 1920.

dehara, it indicated that the Japanese were moving toward the denouement the Americans were waiting for. It was the first solid sign that Tokyo was weakening in its opposition to the Hughes formula. "It is necessary," Count Uchida wrote, "to avoid any clash with Great Britain and America, particularly America, in regard to the armament limitation question." The telegram contained specific instructions for the acceptance of the American proposal, provided the final agreement would include "a guarantee to reduce or at least to maintain the *status quo* of Pacific defenses."

On December 8, in a telegram to Tokyo that sounded like an ultimatum, Minister Kato demanded that he be authorized either to reject or accept the American formula. Permission to accept it was granted on December 10, in the historic telegram No. 155, which Prince Tokugawa read at the conference on December 11:

"We have claimed that the ratio of strength of ten to seven was absolutely necessary to guarantee the safety of the national defense of Japan, but the United States has persisted to the utmost in support of the Hughes proposal, and Great Britain has also supported it. It is therefore left that there is practically no prospect of carrying through this contention.

"Now, therefore, in the interest of the general situation and in a spirit of harmony, there is nothing to do but accept the ratio proposed by the United States."

The jubilant American diplomats generously shared their triumph with Yardley and his anonymous helpers in that mysterious brownstone in New York. "Christmas in the Black Chamber was brightened," Yardley wrote, "by handsome presents to all of us from officials in the State and War Departments which were accompanied by personal regards and assurances that our long hours of drudgery during the Conference were appreciated by those in authority."

But Yardley regarded himself as the chief architect of this great American victory. In particular, he was not unduly impressed with Secretary Hughes's performance.

"Stud poker," he remarked wryly at the end of these exciting days, "is not a very difficult game after you see your opponent's card."

3　　The Secrets of Room 2646

On January 7, 1923, Herbert Yardley received word from the War Department that he had been awarded the Distinguished Service Medal. Although the citation said that he had been given the coveted decoration for his "exceptionally meritorious and distinguished services . . . during the World War," he actually received it for breaking the Japanese code in time for the Washington Conference.

The "black chamber" was still this country's best-kept secret. So few people were privy to its existence that Yardley doubted that even John W. Weeks, Secretary of War in the Harding Administration, knew why he was decorating this ex-major in Military Intelligence. But when the medal was pinned on his lapel, Yardley thought Mr. Weeks had looked at him knowingly with a twinkle in his eye. "The wink," he later wrote, "pleased me immensely."

Yardley had reached the peak of his clandestine career, but his halcyon days were over. His "black chamber" was idle most of the time. Sometimes weeks elapsed before he heard from his "Washington clients." The "black chamber" no longer was the indispensable tool of American diplomacy.*

* For want of anything more important to do, Yardley began to crack the codes of picayune South American republics. But then he hoped to score again by compromising one of the "great ciphers" of secret diplomacy, the venerable system of the Vatican in which, he assumed, all the state secrets of the world were carried, thanks to the Papacy's fabulously efficient intelligence service. He succeeded in breaking the Vatican code but antagonized Bill Hurley, his mentor in the State Department. A devout Catholic, Hurley so resented this

Moreover, the world-wide acclaim that greeted Secretary Hughes's triumph, and the furtive tribute Yardley received from his patrons and associates, were by no means unanimous. The United States Navy, in particular, was bitterly opposed to all that the conference had stood for and produced. And the faceless professionals in the Office of Naval Intelligence despised Yardley for what he had done, not only to the Navy but to them personally, because Yardley, who was the man of the hour behind the scenes as much as Hughes was in the public eye, had overshadowed them for the second time in only four years.

In 1918, after attempts at cryptanalysis on the Yardley pattern, ONI had peremptorily been ordered to relinquish its secret cipher work to Yardley's bureau in Military Intelligence. ONI was then further humbled when it was forced to give up its Secret Ink Laboratory to M.I.8. As a result, at the time of Yardley's triumph the Navy had only a small cryptographic bureau. This crippled little branch had nevertheless made a valiant attempt to solve the Japanese diplomatic code in the hope that it could beat Yardley at his own game. But the Navy cryptographers lost again. Although they managed to crack the system in its basic principles, they failed to recover the code, chiefly because they could not break down the formidable language barrier.

The small band of Navy cryptologists subsisted more or less in a vacuum, without the slightest encouragement from topside. It is indeed difficult to find a rational explanation for the United States Navy's neglect of this activity at the time. The American Navy was sluggish in recognizing the need for security in transmitting orders and intelligence, and even slower—much slower—in exploiting this highly productive and easily accessible source of intelligence. It was not until two years after World War I that the Navy became interested in operational cryptology, and even then

---

trespass on the Pontiff's sacrosanct cipher that he moved promptly to abolish Yardley's establishment in New York. The "black chamber" was saved only by Hurley's own abrupt transfer from the State Department, in retaliation for a quaint diplomatic indiscretion on his own part. He was so carried away by an animated conversation with the wife of the British ambassador during a reception that he slapped the lady on the back, creating what threatened to become an international incident. The embarrassed State Department made him ambassador in Rome, not so much to punish him as to remove him from Washington and the lady's wrath.

only on a very modest scale. And the initiative came not from the high command or from the Naval Communications Service, but from a few imaginative and venturesome officers in the Office of Naval Intelligence.

Established in 1882 as a "device" for keeping the Navy Department informed of the characteristics, ships, installations and policies of other navies, the Office of Naval Intelligence—with its quasi-intellectual functions and egghead personnel—had never been trusted, liked or properly appreciated by the pragmatic, anti-intellectual, line-oriented naval brass.

"Arguments," wrote Admiral Julius A. Furer, "as to the scope of Naval Intelligence responsibility were frequent." And they usually ended with some further curtailment of its scope. The admirals regarded ONI as a mere "post office charged with forwarding intelligence reports." They never conceded to it any ability "to search for obscure leads in the reports pointing to enemy intentions."

ONI survived as best it could by being humble, exiguous and dormant. It left the gathering of intelligence almost exclusively to the elite corps of naval attachés. But what was called their "barter method" (friendly exchange of just enough information at their posts to provide data for their periodic reports) and the Navy's strict policy against "the buying of information" (euphemism for espionage activities) militated against obtaining closely guarded data.

In 1920, however, a set of circumstances combined to develop ONI into an efficient secret intelligence service, even though it had only about half a dozen trained officers for the delicate job. For one thing, the controversy with Japan had flared up over Yap. For another, ONI had a substantial slush fund from the war stashed away in a blind account at the Riggs Bank in Washington, from which many secret transactions could be financed. And lastly, ONI had an energetic, ambitious and daring director (for a change) in the person of fifty-four-year-old Captain Andrew T. Long, a native of Iredell County in North Carolina. He had served in ONI before, for a brief period in 1909, and had been naval attaché at such key posts as Rome, Paris and Vienna.

Long came to ONI in the late spring of 1920, and moved quickly to make it a real center of naval intelligence. He sent a high-powered group of intelligence officers to Japan, the largest such contingent of "legal spies" the United States had ever had there. Before long, eleven members of the American embassy's seventeen-man diplomatic staff were performing specific intelligence functions.

Captain Watson, the naval attaché, had five assistant attachés under him—including a major of the Marine Corps, a submarine specialist and a naval architect. Even the embassy's medical aide, Chief Pharmacist Karl Zembsch of the Navy, was doing a little spying for Long in addition to running the infirmary.

The Japanese had two naval attachés in Washington at this time—Commander Yoshitake Uyeda and Lieutenant Commander Kiyoshi Hasegawa. Uyeda had his combination office and living quarters in the Benedick, an elegant little apartment hotel for bachelors near the Army and Navy Club. A fun-loving, sensuous man, he took full advantage of the Benedick's liberal rules regarding women visitors. Several nights a week he gave wild parties in his suite, with comely young American ladies in the role of "geishas."

Lieutenant Commander Ellis Zacharias had just arrived in Washington from Tokyo on his first assignment at ONI headquarters, and Captain Long commissioned him to keep a watchful eye on Naval Attaché Uyeda. Zacharias checked into the Benedick and arranged for an apartment just above Uyeda's. Night after night he heard the shrill sounds of typically Japanese merriment, interspersed with unmistakably feminine giggles. Naturally interested in the naval attaché's pretty guests, Zacharias established that they were, without exception, secretaries in the Navy Department. One of them was, in fact, a confidential stenographer in the office of the Secretary himself.

Zacharias reported his discovery to Long, but the captain was no kill-joy. Taking his cue from Gilbert and Sullivan, the ONI director apparently did nothing to spoil the fun, but he did it very well indeed. Soon after Zacharias' findings the guests of Commander Uyeda became victims of a sudden retrenchment in the Navy Department. But Long arranged for what Zacharias called "carefully briefed replacements." Commander Uyeda's social life then continued merrily—both for him and for ONI.

One of the "replacements" was instructed to lavish her attention on Commander Hasegawa. Uyeda's shy assistant was trying to keep up with his chief's amorous technique of intelligence procurement, but he was inexperienced and far less security-conscious, especially when in his cups. The young lady had therefore no difficulty in finding out from Hasegawa that at least one copy of Japan's operational fleet code was somewhere in the United States outside the Japanese embassy's inaccessible strong room in Washington.

This was a most important bit of intelligence. The Imperial Navy's communication system was generally very good; its *cryptographic* security was close to ironclad. Extreme care was taken to protect the codes, few of which were ever allowed to leave Japan. The naval attachés had to use the Foreign Ministry's encoded ciphers. Aboard the warships all crypto-material was kept in leaded metal boxes to make sure the code books would sink in case the ships went down.

It was therefore nothing short of sensational when it was learned that a copy of the Japanese navy's operational code was kept in this country after all. To the seasoned investigators of the ONI this meant that it was "accessible."

Further probing revealed that the precious commodity was at one of the Japanese consulates general in the United States, in care of a vice-consul. ONI knew that the consul was using the cover to conceal his true identity. He was a lieutenant commander in the Imperial Navy on intelligence duty in the United States.

Arrangements were then made with the intelligence officer of the naval district to "procure the code book by whatever means." District intelligence officers (DIO) are chiefly engaged in counterespionage work under the "B," or Domestic, Branch of ONI. But that activity covers a multitude of authorized sins, such as the surreptitious entry of privileged premises, the cracking of consular safes and, indeed, the copying of confidential papers reposing in them.

By the late summer of 1920, all arrangements had been made to stage the coup de main. The office building where the Japanese consul general had his quarters had been thoroughly "cased." It had been ascertained that the consulate offices were usually deserted at night and that they had no special guard but were protected by the regular night watchman of the building. The man turned out to be a patriotic American. Without asking any questions, he permitted himself to be distracted one night when a team of five strangers showed up to call at the consulate.

The team was from the office of the DIO. It was made up of the DIO himself; a couple of "gumshoes" (operatives of the "B" Branch); a surreptitious-entry expert; and a locksmith who practiced safe-cracking as a legitimate sideline.

Not too long after this nocturnal adventure, the secret Japanese code book arrived in Washington. It was an exact photocopy of the original, except for a minor and incidental addition. On each sheet, in white on black, was the silhouette of a thumb. It was the DIO's; the camera had caught it as he was holding the book open for the photographer, page after page.

The code book was given the official designation of "JN-1," because it was the first *Japanese Navy* code to come into American hands.* But colloquially it came to be called the "Red Book," after the color of the binder in which the loose pages of the photocopy were kept.

Thus, exactly when Yardley succeeded in breaking down Japan's major *diplomatic* crypto-system, the United States Navy managed to gain possession of a Japanese *naval* code. The manner in which the latter was obtained had little in common with the plodding methodology of scientific cryptanalysis.

The physical acquisition of a code book simplifies things considerably. It automatically and immediately supplies the key to the encoded text, without the backbreaking effort required to solve its code or cipher by analysis. The so-called processing of the pilfered code could therefore be confined to an examination of its system and the translation of its Japanese contents into English.

Upon closer scrutiny at ONI, the code book turned out to be of 1918 vintage, but that did not make it any less valuable. It also contained all the changes the Japanese had made in 1919 and 1920, and was in current use. And though it was a fleet (or operational) code, it also included administrative, logistic and

---

* At the time of Pearl Harbor, American Navy cryptologists were reading Japanese messages with the help of JN–25—the twenty-fifth variant of the code. Each time the Japanese changed it, the Navy's cryptanalysts succeeded in recovering the changes without any more need to crack consular safes.

geographical material, affording almost complete coverage of the Imperial Navy's confidential dispatch traffic. The geographical section was regarded as especially significant because it seemed to indicate Japan's interests abroad. More than half of this section was devoted to China. The book listed even obscure inland towns that could be of no possible direct interest to a navy.*

The book was made up of ledger pages with four columns on each page running vertically. The numeral code groups, listed seriatim, were printed in the far left-hand column. The other three columns, from left to right, had Chinese ideographs, the code words, and their plain-text equivalent in Japanese. The Chinese characters supplemented the code words, and had been included to improve security.

The vocabulary contained names of vessels, common-usage phrases, command expressions, geographical place names, time signals, technical terms. There were also a number of blanks.

The code's basic system appeared to be simple even by the rather primitive standards of cryptography in those days. The cipher text was limited to ten numerals. The code groups were also in numerals, to which an "additive" or "subtracter" key had been applied.

The next step was to translate the text into accurate English, and this developed into a difficult task requiring several years. It was decided to keep the possession of the code a secret even inside ONI. As one of the analysts put it: "Very few people in the Navy and none in the Army *ever* learned of the existence of the 'Red Book' and of the manner in which its photocopy had been obtained."

The ironclad secrecy necessitated special arrangements for the custody and use of the code book, and it was not easy to find someone fluent in the Japanese language who could also be trusted implicitly. The Navy had only a few officers of its own who spoke Japanese, but their command of the language was not considered adequate for such an exacting task.

Somebody had to be brought in from the outside, a civilian linguist whose discretion matched his proficiency in the difficult

---

* The code's emphasis on Chinese localities prompted one ONI analyst to remark: "I am convinced that the Japanese are planning the conquest of China, and have been planning it for many years."

language. Such a man was eventually found in the person of Dr. Emerson J. Haaworth, a former Quaker missionary in Japan and teacher at Tokyo University. Dr. Haaworth was hired, together with his wife to act as his secretary. Her chief qualification for the job was that she was the only person in the world who could read the doctor's handwriting.*

Office space was found for the Haaworths in Room 2646 at the far end of the sixth wing on the second floor in the ramshackle old Navy Building. Unmarked and isolated from the other offices in the wing, the room required a special permit for entry. The Yale lock on its door was periodically changed, and only two keys were issued to it. One was kept by Dr. Haaworth, the other by Lieutenant Commander McClaran, who had returned from Tokyo to take over the Far Eastern Section in ONI and was chosen by Captain Long to supervise the translation of the code book.

For eight to twelve hours each weekday, Haaworth was at his cluttered roll-top desk in Room 2646, working on the translation. Despite his fluency in the language, Dr. Haaworth required eighteen months to translate the "Red Book," and even then he left a great number of what he called "doubtful portions." The Japanese spelling of certain obscure words had stumped him; and several phrases just did not make sense to him. For example, he had come up against what seemed to be a five-word sentence—*"Haru endo Sutarodo reinji fuainda"*—but proved untranslatable no matter how he tried to juggle the spelling and unscramble the words.

"I don't know what you have there," he told McClaran, "but it isn't Japanese. They may be Japanese words, at least they *seem* and *sound* like Japanese words. But they have absolutely no meaning in this form."

Commander McClaran finally realized that the proper translation of many of the elusive words and phrases needed, in addition to a classical scholar like Haaworth, a language officer familiar with Japanese military, naval and technical terms. McClaran tried to find someone who could teach the scholar some technical

---

* The Haaworths were not carried on the rolls of the Navy Department, nor did they have Civil Service status. They were paid twice a month from the director's "slush fund," as were all expenses incurred in this operation. Aside from typing up her husband's scribbled notes, Mrs. Haaworth also had to clean the room because the regular char force was barred from it.

Japanese, but it was a big order and he despaired of locating the right man.

By then it was 1925.

Lieutenant Commander Ellis Zacharias had become the Navy's foremost Japanese linguist, and Commander McClaran, who remembered him most favorably from their tour of duty in Tokyo, finally decided to bring him into Room 2646 in the hope that he might be able to fill in the gaps Dr. Haaworth had left in the "Red Book." A search found Zacharias at the Canal Zone, serving as navigation officer aboard the *Rochester*. In January 1926 Zacharias was abruptly detached from the cruiser and ordered to report at once to the Chief of Naval Operations in Washington "for temporary duty in the Office of Naval Intelligence."

Mystery surrounded his new assignment. He was not told what he would be doing in ONI. Nor was he aware that a branch like the one working in Room 2646 even existed. It was not easy for Zacharias to adjust himself to his new environment among the "taciturn, secretive people" who worked in that locked room. A gregarious man who liked intelligence work chiefly because of its excitement and glamour, he was to share a strictly quarantined office with an old couple singularly unimpressed with the romance of their work. When Zacharias entered this inner sanctum he felt, as he put it, like a monk going into a monastery. But he solved the personality problem of his new assignment by adapting the job to his own ways rather than adapting himself to the job.

One of the first problems with which McClaran confronted Zacharias was the phrase that had nonplused Dr. Haaworth. But it did not baffle the newcomer. He read the enigmatic entry, "*Haru endo Sutarodo reinji fuainda,*" then exclaimed: "Why, this is simple! *Reinji fuainda* obviously stands for 'range finder.' So this must be Jap for our Barr and Stroud range finder, *Haru* means 'Barr' and *Sutarodo* stands for 'Stroud.'" And he was right, too.

For five years key parts of the stolen code had remained shrouded in mystery. Then, in only five months, Zacharias had the "Red Book" completely clarified, down to its last "untranslatable" phrase.

4 The Mission of the Marblehead

Back in the fall of 1923, thirty-year-old Lieutenant Laurence Frye Safford, a tall, lean, sandy-haired New Englander, was in Manila Harbor, looking forward to the bleakest Christmas of his life. As skipper of the *Finch*, a 950-ton mine sweeper in the Asiatic Fleet, he probably had the dullest command the United States Navy had to offer.

It was the low point in Safford's career. In the seven years since he graduated from the Naval Academy, he had seen action in the Atlantic, commanded a couple of submarines, and served as navigator in the *S-7* on her historic cruise from Portsmouth, New Hampshire, to the Philippine Islands. But when he arrived in Manila he was given the *Finch*, of all things. From then on he suffered all the frustrations that come from commanding a mine sweeper when there are no mines to sweep. Once in a while he was allowed to take his little ship on patrol duty up the Yangtze River. But most of the time he was given only humdrum missions around Manila Harbor—mainly towing and simple salvage work—for which no man needed an Annapolis diploma.

But just when his future seemed least promising, a signal from the Chief of Naval Operations ordered him to proceed forthwith to Washington, D.C., and report for duty in the Office of Naval Communications. He was made officer in charge of a newly created "Research Desk" * in the Code and Signal Section.

---

* The words "research" and "special" are used alternately in the armed forces in naming secret branches whose functions cannot be spelled out for security reasons or would prove embarrassing if publicly known.

Though this sudden upturn in Safford's fortunes seemed to be but an accident of fate, there was serious purpose behind his transfer. The acquisition of a Japanese code in 1920 had created a new situation for which the United States Navy was neither mentally prepared nor physically equipped. The only cryptographic establishment it had then was the small Code and Signal Section, and its functions and responsibilities were limited to the compilation and handling of the Navy's own codes.

Something had to be done if the Navy were to exploit the breakthrough. The Office of Naval Communications was the logical place to accommodate these activities, but Rear Admiral W.H.G. Bullard, its able director since 1916, had neither time, men, money nor facilities, nor, indeed, even the slightest desire to add communications intelligence to his responsibilities and headaches.

Yet toward the end of his tenure in 1923 the problem could no longer be ignored, nor could its solution be delayed. In December the activity was added to the Code and Signal Section's functions with the establishment of a Research Desk. According to the order setting it up, the Desk was to "study means of improving communications security in the United States Navy" through the development of cipher machines, and to conduct "communications intelligence" by monitoring the radio transmissions of other navies and prepare traffic analyses. However, nothing was said about a frontal attack on their crypto-systems.*

The designation of the new subsection as a "Desk" indicated by itself how modest these beginnings were. A "Desk" was the administrative amoeba, the smallest unit in the Navy's table of organization. In most cases, up to World War II, a "Desk" consisted of a single desk in physical fact, and a young officer who sat behind it. It was, indeed, a rather battered old desk in Room 1649 that now

---

* In October 1925 another pioneer in American cryptology was transferred, from the battleship *Arizona* to the Cryptographic Section. He was Lieutenant Commander Joseph J. Rochefort, who had made his way up from the ranks, having enlisted as a seaman in the Naval Reserve in World War I. An expert cryptographer (regarded by many as the Navy's best) and a Japanese linguist, he was destined to go far in communications intelligence. His greatest triumph came seventeen years later, when he supplied the intelligence from intercepted Japanese messages which Admiral Nimitz needed to win the battles of the Coral Sea and Midway.

awaited Lieutenant Safford in January 1924, at the end of his long journey from Manila.

Lieutenant Safford had been drawn out of the familiar duffel bag from which the Navy usually picks officers for offbeat duties. At Annapolis, where he was an expert rifle shot, won his class numeral in soccer and acquired the nickname "Sappho," he attracted attention as a keen chess player, a better-than-average student in mathematics, and something of a wizard with precision instruments. But he had no experience in cryptography and the only language he knew was English, which, however, he spoke with persuasive eloquence.

And yet the seemingly random selection of Lieutenant Safford proved fortuitous, fitting an odd man to an odd job. What the Research Desk needed at this stage was not yet an expert cryptologist. It needed a promoter.

Safford had no illusions about his new job. He realized as soon as he sat down at his desk that he would have to fight an uphill struggle with the entrenched powers in Naval Communications against their traditional opposition to change. He found that they regarded him as a kind of freak in a side show, but this did not discourage him the slightest. He was cut out by nature to tackle new things. And he functioned best when left to his own resources.

The Code and Signal Section had a collection of cipher machines in various stages of development, and the blueprints of others yet to be built. Safford was to study them, establish their good and bad points, then develop machines which Admiral Bullard hoped would improve the fleet's woeful signal security. With his interest in precision instruments and his aptitude for this sort of gadgetry, Safford was soon producing the ingenious inventions that would eventually, as one of his citations phrased it, "give the United States Navy the finest system of encipherment in the world." *

Soon two events abruptly changed the entire direction of Safford's mission. In the summer of 1924 Bullard retired and was

---

* After World War II, Congress voted Safford a grant of $100,000 to compensate him for his inventions, which, under the Navy's strict security regulations, he could not patent and exploit commercially.

succeeded by Captain Ridley McLean, an alert and progressive Tennesseean, who, like Captain Long in ONI, was a courageous innovator willing to step on sensitive toes.

Just as important, Safford had stumbled upon the secret of Room 2646. Very soon he was spending more time in ONI's *cabinet noir* than in his own office on the deck below, studying the pilfered code and watching Dr. Haaworth as he struggled with its stubborn mysteries.

What he saw in Room 2646 determined Safford to burst the narrow confines of his Research Desk. He pleaded in his most persuasive manner for permission to branch out in two directions —to set up interception stations to obtain the Japanese dispatches which ONI needed to put its "Red Book" to practical use, and to add code-cracking to the functions of the Research Desk.

Captain McLean was amenable, and in August (only a month after McLean had become DNC), the first electronic listening post was put up in the Pacific, on Guam. Then McLean authorized Safford to hire a small staff of cryptanalysts to start work on the other Japanese codes. Barely ten months after Safford's arrival in Washington, the Navy had the beginnings of its own "black chamber."

In a sense Safford was the Yardley of the Navy. But whatever similarities their characters possessed stemmed from certain innate traits that ordain some people for work in cryptology. Though Yardley himself was an expert cryptanalyst, while Safford was only a lay administrator of cryptologists, they both suffered from what Colonel Étienne Bazèries, the great French code expert, called *cryptographitis*—"a sort of subtle, all-pervading, incurable malady." It gives them, as Bazèries put it, delusions of grandeur. It subjects them to hallucinations. It wrecks them, makes them sad nuisances to their families and friends, and often to their governments.

All these characteristics Safford had in common with Yardley. He also had Yardley's hypertrophic ego and adventurous streak, and was, like the other man, intense, eager, obstinate and domineering. And yet he was not just another Yardley. He had none of Yardley's overweening ambition, flamboyance and arrogance. He understood how to keep his restive energy under control and knew by instinct how far he could stretch his independence. With the other man's exhibitionist traits he could not have survived in the Navy, where an ounce of vanity, as the saying goes, invariably spoils a ton of merit.

Safford spent 1925 laying the groundwork for a systematic attack on the Japanese crypto-system. Then, in February 1926, as abruptly as he had been summoned to Washington, he was ordered back to sea. After a brief tour of duty in the battleship *California*, he was assigned to the destroyer *Hull* as executive officer and navigator, with not even collateral duties in his new speciality. Since he would be gone for several years, his friends feared that the Research Desk would disintegrate during his long absence.

But he had laid its foundations too firmly to justify such apprehensions. He was leaving behind a viable organization with a small but brilliant staff of cryptanalysts. It was no mean accomplishment by itself to assemble such a competent group. In those days there were very few people in the country working in this field, and even fewer on whom he could draw. Before the computers took over, cryptanalysis seemed to be akin to alchemy, with its speculative processes, deep mysteries and preternatural hocus-pocus. The science (or art, as some preferred to regard it) attracted a certain breed of seemingly odd people, not easy to fit into the naval establishment even if only as civilian employees tucked away in a locked room. But Safford managed to hire the best of them, who compensated with their skill, industry and discretion for whatever idiosyncrasies they otherwise had.*

Among the experts Safford had recruited for Room 1647 was a young woman, the daughter of a great patrician family whose name she bore but from whom she was separated by her compulsive love affair with cryptology. She was closest to being the perfect cryptanalyst. She had what is called a "cipher brain," that

* When Zacharias got his chance to enter Safford's inner sanctum, what impressed him most were the people he found there "sitting in front of piles of indexed sheets on which a mumbo jumbo of figures or letters was displayed in chaotic disorder." They were selfless, hard-working people who passed up meals and forgot Sundays when engrossed in the solution of a code or cipher. "It was an inspiration to watch these people work," Zacharias later wrote, "training themselves and improving their art in the secrecy which is part of their craft."

unique quality of mind and sixth sense which go into the making of great cryptologists. Since her identity has never been disclosed, we will call her "Miss Aggie," the name she used in Room 1649. Though she was a woman in a world of men, it was in her care Safford had left the Research Desk and its top-priority project— the solution of the Japanese FLAG OFFICERS (or ADMIRALS) system.

It was, as Safford put it, "the most difficult as well as most important system the Japanese navy was using." He chose it, therefore, as the first code to be attacked by the Research Desk. Basically a transposition cipher, it was so complex even in its cipher element that its solution presented seemingly insurmountable difficulties. To make things worse, the cipher was superposed on a code made up of four-character groups, an added complication that made the task of recovery seem hopeless.

But Miss Aggie was working on it, convinced as she was that every man-made secret could be unraveled by man—or, in this particular case, by a woman. Even before Safford's departure she had succeeded in breaking into the code. And then, late in 1926, she finally recovered it, as completely as Yardley had solved the major Japanese diplomatic system six years before. The second high-grade Japanese naval code to come into American hands (and the first to be solved solely by the analytical method), it was given the designation "AD code" (short for ADMIRALS code) to distinguish it from the JN series, the successors of the FLEET code ONI had obtained in 1920.

The importance of Miss Aggie's feat cannot be overstated. Since it was the system the Imperial Navy reserved for the concealment of its admirals' dispatch traffic, the messages it was supposed to cloak contained data of the utmost secrecy and significance. The compromised code thus became, in Safford's words, "our main source of information on the Japanese navy." Its solution was the crowning achievement of the Navy's entire cryptological effort, and it was especially astonishing and gratifying since it came so early in the game.

Miss Aggie's triumph had a salutary effect on the Office of Naval Communications. The Research Desk became respectable overnight. Its value was recognized all the way up to the Chief of Naval Operations. Its continued existence was assured.

The agency that greeted her victory with the greatest expectations was the Office of Naval Intelligence. Captain Long was gone from ONI.* Now, in late 1926, the Director of Naval Intelligence was forty-nine-year-old Captain Arthur Japy Hepburn, one of the Navy's brainiest officers and a naval diplomat of the first rank, destined to become commander-in-chief of the United States Fleet within a decade. But he was in ONI only in transit, to prepare himself for the 1927 disarmament conference, which he was to attend in Geneva as a member of the American delegation. ONI was actually managed by his deputy, Captain William W. Galbraith, an officer who had Long's dash and daring. He and a small group of activists around him recognized at once that the AD code could be an invaluable tool of intelligence. But how to put it to its most effective use?

Obviously the first prerequisite was the improvement and extension of the Navy's monitoring facilities. Galbraith urged Captain McLean to build up a network of fixed shore stations as rapidly as possible. And he persuaded him to develop mobile listening posts by installing interception equipment on board ships to enable ONI to "penetrate the screen with which Japan hoped to shield the secrets of her fleet." The idea was to place the Imperial Navy under surveillance, by monitoring its transmissions from closer proximities.**

In October 1926 an American destroyer steamed out of Chefoo, her base on the Shantung Peninsula, and sailed down the Yellow Sea. She was the *McCormick*, a compact, six-year-old Chandler-class destroyer of 1190 tons, ostensibly on one of the regular cruises which units of the Asiatic Fleet took each year to show the flag in the Chinese treaty ports.

In actual fact, the *McCormick* was a floating radio-interception

* He had been given his flag and made commander-in-chief of the Atlantic Fleet in European waters.
** It should be remembered that forty years ago radio communications in all navies were poor in both ship-to-shore and ship-to-ship transmissions. Facilities, equipment and personnel were all inadequate. The problem of skip distance, for example, made it impossible to cover all ocean areas entirely from shore locations. Even high-power stations, presumably capable of transmitting at a range of three thousand miles, could not be used for direct communications with the ships at sea, and employed the so-called intercept method. The same conditions placed serious limitations on monitoring and interception efforts.

station on a secret mission. She had been chosen to test the feasibility of Galbraith's idea because she was stationed in the Yellow Sea and was a familiar sight on its busy ship lanes frequented by a great many Japanese warships. Nothing in her outward appearance distinguished her from the other ships of her class, except her system of multiplex aerials that seemed a bit too ornate for an ordinary DD. But there was more than just a new set of antennas to set her apart from an ordinary destroyer on a routine cruise. She carried an assortment of special monitoring equipment in addition to her regulation battery of eight RD-type radio sets. She had 101 enlisted men on board instead of her normal complement of 95—an added crew of six radiomen especially trained for the venture. And she had a new skipper, the ubiquitous Lieutenant Commander Ellis M. Zacharias from Naval Intelligence.

Cruising at a leisurely speed and breaking the trip with calls at Amoy and Foochow, Zacharias took the *McCormick* to Hong Kong, monitoring the dispatch traffic of the Japanese all the time and all the way. The voyage proved beyond doubt that electronic snooping was technically feasible even with the *McCormick's* improvised facilities, and that it was capable of yielding considerable intelligence that could not have been obtained otherwise.

Commander Zacharias left the *McCormick* in Hong Kong and went on to Manila on the second prong of his mission. The United States already had a few radio stations operating overtly, but they were used solely to expedite official communications between Washington and the American diplomatic and naval outposts in the Pacific and in Asia.* Up to this time, none of these installations were used for radio intelligence. Zacharias was therefore sent to the Philippines to revamp the two navy radio stations and to add radio surveillance to their functions. Then he went on to Shanghai to convert the radio station, located on the fourth floor of the American consulate, into the United States Navy's major listening post in Asia.

---

* Two of these stations were in Hawaii, two in Samoa, one was on Guam, two were in the Philippines, and one was in Shanghai. Only the Shanghai station was on foreign soil, but under the old treaty that had established the international concessions, it had every right to be there. All the great powers had their own radio stations at Shanghai and, presumably, their monitors as well.

By the summer of 1927 Commander Zacharias had intercept stations in action in the Philippines, on Guam and in Shanghai. In Washington the Research Desk had updated the "Red Book" and recovered the keys of the AD code, together with whatever changes had been made in it. Everything was thus functioning smoothly even in Safford's absence, when a series of developments persuaded ONI to embark on the first full-scale radio intelligence operation ever staged by the United States Navy.

Tokyo had announced that a training squadron, consisting of the *Asama* and the *Iwate*, would visit the United States in the fall. Washington responded with the announcement that the *Marblehead*, a cruiser with the Asiatic Fleet, would return the courtesy by calling at Nagasaki and Kobe.*

Elsewhere other events had less felicitous overtones. In Japan a retired admiral named Baron Sakamoto urged in an article that Japan "take measures in good time to assure its mastery . . . over a sufficiently broad area [of the Pacific]" to guarantee, as he put it, her "life line of communications with the continent of Asia in both war and peace."

An impressive doctrinal-tactical-technical revolution in the Imperial Navy appeared to lend weight to Admiral Sakamoto's statement. The speed of cruisers and destroyers, and the cruising range of the I-class submarines, were increased. Plane-carrying submarines were added to the fleet. A superior oxygen-fueled torpedo was developed. Special stress was being placed on ship-based air power.

Japan's newest aircraft carrier, the *Akagi*, had been completed and was shaking down prior to joining the fleet. Mysterious items in the budget hinted at other developments of acute interest to ONI—such as an appropriation for certain unspecified "installations aboard ships," and another for "improved naval communications."

The American Navy was keenly interested in these developments and was anxious to obtain detailed information about them. In the almost total absence of other means, this intelligence could

* A number of festive celebrations and parties were arranged both in Japan and the United States, including a luncheon at the White House given by President Calvin Coolidge for Rear Admiral Osami Nagano, who commanded the training squadron. Fourteen years later, as Chief of the Naval General Staff, Nagano was, next to Admiral Yamamoto, the strongest advocate of the Pearl Harbor attack.

be procured only by tapping the signal traffic of the Imperial Navy.

On August 30 Tokyo announced that the Japanese navy would hold grand maneuvers of its Combined Fleet in October, to "test the value of air reconnaissance on a large scale." Although in a sense the Japanese navy was exercising all the time, 1927 was an especially busy year for the Combined Fleet. Its units had been engaged in almost continuous war games—off Tateyama and Maizuru, in the vicinity of the Amami islands, and off Mihonoseki.* They were held to prepare the vessels and their crews for the Fleet Problem of the year, which was rendered more important than usual by the *Agaki*'s presence.

At his monitoring sets in Shanghai, Commander Zacharias deduced from the crescendo of messages he was intercepting that the Japanese fleet maneuvers of this year would be more elaborate and important than any held before. He thought it might be possible to reconstruct the pattern of their tactics and gain other operational and technical intelligence by intercepting the signals of the ships taking part in the games.

But his shore-based listening posts were too distant from the maneuver area to assure adequate reception. It occurred to Zacharias that the Combined Fleet could be caught in what he called an "ambush by radio." The idea was to move an American ship with special monitoring equipment on board into the area where the Japanese fleet would be exercising, and to intercept its traffic from close quarters.

He submitted his idea to ONI in Washington, where it was endorsed enthusiastically. Admiral Josiah Marvell, commander-in-chief of the Asiatic Fleet, agreed to give Zacharias one of his cruisers for the operation. Since the *Marblehead* was going to Japan on the prearranged courtesy visit, Zacharias was assigned to her. He then replotted her course so that she would sail through the maneuver area on her way to Kobe.

* The United States Navy had a generally low opinion of the seamanship in the Combined Fleet, and the exercises off Mihonoseki did little to change it. Designed to train the crews for action at night, they ended in disaster when two cruisers and two destroyers collided in the dark. The vessels were seriously damaged and some two hundred sailors lost their lives in the embarrassing accident. The commanding officer of one of the cruisers "atoned" for the mishap by committing suicide.

Shortly before midnight on October 16, all the monitoring equipment Zacharias could assemble in Shanghai and obtain from the United States was brought to the *Marblehead*. Then at midnight Zacharias sneaked aboard the cruiser, which left immediately afterward. Simultaneously a squadron of American destroyers sailed from the Philippines, ostensibly for a regular exercise—but actually on a cruise to the area where the Japanese hoped they could stage their war games without being disturbed. Teams of specially chosen officers were stationed on each of the destroyers, with orders to subject the maneuvers to visual observation.

In the meantime 170 vessels of the Imperial Navy deployed for the grand maneuvers. They were divided into a "Red Fleet" to defend Tokyo and a "Blue Fleet" to attack the capital from the direction of Formosa. The "Reds" concentrated on October 19. The next day the "Blues" left Tokuyama, at the southwestern end of Honshu in the Japan Sea, reappearing from the Pacific as the "enemy" fleet. A violent storm was blowing, adding considerable realism to the mock battle.

On October 24 the battle fleets met two hundred miles southeast of the Kii Peninsula. "As usual," the *New York Times* reported on October 27 in a dispatch from Tokyo, "both the problem set and the results achieved are kept secret, but the defenders evidently benefited by aircraft, as the final battle occurred three days before the allotted time and some hundred miles farther from Tokyo than expected."

Commander Zacharias reached the general area of the maneuvers on October 20—on the *Marblehead's* fourth day at sea—and though the cruiser made no visual contact with the Japanese fleet, he succeeded in getting what he sought. Throughout the maneuvers he and his team of radiomen listened to the Japanese traffic and transcribed the messages passing to and from the flagship. He decrypted them with the help of the Japanese code books he had with him in the *Marblehead*.

The American destroyers, on the other hand, actually sighted the "Blue Fleet" in the vicinity of Formosa, and steamed across its path. The intelligence officers aboard could thus observe the *Akagi* as she was launching and recovering her planes.*

* From intelligence reports produced by these teams, ONI developed the erroneous theory that Japanese carrier pilots lacked the 20/20 vision needed

Listening to the Japanese, Zacharias could hear "sounds of excitement and annoyance," caused by the sudden appearance of the American destroyers. He heard, too, signals from the flagship ordering fast vessels to raise a smoke screen between the *Akagi* and the American destroyers. "But no smoke screen could interfere with the radio waves," Zacharias wrote smugly, "and we learned much that we wanted to know by reading their messages, even if we could no longer observe the action through our binoculars."

From what he heard and what the destroyers saw, Zacharias reconstructed "the complete and accurate plan of the entire operation," as he put it, "together with their confidential findings not available to their own observers, who were permitted just a modicum of insight into real events from the narrow bridge of the Japanese flagship."

On October 28, when the *Marblehead* arrived in Kobe on the first leg of her courtesy cruise, Zacharias had his preliminary report ready. He passed it on to Captain Cotten, the American naval attaché in Tokyo, who had come to the big port city on Osaka Bay with the official Japanese reception committee. On November 4 Zacharias returned to Shanghai to prepare a fully documented final paper on everything he had learned in the "ambush." It was the first comprehensive intelligence report in the United States Navy on the Combined Fleet in action.*

"Sappho" Safford had been at sea in the *Hull* during Zacharias' adventure in the *Marblehead*. But he had been bitten by the bug of *cryptographitis*, and moved heaven and earth to get back to his old Desk in Washington. He got his wish in June 1929, together with a promotion to lieutenant commander. From then on—with the exception of another four-year stretch at sea (from May 1932 to May 1936)—he remained with the activity for the rest of his service in the Navy.

His own opportunity to participate in an "ambush by radio"

---

for this intricate maneuver. This was "confirmed" by later intelligence, and added to the notorious underrating of Japanese carrier pilots by the United States Navy.

* "I consider this report excellent," the Director of Naval Communications wrote to Zacharias in a letter of commendation, "as it covers a line of naval information which is very important for us to get hold of, and the value of which we so far have failed to appreciate."

came in 1930. The Japanese navy was ready for another of its periodic Fleet Problems. But remembering the intrusion of those American destroyers three years before, the Naval General Staff now decided to prepare these war games in secrecy. Captain Isaac C. Johnson, the American naval attaché in Tokyo, had no inkling that any maneuvers had been scheduled at all.

But Washington knew, thanks to Safford and his enlarged Research Desk. Upon his return he had introduced a *continuous* surveillance of the Imperial Navy's dispatch traffic, using the station on Guam with back-up from the Shanghai listening post. Their intercepts had alerted Safford to the impending war games, and he made his arrangements in ample time for a repeat performance of the Zacharias operation.

Everything was set for the operation when an unexpected hitch placed it in jeopardy. The Japanese issued a new code. Working around the clock, Safford's team of cryptanalysts managed to solve it in time for the maneuvers, then followed through with another perfect coverage.

But just when this intricate activity was becoming a permanent fixture at last and an important safeguard of American security, a sudden crisis in Washington threatened to destroy the entire cryptological establishment of the United States.

5   "Gentlemen Do Not Read Each Other's Mail"

Beset by the kind of qualms that made King Solomon formulate proverbs, Americans have a penitent feeling about their own involvement in what they call the dirty business of espionage. Their hero figure in this field is the pathetic Nathan Hale, who accomplished nothing as a spy and was hanged for merely trying. And one of the best known among our pertinent maxims is the famous phrase, "Gentlemen do not read each other's mail," which Henry L. Stimson coined in 1929, shortly after he had been made Secretary of State in the new Hoover Administration.

As Governor General of the Philippines the year before, Mr. Stimson had had ample opportunities to observe the rebirth of Japanese militarism. By the time he left Manila, in March 1929, to head the State Department, the Japanese officers' clique was on the rampage, determined to seize power by murder at home and conquest abroad.*

Because of his failure to strike a balance between his ideals in international relations and the realities of these years, and because of what he himself described as his "inexperience in power poli-

---

* In May 1928 Japanese troops clashed with the forces of Chiang Kai-shek and checked the Kuomintang's advance into North China. On June 4 Chang Tso-lin, military governor of Manchuria since 1911 with Tokyo's blessings, was assassinated near Mukden by Japanese officers because he had suddenly refused to take "any more advice" from them.

tics," Mr. Stimson's mental seismograph failed to register these rumblings. "In 1929," he wrote, "the world was striving with good will for lasting peace, and in this effort all the nations were parties." He approached his new responsibilities with evangelistic fervor, determined to work for peace and "deal as gentlemen," as he put it, "with the gentlemen sent as ambassadors and ministers from friendly nations," including Japan.

At the time of Stimson's advent, the "black chamber" of Herbert O. Yardley was still in business, even if it was wasting its skill on such minor assignments as, for example, the breaking of the Peruvian diplomatic code. The Department needed it to gain some insight into a dispute between Peru, Chile and Bolivia over Tacna-Arica that harked back to 1883.

But then Yardley perked up. A number of intercepts passing through his hands recalled the exciting days of 1921. He learned from these messages that another naval disarmament conference was in the making. Yardley expected the new Secretary of State to make use of the "black chamber's" services exactly as Secretary Hughes had done eight years before. As yet, however, Mr. Stimson was still ignorant of its existence. It was the custom to let a new Secretary become more firmly settled in the Department before confiding to him the existence of the "black chamber" and the nature of Yardley's activities.

During the briefings for the conference, scheduled to open in London on January 21, 1930, Stimson was at last acquainted with his Department's cryptanalytical annex, and was shown a number of messages it had decrypted. Stimson exploded. He had adopted as his guide in foreign policy a principle he always tried to follow in his personal relations: "The way to make men trustworthy is to trust them." The whole concept of the "black chamber" was a crass violation of this principle. "Gentlemen do not read each other's mail," he exclaimed, and gave orders that "all State Department funds be withdrawn from [Yardley's] support" at once.

By then the "black chamber" existed solely for the benefit of the State Department, which was footing its entire bill. Yardley had no advance warning and was stunned when the blow fell. "There was nothing to do," he wrote ruefully, "but close the Black Chamber. . . . Its chapter in American history was ended."

· · ·

Secretary Stimson's seemingly naïve decision to dismiss Yardley was, unbeknown to him, one of the most fortuitous acts of his distinguished public service. Despite the secrecy in which the "black chamber" was shrouded within the American government, the Japanese knew all about Yardley's activities because none other than Herbert O. Yardley had sold its secrets to them. And he was not even the first one to betray to the Japanese the cryptological efforts of the United States.

It is the scourge of a secret service that it is sometimes less successful in safeguarding its own secrets than in procuring those of others. The very atmosphere of the institution—its basic melodrama, its lack of moral scruples, its dependence on people with aberrant personalities—renders it highly vulnerable.

The American cryptological establishment was no exception. For all its many loyal workers, it also had its quota of traitors. They were lured into treason by their unbridled ambition and an exaggerated notion of their own importance.

On March 7, 1925, an American employee of the War Department's cryptographic bureau contacted the Japanese embassy in Washington and warned Counselor Isaburo Yoshida, the acting chief of the mission in the absence of Ambassador Masanao Hanihara, that "the War Department was maintaining a supersecret code-breaking bureau." According to Yoshida's informant, "there was no foreign code that could not be decrypted" by this mysterious agency. The man went even further. He volunteered the advice that "the only possible means of protecting the [Japanese] codes [would be] to change them as frequently as possible."

The sensational information was immediately forwarded to Tokyo, in document "Secret—No. 48," dated March 10, 1925. But nothing in the Japanese archives indicates that they undertook anything to tighten up their crypto-security as a result of this warning, or that Yoshida's informant followed up his "advice" with additional information or other useful services.

In the summer of 1928 Yardley attended a party at a friend's house in New York because he hoped to pick up some intelligence from one of the other guests, Koshiro Takada, who represented a Tokyo newspaper in the United States.

By then Yardley was thoroughly disillusioned and disgruntled. Even as a telegraphist in the State Department he had had the dream of running a vast *central* cryptological agency in the United States, with hundreds of men and women working under him. His pioneering work in M.I.8 and his great coup in 1921–22 turned the dream into an obsession. But instead of gaining the authority, influence and scope he craved, he was gradually cut back while a "bunch of amateurs," as he called his colleagues in similar agencies, were established in positions of importance.

In his isolation, Yardley had persuaded himself that his government was ungrateful and disloyal to him. And he decided that this ingratitude had automatically released him from any moral bonds on his part. Moreover, he was troubled by increasing financial difficulties. He needed more money to finance his private life, his gambling for high stakes and his huge consumption of liquor during those Prohibition days. Now he was ready to have his revenge and also to get the money he urgently needed.

A few weeks after their meeting in New York, Yardley called on Takada and told him that he had some valuable information that would interest the Japanese embassy. Could Takada introduce him to Ambassador Tsuneo Matsudaira in Washington? Takada made the arrangements and suggested that Yardley, on one of his next trips to Washington, call at a house on Crescent Place where he would find someone to whom he could give the information.

At 1661 Crescent Place, an elegant little graystone house off Connecticut Avenue, he was received by Setsuzo Sawada, counselor of the Japanese embassy. Yardley went to the heart of the matter at once. He introduced himself as the United States government's senior cryptologist, briefly sketched his background, then told Sawada that he was prepared to sell his country's most closely guarded secret—for $10,000 in cash.

The offer was so staggering that it aroused Sawada's suspicions. According to his first report to Tokyo, in which he described this strange encounter, he had said to Yardley: "But you're making a lot of money in your job! Why are you willing to sell your country?"

"Simple, sir," Yardley replied, according to Sawada. "It just so happens that I need *more* money."

This was an unparalleled opportunity and Sawada acted quickly to make the most of it. When his report reached Tokyo the two most important Japanese officials in cryptography were sent to

Washington, under assumed names on diplomatic passports, to examine Yardley's proposition and advise Sawada. One of them was Captain Kingo Inouye of the Imperial Navy, on loan to the Foreign Ministry to organize a Code Research Group within its Cable Section. The other was Naoshi Ozeki, chief cryptographer of the Foreign Ministry.

A deal was made, but not without some haggling. Contrary to the popular belief that the Japanese had unlimited funds for such transactions, the Foreign Ministry operated on a very tight budget from secret funds. Sawada countered Yardley's demand by offering him $3000 at first, and then $5000. For a while Yardley refused to lower his price, but an agreement was finally reached. Yardley received $7000, with the understanding that he would be paid more if he decided to continue to work for the Japanese.

It was an amazing bargain at any price. In return for their money, the Japanese obtained all the secrets of the "black chamber"—Yardley's methodology in breaking their codes, copies of his work sheets, and his solutions of other codes as well, including those of the British Foreign Office, which they were especially anxious to get. Moreover, Yardley agreed to cut back his work on Japanese messages.

For a while Counselor Sawada remained in Washington to maintain liaison with Yardley. In 1929, however, he was recalled to Tokyo to take over the *denshin-ka*, the Cable Section of the Foreign Ministry. He went to work to revamp the entire cryptographic establishment of the *gaimu-sho* (Foreign Ministry). The security of the Cable Section, he found, left much to be desired. Its doors were never closed, much less locked. Access to the Code Room was easy for anyone, including messengers from nearby restaurants delivering food ordered by the personnel. The old-fashioned safes in which the code books were kept were left open even after the last clerk had left for home.

Many of the diplomatic missions abroad—including some of the major embassies and legations—had only primitive safes, none of them equipped with combination locks. The encoded telegrams and their plain-text copies were filed in wooden boxes that could not be locked at all. The code books were carelessly handled in transit—to and from the missions abroad—and there was reason to believe that at least one set had been compromised en route as a result of the courier's lax security measures.

Sawada now issued a six-point instruction sheet—entitled "Protection of Secrecy of Telegraphic Codes"—to remedy the situation. He sent them to some forty-odd missions abroad, with a questionnaire for suggestions of how to improve crypto-security still further. He admonished the code clerks to keep the code books not in actual use always locked up in the safes, and to remember the exact spot where they left them so that they might notice at once if the books had been moved or replaced during their absence.* Sawada then proceeded to develop a new system of codes and ciphers that, if not impossible to break, would at least resist cracking long enough to protect messages while their secrecy was imperative.

Most important—and, indeed, most crucial in the historic context—Sawada decided to automate Japanese cryptography through the introduction of cipher machines. The idea of using an instrument or apparatus or machine for the encrypting of secret messages was not new, of course. Thomas Jefferson had invented such a machine, as did Colonel Bazèries a century later. Innumerable others followed in a mushrooming industry to mechanize cryptology. When Dr. Siegfried Tuerkel, director of the Criminological Institute of the Vienna Police Department, compiled a list of patents in 1927, he found that a total of 196 had already been issued in six countries, forty-eight in the United States alone.**

Whether it was on Yardley's suggestion or on his own initiative, Section Chief Sawada sent Chief Cryptographer Ozeki to Europe to inspect the various machines on the market and purchase one or two of the best for adaptation to Japanese requirements. In Germany, Ozeki visited two firms making cryptographs—the Chiffrier-

---

* "A special, securely located office must be set aside at every mission," he wrote, "to serve as the Code Room. It must have steel doors with Yale locks and thick walls all around. The locks must be checked frequently and changed periodically." He introduced night watches, even at consulates, and initiated a system of what he called "code inspections," to take place every month on the 15th, instead of once a year as under the old regime.

** The first patents for so-called cryptographs were issued in 1877 in Germany, in 1893 in England, in 1904 in France, in 1899 in Austria, in 1892 in Switzerland and in 1893 in the United States.

Maschienen Co., which manufactured a device called Enigma by
its trade name; and the Ingenieurbureau Securitas, Ltd. At the
latter he met a Polish-Austrian engineer, Dr. Alexander de Kryha,
and was immensely impressed by the man.

Under Dr. de Kryha's spell, Ozeki purchased two Cryha machines. Back in Tokyo, he developed a Japanese version of the
Electro-Cryha, an electrically operated cipher machine of the type-
writer-combination type. The results were disappointing. The
modified Cryha proved difficult to handle, because the cipher text
had to be written down by hand. Moreover, the crypt produced by
the machine was easy to decipher, as the substitution series was
very short, consisting of less than twenty letters.

Sawada asked the navy's cryptographic branch to build a machine for the *denshin-ka*, basing it on the technical features of the
Cryha but improving them as far as possible. By the time the next
naval conference opened in London in January 1930, the code
clerks of the Japanese delegation had a machine with them—the
very first used by any Japanese diplomatic mission. It had hur-
riedly been put together by Captain Jinsaburo Ito's special group
in the navy.

However, it was far too big and too complex, and was plagued
by innumerable technical defects. The clerks, who had been
trained in a hurry to operate the machine, were not capable of
handling such a recalcitrant monster, and soon reverted to the old
systems. But good or bad, it was the beginning of a new era in
cryptology, introducing a novel element into the secret war between Japan and the United States, and casting its long shadows
far ahead.

Although Mr. Stimson's decision to abolish the "black chamber"
had removed a traitor from one of the most sensitive branches of
the government, it had other effects as well, not all of them as
fortunate. The Secretary's vehement objection to cryptographic
espionage reverberated in other government departments and created near-panic in the Office of Naval Intelligence.

The venturesome Captain Galbraith had left ONI, and with
the new directors cast in the old do-nothing mold, ONI was
reverting to its slumbering past. The director now was fifty-year-
old Captain Harry A. Baldridge, a sick man who was due to retire

momentarily. ONI was actually run by the assistant director, a martinet with reactionary concepts of intelligence activities. He was generally disliked in ONI, as his nickname, "Bill the Bastard," clearly indicated.

When word of Mr. Stimson's peremptory move became known in ONI, the assistant director prevailed upon Captain Baldridge also to retrench. All cryptological work was taken out of Naval Intelligence; and the old slush fund was turned in to the Treasury, with only half of its original amount having been expended. Room 2646 was evacuated, to become the office of the Naval Examining Board. All cryptographic co-operation with Naval Communications was terminated.

However, while the Navy was clamping the lid on cryptology and the State Department was abandoning it altogether, the Army suddenly embraced the cause with surprising vigor. As is so often the case in pioneering ventures, the Army's interest was inspired by a single zealot.

He was William Frederick Friedman, a native of the Bessarabian part of Czarist Russia, where he was born in 1891 at Kishenev, a huge ghetto town notorious for its pogroms. Brought to the United States at the age of two, he was destined for a remarkable career.

A graduate of Cornell University, where he majored in genetics in 1912, Friedman was employed by an eccentric textile millionaire, Colonel George Fabyan, at Riverbank Laboratories in Geneva, Illinois. This was a private research compound working on various projects in which the colonel had a personal interest. A romantic dabbler, Fabyan was fascinated by cryptology, chiefly because he hoped to prove, with the help of cryptanalysis, that Francis Bacon was the real author of the works attributed to William Shakespeare. At Riverbank, "Billy" Friedman met the young Canadian woman who was helping Fabyan to prove Bacon's authorship of Shakespeare's works. He fell in love and married Elizabeth Smith, and became a cryptologist like his wife. Although he was initially hired by Fabyan as director of his department of genetics, he threw himself into cryptology. Since he was an erudite man with a vast capacity for work, he was soon made director of Fabyan's department of ciphers.

At the time of World War I, the United States Army was unprepared for cryptological challenges.* In 1917 the Army had fewer than half a dozen experts on enemy code and cipher systems, not one of whom could be spared to work with MID. In this emergency Fabyan offered the War Department the use of his laboratory to train a group of officers and enlisted men in cryptography and cryptanalysis. The offer was accepted. At his own expense, Fabyan set up a cryptographic school at Riverbank for hand-picked Army personnel, and delegated Friedman to organize and direct a faculty. Friedman was later made a lieutenant in the Signal Reserve, and sent to France for service with the AEF's Military Intelligence Division.

After the war he returned to Riverbank, but only because he had no other place to go. By then his relations with Fabyan had deteriorated. Although Friedman appreciated the opportunities he had found on the millionaire's estate, he came to regard Fabyan (a colonel by courtesy of the Governor of Illinois) as a humbug artist like the Wizard of Oz.

He was therefore relieved when, in January 1921, the Signal Corps invited him to take charge of its Code and Cipher Section —to develop "new systems and devices, and improve security procedures in the handling of the Army's crypto-system." Friedman moved to Washington, and with only a single assistant, carried on the task until 1929.

Cryptanalysis—a term he himself had coined, thus dignifying the function of code-cracking with a scientific-sounding name— was not among his responsibilities, but he regarded it as an integral part of his duties. He held with the view expressed by Major General Earl F. Cook, chief signal officer in the early sixties, that "those who have the responsibility of creating the Army's security system should also be assigned cryptanalytical duties."

Friedman set himself up as a one-man lobby in the War Department to gain recognition and scope for the activity. An eloquent little man, and an intense and apparently sincere person of conta-

* What little there was of the activity was subdivided among the Military Intelligence Division, the Adjutant General and the Signal Corps. The war then created yet another split, between Washington and the AEF. In France, Brigadier General Edgar Russell, Pershing's chief signal officer, was charged with the collateral functions of signal intelligence, while G-2 in Washington took over cryptological work and hired Yardley to manage it.

gious enthusiasm, "Billy" Friedman emerged in the Munitions Building as Larry Safford's counterpart—the mastermind, the organizer, the defender, the very personification of aggressive cryptology as a major instrument of intelligence.

His relations with Safford were excellent. Ties of close personal friendship and a communion of interests bound them, enhancing their appeal and bolstering their case. Safford, on his part, relegated himself to second place in this partnership. He was leaning heavily on his friend and colleague in whom he admired a rare combination of old-world sophistication and broad intellectual vision.

In the spring of 1929 Friedman persuaded Major General George S. Gibbs, the chief signal officer (who, in 1917, had foisted Yardley on MID), to effect a change in Army regulations placing all work connected with codes and ciphers under his office. In the course of the change the Signal Intelligence Service (SIS) was created, and Friedman was named its director. Its duties now explicitly included "interception of enemy radio and wire traffic, the goniometric location of enemy radio stations, the solution of intercepted enemy code and cipher messages, and laboratory arrangements for the employment and detection of secret ink."

It was obvious that Friedman could not handle his new job with only the one assistant, so Gibbs gave him five more. For years afterward the staff remained small, but according to the official history of the Army's Signal Security Agency, these seven persons "accomplished valuable spade work toward emergency war planning." *

---

* From May 1929, when he was made director of SIS, until his retirement from active service in 1950, Colonel Friedman remained the central figure in American cryptology, in perfect partnership with Captain Laurence Safford.

PART II

Into the Dark Valley

6 **Nothing Sacred, Nothing Secret**

In the late spring of 1931, when American diplomats were occupied with a crisis created by Germany's refusal to pay her debts and reparations, the State Department found itself involved in two perplexing incidents much closer to home. The Washington police had uncovered a flourishing bookmaking racket and traced its ringleaders to the State Department mailroom. Then a book appeared with the provocative title *The American Black Chamber*, revealing all the awkward secrets of the code-cracking operation in that New York brownstone. There could be no doubt about its authenticity. Its author was Herbert O. Yardley. Determined to avenge his humiliation, he had hit upon the idea of writing a book; he knew that his revelations could not hurt him but would deeply embarrass the American government.

He plotted his revenge under the guise of a patriotic stance. Since the "black chamber" had been abolished, he rationalized, there could be no valid reason for keeping mum about it. He would share its secrets with his countrymen so that, as he put it, the United States "may protect herself from the prying eyes of skillful foreign cryptographers." He entered into a publishing contract with The Bobbs-Merrill Company in Indianapolis, then retired to his home town, Worthington, Indiana, to write the book.

It came out on May 31,* when the State Department was

---

* "It is my aim," Yardley wrote in the Preface, "to unfold in a simple dispassionate way the intimate details of a secret organization that I fostered for the American Government; an organization which, at its height of power, employed one hundred and sixty-five men and women."

disconcerted by the discovery of that "bookie joint" in its mail-room. Besieged by reporters on the scent of a scandal, the Department spokesman resolved to meet the truth halfway. He admitted that the police had, indeed, found two men among its messengers who had made book on the ponies, but he denied categorically that anything like a "black chamber" had ever existed, either in State or anywhere else in the entire government.

William R. Castle, Jr., the Undersecretary of State, asserted to the press that he "had not heard of the existence of such a bureau in all of his years in the Department." The *New York Times* reported from Washington: "Officials are inclined to be indignant over Major Yardley's assertions. . . . Nothing of the sort happened, they said, and denied that any such practice ever had been sanctioned."

The reporters tried to check out the Yardley story with Secretary Stimson by phoning him at his residence. Mr. Stimson refused to take their calls, but authorized someone in his household to state that "the Secretary has never heard of any such organization." A similar denial was issued by General Douglas MacArthur, the Army Chief of Staff.

In off-the-record briefings, however, representatives of the State and War departments confirmed parts of Yardley's exposé, but insisting that "no such bureau was now in existence," pleaded that the press play down the revelations. And they did all they could to discredit Yardley, mostly by harping on his more patently absurd assertions, such as his bizarre claim that an attempt had been made to poison President Wilson in Paris.*

Probably because the newspapers themselves were taking many of Yardley's revelations with a grain of salt, the press went along with the government's plea. The *New York Times* buried the story on page 18 in its June 2 issue, giving it just seven inches of space under a one-column headline: "Deny Our Statesmen Read Envoy's Ciphers: State Department Officials Discredit Yardley's Story of a 'Black Chamber.' " **

---

* Major General Peyton C. March, who had been Chief of Staff of the Army at the time of the Paris peace conference, came out of retirement to avow that he "never had heard of any such 'plot.' "

** On June 15 the New York *Evening Sun* came out with a sharp editorial against Yardley. "We wish that Theodore Roosevelt were alive," the paper

Yardley tried desperately to stay in the limelight and exploit the publicity. Press releases pouring from his publisher's mimeograph machines announced that the Pathé Studios would make *The American Black Chamber* into a motion picture starring Constance Bennett (Yardley was to serve as technical adviser), and that he had been hired by Northwestern University to fight crime in Chicago by cracking the gangsters' codes. He also went on a lecture tour, but when the response turned out to be much less enthusiastic and lucrative than he had expected, he returned to Worthington again and went into business with W. I. Pryor, a local printer, to exploit an invention of his which he described as "secret printing."

Yardley's indiscretion induced the government to pass a bill in Congress prohibiting its "agents . . . from appropriating secret documents." When it became known a year later that Yardley was planning another book on the theme, called *Japanese Diplomatic Secrets*, federal agents seized the manuscript in the office of his literary agent. An attempt was then made to have him indicted by a New York grand jury, but the government did not pursue the case. He was never tried for security violations. And nothing on the record shows that the United States government ever found out about his arrangement with the Japanese. Yardley vanished from public view, pushed into limbo by a quiet campaign of obfuscation.*

· · ·

said, "to read to the author of this book a lecture on betraying the secrets of one's country." Yardley replied with a letter of righteous indignation. "It seems to me," he wrote on June 20, "that my book may possibly render a real public service in at least pointing out the conditions existing as a first step toward achieving their remedy."

* In subsequent years, Yardley published a number of books: *Yardleygrams* in 1932, *The Blonde Countess* and *Red Sun of Nippon* in 1934, *Crows Are Black Everywhere* in 1945 and *The Education of a Poker Player* in 1957. In 1937 Metro-Goldwyn-Mayer bought *The Blonde Countess* as a starring vehicle for William Powell, under the title *Rendezvous*. That year Yardley went briefly into the real estate business on Long Island; in 1940 he opened a restaurant in Washington. For a short spell in the late thirties Yardley had returned to cryptology, ostensibly working for China on Japanese codes. During World War II he was employed as an enforcement officer in the Food Division at the headquarters of the Office of Price Administration. He died on August 7, 1958, at his home in Washington, D.C., at the age of sixty-nine, and was buried at Arlington Cemetery with the usual military honors.

In the morning of June 4, 1931, Shin Sakuma, Sawada's successor as chief of the Cable Section, rushed a freshly decoded telegram to Foreign Minister Baron Kijuro Shidehara. It was from Katsuji Debuchi, the Japanese ambassador in Washington, advising the Foreign Minister of the appearance of *The American Black Chamber*. The long message included a summary of the book, placing special emphasis on its chapters about the cracking of the Japanese codes during the Washington Conference. That same morning the newspapers *Nippon* and *Nichi-Nichi* printed the first dispatches of their Washington correspondents about the Yardley book. The Osaka *Mainichi Shimbun* announced that it had purchased the Japanese rights and was planning to print the book as soon as the translation was completed.

Baron Shidehara recognized at once the extraordinary significance of the event. A sensitive man of integrity, he was chagrined that his American friends had stooped to such means to take advantage of Japan, and as he saw it, to hurt him personally. He had spent the itinerant years of his distinguished diplomatic service in London, The Hague and Washington, and prided himself on his knowledge of Western history and mores, and on his fluency in the English language. The fifty-nine-year-old Foreign Minister—probably the most pro-Western of Japanese statesmen —was the courageous spokesman of all the conciliatory policies of these years. While he was ambassador in Washington in the early twenties he was instrumental in relaxing the tension with the United States and in bringing about a rapprochement with China.

The appearance of the Yardley book threatened to shatter all his efforts and hopes. He was all the more shocked since after his return to the *gaimu-sho* in July 1929 as Foreign Minister in Premier Yuko Hamaguchi's Cabinet, nobody in his Ministry had thought it necessary to tell him that the Japanese diplomatic cipher had been cracked by the Americans.

He summoned a ranking official of the Ministry of Communications, a certain Watanabe, to find out how Yardley could have obtained the privileged Japanese cables. Watanabe was a realist. He explained to the Foreign Minister the facts of diplomatic life —how simple it was to get, buy, steal or borrow such raw material in the black market. Watanabe was in charge of the very section in the Communications Ministry that was "rerouting" the cables of the diplomatic corps in Tokyo to the Code Research Group in Shidehara's own Foreign Ministry, where they were read exactly as Yardley had examined the Japanese telegrams in his own time.

This was a sobering bit of information that considerably dampened the Foreign Minister's pious anger. But when he learned that Yardley's operation was not only a breach of confidence but actually a breach of certain American laws that explicitly prohibited intrusions on the privacy of telegrams, he insisted that the legal issue be raised in protest to the United States. However, Section Chief Sakuma prevailed upon him to drop the idea of instituting any action in Washington.

Early in July the *Mainichi Shimbun* began publication of the Yardley book, creating consternation throughout Japan. This became the signal for the anti-Shidehara elements to go into action. A group of deputies in the Diet demanded that the case of the "*Amerikan Burakku Chiemba*" be aired thoroughly in a full-scale debate. In the Foreign Ministry, the harassed Sakuma dutifully drafted a long memorandum for Shidehara with deftly worded answers to all possible questions he expected the hostile deputies might ask. But the Foreign Minister was never given an opportunity to read them in the Diet.

On August 15 an editorial in *Nippon* made the Foreign Minister personally responsible for Japan's humiliating defeat at the Washington Conference, where he had been a delegate. It asked for his removal from office and demanded that the whole Wakatsuki Cabinet resign with him. By then Shidehara had some reason to suspect that the turmoil Yardley's exposé had created in Japan was being exploited shrewdly by the army clique to remove him from their path.

Shidehara had been receiving reports from his representatives in Manchuria with the warning that some kind of "direct action" was being planned by the Kwantung Army against the Chinese. On September 18, acting on the pretext that Chinese soldiers had tried to blow up the tracks of the South Manchurian Railway just north of Mukden, Japanese soldiers attacked the Chinese garrison. The next morning they seized the arsenals of Mukden, Antung, Yingkou and Chang-chun. The first shot had been fired in what became known as the Manchurian Incident.

Shidehara was thoroughly discredited. The Wakatsuki Cabinet was doomed and the government fell in December. Shidehara vanished through a trap door in history, to reappear fourteen years later—by then an old man of seventy-three, yet the symbol of a new Japan—as the first postwar Premier of his vanquished country.

What had begun as a mere political scandal, unleashed by an unscrupulous adventurer, developed into an international tragedy. Japan entered *kurai tanima* ("the Dark Valley") as the hectic period between 1931 and 1941 came to be called.

She had taken the first step on the road to Pearl Harbor.

Cabinets are toppled and ministers come and go, but the departments of state continue the business of government as usual. Baron Shidehara was gone. But Shin Sakuma remained at the head of the Ministry's Cable Section, in supreme command of the secret war with the United States.

Sakuma, too, had been jolted by the appearance of *The American Black Chamber*, but he was not surprised. In a memorandum reviewing this battle of cryptology in all its ramifications, he dismissed the wayward American who had created the stir. "What can you expect of a rascal," he wrote, "who was willing to sell his country?"

By this time Sakuma had every reason to be pleased with the state of cryptology in his Cable Section. It had grown and improved under his supervision. Three government agencies now maintained elaborate cryptological bureaus, and he was satisfied that the Japanese combine—for it had indeed become a combine in just three years—was better and bigger than anything the Americans had been left with after the dismantling of the "black chamber."

The establishment included cipher bureaus in the Foreign Ministry's Cable Section, and in the Navy and Army General Staffs. Under an arrangement with the Communications Ministry, which controlled all telegraphic traffic, the Foreign Ministry was obtaining copies of the coded telegrams of the foreign diplomatic and consular missions in Tokyo, "for the purpose of research in coding techniques." They were "processed" by the branch of the *denshinka* called the Code Research Group, headed by Captain Inouye on loan to the Foreign Ministry from the navy. By 1931 most of the diplomatic codes had been solved by the Group, enabling the Ministry to read telegrams of foreign envoys on the scale of Yardley's defunct organization.

In 1925 the Imperial Navy had added a communications intelligence branch to the Fourth (Communications) Bureau of the Naval General Staff. Headed by Captain Jinsaburo Ito, it had a "radio detection center" at Tachibana Mura and a "research" section in Tokyo, then occupying a single room, to "analyze" the crypto-systems of other navies. A Polish expert, Captain Jan Kowalewski, was hired to teach Japanese personnel cryptology in all its ramifications.

The network was then gradually expanded. By 1938 it included (now under Captain Gonichiro Kakimoto) the so-called 11th Section, engaged in (a) cryptanalysis (Group A under Commander Imaizumi attacking the American and Group B under Captain Tabe the British crypto-systems), and (b) radio detection (First Combined Communications Unit, under Commander Naosada Arisawa) with the Oowada Signal Intelligence Corps, near Tokyo, and monitoring stations at Wakkanai, Ominato and Maizuru in Japan, Takao in Formosa, and Chinkai in Korea, and a station on Marcus Island in the Pacific. The Oowada station alone had 181 radio-monitoring and 20 direction-finding units.

The army's communications intelligence branch worked on the entire spectrum of secret communications. Maintained as Group 18 of the Army General Staff's Signal Division (Tanashi Signal Intelligence Corps) and headed by Colonel Tomokatsu Matsumura, it was preoccupied mainly with the monitoring and analyzing of Chinese and Russian crypto-systems.

Section Chief Shin Sakuma brought a wholesome sense of proportion to his approach to cryptology, probably because he himself was not a professional cryptographer but a career Foreign Service officer. He was doubtful whether absolute secrecy could be sustained in diplomatic or, for that matter, any communications unless the exchange of encrypted messages was kept to a minimum and limited to an infinitesimally small number of parties.

Despite his skepticism, Sakuma decided to seek means to improve the safety of his Ministry's classified traffic. The Japanese imported a Frenchman, regarded at that time as the world's foremost cryptographer. He was Brigadier General Henri Cartier, whose *verts*—transcripts of decrypted German messages distributed in France on green foolscap—had contributed materially to the Allied victory in World War I.*

He did much to improve Japan's crypto-system by training a new generation of native cryptologists and by developing a series of complex codes and ciphers. His most important contribution, however, was his contagious enthusiasm for cryptographic machines at a time when many of the professionals were still opposed to them.

Nothing was done until 1931, however, perhaps because of the dismal experience with the Cryha-type machine at the London naval conference. But on July 29—in the midst of the Yardley crisis—Sakuma was invited by Captain Ito to a conference at his office in the Naval General Staff. Sakuma went with Ozeki and Captain Inouye to the meeting, and was introduced to a man named Ichiro Hamada, a civilian inventor who had with him the blueprints of an "undecipherable cryptomachine" which he was trying to sell to the navy.

Both Ozeki and Inouye were favorably impressed with Hamada's design. His yet-to-be-built machine promised several important advantages. It would be small and light, relatively simple in construction, easy to operate, and since it could be broken down into four parts, easier to transport.

Captain Ito then startled Sakuma by inviting him to join the navy in developing the machine. Sakuma had been aware that the navy was experimenting with improved cipher machines for its own crypto-communications. But all his previous efforts to participate in the experiments for the benefit of his Cable Section had been rebuffed because the navy considered all coding equipment "secret weapons."

* As an officer of the Reserve specializing in cryptology, Cartier worked between 1900 and 1912 as secretary for the French Commission for Military Cryptology under Generals Penel, Berthaut and Castelnau. In 1912 he was made chief of the Cipher Section at the Ministry of War, then became head of the cryptological services of the *Deuxième Bureau* of the General Staff, remaining until 1914. After leaving the French army in 1919, he became available as a consultant and thus worked for various foreign governments as well as individuals.

The reason why Captain Ito was suddenly willing to share the machine with the Foreign Ministry was similar to the United States Army's willingness to share Yardley's "black chamber" with the State Department. On his own limited budget Ito could not afford to finance the building of the Hamada machine. He hit upon the idea of obtaining a prototype by persuading the Foreign Ministry to pay for it. As a matter of fact, not too much money was involved. One of the attractions of Hamada's device was its low cost—about half the price of the huge contraption the navy had produced for the London Conference in 1927.* But Ito did not have even this small sum.

The proposal was approved, the funds were transferred, and Ito had twelve machines built by a small group of hand-picked mechanics in a sealed workshop at the Naval Technical Institute.

This was how the first practical cipher machine was born in Japan. In the navy it was named TYPE NO. 91 after the year of its inception (1931 was the year 2591 according to the Japanese calendar). The slightly modified version which Ito gave the Foreign Ministry was given the designation A machine in the *denshinka*. Four of the machines were completed in time for the Geneva Conference—two kept in the Cable Section, and two sent abroad. When all twelve machines became available, two were sent to the mission in Washington, and one each to the embassies in Paris, London, Berlin, Rome and Moscow, and to the consulate general in Shanghai.

After that Sakuma—according to his own account—slept more easily. He was still not completely convinced that perfect security had been achieved with the A machine. But he was confident that it would take some time before the Americans could crack its automated ciphers.

* The bulky 1927 machine had cost 4500 yen to build. Hamada budgeted his machine at 2300 yen (about $1250 and $600, respectively, at the rate of exchange in those days).

The RED Machine

The cryptanalysts of the United States Navy immediately recognized the complexity of the new Japanese cipher, and they assumed that it was tied to some sort of a machine.

At the time of the discovery the Research Desk was again in the throes of one of its periodic internal crises. Commander Safford had been removed from his job and was on sea duty. His departure in 1932 brought cryptanalysis in the Navy almost to a standstill, at a time when Japan was again ready to hold one of its grand maneuvers with what appeared to be an especially intriguing Fleet Problem. To make things worse, the Japanese had changed their FLEET code on the eve of the exercises, and the small, leaderless staff of the Research Desk could not solve it in time. So for the first time since 1927, the Japanese staged their war games in privacy.

And yet this was but a transient period of crisis. The Navy continued to have a pressing interest in Japan and needed whatever intelligence it could assemble about the Imperial Navy. Since cryptanalysis was not only the best but almost the only means to obtain this information, communications intelligence survived in the Navy even during Safford's long absence. A handful of younger officers were assigned to the Desk, both to fill the vacuum and to aid in the growth of the organization.

One of them was Lieutenant Thomas Harold Dyer, a thirty-one-year-old Kansan, Annapolis class of 1924. He had taken special instruction in communications intelligence in 1927, and served as communications officer both afloat and ashore until his transfer to the Research Desk. Another newcomer, Lieutenant Wesley Arnold Wright of Brooklyn, had attended the Academy after three years of service in the old *Florida,* then served as gunnery officer in the *New York* and as ordnance officer in training before joining the Research Desk.

He and other young officers embarking on a lifelong career in communications intelligence at this time formed a remarkable band of lieutenants from all branches of the service. The group included Thomas A. Huckins, Jack Sebastian Holtwick, Jr., and Henry Williams, Jr.—names to remember because they were all destined to shine brightly, even if anonymously, during the climactic stage of this endeavor.

It was a strange group. Impatient, intolerant, vibrant and gregarious within the confines of their craft, they could also be rude in their relations outside their own circle. They were the "nuts" Rochefort once said make the best cryptologists. Though they were Regular Navy, they regarded themselves anything but regular. Dyer once persisted in growing a beard, although it was against regulations, doing it only to antagonize a superior officer he loathed. Another officer refused to work during the day, insisting he was suffering from a condition he called "nyctitropism," which made him sleep all day and work all night.

The young officers lacked a sense of reality but regarded themselves as the most realistic of men. And they had a kind of superman complex that conceded no flaw or inferiority as far as they were concerned. When one of them was invited to play tennis, he refused to admit that he didn't know how. He obtained a book about the game, studied it and became an excellent player.

But whatever idiosyncrasies they had, they were superbly qualified for their assignment. The new Japanese cipher was their first test with a machine, and it proved a formidable one.

Since the Japanese were using the A machine almost exclusively to encrypt their diplomatic dispatches, its recovery should have been of primary importance to the State Department. However, State was still in its gentlemanly mood as far as code-cracking was concerned. When it became evident that the A machine was also being used to encode the dispatches of the Japanese naval attachés and that some of the reports of their secret agents were in this cipher as well, the A machine became of immediate interest to the Navy, and its cryptanalysts were instructed to go to work on it.

Attack on a sophisticated cipher is a difficult undertaking in which analysis is regarded only as a last resort. Determined efforts are made, therefore, by all intelligence agencies to gain direct access to the other fellow's crypto-systems without the backbreaking (and often heartbreaking) chore of cracking them in the tedious analytical process.

As a matter of fact, the greatest danger to codes and ciphers is not the analytic approach. "If one evaluates realistically," wrote Boris Hagelin, Sr., one of the master builders of modern crypto-machines, "the various ways by which an enemy can successfully recover a cryptographic usage, one is forced to the conclusion that by far the greatest source of danger is from unauthorized access to cryptographic instructions, key lists and related documents."

In this case, too, it became essential to obtain at least some clues to the machine itself—an instruction sheet, if possible, or the keys used in setting the machine. Nothing of this nature was available to the analysts of the Research Desk and it seemed, therefore, that the new machine-based cipher would defy solution. But then help came—from the Office of Naval Intelligence.

Several times during the sultry nights of July 1935 Captain Tamon Yamaguchi, the Japanese naval attaché in Washington, was annoyed by recurrent failures of the electricity in the Alban Towers, a fashionable apartment house on Wisconsin Avenue where he had his living quarters and office. The lights would flicker, grow dim, then go out altogether. But before he could summon an electrician, they would return and everything would be all right—until the next time.

On July 26 all the officers of Captain Yamaguchi's staff were attending a dinner party given by Ellis and Claire Zacharias at their house on Porter Street. The couple had recently returned to Washington when Commander Zacharias was reassigned to ONI as chief of the Far Eastern Section.

Yamaguchi and Zacharias were on friendly terms. In fact, one reason for Zacharias' being ordered back to Washington was because ONI thought Yamaguchi could bear more than routine watching. The presence of these two mercurial intelligence officers in Washington led to a spirited bout behind the scenes—an affair of honor rather than a stand-up fight—as each tried to outwit the other. Their friendship was kept in constant repair by the small triumphs each man scored.

Yamaguchi (who appreciated a good meal and knew that he would be served an exquisite one at Claire Zacharias' table) was pleased, therefore, to accept his friend's invitation to the party. Zacharias told him that it would be held to celebrate the *chugen,* a popular midsummer festival in Japan, during which people exchange gifts as compliments of the season. The naval attaché took all his aides along, leaving only his chauffeur (who doubled as bodyguard and watchman) and his young yeoman (who was also his code clerk) at the apartment.

Captain Yamaguchi was having his third martini when the lights in his apartment on Wisconsin Avenue went dim again, then flickered and went out. When they did not come back, the code clerk called the desk downstairs. Shortly afterward two men dressed in overalls and carrying a huge tool box showed up, identified themselves as electricians and proceeded to subject the entire apartment to the most minute inspection. They checked all electrical equipment, examined the wiring in the walls, tested the sockets, tried out the switches and scrutinized whatever fixtures they could find.

In the Code Room their powerful flashlights traced the contours of the safe and various crypto-paraphernalia on the clerk's worktable. By the time Captain Yamaguchi settled down to Claire Zacharias' turtle soup (served in lacquered Japanese bowls), the inspection had been completed, the trouble spot found and the short circuit fixed. The lights were on again, enabling the clerk to go back to encoding the message he had been working on at a typewriterlike machine when the power failure had interrupted him.

Needless to say, the blackout had been staged by Zacharias to clear up certain mysteries that were baffling the Research Desk. Dyer and Holtwick had asked ONI to find out whether Yamaguchi kept an electric cipher machine on his premises, and if so, to try to determine what it looked like. The electricians were a pair of ONI operatives. "Their inspection by flashlight," Zacharias later wrote, "had covered *everything* we desired." And "everything" in this case included clues to the coding machine—the typewriterlike apparatus on the clerk's worktable—that Yamaguchi was using.

This was only one part of a two-pronged attack. Many miles from the search on Wisconsin Avenue, another Japanese naval officer was trapped by ONI agents in the hope that he would supply the missing link the Research Desk was clamoring for.

He was Lieutenant Toshikazu Ohmae of the Imperial Navy. From a Miss Sakanishi, a double agent working in the Library of Congress, Zacharias had learned that Ohmae was in the United States to deliver a set of keys for the naval attaché's new cipher machine. Then he found out from Miss Sakanishi that Ohmae would be driving back to the West Coast on his return trip to Japan, stopping, among other places, in Davenport, Iowa, an important rail and industrial center on the Mississippi River.

Arrangements were made to spice the lieutenant's brief stay at Davenport with some controlled divertissement. A comely young woman who (either for patriotic or purely professional reasons) was willing to share her bed with Ohmae was planted at his hotel, and she succeeded in enticing the lieutenant to her room. It was a brief tryst, but it lasted long enough to enable an ONI operative to examine Ohmae's briefcase and find what was later described as "a document of the greatest significance." From these and other clues the young cryptologists of the Research Desk assembled a working copy of the A machine, which the Japanese had developed four years before.

The reproduction of the machine was a milestone. It was the first time that a cipher machine of such complexity had been "solved" anywhere. The possession of the machine itself now made it possible to decrypt the dispatches by machine. This reduced the work to the analytic task of solving the keys, a considerably simpler chore and faster process than the solution of the cipher.

The reconstructed TYPE NO. 91-A machine was arbitrarily given the name "RED machine" by the Americans.* Although its "solu-

* Up to December 7, 1941, five of these machines were built for use in the United States Navy. One each was allotted to Washington, Pearl Harbor and Cavite. The other two were later bartered to the British, who installed them in London and Singapore, respectively. None was given to the United States Army, which continued to be kept in the dark about the remarkable achievements of the Navy's cryptanalysts.

tion" did not create either the sensation or the jubilation that would greet the cracking of the PURPLE code in 1940, the importance of this achievement cannot be overstated. For one thing, some of the important Japanese dispatches continued to be encrypted on the RED even after its far more sophisticated successor had come into use. For another, without the technical clues gained from the RED machine, the PURPLE would have been even more difficult to crack.

Such are the exigencies of their trade and so rapid are the changes that no cryptologist is ever allowed to rest on his laurels. No sooner had the A machine been solved than the Americans were confronted with much bigger challenges.

As the Japanese accelerated their march into "the Dark Valley," ironclad secrecy became a crucial element in their transactions, to cloak their moves. They needed bigger and better secret services to accommodate their vastly grown needs. The intelligence services became an operational arm by themselves—"the major instrument abroad," as Allen W. Dulles has phrased it, "probing and preparing for foreign expansion."

Japanese-American relations continued in a flux, but from 1931 on, the Japanese felt not merely justified but actually compelled to cover the United States with "cryptographic espionage" as well as their best secret agents. They saw in the American government the major stumbling block in the path of their aspirations. Determined American opposition to Japanese moves in Manchuria and Shanghai, and the introduction of the so-called Stimson Doctrine, moved this country into the front line of the enemies of this new Japan.*

The Stimson policy then continued under Franklin D. Roosevelt. On March 7, 1933, only three days after his inauguration, Mr. Roosevelt raised the issue of a possible war with Japan, concluding that all the United States would have to do in such a war would be "to starve Japan into defeat within three to five years."

---

* Under the Stimson Doctrine, enunciated on January 7, 1932, the United States would not "recognize any situation, treaty or agreement which may be brought about by means contrary to the covenants and obligations of the Pact of Paris," the so-called Briand-Kellogg Pact, signed in Paris on August 27, 1927, which outlawed aggressive wars.

The President told his Cabinet that in a war with Japan the Navy would have to do the fighting while the Army watched from the side lines. The Japanese had pretty much the same idea as far as their own navy and army were concerned. This determined the orientation of their secret services. In this division of labor, the Naval Intelligence-Naval Communications combine of the United States was assigned to Japan. In Tokyo the Third (Intelligence) Bureau of the Naval General Staff was given the job of covering the United States.*

This was a seesaw battle. But by the mid-thirties the initiative had shifted back to the Japanese.

---

* In his book, *The Craft of Intelligence*, Allen Dulles wrote: "Our Army and Navy had, fortunately, begun to address themselves to the problem of cryptanalysis in the late 1920's, with particular emphasis on Japan, since American military thinking at that time foresaw Japan as the major potential foe of the United States in whatever war was to come next." This is a fair statement except for the fact that the Army and Navy began to become involved in cryptanalysis with emphasis on Japan not in the late but already in the early 1920's, and kept up their coverage for the next twenty-five years.

8 The **Burakku** **Chiemba** and TYPE NO. 97

One evening in September 1935 a German businessman named Friedrich Wilhelm Hack gave a smoker in his suburban villa near Berlin for his good friend Joachim von Ribbentrop, a former champagne salesman who had become Hitler's diplomatic adviser. Dr. Hack had many Japanese friends from his days in Tokyo, where he had worked for the South Manchurian Railway Administration. Ribbentrop was using him as a pipe line to some of the more militant Japanese imperialists stationed in Berlin.

There were only two other guests at the party—Admiral Wilhelm Canaris, head of the *Abwehrabteilung,* the secret intelligence department of the German armed forces, and Colonel Hiroshi Oshima, the Japanese military attaché. It was a smoker with a purpose. Ribbentrop had the vision of a formidable military alliance with Japan against the Soviet Union, and had asked his friend Hack to arrange an informal party at which he could propose the idea to Colonel Oshima.

Canaris was there because he, too, had a vision. Still new in the *Abwehrabteilung* (he had been appointed its chief the previous January), he was trying to broaden its base, particularly to improve the collection of intelligence in the Soviet Union. He was seeking an agreement with the intelligence services of Japan under which they would divide the world and exchange information—

the Japanese covering the U.S.S.R. and Asia while the Germans would specialize in Europe and the Western Hemisphere.

The Ribbentrop plan for a military alliance was opposed by the army authorities in both Germany and Japan, and became merely the ephemeral anti-Comintern pact in the end. But the Japanese navy welcomed closer co-operation with the Germans, for more reasons than one. First of all, the *joho kyoku*—the Third (Intelligence) Bureau of the Naval General Staff—was eager to obtain some of the remarkable new German gadgets, like the Mikropunkt and the Aku-Gerät, that Section I-G of the *Abwehrabteilung* was developing for operatives in the field.*

But most of all, the prospect of Germans or other Caucasians spying for them in the United States appealed enormously to the Japanese. They were losing ground in America, where it was becoming increasingly difficult to operate with their own conspicuous nationals.

The *joho kyoku* not only agreed to the spy alliance but also pressed Canaris for the immediate implementation of its part aimed at the United States. On October 5, therefore, a convention of German and Japanese intelligence officers assembled at Cuernavaca, a resort town near Mexico City, to formalize the compact and work out details of the co-operation. The Germans were represented by Dr. Heinrich Northe, chief of the *Abwehrabteilung* in North America, and by Hermann von Keitel, his resident director in the United States, who had come down from his headquarters in New York. The Japanese sent Captain Kanji Ogawa, chief of the Naval Intelligence Division's America Section. He was joined at Cuernavaca by Commander Bunjiro Yamaguchi, the assistant naval attaché in Washington, and two newcomers to the American scene, Commander Inao Ohtani and Lieutenant Commander Ko Nagasawa, who were to serve as liaison with the Germans on the West Coast.

---

* Called "the masterpiece of German espionage" by J. Edgar Hoover, *Mikropunkt* (or "microdot") was an amazing process by which an entire page of copy could be reduced to the size of the dot of a typewriter. The full-stop periods of a letter would then be punched out by a special machine and replaced by the microdots. The message could be read under a microscope or enlarged by another ingenious process. The Aku-Gerät was a compact but tremendously potent radio sender-receiver set that could be accommodated in the false bottom of an ordinary suitcase.

At the conclusion of the meeting Commander Yamaguchi boarded a train, apparently to return to Washington. But he went only as far as Phoenix, Arizona. There he was joined by a distinguished-looking Japanese gentleman traveling on a passport made out to Dr. Kenji Iwamoto, a dentist residing at Cananea, a Mexican city near the United States border. During the next few weeks Dr. Iwamoto was to act as Yamaguchi's guide on a brief sightseeing tour around the Gulf of California.

In Phoenix the two men took a Southern Pacific train south to Nogales, a point of entry to Mexico from the United States, where a certain L. Z. Okumura was waiting in a new Ford V-8 truck. Okumura drove them through the broad, low coastland to Guaymas, a small port city on the gulf popular as a fishing resort. The journey ended in a soda-water bottling plant on Avenida XIV, where Dr. Iwamoto introduced Commander Yamaguchi to the owner, a certain Keigo Matsumiya, who had come to Guaymas in 1930 and was the senior member of the city's Japanese community.

In Matsumiya's office Yamaguchi met a man named Edisioka, the local agent of the Nippon Saison Kaisha Company, which operated a number of fishing boats in the Pacific, and two other men—Saichi Imamura and Yokichi Matsui. The group was then joined by a Caucasian who had come up from Mexico City and registered at the Club de Pesca, one of the better hotels in town, as "Juan G. Lübke."

They all boarded Matsumiya's yacht for a leisurely cruise across the gulf to Santa Rosalía and then down to San José at Cape San Lucas, on the southernmost tip of the long, barren Baja California Sur peninsula.

The movement of the group did not escape the attention of the "Jap-watchers," certain Americans and Mexicans in Sonora whom ONI and the FBI had organized to keep tabs on the state's substantial Japanese population of small farmers and fishermen, doctors, dentists, barbers, photographers and haberdashers. Two of the men in the group were known to ONI as commanders of the Imperial Navy on intelligence duty in the strategic area. Posing as director of the NSK Company in Mexico, Imamura had been identified as chief of the Japanese naval intelligence network along the Mexican Pacific coast. Matsumiya, the prosperous owner of the bottling plant, was his ranking agent for the Sonora region.

Matsui, who was carried on the roster of the Japanese legation in Mexico City as a fishery expert, with the rank of third secretary, was actually a communications specialist supervising all Japanese activities of this kind in North America.* The man who gave his name as "Lübke" at the Club de Pesca was the *Abwehr's* communications specialist in North America.

A report sent to ONI by one of its local observers speculated that these Japanese had been on a "fishing expedition" to survey the sheltered inland sea with its many excellent natural anchorages as a possible haven for an invasion fleet. From then on, ONI was on the lookout for signs of surreptitious fortifications of the fishing villages in the gulf and for work on the anchorages. But nothing of this nature ever developed.

Actually, the Japanese explored the area to find secluded spots where they could set up stations to monitor the radio traffic of the American Navy. Admiral Gonichiro Kakimoto's Section 11 already had listening posts in Japan proper, in China, Formosa, Korea and the Pacific Ocean, to cover the Royal Navy and the U.S. Asiatic Fleet. At the conference in Cuernavaca, Captain Ogawa had suggested that the network be extended to the American West Coast by setting up a station in Mexico, and Dr. Northe volunteered to donate the best German equipment he could find in Mexico or obtain from Germany.

With the help of their German friends, the Japanese established two monitoring stations in the area—one in Guaymas, in a secluded little house on Calle 22, the other on the southernmost tip of Baja California Sur. Both were managed by a lieutenant named Yamashita, who had been sent from Japan with a crew of signalmen. Their equipment included sensitive Telefunken radio search devices, and also such sophisticated monitoring gear as the GHG-Apparat, which could pick up propeller sounds at considerable distances: as well as a number of direction finders, like the Olympia and the Michael, which Northe and Herr Lübke obtained from the *Kriegsmarine* (German navy).

The new stations in Mexico now extended the coverage to three

* Matsui was still in Mexico City in 1941, whence he directed the dismantling of Japanese communications equipment and the destruction of all crypto-paraphernalia in the United States on the eve of Pearl Harbor.

American naval districts embracing eleven Western states, all the naval installations on the West Coast and the communications net. They could monitor the movements of ships and the American fleet exercises as far as Hawaii. All these machinations had become a kind of war. And like war itself, it was a continuous interplay of measures and countermeasures.

In the United States, Safford had returned to the activity in May 1936. He was no longer running a mere Research Desk within the Code and Signal Section. He had a section of his own —called Communications Security Section in the Office of Naval Communications, or Op-20-G by its shorthand designation on the Chief of Naval Operations' organization chart.

He had a dual assignment. He was expected to develop a machine-based crypto-system the Navy needed to ensure the security of its own dispatch communications.* But he was also continuing —and, in fact, broadening—the assault on the crypto-systems of the Japanese.

Safford had returned at a most propitious moment, when this clandestine contest between the United States and Japan was flaring up in earnest for the first time. The Americans no longer had a monopoly on radio intelligence in the Pacific. Communications intelligence had come into its own to dominate the espionage activities of both sides.

The first head-on clash of the two countries' radio intelligence organizations occurred at the Japanese and American fleet maneuvers held a few months apart. The Japanese exercises came first. In October 1936 the entire fleet was assembled for another war game, staged under simulated combat conditions close to the Japanese coast.

The United States Navy's new Communications Security Section was perfectly geared to eavesdrop on them. Commander

* In this field, he modernized the existing equipment; adapted it to teletype and other rapid means of communications; tightened communications security by developing various concealment and scrambler systems; started a program of miniaturization; and eliminated practically all the old paper-and-pencil systems. In addition he worked on the expansion of the Navy's direction-finding network. As his biography sheet put it: "In anticipation of the United States' entry into World War II, he greatly expanded the Communications Intelligence Organization and had it on war footing prior to the Japanese attack on Pearl Harbor."

Safford had all the Japanese codes and ciphers cracked in time, and he had a string of monitoring stations operating fairly close to the maneuver area. He utilized them all, but leaned most heavily on the station at Cavite in the Philippines. Operated with efficiency and zeal under a lieutenant named Wenger, it produced the best intercepts of the operation.

The information culled from this surveillance enabled Captain Royal E. Ingersoll, one of the best American naval strategists and head of Chief of Naval Operations' War Plans Division, to reconstruct the *zengen sakusen* ("Operation Attrition"), one of the basic war plans of the Imperial Navy. Thoroughly defensive, the plan had been built on the premise that the Imperial Navy would be at a grave disadvantage in a war with the United States because of the numerical inferiority of its fleet. The Japanese hoped to compensate for this by luring the enemy to the coastline of Japan, where shore-based aircraft could be brought into action.*

Captain Ingersoll then revised the strategic plans of the United States Navy and adapted them to the Japanese design. This Ingersoll plan was put to its first test in Fleet Problem XVIII, exercises and maneuvers the Navy held in the spring of 1937.

The sour smell of war was in the air. In Europe, Germany, Italy and the Soviet Union were exploiting the Spanish Civil War to test their doctrines, tactics and weapons. The Nazis plotted in Austria, Czechoslovakia, Hungary and Rumania; the Fascists in Albania and around the Red Sea. In Japan, the militarists had gained control. They provoked an "incident" in China, but they served notice on the world that they regarded it as a war in all but name. They established the Imperial Headquarters, the Japanese version of a Joint Chiefs of Staff, which the constitution explicitly stipulated should be called into being only in the event of a major war. In the United States, President Roosevelt reinforced the Neutrality Act. But at the same time he castigated the dictators, demanding that they be quarantined, a fate nobody expected they would accept without a fight.

* According to the *zengen sakusen*, the enemy fleet would be attacked by submarines throughout its approach march across the Pacific. By the time it reached the waters of Japan, "it would be bruised and crippled with most of the fight taken out of it." In the meantime the defensive forces would be held back for a stupendous last battle, in which the Japanese planned to open up with everything they had. Under this attack the enemy was expected to flounder like Admiral Rozhdestvenski's hapless fleet at Tsushima in 1905.

It was in this atmosphere that the American Navy assembled its battle force in the Hawaiian area for Fleet Problem XVIII. It was described as "the greatest game of mock naval warfare ever staged." The "enemy" was openly identified as "Orange," the code name for Japan in the American war plans. The basic mission of the Fleet Problem was "to bring the war to American shores to test whether a breakthrough by a hostile naval force is possible." According to the strategic concept inherent in the problem, the United States had a life line in the Pacific extending from Dutch Harbor in Alaska to Pago Pago in Samoa. The line had to be sustained and defended at all costs if the security of the United States was to be assured.

It was now the turn of the Japanese to place an American war game under surveillance. With their *burakku chiemba* already operational in Mexico, their other monitoring stations working in the Far East and a number of floating listening posts dispatched into the maneuver area, they tuned in on the fleet's radio communications to penetrate to the secrets of Fleet Problem XVIII.*

It seemed to the Japanese that what the Americans regarded as a line essential for their security was, in actual fact, a fence behind which they could be contained. The strategic picture that emerged from these war games was breath-taking. It indicated that a determined and skilled aggressor could paralyze the United States by bottling it up behind its Dutch Harbor–Pago Pago life line. And it suggested that the United States could be checkmated in a war by the seizure of its outposts—like Guam, Midway and Wake—and especially through the destruction of its fleet in the Pacific, its only means for breaking out of the quarantine.

But unlike the United States Navy, which had moved promptly with the revised plans of Captain Ingersoll to draw strategic conclusions from the Japanese scheme, the Japanese Naval General Staff hesitated to revise its own war plans in the light of information gained from eavesdropping on Fleet Problem XVIII. The basic defensive plan, originally devised as far back as 1907, was too deeply embedded in tradition. It continued to dominate the strategic thinking of the General Staff. There seemed to be no

---

* According to K. Kato, the Japanese did not actually succeed in breaking the American crypto-system. But sheer monitoring of the U.S. Navy signals provided them with considerable strategic and tactical information, and intelligence about the composition and condition of the participating forces.

real or urgent reason to change it, even in the light of the Fleet Problem's startling lessons. It was, indeed, left to Admiral Isoroku Yamamoto, an officer of the line far beyond the orbit of the Naval General Staff, to apply those lessons and bring about the change.

At this same time in the mid-thirties, the Imperial Navy's Special Duty Group and the Cable Section of the Foreign Ministry joined forces again to advance their communications security another giant step forward. Although neither Captain Ito nor Section Chief Sakuma had any reason to suspect that the Americans had succeeded in compromising their cipher machine, they decided nevertheless to build a better and safer one. Japan was on the warpath. She was engaged in increasingly complicated diplomatic maneuvers. It had become imperative to conceal her secrets and, especially, to ensure that the United States would not gain access to them by cracking the Japanese codes again in the style of Yardley's old coup.

Throughout 1935 and 1936 Captain Ito had been experimenting with a novel type of "cipher equipment." In 1937 he had a model ready for a test. It was so original in its construction, so unique in the basic components of its cryptographic element that it seemed the closest human ingenuity could get to the ideal—the invulnerable machine capable of producing the dream of all cryptologists, the unbreakable cipher.

It had no key wheels or pin discs, no motor. It consisted of a battery of standard, off-the-shelf, six-level, twenty-five-point relays (electrically controlled switches) and an intricate rat's nest type of wiring. It looked like a telephone switchboard and actually operated on its principle.*

* Simple though the switching mechanism is believed to be, an entirely new mathematics principle had to be formulated before engineers could design the complex systems required in all sorts of modern appliances, from the ordinary telephone to missile controls and, indeed, cipher machines. In the relay setup the current goes into the primary circuit (a coil of wire wrapped around a soft iron rod called solenoid), turns it into an electric magnet, attracting the armature (secondary circuit), which is so pivoted as to swing freely to or from the coil's point. The diagram below shows a simple relay system in which a single solenoid controls several sets of contacts, interconnecting one and disconnecting another with a single signal at high speed. The primary circuit determines whether or not electric power goes to the secondary circuit, thus controlling the armatures.

The machine operated in two separate parts. One was the printing mechanism, kept in its own box, made up of two keyboards resembling those of ordinary typewriters. The other part, housed in a rectangular box, was the so-called cryptographic element—the cipher unit itself. The two boxes were connected by cords.

One typewriter was used in encoding, the other in decoding. For example, when the machine was set to encode and the plain text was typed out on the keyboard, the board produced the encoded text in accordance with the key set in advance. By typing out the encoded text on the other keyboard, the machine returned the clear text. The relays yielded both cipher and clear text. The secret of the cipher lay in the machine's unique and unpredictable method of providing "offsets" through the relays.*

Although the unique construction of the machine and its unprecedented employment of stepping switches convinced Captain Ito that "it was impossible for an unauthorized person to discover how the machine worked," he had certain security features incorporated in it to mislead onlookers. For example, one of its many screws was actually the electric switch that turned it on. Unless this was known and the switch-screw identified, an outsider could

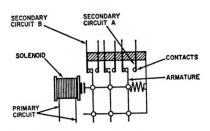

In this diagram (as in Captain Ito's machine) several armatures are ganged together so that a single flip of the toggle opens or closes different pairs of contacts at the same time. Such multipole switches are common in electrical work.

* When enciphering is done on the transposition principle (in which the letters undergo merely a single shift), a key is chosen to determine the position of the letters in the transposed crypt. To demonstrate the procedure on a typical paper-and-pencil sample of single transposition, we use the word COURTESAN as the key in a fifty-four-box matrix composed of nine horizontal

not know even the first and simplest thing about the machine—
how to turn it on.

Captain Ito named the machine TYPE NO. 97 for the Japanese
calendar year 2597 (A.D. 1937 by our reckoning). In view of the
fact that the development of the machine had again been financed
from funds of the Foreign Ministry's Cable Section, Ito knew he
had to share it with the *denshin-ka*, as was the case with TYPE NO.
91. The machine he placed at the disposal of the Cable Section
was a slightly modified version of the navy's. In the Foreign
Ministry it was named the BEI-GWA, the B machine.

Although some diplomatic dispatches continued to be encrypted by the old paper-and-pencil methods, while others were
still being sent out in the cipher of the A machine, all communications specifically classified as "state secret" were now shifted to
the B machine. It was used in two versions.

With the advent of TYPE NO. 97, cryptology reached the summit
of its development. "Let the Americans or British 'solve' this
cipher," Captain Ito said, "if they can!"

---

and six vertical lines, to encrypt the sentence "Seven battleships arrived Friday
morning," as follows:

C	O	U	R	T	E	S	A	N
2	5	9	6	8	3	7	1	4

} KEY

S	E	V	E	N	B	A	T	T
L	E	S	H	I	P	S	A	R
R	I	V	E	D	F	R	I	D
A	Y	M	O	R	N	I	N	G

} CLEAR TEXT

The letters of the key word are numbered in the relative order of their
appearance in the ordinary alphabet. Enciphering is done by reading the
letters vertically downward in the sequence of the key numbers, column no. 1
first, column no. 2 next, and so forth. Arranging the crypt in five-letter groups,
we obtain the cipher text, TAINS LRABP FNTRD GEEIY EHEOA SRINI DRVSV M.
The letters did not change their identity but merely had their position altered.
In double transpositions the letters undergo two successive shifts as the
enciphered text is transposed again with a different key. Ito's unit produced
multiple transpositions with possible variations of 10^4 or 10^5.

𝒥 The PURPLE Code

In the morning of December 12, 1937, just as he was about to leave for a golfing date at the Takenodai course, Ambassador Joseph C. Grew was handed a triple-priority telegram from Washington informing him that an American gunboat had been sunk in the Yangtze River by bombs from Japanese *naval* aircraft.*

Later telegrams brought additional details—how the *Panay* had been attacked without warning while escorting three Standard Oil tankers filled with refugees from Nanking; how a couple of motorboats machine-gunned the survivors in the water; and how the Japanese mowed down the wounded after they had reached the banks of the river and tried to escape by crawling into the thicket.

"This was a black day indeed," Mr. Grew noted in his diary.

General Matsui's 10th Army was attacking up the river under orders to take Nanking by December 15. The diplomats watched in stupor as the pent-up, compulsive aggression of the Japanese militarists erupted in South China.

It seemed almost as if Japanese firebrands were trying to instigate war with the United States. Since August 11, when the drive began, one provocation had followed another. Schools and hospitals of American missionaries were attacked. Five Americans on an outing in Shanghai were strafed by Japanese planes. An American church in Chungking was bombed eight times before it was finally destroyed in the ninth bombing. And now the *Panay*.

The Japanese government professed to be deeply disturbed.

* The British gunboat *Ladybird* was also sunk in the same attack.

Foreign Minister Koki Hirota motored to the American embassy in person to commiserate with Ambassador Grew, express his government's abject apologies and promise "the most thorough investigation of the unfortunate incident." He instructed Ambassador Hiroshi Saito in Washington to call on Secretary Hull with the pledge that "such misconduct" would be avoided in the future.

But behind the apologies was the swagger of the militarists. Naval officers were seen toasting the mishap of the *Panay* at Tokyo geisha houses. Spokesmen of the Foreign Ministry told Ambassador Grew that the matter was really out of their hands: the incident could not be "clarified" until a report was received from the Imperial Navy. When could it be expected?

"Oh," a spokesman said, "that is indefinite." He then added, with a shrug of his shoulders and a reproachful glance in the direction of the nearby Naval General Staff building: "Maybe in a hundred years."

In the meantime the United States Navy called its own court of inquiry. Meeting in camera, it heard evidence in such "circumspect detail" that it seemed to emanate from the Japanese themselves. The planes had come from the carrier *Kaga* steaming over from Sasebo ostensibly to participate in the blockade of South China, but actually to give the pilots a chance to "participate in the fun at Nanking." The officer who had conceived the idea of the raid was identified by name, as were the pilots in the cockpits of the attack planes. "The reports," the inquiry found, "give every definite indication of deliberateness of intent."

The evidence before the court did come from the Japanese— from the dispatches of Admiral Keizo Mitsunami, commander of the carrier squadron, sent to Combined Fleet headquarters and the Naval General Staff. They had been intercepted and read by Commander Safford's Group, and gave the court of inquiry the "eyewitness" account it needed for its findings. It exposed as a deliberate lie Hirota's assertion that the bombing was due to "the mistaken identity of the ship," and showed that Ambassador Saito only "pretended," as Mr. Hull put it, when he appeared to be "downcast and humbled" by the incident.*

* Saito died in the United States on February 26, 1939, and the American government, willing to overlook the many irritations he had caused as ambassa-

It was, however, one of the few opportunities Safford had to show what his Section could do. Op-20-G had enlarged its personnel and had better facilities, but was still a minor cog in the naval intelligence effort, as was intelligence itself. It needed an emergency like this or a Fleet Problem to assert itself. Otherwise, the Section was occupied with its routine chores—keeping the codes open and guarding the Japanese naval circuits, picking up tid-bits of intelligence which nobody in the United States Navy seemed to be particularly interested in.

In the Army, too, cryptographic intelligence had undergone some changes, but they were mostly of an administrative nature. In 1935 William F. Friedman had been replaced as chief of the Signal Intelligence Service by Major Haskell Allison of the regular Signal Corps. Friedman remained as principal cryptanalyst with a staff of only six assistants.

Conditions in the world at large were such as to make the intensification of intelligence activities imperative and urgent. But Op-20-G and SIS were kept barely alive, mostly only by the zeal and dedication of the handful of people working in them. The fact that they were concentrating their attention on Japan did not make things any better. The eyes of America were focused on Europe.

But the situation was due for a radical change.

The first Japanese telegrams to indicate some departure in Tokyo's crypto-system began to appear early in 1938. Although the new cipher showed up mainly on the Foreign Ministry's circuit, in which Safford had only an indirect interest, it was natural for him to probe the mystery, especially when it was discovered that scattered naval dispatches were also sent in the enigmatic new cipher. The probe began with attempts at breaking *into* the system, a prodigious task by itself which required several months.

Safford and his group spent part of 1938 on this effort, in addition to their regular work. The more they got into the new

---

dor, sent his ashes home aboard the cruiser *Astoria* as "a gesture of friendly courtesy." At the other extreme, Hirota was sentenced to death after the war for his "criminal negligence" in failing to curb the atrocities during the Nanking campaign.

cipher, the more intrigued they became with it. By the end of the year some of its important features had become evident. First, it was obviously an encoded cipher, tied to a machine that differed radically from the RED. Second, the few messages the Group managed to unravel turned out to be top-priority diplomatic dispatches of considerable intelligence value.

These discoveries were kept under the lid the Navy had tightly clamped on all its cryptological efforts. At this point, however, the Navy did make a rare concession. It decided to take the Army into its confidence and disclose to SIS its work on the new Japanese cipher. This exception was made entirely on Safford's initiative. He had made up his mind to break down the whole cipher instead of just nibbling at it. But in the face of his existing commitments and of the evident complexity of the new machine, he doubted that his Section could accomplish this task with its own resources. He was convinced that his friend at the Army could make a major, if not *the* major, contribution to the recovery of the mysterious new machine.

William Friedman had made attacks on machine-based systems one of his specialties. Already in the 1920's he thus "solved" the rotor machine invented by the American Edward H. Hebern in 1917 (and independently developed later by others in Sweden, Germany and The Netherlands), and he had perfected a "test" that promised to open the way to the "solution" of even the most sophisticated such devices, by statistical and mathematical methods. In particular, he had developed the principle by which the wiring of the device, the crucial ingredient of the machine's cryptographic element, could be reconstructed.

Safford broached the subject to "Billy" Friedman informally at first, for he was not allowed to share any of the Navy's cryptological secrets with the Army or, for that matter, with any other agency of the government. Safford coaxed permission from his superiors to explore the possibility of a joint Army-Navy venture. In late 1938 SIS was headed by Major William O. Reeder, who agreed to co-operate with Op-20-G on the solution of the new cipher. From Safford and Reeder the idea of the joint project moved up to Rear Admiral C. E. Courtney, Director of Naval Communications, and to Major General Joseph O. Mauborgne, the chief signal officer.

Courtney approved, partly because he was on his way out as

director and partly because there was a recent precedent involving
an even more jealously guarded "secret baby" of the Navy. In the
summer of 1937 the Naval Research Laboratory had been authorized to disclose to the Army its work on radar.

In General Mauborgne the Signal Corps had a chief who was an
expert cryptologist himself and had been deeply concerned with
code and cipher matters throughout his military career. He gave
his enthusiastic endorsement and became Friedman's most stal-
wart supporter during his period of trial and error.

Before the year 1938 was out, an arrangement had been made
with the Army. SIS was to discontinue everything it was doing and
devote all its resources to the solution of the new Japanese cipher
and the reconstruction of the machine. The Navy gave the Army
the intercepts SIS needed and the solutions of the cipher thus far,
and agreed to disclose the technical details of the RED machine.
When it developed that no funds were available within the Signal
Corps to finance this project, the Navy accepted the burden. The
money was eventually found in the Bureau of Ships, which made
it available without any questions asked. The Communications
Security Section then took over all the normal cryptanalytical
functions of SIS to allow Friedman to concentrate on the elusive
cipher and machine.

General Mauborgne assigned additional assistants to SIS for the
task, and with his staff now grown to nineteen men and women,
Friedman began to work. If his proven technique was used (as
most probably it was), his team applied the statistical-mathemat-
ical "test" he had perfected, trying to reconstruct the machine's
wiring from certain basic information obtained from intercepted
messages. In this method, clues are developed first by comparing
such known texts as, for instance, notes handed to Japanese diplomats in Washington with their cipher version produced by the
machine for transmission to Tokyo. Then the wiring is converted
into algebraic terms by counting the number of places between an
input contact and an output contact, and by setting up a number
of equations in which the numerical form of the plain-text letter
plus the X quantities of the machine displacements equal the
numerical form of the cipher letter. In his previous experience
with rotor machines Friedman had found that if a sufficient
quantity of intercepts was available to experiment with, such
equations could be solved and the wiring of the machine recon-

structed. It was a slow and tedious process that strained the imagination, taxed the patience and tested the perseverance of this secret band of twenty people.

There seemed to be enough superficial similarity between the RED machine and the new one to get the Friedman task force off to a promising start. Within the first few weeks they succeeded in reconstructing what was estimated at "25 percent of the new machine"—but that was as far as they got.

The work progressed fitfully, from crisis to crisis. The strain became arrant for most and almost unbearable for Friedman. The effort was so frustrating that several times he was on the verge of giving up the struggle. He pushed himself to the brink of exhaustion in both body and spirit. Only with the reckless exertion of the last ounce of his physical energy and mental strength did he manage to stay with the job.

Intermittent progress was made in breaking down the cipher. Some encouraging results were achieved in the unscrambling of the linguistic and idiomatic peculiarities of the Japanese language, complicated by encoding and/or enciphering. But the machine itself resisted all their efforts. For eighteen fatiguing, disappointing months, the work barely advanced. Some 75 percent of the machine remained shrouded in mystery. It became evident to Friedman and his associates that the Japanese had devised a machine along entirely novel lines. Innumerable attempts were made at divining these novelties, but none worked.

The breakthrough finally came with dramatic suddenness.

One morning in August 1940, in the nineteenth month of the effort, a young cryptologist named Harry Lawrence Clark arrived at work in an almost euphoric mood. He sought out Friedman and told him he had stayed up night after night studying the problem, and had stumbled upon what he confidently believed was the key to its solution. "I wonder," he said, "if those monkeys used stepping switches instead of discs in the cryptographic element of the unit."

The whole concept of using switches in a cipher machine was so unorthodox that it stunned Friedman. But he immediately decided to subject Clark's idea to a practical test by putting together a rudimentary contraption using relays wired according to the young man's ideas.

When no stepping switches could be found in the Munitions Building, an assistant was sent downtown to buy several dozen in the dime stores and electrical supply shops. A primitive machine was then assembled on an insulating board, in which the relays were buried in desultory order in a maze of loosely hanging wires. When turned on, the contraption swished and fluttered fiercely as the current kept flowing from contact to contact with intensely bright sparks jumping across the gaps.

Now it took only two more days to establish the actual cryptographic features of the machine—the manner in which it functioned to produce a cipher—but what forty-eight hours they were! The team worked around the clock. The wiring had to be rearranged and adjusted again and again, until the crazy jumble of interconnected wires properly linked the various levels of the switches to yield the circuits.

Compared with the technological task of assembling the machine, the solution of the keys was a matter of simple routine. An ordinary commercial plug board was used to facilitate the setting of the keys without having to open the machine each time it had to be programmed. The entire circuitry could thus be altered by simply changing the positions of the plugs in the board.

The machine still did not return a completely intelligible text, even when the original message was in English. Since the Japanese were mixing the machine-produced cipher with a three-character code consisting of numerals, dates, punctuation and certain recurrent technical terms, further decoding became necessary whenever coded passages appeared in the cipher. And as a final step, the decrypted messages had to be translated into English. By the end of the month nothing about Captain Ito's machine remained a secret to SIS. The first fully intelligible, ungarbled text was recovered from it on September 25, 1940.

The assault on the "unbreakable" TYPE NO. 97 machine stands out as the most remarkable episode in the history of American cryptology. Its success is a monument, not merely to the ingenuity and tenacity of this country's anonymous cryptologists and technicians, but also to their selfless dedication.*

It was nothing short of miraculous that they succeeded in

---

* Friedman could not enjoy the triumph. He collapsed under the stress, and had to be hospitalized for months with a nervous breakdown.

building a machine the prototype of which they had never seen and whose cryptographic principles and components were unknown to them. They did it from the laboriously gained clues of the cracked cipher the original machine had produced. Henceforth this strange gadget, which was given the designation PURPLE, would do the job that it would have taken dozens of men and women weeks, if not months, to achieve without the machine.*

General Mauborgne reported SIS's achievement to General George C. Marshall, the Army Chief of Staff; and Captain Leigh Noyes, who had succeeded Admiral Courtney as Director of Naval Communications, advised Admiral Stark, the Chief of Naval Operations, of the breakthrough.

At the suggestion of Admiral Anderson of ONI, the word "Magic" was chosen as a generic cover name for the entire operation involving all of Japan's *diplomatic* systems: the PURPLE (B) as well as the RED (A) machines, and the other codes and ciphers—such as the J series (TSU), P or PA series (OITE), L and S—which the Army and the Navy had cracked prior to the recovery of purple.

"Magic," when used with a capital M, denoted the whole operation in all its various phases; "magic" with a lower-case m stood for the decrypted intercept which it produced. The term was also designed as a security classification, higher than "top secret." In the quaint vernacular of the project, the handful of people cleared for "Magic" were called Ultras.

The choice of such a melodramatic-romantic name as "Magic" reflected the awe and admiration with which the operation was regarded. However, broad though it was, "Magic" still did not include all American efforts aimed at the Japanese crypto-systems. The Navy continued to handle the Imperial Navy's codes and ciphers separately, by itself and in complete secrecy, withholding

---

* To this day Japanese cryptologists refuse to concede that their American colleagues solved the code by actually reproducing the B unit from telltale clues gained through pure cryptanalysis. According to Noboru Kojima, "it is assumed in Japan that a machine was stolen either by an official of the Japanese embassy in Washington or by a British intelligence agent from a Japanese diplomatic mission in a neutral country." In the opinion of Japanese code experts, the kind of ingenuity Friedman and his associates claim to have had, simply does not exist.

all information about them, not only from the civilian agencies of the government but even from the Army.

The care with which General Marshall decided to safeguard the "Magic" operation could not be surpassed. Taciturn and secretive by nature, he resolved that ironclad discretion must be the dominant factor in all activities connected with it. By agreement with Admiral Stark, he restricted access to the decrypted dispatches only to those few in the War Department who, in his opinion, absolutely had to be "cognizant" of the operation and indispensably needed the "ultrasecret" intelligence contained in the intercepts for their work on the highest policy or planning level.

Within the Army, the secret was shared with only a single civilian. Eleven years after he abolished Yardley's bureau Henry L. Stimson, now Secretary of War in the Roosevelt Administration, was told by Marshall himself that the United States had a far better cryptological tool than the "black chamber" ever was. This time Mr. Stimson had no qualms about its use. "The situation was different," he remarked in his memoirs.

Aside from Marshall and Stimson, access to "Magic" within the Army was restricted to Brigadier General Leonard T. Gerow,* chief of the General Staff Operations Division, Brigadier General Sherman Miles, acting assistant chief of staff for Intelligence, and Colonel Rufus S. Bratton, chief of G-2's Far Eastern Section. Bratton, designated "the custodian and processor of the Japanese diplomatic messages," had charge of the material from the time it reached the Military Intelligence Division from SIS.

How closely Marshall held the secret can be shown by the fact that not even General Henry H. Arnold, head of the Army Air Corps, was told of "Magic." Both Colonel Walter Bedell Smith, the secretary of the General Staff, and Colonel Ralph C. Smith, executive officer of the Military Intelligence Division, were denied clearance as Ultras. The brown leather pouches containing the intercepts were delivered to them, but only for forwarding to Marshall and Miles, respectively, who had the keys to unlock them.

---

* While in Marshall's personal entourage the restrictions were rigidly enforced, General Gerow relaxed them a bit to enable two of his top aides in the Operations Division—Colonel Charles K. Gailey, Jr., and Colonel Charles W. Bundy—to inspect some of the intercepts.

In the Navy, the sole civilian official among the Ultras was Secretary Frank Knox. In the Office of the Chief of Naval Operations, the tiny group of initiated consisted of Admiral Stark; Rear Admiral Richard Kelly Turner, chief of the War Plans Division of CNO; Captain Royal E. Ingersoll; the Director of Naval Intelligence; * Commander Arthur Howard McCollum, forty-three-year-old chief of ONI's Far Eastern Section; and Lieutenant Commander Egbert Watts, chief of the Japanese Desk. Both custody and the job of distribution became the responsibility of Lieutenant Commander Alvin D. Kramer, chief of the Translation Section of ONI.

With the prototype machine functioning, the project was returned to Safford in the Communications Security Section, which, under agreement with the Army, was responsible for fabricating the machines. Facilities to assemble them were set up in the Naval Code and Signal Laboratory at the Washington Navy Yard, under the supervision of Commander D. W. Seiler. Funds were again provided by the Bureau of Ships on work orders issued and signed by Lieutenant Commander Dundas P. Tucker. Neither officer was told what was involved.

The initial work order called for the construction of four PURPLE machines. They were assembled and wired by a master electrician at the laboratory, identified only as "Buzz." He was assisted by "Tom," a precision mechanic. When "Buzz" had finished his part of the work he returned to his regular job, leaving "Tom" alone to work on the construction and wiring of a few more machines.**

The first units were delivered early in November 1940. In the Navy a PURPLE device was set up in the room assigned to the Section's Cryptanalytic Branch (Op-20-GY), headed by Lieuten-

* During the initial (1940–41) period of the "Magic" operation, ONI had four directors: Rear Admiral Walter S. Anderson (until January 1941), Captain Jules James (from February 1 to March 31), Captain Alan G. Kirk (from April 1 to October 15) and Captain Theodore S. Wilkinson (who was DNI during the crucial last fifty-two days before Pearl Harbor). The prestige of ONI was at an all-time low. According to John W. Thomason, Jr., a Marine Corps colonel who headed the Latin American Desk, ONI was "a haven for the ignorant and well connected."

** By the day of Pearl Harbor, eight PURPLE and five RED machines had been completed. The Japanese had twenty-five B and forty A units, two of each at the embassy in Washington.

ant Commander L. W. Parke. A special cage was built for its machine by the Army, next to the room occupied by Colonel Spencer B. Akin, the Signal Corps officer who had been director of SIS since August 1939.

Within days, decrypted intercepts flowed from the machines. So perfect had this remarkable precision instrument become in American hands that messages the Japanese were sending in this system became available in SIS and Op-20-G even before they reached their own embassy on Massachusetts Avenue.

Before long the American cryptologists proved superior even to the Japanese code clerks who handled the same traffic on their B units at the embassy. The Americans, for example, could compensate for any malfunctioning of the unit at the Tokyo end and obtain copies free of garbles, while the code clerks invariably were forced to call Tokyo for verification. The embassy had its own 1-kw. radio transceiver, but all its dispatch traffic was handled by the commercial cable companies. Telegrams addressed to the embassy were picked up in San Francisco, routed to New York for relay to Washington by teletype and delivered by messenger.

The physical operation of "Magic" was complex, involving separate quasi-autonomous units of the Signal Corps and Naval Communications. Every one of the Army and Navy monitoring stations operating at this time was drawn into the activity to ensure continuous good interception in the face of varying conditions of reception.* The monitoring of PURPLE on the Tokyo–Washington circuit was assigned primarily to the Navy's Station S on Bain-

---

* Until March 1939 the Signal Corps had monitoring stations at Fort Monmouth, New Jersey; Quarry Heights, Canal Zone; Fort Sam Houston, Texas; at the Presidio in San Francisco; Fort Shafter, T.H.; and Fort McKinley, P.I. They were operated by the 1st, 7th, 8th, 9th and 10th Signal Service companies respectively. On January 1, 1939, the 2nd Signal Service Company was established under Lieutenant Earl F. Cook. On March 22 one of its detachments set up a monitoring station in New York Harbor, at Fort Hancock, New Jersey; and in October another detachment organized one at Fort Hunt, Virginia, with headquarters in the Munitions Building, adjacent to the offices occupied by SIS. Another station (MS-5) was added in the late spring of 1941, at Fort Shafter on Oahu, T.H. It was so secret that not even the Commanding General, Hawaiian Department, knew of its existence. The Navy stations were on Bainbridge Island in Puget Sound; at Cheltenham, Maryland; Winter Harbor, Maine; Jupiter, Florida; and Corregidor, P.I. A highly secret station was located at Aiea on Oahu, T.H., but had nothing to

bridge Island and to the Army's MS-2, located at the Presidio in San Francisco. The Tokyo–Berlin and Tokyo–Moscow circuits were guarded by Cavite in the Philippines, and later by MS-5, set up on Oahu in the spring of 1941.

A station like S recorded the whole so-called schedule of transmissions from or to Tokyo, but had orders to ignore the commercial and personal telegrams. All official communications, however, were transcribed and punched on a teletype tape. Then it was sent to Op-20-G by TWX at the rate of sixty words per minute. The Army had no such facilities. A teletype linking Washington with MS-2 in San Francisco was installed only in the afternoon of December 6, 1941. Until then the Army stations forwarded their intercepts to SIS by confidential mail, MS-5 by the Pan American Clipper on its regular schedule, usually once a week.

In Op-20-G the intercepts were received on a WA-91 teletype printer located beside the desk of the watch officer in the Cryptanalytic Branch, who operated the PURPLE machine with the aid of a petty officer. The encoded intercepts were reproduced by the printer on the familiar yellow teletype paper, and were transcribed on a typewriter the Navy had especially constructed for the purpose. In the Army the leather pouch with the raw intercepts was delivered by armed messenger into the hands of Captain Robert E. Schukraft, who was chief of Section A (Interception) in Signal Intelligence. From Schukraft the raw intercepts passed to Captain Harold Doud in Section B (Code and Cipher Solutions).

The so-called processing, which was the next step, consisted of decrypting the intercepts by machine if encoded in RED or PURPLE, or by the analytical method if they were in any of the other Japanese systems that SIS or Op-20-G had compromised. The work load was split between the Army and the Navy. Signal Intelligence processed the intercepts on the even days of the month, Communications Intelligence on the odd days.

The Army was still keeping normal Civil Service hours, and so SIS, which employed mostly civilians, closed down at four-thirty

do with the "guarding" of Japan's diplomatic traffic. The intercepts were obtained mainly from radio transmissions. A relatively few dispatches (mostly cable transmissions) were procured by what was called the X process—photographing the original dispatches at the offices of the commercial companies which handled them (in San Francisco or Washington).

from Monday to Friday, and at one o'clock on Saturday. But Safford, who had few civilians working for him, had his Section operating around the clock. He had one of four watch officers in the Cryptanalytic Branch always on duty in eight-hour shifts. The one standing watch set the key and put the intercepts through the machine as soon as they were taken from the teletype.

The machine made the work of decrypting both simpler and faster (it deciphered at the rate of five words a minute). The only continuing problem to be solved was the recovery of the keys, and the machine, if properly "programmed," took care of the rest. Virtually all PURPLE keys yielded to solution, most of them quickly, many even in advance of their use by the Japanese. On the other hand, only about 80 percent of the J series (TSU) keys could be solved.

The mechanical process of decrypting on the PURPLE machine produced clear texts instantly. However, the decrypting of a J-message needed from a minimum of twelve hours to as much as five days. The less sophisticated P system (OITE) (used for low-grade security traffic) required only from half an hour to a few hours for decrypting.

In the Army, translations of the Japanese messages into English were made within SIS, and the fully processed intercepts were routed to Colonel Bratton for "information, evaluation and dissemination." In the Navy, Commander Kramer functioned in a dual capacity, with one foot in Op-20-G (whose GZ, or Translation Branch, he headed) and another in ONI, where he was responsible for evaluating the intercepts and distributing them to the Navy's Ultras.

Bratton and Kramer were given full discretionary powers as far as the screening of the messages and their distribution were concerned. It was entirely up to them to decide which ones warranted distribution and which ones to set aside or even discard altogether.

The system, evolved in exemplary collaboration by the directors of Military and Naval Intelligence, promised to work out well. "Magic" appeared to be off to an excellent start.

In the midst of all the exultation over the recovery of the PURPLE code, nobody in Op-20-G seemed to be particularly concerned about a sudden setback that occurred at this same time.

On November 1—the day when the top-secret crates containing the Section's first PURPLE machine arrived from the Navy Yard—the watch officer in the Cryptanalytic Branch greeted Safford in the morning with the news that the Japanese had changed their FLAG OFFICERS system during the night.

This by itself was nothing unusual. Innumerable changes had been made in this code since Miss Aggie compromised it the first time, in 1926–27. As a result of this rigid adherence in the past to the system's basic principles, the Navy's analysts had invariably succeeded in solving the changes without too much difficulty, usually in a relatively short time.

Now, however, instead of introducing changes which kept the system basically intact, the Japanese had scrapped the entire old FLAG OFFICERS code, and the new one apparently had nothing in common with the discarded system.

The loss of the AD code would have caused irreparable damage, for it was, as Safford had put it, "the main source of information we have about the Imperial Navy." But he was confident that the new system would be recovered, if not at once then soon enough, for no major crypto-system of the Japanese navy had ever succeeded in eluding the Section's seasoned analysts for any length of time.

This time the initial assaults failed completely even to break into the new system. It was evident that this was probably the toughest Japanese code ever to confront the Safford group, and that the best of the Navy's cryptanalysts would be needed to solve it—if it could be broken at all.

At this crucial juncture those "best men" Safford needed urgently and desperately were scattered widely, serving in radio intelligence but either at sea or at distant shore stations. Lieutenant Commander Dyer was with the Fleet Radio Unit at the 14th Naval District in Pearl Harbor, as were Lieutenant Commander Huckins and Lieutenant Holtwick.

Lieutenant Commander Wesley Wright was serving as communications officer in the cruiser *Philadelphia*. Lieutenant Rudolph J. Fabian was at Cavite, and Lieutenant Commander Williams was on Guam. Commander Rochefort, senior member of this secret fraternity and the Navy's foremost cryptologist, was at sea in the cruiser *Indianapolis*, flagship of the Scouting Force, Pacific Fleet.

As persistent efforts in Washington to crack the new code continued to fail, just as persistently Safford set out to reassemble the superb team that had started American cryptology off on the road to PURPLE, with its pioneering recovery of the RED machine. Dyer, Holtwick and Huckins were the first to participate in the effort, then the others joined them one after another, until Rochefort himself was drawn into it, in May 1941.

But unfortunately for the United States, Op-20-G was now destined to suffer its first defeat. As we shall see, the abrupt scrapping of the FLAG OFFICERS system was to be historic in its consequences. The decision of the Japanese to replace it with a system so difficult that it frequently stumped even the signalmen who handled it within the Imperial Navy was to prove catastrophic for the United States.

For the time being, however, "Magic" was all the United States needed to follow the diplomatic maneuvers of the Japanese. The contours of their aggressive designs had begun to show up in the dispatches of the Foreign Ministry at the time PURPLE became a working reality in American hands. Poland, Denmark and Norway as well as the Low Countries had been conquered by the Germans, France had fallen, and Marshal Henri-Philippe Pétain had his puppet government at the famous spa in unoccupied France.

Japanese dispatches sent on the RED machine during the summer of 1940, intercepted and processed by the Communications Intelligence Unit at Cavite, revealed that Tokyo was coercing the Vichy regime to agree to the occupation of parts of Indochina. This advance intelligence was borne out on September 23. Japanese forces moved into the northern provinces under an "agreement" with Vichy-France which Pétain had neither the power nor the will to resist.

The first diplomatic dispatches recovered on the PURPLE produced other straws in the wind. Cables between Tokyo, Berlin and Rome, which were now read regularly in Washington, revealed that negotiations were in progress to arrange for Japan's closer cooperation with the Germans and Italians in the war. This intelligence was also confirmed when, on September 27, Japan signed the Tripartite Pact with Hitler and Mussolini. The three powers agreed to assist one another by political and economic as well as military means should one of them be attacked by any power not involved either in the European war or in the so-called China Incident.

The Japanese aggression in Indochina and the conclusion of the Tripartite Pact became the turning point in Japanese-American relations. The President and the Secretary of State viewed these moves with the gravest misgivings. They were especially disturbed by Japan's pact with Germany and Italy, whose object ostensibly was to embarrass Britain in the Far East. But its sharp edge was directed at America, designed as it was to confront the United States with the threat of a two-front war if it went to the aid of Britain.

However, none of these intercepts about Japan's move into Indochina and the conclusion of the Tripartite Pact had been forwarded by the Army or the Navy to either the White House or the State Department. "Magic" was the exclusive property of the War and Navy departments, and it was jealously guarded in a somewhat too-literal interpretation of General Marshall's security instructions. Marshall himself was opposed to sending *any* of the intercepts out of the Munitions or Navy buildings, so afraid was he that the secret of "Magic" might be compromised by people around Roosevelt and Hull whose security consciousness (and indeed security) was open to doubt.

It was a situation that Secretaries Stimson and Knox recognized as intolerable under the American system of government. They decided to make the intercepts of "Magic" available to Roosevelt and Hull.

On January 23, 1941, at last—140 days after the first Japanese dispatch had been recovered from PURPLE—the White House and the State Department were finally placed on the "Magic" distribution list. Under this arrangement the intercepts were to be taken to the White House and to State by Colonel Bratton and Commander Kramer, in locked leather pouches to which only Mr. Roosevelt and Secretary Hull would have keys.

The timing was perfect. Japan had abandoned its posture of "wait and see." Powerful forces in Tokyo had begun to move in earnest, pushing Japan inexorably toward a far bigger and much more perilous adventure than her interminable conflict with China.

PART III

The Crooked Road
to War

10   **War on a Shoestring**

During one of the moonless nights of early January 1941, a slim Malayan fishing boat, its rectangular sail set jauntily to the nocturnal breeze of the cool season, glided quietly through the Andaman Sea. It sneaked by the myriad little islands of the Mergui Archipelago to a deserted spot at the trunk-shaped southern part of Thailand, put a man on the white-sand beach and sailed away.

Alone in the dark at the foot of tall green hills sloping toward the beach, the man picked up his bag and trudged inland toward Marang, a border town where Thailand faded into Malaya. He looked like a wandering coolie roaming about in search of work, driven by hunger or just wanderlust. There were many like him in Thailand and Malaya.

From Marang the man moved down the Malayan coast, from Chumphon to Penang, on to Kuala Lumpur, crisscrossing the whole peninsula. In mid-February he reached Johore Bahru, on the southernmost point of the Asian mainland across the mile-long causeway from Singapore. He turned north again, and walking east on the road through Kota Tingii, arrived at Mersing, a teeming port city on the South China Sea. There he boarded one of the fishing craft bobbing in the bay, set the canvas and vanished with the boat in the direction of Cochin China, a forbidding four hundred miles away.

About a week later he was on Taiwan, on the outskirts of Taipeh. Squatting on a rush mat in the back room of a frame house and sipping *tosozake,* a thick sweet wine, in belated celebration of the New Year, he related the story of his journey to a bespectacled, frail man in the uniform of a staff officer of the Japanese Imperial Army.

The itinerant little "coolie" was, of course, no coolie at all, but Major Shigeharu Asaeda, an honor graduate of the Army War College and a former staff officer of the Kwantung Army. And the officer he was reporting to was Lieutenant Colonel Masunobi Tsuji, an intelligence specialist with a consuming interest in Malaya.

Outside, nailed over the door, a newly painted sign identified the house as headquarters of "Unit 82." Living apart and working feverishly in an aura of mystery, the occupants of the house baffled and irritated the regular headquarters staff of the Taiwan Army, and were ostracized by them in turn. The group was nicknamed the "*doro nawa* unit," the popular phrase for eager beavers who try to accomplish too much with too little, and too late.*

Everything about the unit seemed improvised and irregular. Yet there was real purpose in its presence at Taipeh. The handful of men working in that off-limit house in a remote corner of the Taipeh Army compound were the vanguards of the "march to the south." Even at this late date (though few people then knew how late it really was), Unit 82 was all the Imperial Army had actively engaged in preparation for what, in only ten months, was to become the "Greater East Asia War."

The Taiwan Army Research Group—as the unit was called by its proper official name—had come into being because the generals could not make up their minds whether to go to war or not to go to war. And even those who, stimulated by events in Europe and Hitler's lightning conquests, saw in war the only solution for Japan's growing plight at home and in China could not agree on the direction in which it would be best to strike.

In the high councils of the army, two powerful groups were pitted against each other. One group, led by General Gen Sugiyama, square-jawed, bulldog-faced Chief of the General Staff, preferred a war with Japan's "historic enemy," the Soviet Union.

* The phrase defies literal translation. *Doro* means "robber," and *nawa* means "rope." The words are used together to say: "Trying to catch a robber without having rope to hold him."

The other group, led by the War Ministry clique under General Hideki Tojo and Major General Akira Muto, chief of the Ministry's Military Affairs Bureau, saw the panacea in what they called "the southward advance"—to Thailand, Singapore and Malaya, to the East Indies and maybe points beyond, including the Philippines.

Muto was the theoretician of the Tojo group, and his argument was simple and logical. Japan was already woefully short of raw-material resources and foodstuffs even to sustain its costly conflict in China. There was not enough left of anything for a major war with Russia, and even conquest in the arid north could not yield the oil and rubber and rice Japan desperately needed. On the other hand, a move to the south would fill the larder. The question was whether Japan could afford such a venture. Was she strong enough to escalate the war in China into a Greater East Asia war? And what would the United States do? Washington's growing opposition to what Muto called "Japan's legitimate aspirations" threatened to make a showdown with America inevitable. It need not come in a head-on clash. But it was likely to lead to one if Japan suddenly erupted all over East Asia.

Perhaps it was a vicious circle. But whatever it was, Tojo and Muto were convinced that the military program of the General Staff was antiquated, unworkable and inexpedient. It had to be reviewed, replanned and reoriented, from preoccupation with the Soviet Union to designs on South Asia.

The Army General Staff, like all higher staffs in every army, had a number of operations plans prepared for all possible and probable military eventualities. This planning had begun in 1907, when the so-called National Defense Policy was first formalized and the army prepared a program for its implementation. They had a plan for war with The Netherlands over the East Indies, another with Britain over Singapore and Malaya, and one with the United States over the Philippines. But they were vague, inert designs drawn in broad strokes. Even the plans for the real war which Japan was already waging in China were amorphous, full of gaping tactical and logistic holes.

The only firm and detailed war plan on file in the General Staff was the one prepared against the Red Army in the Far East. It was fully developed and kept up to date. The General Staff was mesmerized by it. The Tojo group regarded it as impractical, if not suicidal, hardly the kind of program Japan needed for her salvation.

The plans were reviewed and revised annually in special sessions of the General Staff; the next conference was scheduled for January 1941. However, a two-pronged pressure compelled the General Staff to advance the date. The international situation made a review of the plans urgent, and the Tojo group insisted that they be revised at once. Sugiyama agreed to hold the session already in November 1940.

The meeting took place on the second floor of the *shunobu* (General Staff) building in the Chief of Staff's simply furnished conference room, whose windows opened on the stale old moat of the Emperor's palace. It was November 16, the day after *miyamairi*, one of the three festive days of the month when Japanese children were taken to their tutelary shrines to pay homage to the gods. The fresh memory of their own children's solemn pilgrimages left the younger men in the room with what Colonel Takushiro Hattori, senior staff officer in the Operations Section, described as a "profound feeling of trepidation." *

General Sugiyama presided ponderously over this assembly of stiff-backed, solemn-faced military bureaucrats. Seated around two long tables in strict order of seniority were all the leading members of the General Staff. Only two outsiders were permitted to attend the conference—Colonel Kenryo Sato and Lieutenant Colonel Joichiro Sanada. They were from the War Ministry's Military Affairs Bureau and represented General Muto.

Flanking Sugiyama at the head of the table were Lieutenant General Osamu Tsukada, the Vice-Chief of Staff, and the bureau chiefs—Major General Shinichi Tanaka of the *daiichibu* (Operations), Major General Seifuku Okamoto of the *dainibu* (Intelligence), and Major General Kyoji Tominaga, director of the Personnel Bureau—the most powerful men in the General Staff. Farther down sat the *ronin* of the *chuken shoko*, the younger staff officers

* Coincidentally, the United States Army General Staff was also meeting in Washington, to revise the American plans in the light of the year's upheavals in Europe and to update its "Rainbow Plans," including "Plan Orange," the old war plan against Japan.

who did the actual thinking and planning for their elders. The whole brain trust of colonels, lieutenant colonels and majors was assembled in the board room: Hattori, Akio Doi and Yadoru Arisue from Operations, Yasuo Karakawa from Combined Intelligence, Aribumi Kumon from Air Operations, and the others, with their assistants.

The agenda mirrored the confusion of the times and the perplexity of the General Staff. The keynote speaker was Colonel Arisue, who, as chief of the War Guidance and Co-ordination Section, acted as the devil's advocate. He presented a long paper proposing "three possibilities" for consideration by the conference: (1) "War in the south" in association with Japan's partners in the Tripartite Pact; (2) "solution of the northern problem [war with the U.S.S.R. in Siberia] in co-operation with the United States"; * and (3) maintenance of the *status quo*—to do nothing.

The generals sat back in their chairs, listening mutely as their ranking aides rose one after another to discuss the alternatives. Colonel Sato was the first to speak. Conveying the ideas of the Tojo-Muto group to the conference, he argued vehemently in favor of the southern advance, and was supported by Colonels Doi and Karakawa. But Arisue and Kumon opposed the idea just as strongly, and spoke in favor of war in the north.

As Hattori later described it, "heated arguments arose but no decisions could be reached." In the end the General Staff resolved to shelve "the solution of the northern problem." Several alternate propositions were adopted, including a recommendation that the lodgment area in Indochina be enlarged. Another resolution "acknowledged" the need to solve Japan's acute fuel problem by "advancing into the Dutch East Indies."

But action in Indochina was dismissed out of hand, and the move into the East Indies was tabled on the ground that it would "leave the flanks wide open unless Manila and Singapore could also be occupied simultaneously." The underlying reason for this indecision and timidity was simply that the General Staff did not consider the Imperial Army strong enough or sufficiently well

* This strange assumption—that the United States would join Japan in a war against the Soviet Union— was based on the belief that America was more opposed to Communist than Japanese imperialism.

prepared for a major war, either with the Soviet Union in the north or with the British and the Dutch in the south, and especially with the United States—anywhere.

At this point Japan had only 51 divisions in her entire army—a fraction of the 209 divisions Germany had mobilized by the end of 1940, and of the 169 the Red Army had in Europe and Asia. Moreover, Japan's widespread commitments had laid pressing claims to most of those divisions. They had 13 in Manchuria, 26 in China and one in Korea. This left only 11 combat-trained divisions for the venture in the south.*

The matériel situation was not better. Half of Japan's ammunition and fuel stocks had been committed to the war in China and to the Kwantung Army in Manchuria. No ammunition or aviation gasoline was stored on Formosa or in Indochina.

A study of the world situation, Hattori wrote, persuaded the General Staff that "no changes were necessary in the long-standing national policy." The men at the conference went even further. They concluded that Japan should not unleash a major war, in either the north or the south, before the China Incident had been liquidated. The meeting adjourned—without formal and binding agreements on anything. No teeth were put into the old plans. No agreement was reached to draft any new ones.**

The conclusions of the General Staff did not impress the Tojo clique as sound. If anything, the cautious procrastination of the "do-nothing conference" enraged them. They insisted that the General Staff's apprehensions were unduly pessimistic. Their caution they regarded as defeatism. They argued that Japan did have the resources needed for a lightning campaign in the south

---

* In the north the Japanese had but 16 divisions available for an attack on the Soviet Union, while the Red Army had 30 in the Maritime Territory and Siberia. The discrepancy was just as great in the relative strengths of armor and planes. The Russians had 2300 tanks, compared with Japan's 800, and 1700 aircraft versus the 600 planes the Japanese had.

** According to General Tanaka, another element in the General Staff's indecision was the refusal of the Imperial Navy to commit itself one way or another. As Hattori put it, the admirals "wanted to await the clarification of the situation before deciding whether to strike north or south." In a subsequent meeting the admirals expressed "no desire to go to war," but assured the army people that they would organize the Fifth Fleet for operations in the north and "continue preparations against the United States."

(which they envisaged on the pattern of the German blitzkrieg in Poland and France)—not because she was strong by any means, but because her enemies were weak and even more poorly equipped and prepared.

Tojo and Muto had some hard intelligence to support their contentions. It was coming into their hands from an unimpeachable source—the code-cracking enterprise in which the army's own radio intelligence bureau co-operated with the Communications Ministry. All the incoming and outgoing telegrams of the diplomatic corps in Tokyo were continuously monitored and transcribed by the Ministry's Censorship Section under Tateki Shirao, its chief. Each evening he handed copies of the intercepts to Colonel Morio Tomura from Group 18, the communications intelligence branch of the General Staff. They were intended for use only within the staff. But Colonel Tomura passed them on to General Tojo via Muto, making available to them crucial information the General Staff was actually anxious to withhold from their eyes.

Among these intercepts the American telegrams were not especially productive. The State Department knew that the Japanese had succeeded in compromising several codes of the American diplomatic crypto-system. As a result, no highly confidential matter was sent by telegram but rather by courier or in the so-called brown code, a two-part system, which Ambassador Grew had reason to believe the Japanese had failed to crack.* Otherwise the American telegrams abounded in generalities, much of which Mr. Grew actually wanted the Japanese to read.

On the other hand, it is doubtful that the British ever suspected

---

* In this connection Mr. Grew wrote in his diary on August 7, 1941: "It was indicated that any reports which our Embassy might send to Washington would of course become known to the Japanese authorities, although our informant said that he understood that we did have one 'confidential' code (highly significant, but I feel perfectly safe in the use of the one confidential code referred to)." When his friend Admiral Teijiro Toyoda once gave him some information in great confidence and expressed the hope that "no risk would be incurred of [Grew's] telegram being read by others," Mr. Grew assured the admiral that "the telegram would be sent in a code which I hoped and believed was unbreakable." As a last resort, the Japanese cracked the safe of the American consulate in Kobe and copied its code book. According to Katsuji Kameyama, Sakuma's successor as head of the Cable Section, the Foreign Ministry's Code Research Group had compromised all American diplomatic codes but one.

that their coded correspondence had been compromised. Cables to Ambassador Sir Robert Craigie contained much information the British would have had every reason to conceal. Moreover, the Foreign Office kept Sir Robert fully posted about developments in the United States, enabling the Japanese to learn from British telegrams most of what they were vainly seeking from American dispatches.

For instance, on October 27, 1940, in the wake of Japan's occupation of northern Indochina, a cable from Whitehall to Craigie informed the ambassador that the British Chiefs of Staff had recommended that "war with Japan must be avoided" and that the United States had also decided not to do anything that would "aggravate the situation." This dispatch, decoded promptly and presented to Tojo the morning after, reassured Tokyo, as did several others, that Britain, hard pressed as it was in Europe and Africa, was determined to continue the appeasement of Japan.

As a result of this close surveillance of Ambassador Craigie's cables, Tojo and Muto came to the following conclusions, all of them crucial in the development of their plans:

• The United States was not ready to commit itself to entry into the war in Europe, and was much less inclined to become involved in a war in the Far East.

• There was dissension in the Anglo-American staff committees which were trying to draft plans for defensive measures in areas presumably menaced by the Japanese.

• The Dutch had received no assurance of support from either Britain or the United States in the face of persistent Japanese demands for oil and other economic concessions.

• The defenses of Malaya were in a sorry state of repair, and no reinforcements would be forthcoming from other theaters despite urgent pleas from the high command in Singapore.

• The British authorities in London and Singapore were sorely divided over plans for the best possible defense of the Malayan Peninsula and Hong Kong.*

* In January 1941, for example, the Japanese learned from an intercept that the British command in Singapore had suggested to London that the Thai town of Singora be occupied in order to deny it to the Japanese, who might, sooner or later, move in there in preparation for an attack on Malaya. But the recommendation was rejected by the Chiefs of Staff Committee, and even more forcefully by Winston Churchill, who argued that the premises on which the Singapore authorities had based their recommendation were "all wrong."

However, this was mostly intelligence of strategic significance. The telegrams produced little of operational value, none of the tactical information the Tojo clique needed to bolster their arguments and gain acceptance for the "southward advance." For all their notorious curiosity and industry, the Japanese intelligence services had but inadequate coverage of the southern area, and consequently the data which they had on file contained little pinpointed tactical material. Intelligence about Singapore's defenses was scant and mostly old. There was virtually nothing of immediate military value about Thailand; little about the Netherlands East Indies; less about the Philippines.

What Muto needed was first-hand and up-to-the-minute intelligence, such as the exact number of planes the Royal Air Force had in Malaya, the disposition of the British and American fleets in the Far East, the security of the coast and the accessibility of the beaches in Thailand—in other words, the kind of information an amphibious force would need to assure success in an opposed landing.

Without these data the contentions of the General Staff could not be challenged. And in the absence of conclusive intelligence, no plan could be drafted for an operation that the Tojo clique was convinced could be mounted and won with the forces Japan had available for the venture.

And so Unit 82 came into being. Muto's orders establishing it left little to the imagination. They stipulated that the unit must find out, within a six-month period, whether a "march on the Southern Road" was feasible, and how it could succeed in the face of allegedly formidable enemy defenses, whose actual strengths and weaknesses the unit was also supposed to ascertain.

Even at this stage the Tojo clique had a timetable. They scheduled operations in the south to begin in October or November 1941. The unit was therefore given until June 30 to complete its "studies" and draft operations plans based on them.

It was somehow symbolic that the unit began operations on January 1, 1941. The New Year has a special significance in the lore so loved by the tradition-minded Japanese. By midnight, when the temples ring in the New Year with 108 strikes of their bells, old chores must be settled: bills must be paid, houses have to be cleaned, leftover rubbish dumped, the bodies of young and old scrubbed. Life then starts anew, with a set of resolutions that are made far more solemnly and taken more seriously than the light-hearted New Year's resolutions of Occidental revelers.

The unit was put together in such haste that when Colonel Yoshiide Hayashi, the experienced intelligence officer who was chosen to manage it, moved into his new office, he had to share it with carpenters still working on the reconversion of the old house. "The fragrance of fresh wood was still in the air," Hayashi later recalled, "and from early morning until late at night the sound of hammers and planes could be heard."

Hayashi was given no more than thirty men to accomplish this task. Only ten of them were officers, gathered, as Hayashi put it, "from all quarters of the Imperial Army." The others were typists, orderlies, messengers and servants. General Itagaki had appropriated the niggardly sum of 120,000 yen to finance the entire unit, with only 12,000 yen of it set aside to "buy secret information"—this at a time when the Taiwan Army had an annual budget of 300,000,000 yen.

Hayashi and his men embarked on their mission with a zeal that more than made up for their lack of financial means. Characteristic of their spirit was an entry in the diary of Colonel Tsuji, made on New Year's Day in 1941 when he joined the unit. "I vow to the gods," he wrote, "that day and night I will abstain from wine and tobacco, forget instinctive desires and worldly passions, to say nothing of lust and appetite—and even life and death. My whole mind is concentrated on gaining the victory."

Colonel Tsuji was placed in charge of the Malayan project. A colonel named Kogo was assigned responsibility for the Dutch East Indies, and a Major Hata was given the job of reconnoitering the Philippines.

Within a fortnight Unit 82 had a network of secret agents. Thirty-two-year-old Shigeharu Asaeda was typical of the men who worked for the unit in the field. A mercurial young officer, squat and strong, bursting with energy, Asaeda was in his element while serving with the Kwantung Army. His yearning for combat had been satisfied, to a degree, by his frequent participation in bloody punitive missions against Chinese guerrillas and in recurrent skirmishes with the Red Army along the Amur River. But in the fall of 1940 he was abruptly transferred to the General Staff and given

a humdrum desk job in the easy-going, soft-living military bureaucracy of Tokyo, and in the dull Personnel Bureau, at that.

In December, Asaeda went A.W.O.L. and made his way to
Taiwan, where he knew a mysterious unit was being assembled to
work on preparations for the southward march. He sought out
Colonel Tsuji, his superior in their Manchurian days, and volunteered his services. His offer was accepted, but first he had to be
punished. After all, he was absent from his post without proper
leave. Asaeda was tried and sentenced to three months in the brig.
But while he was supposedly serving his sentence, Tsuji smuggled
him out and sent him on the secret mission to Thailand and
Malaya.

In Thailand the unit worked with Major Iwaichi Fujiwara, who
had a modest network of Japanese spies operating out of Bangkok.
In Burma a colonel named Suzuki operated in the garb of a
Buddhist priest, directing a web of agents recruited in the Minami
Organization from among local activists of the Burmese independ-
ence movement.

Most of the intelligence about the East Indies was gathered by
ad hoc agents—sea captains who had been sailing in those waters
for years and Japanese employees of one of the big oil companies.
An official of the Southward Association, En Imugawa, co-operated closely with the unit, as did the Reverend Kozui Otani, a
well-known Buddhist priest who undertook a "pilgrimage" to the
region at the request of Colonel Hayashi.

One sea captain contributed a chart of Malayan waters. A
young Japanese aviation enthusiast with his own airplane at Singapore, which he was allowed to operate freely, supplied excellent
aerial photographs of the fortress. Unit 82 even had its own aerial
reconnaissance branch. It consisted of two pilots, Flying Officers
Omuro and Ikeda, and a solitary two-engined, unarmed Type-100
aircraft which Hayashi "borrowed" from a reconnaissance squadron that had recently been transferred to northern Indochina, and
in which they ferried some of the unit's secret agents to and from
their missions.

Accompanied by Tsuji, Captains Omuro and Ikeda reconnoi-
tered Thailand and Malaya from the air, photographing roads,
harbors and military installations, especially the RAF airfields in
Malaya. The plane was not equipped for photo reconnaissance

and carried fuel for a maximum of five hours in the air. Colonel Tsuji hand-held a camera, taking pictures as best he could. In a technical sense the photo reconnaissance was a failure. "Not even one of the photographs was any good," Tsuji wrote later.

"The image of everything I had seen, however," he added, "was so strongly printed on the living retina of my eyes and on my mind that there was no need for photographs."

On June 30, 1941—exactly on their deadline—Unit 82 delivered its findings, and the result was nothing short of phenomenal. The ninety-three different intelligence reports, which Colonel Hayashi sent to General Muto in Tokyo, conclusively exposed the enemy's weakness and unpreparedness.

Thailand was shown to be almost undefended. Hayashi's agents could find scarcely any Thai troops along the coast. The airfields at Singora and Pattani were crude and neglected. The government was corrupt and complacent. Nothing in the delightful country was likely to present any real obstacle to a determined assault, except the primitive roads and perhaps the monsoon between November and March.

In Malaya the situation appeared to be only slightly less encouraging. Major Asaeda found that coastal defenses were strong in the Mersing area but weak everywhere else. The land forces were poorly equipped and badly deployed, especially in the central region of northern Malaya, in Kedah Province and around Kota Bahru.

One of Asaeda's most important assignments was to ascertain the actual number of RAF planes in Malaya. Published reports claimed the British had as many as 582 aircraft in Malaya, an air force the Japanese would not have dared to challenge. But Asaeda personally inspected the RAF's nine airfields, from Alor Star in Kedah to Tengah, and counted fewer than two hundred planes, many apparently unsuited for combat.*

* At about the same time, an intercepted British dispatch confirmed this crucial intelligence in exact figures. A signal dated January 8, 1941, from Whitehall to the high command in Singapore, specified that the British had only 158 combat-ready planes and 88 reserve aircraft in Malaya, and advised the commanders that they could not expect any reinforcements before early 1942 to bring their strength up to the 336 aircraft they regarded as the "minimum requirement" to give the area "a fair degree of security."

Not even Mr. Churchill knew that the fortress was fatally vulnerable. But a Colonel Tanigawa, who had taken upon himself to explore the ground defenses of Singapore itself, returned with the stunning intelligence that the "fortress was solid and strong on its sea front, but the rear facing Johore Province was practically defenseless."

With the intelligence on hand, Unit 82 turned to the second part of its mission—to the drawing-up of tentative operations plans for the southern campaign, and then to testing them in a series of realistic war games. As far back as February the General Staff had conducted similar amphibious exercises on Kyushu, the southernmost of the main Japanese islands, but the results were far from encouraging. Now, however, Unit 82 was determined to show the staff officers in Tokyo that the dismaying outcome of their maneuvers was caused by faulty planning.

In early June, therefore, a series of large-scale amphibious maneuvers were held for ten days in South China near Foochow and on Hainan Island. Though the exercises were under the nominal command of the 23rd (Canton) Army, they were actually directed in the field by the ten officers of the unit.

Their purpose was to develop tactics for combat in the south for which the Japanese troops were totally untrained, to test the transportation of men and horses, and to rehearse landings on open beaches. It was during these maneuvers that the light uniform the troops were to wear in the southern campaign was designed, and the rations of cooked rice, salted fish and pickled plums, which the men carried in the campaign in cellophane bags, were devised.

Much in the Japanese army's combat methods that so astounded the world in February 1942—and paralyzed the region's defenders—originated with Unit 82, which told Tokyo in definitive terms that the eleven divisions Japan had available for the venture would be enough—and maybe more than enough.

"Our task had been, as it were," Colonel Tsuji wrote, "to warm ourselves at another's fire and to produce something from nothing —a gleam of hope from bewilderment—and to accomplish in a short period a big undertaking by original methods." Unit 82 had completed its mission. And Colonel Hayashi concluded his final report to Tokyo with the words:

"Victory is certain! There is no need for anxiety!"

"Operation Z"—The Pearl Harbor Plan

11

In the Imperial Navy of Japan, planning was divided between the Naval General Staff and the Combined Fleet. Each year the Naval General Staff devised so-called Fleet Problems patterned on its basic strategic concepts, then left it to the commander-in-chief of the Combined Fleet to "design the tactical plans to gain [their] objective." And each year the objective was "the annihilation of the United States fleet."

For thirty-two years, between 1907 and 1939, Japanese naval strategy, defensive in principle, envisaged the showdown with the Americans in a decisive surface engagement, to occur within the first six months of the war in a "battle area" somewhere between Japan proper and the line of the Bonins and the Marianas. For more than three decades the Japanese fleet trained and exercised for such an engagement. The plan did include a proviso for "an attack on the American fleet in Hawaiian waters at the outset of hostilities." But it called only for the deployment of an expeditionary force of submarines in the vicinity of Hawaii, to intercept and, if possible, decimate the American fleet on its approach march to the battle area.

There was no plan whatever for an *air* attack on the American fleet *in* Pearl Harbor. It was left to Isoroku Yamamoto to add this feature to the traditional war plan of the Naval General Staff.

Admiral Yamamoto was the commander-in-chief of the *rengo kantai* (the Combined Fleet of the Imperial Navy). As such, he was supposed to be a flag officer of the line, a leader in combat, a naval tactician, a man of actions and operations. Strategic planning was not among his functions and responsibilities. As a matter of fact, in Japan's complex hierarchy of aggression, he was twice removed from the seat of strategic influence—once by virtue of the fact that the Imperial Navy itself preferred to remain the junior partner in the conspiracy, and again because he was with the fleet, which was supposed to be aloof from the plans and intrigues of Tokyo.

But Yamamoto was dissatisfied with the concepts of the Naval General Staff and its plan for the eventuality of war with the United States. He questioned the efficacy of its defensive principle. He regarded its emphasis on a surface engagement as obsolete and impracticable, unlikely to yield victory over as formidable a foe as the Americans. He considered it too narrow in its anticipation of a fixed battle area.

In his dissatisfaction with the planning of the higher staffs, Yamamoto resembled Tojo and Muto. But unlike them, and since he was not a politician like the two generals, he plotted for war along strictly professional lines, on a higher strategic plane and on the pattern of historic precedents. And he did not need the help of men like Hayashi and Tsuji to see the shape of things. Yamamoto could do his own thinking and make his own plans.

He was still a midshipman, in his third year at the naval academy on Eta Jima, when—on October 17, 1903—another Yamamoto—Captain Morio Yamamoto, then Chief of the Naval General Staff's First Bureau of Operations—called in Vice-Admiral Heihachiro Togo and told him: "To all appearances, there is going to be war with Russia." Then he gave Togo the command of the fleet and ordered him to prepare it for the war.

Togo made his plans on the premise of two basic considerations. First, Japan could not afford to risk her ships on the uncertain gamble of a head-on clash with the Russians—even damage to her fleet would be the end of her existence as a naval power. Second, he had to destroy the Russians' Pacific Squadron before it could concentrate to prevent the Japanese from transporting their army to the mainland. He concluded therefore that he must attack the Russians with a surprise blow before they could sortie for battle on the high seas, and that this advantage would have to be gained with a striking force of torpedo-carrying ships at a minimum of losses.

On February 8, 1904, the war broke out, with a sudden strike on the Russian ships at their moorings in Port Arthur. "Formerly," the correspondent of *Le Petit Journal* of Paris reported from Vladivostok, "when two peoples went to war, they did not do so without an exchange of challenges. . . . Japan has now . . . shown an astonished world that she had no regard for such subtleties."

On the night between February 8 and 9 the Second Russian Pacific Squadron of seven battleships and five cruisers had just returned to its base at Port Arthur and was waiting for new sailing orders. Outside Port Arthur, in pitch-black darkness in an icy storm, was Togo's fleet of six battleships, fifteen cruisers and seventeen destroyers. Then at midnight the destroyers struck. They sneaked up on the Russian ships (whose officers were at a ball in town) and fired their torpedoes without warning, putting out of action two of the Russians' newest battleships and the best of their first-class cruisers.

"Thus war has begun," wrote the French correspondent, "by an act of violence, without previous declaration of war or notification of hostilities; and, suddenly and brutally, Japanese guns have set at naught all the efforts of diplomacy, and the hopes of peace-loving people."

Young Yamamoto at the academy was thrilled and fascinated by Togo's triumph. Then, in May 1905, while still a mere cadet, he participated in the Battle of Tsushima Strait on board the *Mikasa*, the flagship. He lost three fingers of his right hand in the fighting, but gained a purpose for his life. He resolved then and there to pattern his own career on that of Admiral Togo.

He adopted his idol's famous signal as his slogan, "The rise or fall of the nation is at stake in this battle," * and subordinated everything henceforth—his private creed, his friendships, even his family life—to what he regarded as his "personal destiny" in Japan's "historic mission."

Yamamoto got the idea of the sneak attack from Admiral Togo's example at Port Arthur. But the possibility of a Japanese

* On May 27, 1905, the eve of the Battle of Tsushima Strait, Admiral Togo signaled this message to his battle fleet in the z code. The signal was also run up to the *Mikasa*'s mainmast halyards, with the added sentence borrowed from Nelson: "Let every man do his duty with all his might."

attack on Pearl Harbor first occurred to an *American* admiral.

In the fall of 1932, on the eve of his relief as commander-in-chief of the American fleet in the Pacific, Admiral Frank A. Schofield, a remarkable little man with huge strategic vision, devised Fleet Problem XIV as his swan song in the United States Navy.

He posed the problem within the framework of patently imaginary conditions. "An acute situation exists in the Pacific," he wrote. "War is imminent but not declared. The enemy will strike where the fleet is concentrated. The enemy will use carriers as the basis of his striking force. The enemy may make raids on Hawaiian Islands or the West Coast prior to declaration of war. Consider any Black [enemy] forces east of 180th meridian as hostile." *

At that time there were only thirty-eight shore-based aircraft in Pearl Harbor. But this force was regarded as adequate "to detect the approach of a raiding force twenty-four hours before reaching the launching radius of their aircraft." However, when Schofield's seemingly far-fetched "problem" was put to its practical test (in February 1933) in a maneuver area extending from the 180th meridian all the way to the West Coast, the "Blue" forces, assigned to defend Pearl Harbor and the San Francisco area from a sneak attack, failed in their mission. They missed the approaching attackers and permitted them to break through both to Pearl Harbor and to the bases along the West Coast.

During the subsequent critique of Fleet Problem XIV at the Auditorium in Long Beach, California, the failure of the defending forces to spot the attackers created some consternation. And when the lessons of the Fleet Problem became known in wider circles (for such matters were topics of public discussion during those carefree days of peace), the success of the attackers received considerable publicity. But then Admiral Schofield retired, and the flurry of excitement his Fleet Problem had stirred up subsided.

Even in Japanese naval circles the startling outcome of Schofield's experiment aroused only passing interest. But it made a lasting impression on Yamamoto, probably because it was so bold

* The 180th meridian was regarded by the strategists of the United States Navy as the sea frontier of American defenses in the Pacific. It became the crucial spot in the Pacific in 1942 when the Battle of Midway was fought in its immediate vicinity.

and had been patterned along broad strategic rather than the usual tactical and operational lines of Fleet Problems.*

Yamamoto was a strategist *par excellence.* When he was naval attaché in Washington from 1925 to 1927, he showed little if any interest in the *tactical* matters which usually monopolized the attention of his colleagues. He was preoccupied almost exclusively with the *strategic* concepts of the American Navy.

Upon his return to Japan from the United States, he devoted eager attention to air power, in which he recognized a crucial new element of naval strategy. As his first step in 1928, he assumed command of the new carrier *Akagi,* then took over Carrier Division 1, "working out," as one of his biographers phrased it, "the practical problems involved in the developing theories of air warfare."

A captain in 1923 at the age of thirty-nine, a rear admiral when he was not yet forty-five, he was promoted to vice-admiral in 1934 and shifted to the Navy Ministry, where he was needed to shape policy rather than strategy. By 1937, when he was Vice-Minister of the Navy, he had come to regard the traditional strategic plan of the Naval General Staff as hopelessly obsolete and impracticable. But in his ministerial post there was little he could do to influence strategic thinking in the Imperial Navy, except indirectly by promoting the naval air arm, which he recognized as the crucial element of a "new strategy." **

Finally, on August 30, 1939, he was named commander-in-chief of the Combined Fleet. Yamamoto accepted the command avidly. He was convinced that he could push through the changes he had in mind by reversing the usual order of such things—by training his fleet for the new strategy even before the Naval General Staff adopted it or, for that matter, even heard of it.

Isoroku Yamamoto—a handsome man, stocky, black-browed—was fifty-five years old when he was named commander-in-chief. It

---

* Maneuvers at which Fleet Problems are practically tested are concerned with the operational and tactical implementation of certain specific elements of naval strategy, and not with strategic problems *per se.* In this context, "operational" is meant to signify an area between strategy and tactics.
** Strategic planning was the function of the General Staff, whose senior members jealously guarded this prerogative. However, Yamamoto was in a position to promote the air arm because he was concurrently chief of Naval Aviation.

was said after the war that he had been sent to sea to save his life. According to this version, he had been marked for assassination by the extremists in Tokyo who hated him for his alleged opposition to the pact with Germany and for his supposedly moderate views. But his actions in his new command do not bear out his apologists.

He had been with the Combined Fleet for only two months when he made the first revision in the basic strategic plan—by extending its "battle area" eastward to include the Marshalls. It was a seemingly minor change of no apparent significance, and was accepted without resistance by the Naval General Staff.

His next move was to make the Combined Fleet true to its name. When he took over, it consisted only of the First Fleet in fact, although he had nominal command of the Second Fleet as well. Now he joined the two fleets under his direct operational command, combining battleships, cruisers and aircraft carriers of both fleets into a mighty battle force.

During the spring maneuvers of 1940, his first as commander-in-chief, he stressed attacks of carrier-based planes on the ships, then made two more sweeping moves toward his goal. He ordered the fleet to remain on war footing instead of returning to peacetime conditions, as was the customary procedure. And citing the growing influence of air power on naval warfare, he pushed the boundary of the battle area still farther eastward—this time, significantly, all the way to Hawaii.

Since Hawaii had always figured in the plans as the area of operations of an "advance expeditionary force" of submarines, Yamamoto's inclusion of its waters in the anticipated battle area was again approved by the Naval General Staff. So was his decision to maintain the Combined Fleet in combat readiness. After all, war was already raging in Europe, and Japan was tied by the Tripartite Pact to Germany and Italy. Under the circumstances it was considered proper and prudent to keep the Combined Fleet in harness, for it was impossible to foresee what course the war would take and how Japan might be affected by it.

However, Yamamoto was not preoccupied with the war in Europe. He was, as always, thinking of the United States. He feared that the chaotic conditions of the Japanese political system, and the tendency, as he himself later phrased it, to "bandy about glibly armchair arguments in the name of national policy," would push Japan to the point of no return—to war with America.

He was convinced, moreover, that sooner or later the Japanese army would move southward to break the deadlock in China by escalating the inconclusive fighting there into a Greater East Asia war. And he knew that even his own navy was not averse to the conquest of the East Indies, whose immense oil resources it needed desperately.*

As Yamamoto saw it, a southward move against British and Dutch possessions would bring the United States into the war— and without any doubt if the Philippines were also attacked. The American fleet was no longer a potential threat to Japan proper but an actual danger to the flank of Japan's expeditionary forces in southern Asia.

He concluded that the only way to secure the threatened flank once and for all would be to destroy the fleet at its base before it could ever sortie. He told Admiral Ryunosuke Kusaka, a trusted friend: "If we are ordered to fight the United States, we might be able to score a runaway victory and hold our own for six months or a year. But in the second year the Americans will increase their strength, and it will be very difficult for us to fight on with any prospect of final victory." He did not reveal to Kusaka in so many words the alternative he had in mind. But it was implicit in what he said.

This was how Pearl Harbor became the focal point in Yamamoto's plans as early as the spring of 1940, before France fell and Britain came under Göring's air blitz.

"Ever since wooden-walled warships of the Old Navy with their great clouds of canvas first called at Honolulu," wrote Albert Pierce Taylor, "American naval officers have declared that Pearl Harbor presented a natural naval base, upon the shores of whose lochs could be established coaling and repairing stations which

---

* An inventory made at this time by the Second (matériel) Bureau of the Naval General Staff revealed that Japan's oil reserves amounted to only two years' supply in peace and much less in war; and that the country's own production would provide for only some 10 percent of normal requirements. Rigid economy measures had to be introduced to save oil (including reduced training programs).

would be invaluable to any power fortunate enough to gain possession."

It was, however, not until 1911 that the cruiser *California* steamed up Pearl River into the harbor, "thus having the honor of being the first large vessel of the United States Navy to anchor in Pearl Harbor." It was only on August 21, 1919, that Pearl Harbor was inaugurated as an American naval base, and as late as 1940 that the United States fleet came to be based "permanently" there. It was never popular, either with the bluejackets or with the admirals. The sailors loathed it as a liberty port because, as Samuel Eliot Morison pointed out, "white women were few in numbers, and the shopkeepers gypped the men even more unmercifully than those of Norfolk, Virginia."

The admirals disliked it for logistic reasons (it had to be supplied from the mainland, three thousand miles away), and dreaded it on grave operational grounds. One of the American war plans of the thirties postulated that "the strategic freedom of action of the fleet must be assured" and that "the fleet must have no anxiety in regard to the security of its base." But there could be no feeling of security in Pearl Harbor. It had only a single entrance channel that all ships, coming or going, had to use, and even one hostile submarine could bottle up the ships in the harbor by sinking a single vessel in the channel. The fleet needed at least three hours to complete a sortie. The congestion of ships, fuel storage and repair installations made the harbor an enticing target for attack from the air.

The only solution to the problem was for the fleet to be elsewhere. But it had no other place to go. Pearl was the only refueling, replacement and repair station of vessels operating in the Hawaiian area, and the sole place of relaxation for the crews. Moreover, it was firm American policy to keep the battle fleet in Hawaii as a deterrent to Japan, and no amount of argument could persuade Washington to return it to better and safer bases along the West Coast.*

* On March 31, 1940, the Navy Department made it known that the spring maneuvers of the fleet would take place in the Hawaiian area. On April 2 the ships sailed from the West Coast for Fleet Problem XXI in Hawaiian waters, scheduled to return to their mainland bases on May 9. Then, however, the Chief of Naval Operations ordered it to remain in Hawaii, and informed

Admiral Yamamoto knew Pearl Harbor better than any other man in the Imperial Navy. He had studied the great American base meticulously even while he was still in the Navy Ministry. Now, in a locked drawer of a desk in his flagship, the *Nagato*, he had all the information the Third Bureau had accumulated about that strategic spot, summarized in a five-hundred-page mimeographed book. Called *The Habits, Strengths and Defenses of the American Fleet in the Hawaiian Area*, it contained detailed description of the topography of Hawaii, charts of its waters with their many reefs, data about the military and naval installations, the berthing plans of Pearl Harbor and at the anchorage off Lahaina on Maui Island, an outline of the training areas within a radius of five hundred miles, the defenses of the islands including the pattern of air patrols and the zones of reconnaissance, the rhythms of ship movements, and the "habits" of the crews both afloat and ashore.

He knew, moreover, that the assignment of the American fleet command in Pearl Harbor was not to make any strategic dispositions but merely to "prepare the fleet for war through an extensive training and target-practice program."

It did not take any special strategic genius to realize that a fleet in training, bound by the inflexible routine of its mission, had to operate on a regular schedule—going to sea for certain lengths of time and staying in port for fixed intervals between exercises. If the Americans persisted in this program, continued their schedule and made no radical improvements in their defenses, a sneak air attack on the fleet at its base had an excellent chance of success.

Admiral Joseph O. Richardson, the commander-in-chief, that he would be "based at Pearl Harbor until further notice." Richardson questioned the wisdom of the arrangement, but in reply to his inquiry, "Why are we here?" Admiral Stark wrote him on May 27: "You are there because of the deterrent effect which it is thought your presence may have on the Japs going into the East Indies." Richardson continued to protest, but when he carried his objection personally to President Roosevelt during a luncheon conference at the White House on October 8, he was relieved of his command, and Admiral Husband E. Kimmel was sent to Pearl Harbor to replace him. According to Richardson, the President had reassured him that "the United States would not go to war with Japan even if the Japanese attacked Thailand, the Kra Isthmus or the Dutch East Indies, and that he doubted that even if they attacked the Philippines we would enter the war." But it was possible, Mr. Roosevelt had said, that "the Japs might make 'mistakes' which would bring us in."

Yamamoto also had the latest map of Pearl Harbor hanging on a bulkhead in his cabin, bearing marks of his special interest. All he had to do was to look at the map to see how well founded the apprehension of the American admirals was. But what was an obvious bane to them seemed to be a boon to him. If nothing else, the configuration of the base made Pearl Harbor a seductive target, because it imposed a set routine the American fleet could neither change nor evade. With the warships at Pearl, Yamamoto was certain that his plan was feasible.

While he still refrained from sharing his bold ideas even with his staff or closest friends, he now decided to advance them with means within his own jurisdiction. He began to train his forces, not on the pattern of the traditional war plan, but for his own new design—for what he, after Togo's famous Z signal at Tsushima, gave the cover name "Operation Z."

He initiated increasingly more vigorous training programs for his carrier pilots, under conditions simulating those of the prospective attack. He himself scouted the Japanese coast, like a motion picture director seeking locations for a film, to find a place like Pearl Harbor. He found it at the south of Kyushu, in Kagoshima Bay. It bore a striking resemblance to Pearl Harbor, with its many lochs, down to a little peninsula (like that of Pearl City) jutting into the inner bay. And Kagoshima Bay, too, was accessible only through a single-entrance channel.

He moved the fleet carriers to southern Kyushu for special exercises. The planes flew in from the north, low over Shiro Mountain, followed the winding Iwasaki Valley to the shore, releasing their dummy bombs and torpedoes while skimming over the bay. The people who lived in the area soon grew accustomed to this daily spectacle going on over their heads and referred to it as the "navy's aerial circus." But nobody except Yamamoto, not even the captains of the carriers or the pilots in the planes, knew that it was much more than just a circus.

Yamamoto justified the exercises by citing the experience at Nanking in 1937, when the navy's carrier-based planes had to be used to soften up the city's defenses. Who knows, he told his commanders, when they might be called upon again to aid the army in similar situations. The operation at Nanking had revealed many deficiencies, he said, because the pilots were green and lacked training for such missions. He wanted them better prepared the next time, for attacks on inert land targets.

In the summer of 1940 the idea of using torpedo-carrying aircraft against ships in port was in many an admiral's mind. Both the Italian *supermarina* and Sir Andrew Cunningham, commander-in-chief of the embattled British Mediterranean Fleet, were thinking seriously of employing them. The Italians were the first to try out such an unorthodox maneuver, by attacking the *Gloucester*, moored in the harbor of Alexandria. But the two torpedoes loosed at the cruiser by planes skimming low over the breakwater went into the mud.

In September the aircraft carrier *Illustrious* joined the Mediterranean Fleet and brought along Rear Admiral A. L. St. G. Lyster to take command of the carrier squadron. Lyster suggested to Cunningham that a torpedo attack be tried against major elements of the Italian fleet which were habitually riding at anchor in Taranto Harbor, the major naval base in the Ionian Sea. On November 11, "Judgment"—as the operation was code-named— was meted out. The attack was made in two waves one hour apart, with twelve aircraft in each wave.

This was the famous *notte di Taranto*. The raid so crippled the Italian fleet that, as Commander Bragadin put it, nobody then knew if it would ever recover. Its success impressed all navies with both the menace and the opportunity it revealed. In this country, it filled Secretary Knox of the Navy with forebodings. "The success of the British aerial torpedo attack against ships at anchor," he wrote to Secretary Stimson in the War Department, "suggests that precautionary measures be taken immediately to protect Pearl Harbor against surprise attack in the event that war should break out between the United States and Japan."

The defenses of Pearl Harbor were the Army's responsibility. Knox had been repeatedly told, by Stimson and General Marshall, that they were in good shape and getting better, what with the rapid improvement of radar installations and the 125 planes the Hawaiian Department had for the purpose.*

---

* The War Department General Staff considered the defenses of the Hawaiian area better than adequate. According to General Marshall, "it was by far the best prepared that we had." He added: "If the Hawaiian state of

But Secretary Knox was not satisfied. "The greatest danger will come from aerial torpedoing," he told Mr. Stimson. "Highest priority must be given to getting *more* interceptor planes and anti-aircraft guns, and to the installation of *additional* anti-aircraft radar equipment."

For Yamamoto, Taranto was the decisive proof that his idea was as practicable in real war as it promised to be during the exercises of the "aerial circus." He now began to plan "Operation Z" in earnest, giving it priority over everything else.

On January 27, 1941, Dr. Ricardo Rivera Schreiber, Peru's veteran envoy in Japan who had excellent contacts among highly placed Japanese, sought out his friend, First Secretary Edward S. Crocker of the American embassy, and told him about certain rumors he had heard on the diplomatic grapevine in Tokyo. Crocker rushed the information to Ambassador Grew, who immediately sent the following dispatch to the State Department:

"The Peruvian Minister has informed a member of my staff that he has heard from many sources, including a Japanese source, that in the event of trouble breaking out between the United States and Japan, the Japanese intend to make a surprise attack against Pearl Harbor with all their strength and employing all of their equipment. The Peruvian Minister considered the rumors fantastic. Nevertheless, he considered them of sufficient importance to convey this information to a member of my staff."

In Washington, Grew's dispatch was routed to the Office of Naval Intelligence for "information, evaluation and comment." There the experts agreed with Dr. Rivera that the rumors were indeed fantastic. As they put it, Japan would think twice before daring to challenge the United States in such a foolish and suicidal manner.

"The Division of Naval Intelligence places no credence in these rumors," wrote Commander Arthur H. McCollum, chief of ONI's Far Eastern Section, on February 1. "Furthermore, based on known data regarding the present disposition and employment of

---

preparation in men and matériel was 100, Panama was about 25 percent, the Philippines about 10 percent, Alaska and the Aleutians completely negligible." And again: "We were open in a more vulnerable way in the Panama Canal than we were in Hawaii."

Japanese Naval and Army forces, no move against Pearl Harbor appears imminent or planned for the foreseeable future." *

Toward the end of January 1941—just when the rumors about a possible attack on Pearl Harbor became thickest in Tokyo—Admiral Yamamoto decided to draw some of his colleagues in the Combined Fleet into his secret and solicit their opinion of "Operation Z." The first man to enjoy his confidence was Rear Admiral Takajiro Ohnishi, chief of staff of the Eleventh Air Fleet with headquarters at Kanoya on Kagoshima Bay. In a letter dated February 1, Yamamoto outlined the plan to Ohnishi and asked for his opinion regarding its feasibility.

Ohnishi sent for Minoru Genda, a young friend of his, to study the plan and answer Admiral Yamamoto's question. A commander for only a month, Genda was highly regarded in the Imperial Navy. He was, indeed, one of the most brilliant of the younger staff officers, with imagination to match his professional competence and with the courage of his convictions. Locked up in his quarters in the carrier *Kaga*, anchored in Ariake Bay at Kyushu, Commander Genda studied the plan for ten days, made his own estimates and calculations, then returned to Kanoya to present his conclusions to Ohnishi. "I criticized the plan," Genda later recalled, "but concluded that the attack, while extremely difficult to mount, would not be impossible to execute with a reasonable chance of success." **

With Genda's study before him, Yamamoto prepared the first formal draft of the operations plan. The attack was to be mounted by a separate task force—actually called "separate" to distinguish it from other units of the fleet co-operating with the army in the

* Commander McCollum's note was typical of the tone of such communications, conveying inferential rebuke to the State Department for its temerity in sending naval intelligence to the Office of Naval Intelligence. Even specific reports of American consuls in the danger zone, detailing Japanese preparations for war, met with similar responses and usually wound up in the pigeonholes of ONI and G-2.

** Within a month Genda was drawn into the inner circle of "Operation Z." Named deputy chief of staff under Admiral Kusaka, who became chief of staff, he was charged with preparing the tactical implementation of the master plan. He took part in the attack on December 7, then distinguished himself in other actions. He retired from the navy in 1945 with the rank of captain. After the war he was made a general and given command of the air arm of Japan's so-called Self-Defense Force.

southern operations, and to indicate that it was autonomous even within the navy. It was to operate in two sections—a striking force to be built around six fleet carriers, and an advance expeditionary force to consist of about twenty I-class and five midget submarines, and their screen.

The idea was to have the striking force approach the target by taking a northerly course where ships were known to be scarce, then turn south toward Hawaii, launching the planes at a distance of about two hundred miles from the target. The planes were to fly to Pearl Harbor through a corridor where Yamamoto thought American air patrols would be sporadic. In outline the plan was simple, but in detail it presented innumerable problems. This was to be an enormously complex operation which demanded far greater attention to detail than even the most elaborate of conventional battle plans.

By mid-February 1941 "Operation Z" was definitely in the planning stage, not only in the Combined Fleet, but also in several sections of the Naval General Staff.*

While seeking solution for such technical problems as expediting the construction of two fleet carriers, increasing the cruising range of the carriers, improving communications equipment and developing the special low-diving torpedoes needed for the attack in Pearl Harbor's shallow waters, an intangible factor was foremost in Yamamoto's mind. As Admiral Kusaka later said, "Our chief concern during the preparations was whether or not the main body of the American fleet would be in the Hawaiian area at the time the attack was to be made."

In the classic order of preparing operations, the "missions" are developed on the basis of known facts about the enemy, called "evaluated intelligence," and of information that is merely believed to be fact, called "assumptions."

---

* It was claimed after the war that the Naval General Staff had first learned of Yamamoto's Pearl Harbor plan only in the middle of April 1941, after Admiral Osami Nagano, a man under Yamamoto's spell, had been appointed its chief. Moreover, it was said that the Navy Ministry was first advised of the "Z Plan" only in September when the Minister, Admiral Shigetaro Shimada, his private secretary and three of his section chiefs, were invited to attend indoor games at which "Operation Z" was rehearsed. These are undoubtedly spurious claims, designed to confuse the issue of responsibility and place Admiral Yamamoto's surviving colleagues in a better light.

Admiral Yamamoto's plan was extraordinary in many ways. It was nothing short of fantastic in that it seemed to be anchored mainly to a set of basic assumptions. Thus he assumed that (1) the American fleet would be at anchor within Pearl Harbor at the time of the attack, and that (2) a fast carrier force could be moved from Japan across half of the Pacific Ocean to the north of Midway, within striking distance of the Hawaiian Islands, without "undue risk of detection by American defensive reconnaissance." *

To build an operation which would, in Yamamoto's own words, "decide the future of the Empire for centuries to come," on such flimsy premises seemed to be the height of recklessness and irresponsibility. It was simply inconceivable that the Americans would behave as he assumed—that they would overlook an armada crossing the Pacific, miss the flights of strange planes approaching Hawaii and present their battle force at anchor like a flock of sitting ducks.

But Yamamoto, though bold and unorthodox, was not reckless and irresponsible. His biographical card on file in ONI described him as "exceptionally able, forceful, a man of quick thinking." It also noted that aside from being the Go champion of the Imperial Navy, he was a "habitual winner at poker." Those American naval officers who remembered him for his spirited poker parties during his tour of duty in Washington, recalled after Pearl Harbor how good he used to be at bluffing. But they would not characterize him as a gambler. And Go, at which he truly excelled, is a slow, brainy game of skill in which the opponent's pawns are captured one by one and the decision is gained gradually and not by scoring at the outset with a lightning gambit.

"Operation Z" thus did not seem to be in character for Yamamoto. However, its plan was not as preposterous as it seemed, if only because his assumptions were not quite as flimsy as they

---

* These assumptions were actually stated in so many words in "Combined Fleet Operations Order No. 1," the definitive operations plan Yamamoto prepared later. Moreover, he also assumed that the carrier air strike could, if tactical surprise were effected, achieve the strategic result of crippling the American fleet and the tactical result of destroying the Americans' land-based air. This would permit the striking force to withdraw without or with only minor damage. This assumption was not actually spelled out, but it was logically implicit in the plan.

appeared to be. Intelligence did play a part in the shaping of the plan. As a matter of fact, his fanatical confidence in the validity of his "wild guesses" stemmed from abundant information he already had at his fingertips. And from now on he had to keep a steady eye on those ships at Pearl Harbor, to ascertain the *exact* schedule on which they moved, and find out all that was possible about the defensive arrangements of the Islands.

He sent for Captain Ogawa.

Kanji Ogawa was a career intelligence officer, one of the relatively few in the Imperial Navy who spent most of their tours of duty in the Third Bureau of the Naval General Staff, the *joho kyoku*, or Naval Intelligence. A slim, frail man in his middle forties, with close-cropped hair, the shadow of a mustache and deceptively drowsy eyes in his thin, ascetic face, he was chief of the Third Bureau's biggest and most important branch, the so-called Section 5, which specialized in the Americas. He was a hardworking "spy master" totally dedicated to his craft. The section reflected both his industry and ingenuity, as well as his consummate knowledge of America.

Answering Yamamoto's summons, Ogawa flew to Kagoshima on February 3, and boarded the *Nagato* for the conference. When the admiral confided to him the outlines of "Operation Z," Ogawa was, as he himself later put it, stunned and awed, but not by the magnitude of the task Yamamoto was now assigning to his Section.

Although the Japanese coverage of the United States could be spotty at times, the intelligence the Section had on file left little to be desired. It was issued to the Combined Fleet in a series of special monographs, like the big book about the Hawaiian area. It was kept in three loose-leaf binders to enable its recipients to add sheets of supplemental information Ogawa was sending to the fleet from time to time. As recently as December 29, 1940, for example, he had forwarded the intelligence to Admiral Yamamoto that ships of the American fleet in the Pacific had abandoned their anchorage off Lahaina on the island of Maui.

This was a remarkable feat, considering both the importance and accuracy of the information, and the speed with which it reached the Combined Fleet. It was, indeed, only on December 1 that Admiral Richardson had concluded that Lahaina was "extremely vulnerable to submarine attack" and ordered his ships to avoid that anchorage henceforth. The other harbors in the Islands could not be used, for the same reason. If nothing else, the intelligence Ogawa had forwarded lent weight to one of Yamamoto's basic assumptions—that Pearl Harbor was the only target in the Hawaiian Islands he had to consider in his plan.

Though the book with its supplemental data was, indeed, invaluable, he would need much more information in the future—on a week-to-week and maybe even on a day-to-day basis.

And there was something else.

Hitherto Section 5 had chiefly been preoccupied with the American mainland. For all its apparent importance, the Hawaiian area was considered only a secondary intelligence target, inferior to Washington and especially to the vast and teeming naval establishments of the West Coast.*

Yamamoto now asked Captain Ogawa to shift the emphasis to Hawaii.

* Among Japanese naval officers working as espionage agents in the United States at this time were such top operatives as Commander Inao Ohtani, Lieutenant Commander Ko Nagasawa, Commander Itaro Tachibana (alias Hisashi Yamamoto), Lieutenant Commander Sadatomo Okada, Engineer Lieutenant Wataru Yamada and Lieutenant Commander Kumao Ejima. Except for Ejima, who worked out of New York City, all operated on the West Coast, Tachibana in charge of the Los Angeles and Okada of the San Francisco-Seattle-Dutch Harbor branches of the two-pronged espionage network.

12

Eyes on Hawaii

Japanese interest in Hawaii began at the turn of the century when the island group became American territory, establishing the United States firmly in the central Pacific, three thousand miles closer to Japan. The influx of Japanese immigrants in search of legitimate jobs and opportunities enabled the *joho kyoku* to smuggle in an occasional secret agent. For a long time, however, the Islands had only slight military significance and few objectives to justify a more elaborate effort.*

But when Pearl Harbor was inaugurated as a naval base in 1919, and the Army established its Hawaiian Department around Fort Shafter on Oahu, the Japanese began to manifest greater interest in the "military preparedness" of the Islands. Several army and navy officers were sent to Honolulu to see for themselves. One such expedition of naval officers returned to Tokyo with a twenty-three-page report. However, it contained little that could not have been culled from newspapers and similar open sources.

Between March 1922 and December 1923, Japanese Army Intelligence stationed a few resident agents in Honolulu who were required to send weekly reports to Tokyo. By 1926 the various "investigations of the military preparedness of Honolulu" ran to

---

* Even this sporadic and haphazard espionage proved sufficient to alert the American authorities and establish counterespionage as a permanent fixture of the defense plans for the Islands. From 1903 on, teachers in the Japanese-language schools were kept under surveillance, and so-called suspect lists were kept of many Japanese residents. They were restricted in their movements as far as possible—prohibited, for instance, from hunting sea birds, on the assumption that such a pastime might be a cover for espionage.

2042 pages in the files of Army Intelligence. The navy had 1019 pages of similar material in its intelligence archives.

The interest flared up in 1932 when Secretary of State Henry L. Stimson—exasperated by Japanese aggression in Manchuria and angered by "an inexcusable act of cruelty" in the bombing of Shanghai on January 28—persuaded President Hoover to base a major part of the United States fleet in Hawaiian waters. Even so, it was only in 1936, after Captain Ogawa had been made deputy chief of the Third Bureau and director of Section 5, that the coverage of Hawaii was improved.

Ogawa relied heavily—and at times exclusively—on signal intelligence, much in the manner in which the United States was also obtaining most of its information about the Imperial Navy. Four stations—the ones in Canton and Shanghai, and the two "black chambers" in Mexico—monitored the traffic of the Pacific and Asiatic fleets. They obtained first-hand intelligence by analyzing their traffic, and frequently by reading the encrypted dispatches, thanks to Captain Ito's Special Duty Group 20, which had succeeded in compromising several American naval codes.*

Information was also obtained from submarines the Japanese were sending regularly into Hawaiian waters, to cover at periscope depth the other islands—Maui, Molokai, Kauai, and the island of Hawaii—and to observe the Pacific Fleet in its training areas.

Section 5 was getting information from the naval attachés in Washington, from passengers and crews of ships stopping over in Honolulu, from representatives of Japanese commercial firms in the area, and especially from newspapers and periodicals published in Hawaii, and the broadcasts of the two local radio stations. A clerk at the consulate general in Honolulu, Yasumasa Murata, worked full time monitoring the broadcasts and clipping items of intelligence interest from the newspapers, shipping them to Tokyo twice a month.

As far as espionage *per se* was concerned, Ogawa had an organization operating in Hawaii, in two separate "systems." One, called

---

* Special Duty Group 20, the radio intelligence unit of the Communications Bureau in the Naval General Staff, was outside Captain Ogawa's jurisdiction, but it co-operated closely with the Third Bureau. Aside from the listening posts in Canton, Shanghai and Mexico, there were other monitoring stations in Peking and Korea, to cover the Soviet traffic.

the "inside system," was based on the consulate general in Honolulu and its so-called *toritsuginin*, free-lancing consular agents scattered in the Islands. It was, in fact, one of these consular agents, a Buddhist priest named Unji Hirayama, who supplied the information that the fleet had abandoned the Lahaina anchorages off Maui. However, this was the exception to the rule. The "inside system" was restricted to what is called "legal espionage," collecting and reporting only information that could be obtained openly, by sheer observation.* Great care was taken not to jeopardize the consulate and the consular agents by involving them in too-blunt espionage activities.

"Legal espionage" is neither improper, nor was it indigenous to the Japanese. All consulates are required to perform at least some collateral intelligence functions. Those in sensitive water-front areas are expected to send periodic reports to their home offices on the movements of ships, the inflow and outflow of fuel, and whatever information they can pick up about the naval establishment, its installations and personnel. This was done by the seventy-odd consulates the United States had at this time in Japan and East Asia. Their periodic reports—especially those from the American consuls in Saigon, Hainan, Canton and Tsingtao— proved very valuable in charting Japan's march to the war.

Ogawa's "outside system" was composed of secret agents sent to Hawaii under false pretenses and assumed names. Although it was variously estimated that in 1941 the Japanese had as many as a thousand "spies" in Hawaii, closer scrutiny after the attack exposed only about a dozen individuals who had actively engaged in espionage. And they turned out to be rather inferior, at that. Their cover was usually pretty transparent, and the way they used to conduct themselves made it often obvious that they were, in fact, naval officers in disguise.

One of them posed as a grocer, but had been observed visiting the Japanese warships which called at Honolulu from time to time, giving orders to the officers, once even to a rear admiral who

* Even Rev. Unji Hirayama procured the important intelligence about Lahaina by merely driving to the seashore on Maui and *not* seeing the ships at their usual anchorages. Putting two and two together, he felt justified to report to Tokyo via the consulate, on December 20, 1940: "The fleet has not been in [Lahaina] for over three weeks. Apparently training is done elsewhere."

had brought a training squadron to Honolulu on a courtesy visit. Another was the proprietor of the Venice Café, a "hot spot" frequented by American sailors, whose discretion was notoriously lax. When his office was searched after the attack, the American investigators found its walls covered with autographed photographs of Japanese naval officers in full regalia. One of the photographs turned out to be that of the alleged restaurateur. It showed him, too, in the uniform of an officer of the Imperial Navy.

The chief of the "outside system" worked as a chemist at a local *sake* brewery. But whenever he drank more of his own brew than was good for him, he fell to boasting that he was really an officer of the navy and, in fact, the son-in-law of Rear Admiral Hyakutake.

These agents, operating on their own with orders to avoid the consulate, were supposed to obtain information that was not readily accessible by open observation, and even to "buy secrets," as one of them admitted during interrogation after the attack. Their contribution to Captain Ogawa's files was infinitesimal. There were few ironclad secrets in Hawaii that necessitated trained espionage agents to procure. The naval base was as open as a public park. It was fully exposed to anyone gazing down on Pearl Harbor from Aiea Heights or stopping for a soft drink at the stand of Teisaku Eto, an old Japanese alien who was permitted to set up shop at the main gate of the Navy Yard, with its fine view of the inner harbor. Private planes, rented out at nearby John Rodgers Airport, could fly over the base at will; and tourists of any persuasion could go on free sightseeing rides inside Pearl Harbor by courtesy of the United States Navy.

It was therefore not especially difficult for Captain Ogawa to fill his files with intelligence about the Hawaiian area. Ogawa had the mass of incoming data carefully collated and every scrap of information analyzed. He then prepared ingenious statistics from them. This statistical method exposed the "habits" of the Pacific Fleet and the rhythm of the ship movements, producing the basic intelligence Yamamoto needed.*

---

* Combining information supplied by observers of the "inside system" with data obtained by the monitoring stations, the Japanese obtained the schedule of the Pacific Fleet without any need for the employment of precariously placed secret agents. Since the call letters of all American ships were on record

Even at his first meeting with the admiral, in February 1941, Ogawa was able to tell Yamamoto that the number of American planes on patrol flights rarely exceeded three at a time, and that they were patrolling the area from five hundred to eight hundred miles to the north and south on a set pattern. There was, indeed, he told the commander-in-chief, "an unguarded sector" in the American defenses to the north through which the Japanese planes could approach Pearl Harbor without the risk of being spotted.

Aside from the two "systems" and his other sources, Captain Ogawa also had in Hawaii what is called a "sleeper" in the lingo of intelligence. He was a certain Bernard Julius Otto Kühn, a wayward German whom Ogawa had met by chance when once sunning himself at a beach near Tokyo. Kühn claimed to have been an officer of the German navy in World War I, and once, for a brief span, a high official of the Gestapo. However, as he told Ogawa, he had had to leave Germany because "Heinrich Himmler had become jealous of him."

Actually, he was little more than a vagrant in search of adventure and easy living. He had drifted to Japan by way of the United States, supposedly to study the language. Married and the father of a stepdaughter in her twenties and a teen-age son, Kühn was in Tokyo alone, hoping to eke out a living by doing odd jobs that did not involve too much exertion on his part.

Captain Ogawa invited Kühn to go to Hawaii as his "resident agent at large," to wait there, more or less idly, until he was needed in an emergency. Funds (eventually totaling $70,000) were transferred to the Japanese naval attaché in Berlin and were deposited there at the Deutsche Bank in a blind account the Japanese secret service maintained in the name of the Roechling

---

at Special Duty Group 20, the number of vessels in Pearl Harbor or out at training and the identity of the ships could be deduced by the simple process of monitoring their signals. The location of the fleet training areas was determined with the help of direction finders, and by monitoring the radio traffic of planes shuttling between the base and the ships at training, as well as by interviewing passengers and crews of Japanese ships who had observed the American vessels at sea. By a similar method Ogawa deduced the zones of reconnaissance, the schedule and range of the planes, as well as the number of aircraft used on patrol duty.

Steel Works. The money was then sent back to Tokyo to a Dr. Homberg, the Roechling representative in Japan, for disbursements to Kühn on a prearranged installment plan. This way he could claim that his income came from Roechling's and represented revenue from the sale of his German properties to the steel company.

Kühn arrived in Honolulu from Yokohama on October 29, 1936, on the *Tatsuta Maru*. A year later he was followed by his wife Elfriede, who came from Hamburg, where she had been given perfunctory training in simple espionage at the *Abwehr* school. She brought along their son Eberhard. Their daughter (variously called Ruth and Lucy) sailed in from Shanghai on the *President Hoover* on August 28, 1938, to join her parents, who were by then settled comfortably behind a high hedge-fence in a ranch-type house in Kalama, a neat middle-class residential development twenty miles north of Honolulu on the windward coast of Oahu. They also had a beach house at nearby Lanikai.

The Kühns had gone into business with Ogawa's money, but did not fare well. Otto tried his hand at manufacturing steel furniture, but the venture ended in bankruptcy. Elfriede opened a beauty shop in Kalama, but was making only about $80 a month. Even so they continued to prosper, thanks to the spurious debt Dr. Homberg was paying off.

In 1939 Captain Ogawa was appointed naval attaché in Washington.* On his way to his new post, in March, he stopped over briefly in Honolulu to inspect his network. Ogawa met Kühn and toured the island of Oahu with him. The German did his best to impress the captain with his knowledge of the area and the arrangements he had made "for the emergency," even though he had been extremely careful, as he put it, to avoid showing his hand prematurely.

He assured Ogawa that he had invested the Third Bureau's money wisely, especially by buying the two houses. He had chosen them, he said, for their strategic locations, providing excellent

---

* Ogawa's Washington assignment is based on information from Noboru Kojima, but the State Department *Blue Book* did not list a "Captain Kanji Ogawa" either in 1939 or in 1940. It is possible that Ogawa, who was deep under cover in the Imperial Navy as far as his intelligence activities were concerned, had come to the United States on an assumed named with doctored accreditation papers.

views of the Kaneohe Naval Air Station and a Marine Corps training camp at Mokapu Point. Moreover, from them he could observe the American warships in the Kaiwi Channel on their way to Pearl Harbor, and signal to Japanese submarines if such communications became necessary as a last resort. He also told Ogawa that he had assembled a powerful short-wave set to be ready for the "emergency." The captain was pleased with Kühn's arrangements, but cautioned him to "lay low until further notice."

As far as his "inside system" was concerned, Captain Ogawa had less reason to be satisfied. Despite the obvious importance of the spot, the consulate general was not as busy and efficient at this side line as some of the other Japanese consulates at even considerably less sensitive port cities around the world. The casual attention it was paying to its undercover assignment reflected the convictions and sentiments of the consul general, Gunji Kiichi. He was a veteran diplomat and an old-fashioned gentleman who respected the tenets of international morality and the decorum of his profession. Opposed as he was to increasing domination of the Foreign Ministry by the military, he naturally disliked spying for them. He undertook whatever he could to sabotage the covenant his ministry had with Naval Intelligence.

He abandoned the activity, as far as it went, to Otojiro Okuda, his vice-consul, a serious and precise young man who peered quizzically at the world from behind thick glasses. Okuda himself was too busy with his regular chores and was not able to spare too much time for espionage. As a result, most of the secret intelligence work of the consulate general was done by one of the secretaries, Yokichi Seki, a civilian who had spent a year at the naval academy and therefore had some knowledge of naval matters.*

Samon Tsukikawa, the consulate's regular code clerk, also handled the occasional messages sent to the Third Bureau via the

* At this time there was one professional intelligence officer attached to the consulate, a man named Aburashita who used the secret-service alias Kyonosuke Yugi. He posed as a consular secretary and was registered as such with the State Department. He was posted in Honolulu merely to spy on the many Korean refugees settled in the area and on the Korean Independence League. The consular staff consisted of two consuls, three Japanese consular secretaries, four locally recruited Nisei clerks, a Nisei chauffeur, two porters and three female servants.

Foreign Ministry Cable Section. Naval Intelligence had a long-standing arrangement with the Foreign Ministry for handling espionage messages as part of the diplomatic dispatch traffic, using consular codes instead of the navy's cipher system in encrypting them. As a matter of fact, the only naval cipher Tsukikawa had in his custody was the so-called s system assigned to merchant ships. But it was rarely if ever used.

Since Tokyo would not spare one of its cipher machines for Honolulu, Tsukikawa sent all telegrams, including those for the Third Bureau, in one or another of the two paper-and-pencil systems he had. The espionage dispatches went out in the TSU code via the three commercial cable companies operating in Honolulu, the consulate using a different company each month. Toward the very end the OITE code was used because TSU had to be destroyed, on instructions from Tokyo, about a week before the Pearl Harbor attack.

Consul Okuda did not treat his espionage side line lightly. But he was quite cynical about his extracurricular assignment, mainly because he found it so simple. "All you need for this job," he used to tell Seki, "are two eyes and two legs, and not too much brains."

He procured most of the intelligence he needed for his periodic reports from articles in the *Star-Bulletin* and the *Advertiser*, the two Honolulu dailies, and by monitoring KGMB and KGU, the local radio stations. The newspapers were especially useful, since each day they printed columns devoted to news about the varied activities of Army and Navy, both professional and social.

Actually, all the Third Bureau expected to get from the consulate general at this stage were periodic reports on the movements of warships in Pearl Harbor. To give the reports an eyewitness touch, Secretary Seki would make a personal inspection tour once a week, going for a Coca-Cola at Eto's stand or to the landing of the Pan American Clipper on the Pearl City peninsula vantage spots giving him full view of the harbor.

The consulate had hundreds of informants, of course, among the 160,000 persons of Japanese ancestry living in the Islands (of whom 40,000 were aliens), and scores among the Korean refugees. Okuda had a small fund at his disposal to pay for their services, doling out from $5 to $50 depending on the value of the information they supplied. But these people were *ad hoc* informants, not different from those the American embassy had in Tokyo among its many Japanese "friends" who inundated it with information, some useless, other invaluable. By no means could these people be characterized as spies, as was the widespread tendency in Honolulu before the war.

However, Okuda did have at least one major secret source yielding intelligence that could not have been obtained openly by "legal" methods. With so many transients in Hawaii, including the military and naval personnel, Honolulu had a brisk cable traffic handled by the three commercial companies—Mackay, RCA and Globe Wireless. Repeated efforts of the American counterintelligence agencies to obtain bootleg copies of the messages were in vain. The companies refused to hand them over, protesting that the privacy of telegrams was protected by law. However, Okuda managed to plant agents at the cable offices, and they supplied him with reams of messages—more, in fact, than he could handle with his limited facilities.

He was primarily interested in the telegrams of the military and naval personnel stationed in Honolulu. This was a valuable source of incidental intelligence but its actual usefulness in Okuda's hands was open to doubt. The servicemen's cables abounded in the usual gripes, giving him a warped impression of morale at Pearl Harbor. Thus, in December 1940, when the cables were dense with complaints—what with homesickness becoming rampant as Christmas was approaching—Okuda filed a telegram for the *joho kyoku* reporting that "dissatisfaction of the personnel was widespread and morale [appeared to be] at its lowest ebb." *

In the fall of 1940 Consul General Kiichi was recalled to Tokyo in a shake-up ordered by the pro-Axis Foreign Minister Yosuke Matsuoka, who found the old-time career man not quite trustworthy and his sympathies misplaced. For the time being, however, no replacement was sent.

* Okuda sent another report on low Navy morale in February 1941, on the basis of a spate of nostalgic cables sent to their Stateside sweethearts by lovesick gobs. He even quoted one of the messages verbatim. "Blue Hawaii," it read, "would not be so blue if you would be my Valentine." Of course, it was the eve of Saint Valentine's Day.

Okuda became acting consul general. Relieved of Kiichi's inhib-
iting influence, Okuda took it upon himself to improve his side
line and enlarge his crew of legal spies. He gave Secretary Seki a
freer rein and enlisted two "stringers" to aid his coverage of the
Pacific Fleet in and out of Pearl Harbor.

One was a young American of Japanese ancestry, Richard Kotoshirodo by name but called "Masayuki" within the consulate,
where he was employed as one of the Nisei clerks, sharing an office
with Seki. Dick Kotoshirodo, a handsome man with an attractive
young wife, Joan ("Kimie"), who operated a beauty parlor in
Honolulu, lived a double life. In the city he posed as a patriotic
American. In the consulate he was a Japanese patriot. His sympathies were fiercely with the land of his ancestors. Okuda made
him an "honorary spy," to aid Seki on his weekly visits to Pearl
Harbor and drive him around Oahu on more extended surveillance
tours in Kotoshirodo's 1937 Ford sedan.

Dick-Masayuki also made reconnaissance trips on his own, to
the various vantage spots from which the ships in the harbor could
be observed. Thanks largely to his activities, Okuda was able to
increase the number of his reports to Tokyo. He sent twelve
"intelligence telegrams" in January 1941, as against only five in
December 1940, when this surveillance began in earnest after
Kiichi's departure.

The other newcomer to Okuda's little cadre of spies was something of a mystery man. He was a middle-aged, rather shabby
Japanese-American named Yoshie Mikami, owner of a taxi company with a "fleet" of a single dilapidated Oldsmobile which he
drove himself. He seemed to be a simple man, so poorly educated
that he spoke both pidgin English and pidgin Japanese. Known
among the cabbies as "Johnny the Jap," he was a familiar character in downtown Honolulu, where he had worked as a taxi driver
all his adult life.

And yet he had a profound knowledge of naval matters, and
could converse on such intricate subjects as the balance of naval
power, the usefulness of anti-torpedo nets, and the relative
strengths of the American and Japanese navies. He knew technical
details as well, such as the caliber of naval guns and the thickness
of ships' armor.

When asked how he had acquired such a broad knowledge of

naval subjects, Johnny would merely say that he had been reading American publications like *Our Navy* and the *United States Naval Institute Proceedings*. But his suspect card in the Intelligence Office of the 14th Naval District reflected some skepticism. "Whether Mikami [has] actually gained his excellent (though perhaps superficial) knowledge of naval subjects," it noted, "by reading magazines in a language in which he is extremely deficient, or by some other means, remains a matter of conjecture."

Suspect though he was, Johnny Mikami was allowed to drive about as he pleased, even to wait with his cab at the main gate of the Navy Yard for fares of gobs whenever the fleet came in, and drive them to the various places of "relaxation" downtown— pumping them for information on the way. However, the consulate general was his best customer. He drove members of the staff to shopping, golfing, to beach parties, and ran errands for Okuda.

Despite the casual nature of Okuda's espionage effort and the mostly incidental character of the intelligence it produced, his clandestine work was not without importance. He did manage to collect some technical data and present a certain pattern of American naval activities in Hawaii. And he had at least one producing spy at large on Maui, in the person of the Reverend Unji Hirayama.

This, then, was the state of Japanese espionage in Hawaii when, on February 5, 1941, Captain Ogawa went back to Tokyo from his conference with Admiral Yamamoto aboard the *Nagato*. He reported to Admiral Nedo, the director of Naval Intelligence, then held several consultations in the Foreign Ministry, with Kazushige Hirasawa, chief of the U.S. Section in the Bureau of American Affairs; Katsuji Kameyama, chief of the Cable Section; * and a career diplomat named Minode who headed the Ministry's Political Intelligence Department.

Ogawa's purpose was to tighten the co-operation with the For-

* Kameyama had succeeded Sakuma as chief of the *denshin-ka* in June 1937. Prior to this appointment he was in charge of the Soviet Desk in the Foreign Ministry and then made second secretary at the Moscow embassy. Like Sawada and Sakuma before him, Kameyama was a career diplomat with no cryptographic or telegraphic qualifications. He remained Cable Chief until November 1942, when he was promoted counselor of embassy and transferred to Moscow.

eign Ministry during the difficult months ahead. He could not rely on the slipshod operatives of his "outside system" in Honolulu, and there was no time to build up a ring of more competent and better-placed agents. He had to use the "inside system," not only because the consulate general provided the best line of communications, but also because he already had the nucleus of agents inside the consulate. Moreover, he needed diplomatic cover for the changes he would have to make in the organization to assure the coverage Yamamoto had asked him to provide.

His scheme was extremely simple; the personnel involved in it kept at a minimum. Despite the mounting Japanese-American tension, Hawaii continued to be so wide open that not even the intensified surveillance required too great an expansion of his existing consular net. And besides, he was reluctant to make the reorganization too conspicuous or else he might tip off the American authorities and induce them to tighten their security measures.

At first Ogawa toyed with the idea of transferring Commander Tachibana, his best operative in the United States, to Honolulu, either as an independent member of the "outside system" or in a diplomatic guise. Tachibana was in America deeply under cover. At this time he was operating from his base in Los Angeles under the alias Hisashi Yamamoto, posing (rather precariously) as the prosperous owner of a chain of pleasure houses with a seductive oriental atmosphere, and enjoying the protection of the West Coast branch of the Chicago mob.

But Tachibana had been in the United States since 1931, and ten years at a post is far too long a time for an espionage agent to feel safe. Ogawa, who was shrewd in the devious ways of the secret service, suspected that Tachibana might still be at large only because the FBI was "giving him plenty of rope"—leaving him free and seemingly letting him do as he pleased while keeping him under surveillance in the hope that he would lead his "shadows" to his accomplices.*

* How justified Ogawa's suspicion was in the case of Tachibana alias Yamamoto was shown in May 1941 when the FBI suddenly arrested him on the charge of tax evasion prior to charging him with espionage. He had been under surveillance for months, but his arrest had been delayed at the request of the State Department, which feared that the detention of such an important agent would adversely affect Japanese-American relations at that

The idea of Tachibana's transfer to Honolulu was dropped. Ogawa then thought of activating Kühn, his "sleeper" in Kalama, especially since the German seemed to be straining at the leash and was bombarding him with appeals to let him go into action. As a matter of fact, Kühn was violating his instructions and was becoming a nuisance. Beset by financial difficulties, he hoped to obtain additional funds from Tokyo by persuading Ogawa to allow him to start operations. Whether or not he was actually intent on sticking his neck out is open to doubt. But he emerged from obscurity in a most imprudent manner, going to Okuda in the consulate to remonstrate with him about the laxity of Japanese espionage in Hawaii and offering his services to "invigorate" the coverage, as he put it.

Okuda had never been told about Kühn and his dormant mission, so he queried Ogawa, who confirmed Kühn's claim. But since Kühn's entreaties were always accompanied by demands for more money, Ogawa thought it wiser to let him remain a "sleeper" a little longer.*

He decided instead to send a special agent directly from the Third Bureau, a trained intelligence officer whose specialty was information about the movements of ships. He picked an ensign working in Section 8, the British Section, for the mission, and arranged with Director Terasaki of the Foreign Ministry to provide a diplomatic cover for him. In addition he asked the Foreign

---

critical time. Tachibana's arrest led to the collapse of the whole network on the West Coast and New York. By then, however, espionage activities had been shifted to Hawaii, and the destruction of the Tachibana ring was no longer considered a fatal blow. Tachibana was allowed to return to Japan on June 19. He was in Honolulu on June 27, 1941, but only in transit.

* Kühn's cover name was "Friedel," using the German diminutive of his wife's, Elfriede's, Christian name. His decision to "emerge" brought him to the attention of the FBI, where a very well-informed suspect card on him was prepared as early as July 1940: "Formerly (1918) officer in German Navy; cultivates acquaintances among officers in U.S. Navy; at one time received considerable sums of money from European source; frequent trips to Japan; Mrs. Kühn recently (May 1940) returned from Japan and reportedly brought back a considerable sum of money with her; has failed in business but owns considerable real estate." Mrs. Kühn was carried as a "Class A" suspect in the FBI files. "Wife of Otto Kühn," her card read, "suspected of being a German [sic] agent. Friedel Kühn is known to be pro-Nazi. Mr. and Mrs. Kühn are suspected of being 'Mr. and Mrs. Friedel' who are reported as contacts of the local Japanese consulate."

Ministry to send a new consul general to Honolulu under whose sympathetic supervision the consulate could be developed into the focal point of espionage in the Hawaiian area.

After the meetings on February 5, Ogawa sent a telegram (No. 043–1941) to Honolulu, instructing the consul general to shift emphasis in the regular undercover activities of the consulate. "We have decided," Ogawa wrote cryptically, "to de-emphasize our propaganda work and strengthen our intelligence work in the United States."

He followed it up on February 15 with another dispatch (No. 0073–1941), in which he sent a new "shopping list" to Honolulu— or schedule of "the information," as he phrased it, "we desire [to obtain] with regard to intelligence." On the same day, in still another telegram (No. 008–1941), he told Okuda exactly what was expected of him:

"In gathering intelligence material, your office will pay particular attention to:

"(1) Strengthening or supplementing of military preparations on the Pacific Coast and the Hawaiian area; amount and type of stores and military supplies, alterations to airports; also carefully observe the [Pan American] Clipper traffic.

"(2) Ship and plane movements, including the flight of large bombers and seaplanes."

He sent instructions to the *burakku chiemba* at Guaymas for Lieutenant Yamashita to intensify the surveillance of the American fleet's radio traffic. And finally, he increased the number of submarines on patrol duty in the Hawaiian waters.*

---

* The suddenly increased submarine surveillance was noticed immediately at Pearl Harbor. According to Admiral Husband E. Kimmel, he was welcomed to his new post on February 1, 1941, with the report of a submerged-submarine contact only eight miles from the Pearl Harbor entrance buoys. During the ensuing months there were many more reports of "strange submerged-submarine contacts." However, Kimmel had orders from the Navy Department not to molest "suspected Japanese submarines except in the defensive sea areas"— that is, within the three-mile limit—and even then only when "conclusive evidence" was obtained that the strange submarines were "in or near United States territory." The prowlers understood only too well how to remain inconspicuous. "Conclusive" evidence of their presence was not obtained until dawn on December 7, 1941, when the U.S.S. *Ward* made unmistakable contact with an unmistakably hostile Japanese submarine and attacked it. The submarine was from Admiral Yamamoto's advance expeditionary force, in Hawaiian waters since the day before.

In February 1941 Okuda received word from Tokyo that a new consul general would soon be sent to Honolulu to fill the vacancy left by Kiichi's withdrawal. In the immediate wake of Captain Ogawa's conference with Admiral Yamamoto, the *joho kyoku* had made a survey of Japanese consuls at large in the world, to choose the best man for the delicate Honolulu post. They decided on Nagao Kita, the Japanese consul general in Canton.

Born in 1895 in Tokushima Prefecture on East Shikoku, a mountainous region that produced hardy men of courage and resourcefulness, Kita claimed to be a descendant of the legendary Emperor Kwammu and a scion of the famed Taira, a clan crushed by the Minamoto at Dun no Ura in 1185, in the first great naval battle in Japanese history. In native lore the defeated Taira continue to live on in the *heike-gani*, certain crabs thriving on Shikoku which are believed to be the spirits of the Taira warriors killed in that ancient naval engagement.

With such distinguished crabs for ancestors and with a burning ambition to make good, and not much more, Kita entered the Foreign Service. Though his proper colleagues (all of them graduates of Tokyo University, the Harvard of Japan) looked down on this upstart, Kita managed to keep up with them chiefly because he had powerful supporters in the navy, which was making excellent use of such "misfits" in the pursuit of its own diplomacy. Kita was, on the navy's recommendation, always stationed at sensitive posts in which Naval Intelligence had some specific interest—first at Amoy, the old Chinese treaty port on an inlet in the Formosa Strait; then in Shanghai, the perennial powder keg on the Whangpoo River; and eventually in Canton, a city in the shadow of Hong Kong, notorious for its international intrigue.

By the time Kita reached Canton he was a merry widower (with a young son in boarding school in Japan), living much beyond his apparent means. But Kita could afford the good life; he had access to secret funds which he used in his personal pursuit of happiness.

Now, after ten days in Tokyo, where he was briefed for his mission, Kita arrived in Honolulu on March 14, 1941, aboard the NYK liner *Tatsuta Maru*. He took immediate charge of the consulate in the imperious manner which had earned for him the sobriquet *dar-en*, or "the boss," for Kita never left any doubt in anyone's mind that he was, indeed, the boss wherever he operated.

Only twelve days later another NYK liner, the 17,000-ton *Nitta Maru*, sailed into Honolulu after a record-breaking crossing, having made the trip, which normally took eight or nine days, in exactly seven days, five hours and thirty-seven minutes. It brought only one first-class passenger bound for Honolulu—a young man carried on the passenger list as Tadashi Morimura.

There was some incongruity in Morimura's rapid transit from Yokohama to Honolulu. He had traveled in style, occupying the ship's best suite, and dined as the guest of honor at the captain's table every night, although he was but a probationary consul en route to Hawaii. And he had paid 2000 yen for his fare, which was ten times what he was earning per month.

At the consulate the news of Morimura's arrival created a flurry of excitement. Both Kita and Okuda acted mysteriously when the staff inquired about the new consul. Samon Tsukikawa went to the trouble of checking him out in the Foreign Service List of career diplomats and consuls, and was mystified when he could find no Tadashi Morimura in it. The aura of mystery was heightened when Tsukikawa confided to his colleagues that he had dispatched a telegram from Kita to the *Nitta Maru* at sea, instructing Morimura to remain in his cabin upon his arrival in Honolulu until called for by Consul Okuda.

The next morning, March 27, Okuda was at Pier 8 when the *Nitta Maru* docked, then went aboard to greet Morimura, waiting as instructed in his luxurious cabin. The newcomer, a jolly, big man with an easy smile and expansive manners, acknowledged the reception by standing at attention, clicking his heels and saluting smartly, a gesture that impressed Okuda as being more military than diplomatic. At the consulate, when Okuda introduced the new man to the consul general, Kita locked the door and greeted him with a grin. "Welcome to Hawaii, Ensign Yoshikawa," he said. "You are Ensign Yoshikawa, aren't you?" Morimura was, indeed—an ensign of the Naval Reserve, Takeo Yoshikawa his real name. He had come, in the guise of an apprentice consul under an alias, to collect the data Admiral Yamamoto had ordered from Naval Intelligence.

Yoshikawa was a graduate of the naval academy but had been

separated from the service shortly after graduation when it was discovered that he had tuberculosis, the dread disease from which many of the people of his native Shikoku suffered. He then applied for a desk job as a civilian in the navy and was assigned to Section 8, the British Section of Naval Intelligence, where his specialty became the plotting of movements of the Royal Navy's ships in Asian waters. It was this proficiency that made him the choice for the delicate job in Hawaii—had not Yamamoto told Captain Ogawa that he was especially interested in the movements of American warships at Pearl?

The night after Yoshikawa had reached his destination, Kita took his two consuls to the Shunchu-ro, a Japanese restaurant halfway up one of the hills overlooking the harbor, to celebrate the new man's arrival. It was a place of dubious fame run by fifty-four-year-old Namiko Fujiwara, whose checkered past prevented the restaurant from obtaining a liquor license. But it had two huge telescopes on hand, with which tourists could entertain themselves by looking at the sights in the harbor below.

The party was a huge success. Namiko served imported Kirim beer and *sake*, surreptitiously, in enormous teapots. Yoshikawa picked up one of the telescopes, aimed it at the harbor, and peering into the dark night, proclaimed loudly: "This job will be a cinch, and lots of fun besides!"

Okuda paled. Thinking of the trouble he already had with Kühn, he told Seki the morning after, when relating the incident: "I'm afraid we've got another pain in the neck."

With the arrival of Ensign Yoshikawa alias Morimura-*san*, the cast of characters was complete. What had now become the patently primary target of Japanese espionage was receiving the attention of an aging playboy serving as consul general, a scholarly consul apparently too busy with his regular chores to devote proper attention to any clandestine pursuits, a tubercular ex-ensign in a constant state of hangover, a couple of consular clerks, a shoddy cab driver doubling as self-made naval expert and, last but not least, a Teutonic busybody straining to emerge from his enforced hibernation.

13   The Maze of "Magic"

In his story of espionage through the centuries, Colonel Allison Ind, himself a veteran intelligence officer of World War II, bemoaned the fact that Americans had neglected to spy on Japan before the war. "Napoleon said," Ind wrote, "that a spy in the right place is worth 20,000 troops. Japan had that spy at Pearl Harbor. The United States did not have him in Tokyo, or Yokosuka, or Kure."

Ind's statement was the kind of rationalization we contrived in the wake of the Pearl Harbor disaster, to soothe the pain and mend our pride so badly hurt by the defeat. On one score he was right: we had no spy in Tokyo or Yokosuka. But if we had none, it was not because we were either loath to stoop to such means or lax in making use of the craft of espionage.

If we had no secret agents comparable to a Tachibana or a Yoshikawa inside Japan, and were satisfied with a mere lieutenant commander as our naval attaché in Tokyo (who was, besides, an expert on France), it was because we thought that we did not need such an arrangement any longer. After the recovery of PURPLE, "Magic" and the Navy's cryptanalytical effort were satisfying all our apparent needs.

This reliance on "cryptological espionage" became total when the recovery of the PURPLE code placed in our hands the key to what appeared to be Japan's most closely guarded state secrets.

The value of "Magic" was considerable, indeed, both as a source of intelligence and as a tool of statecraft. However, its role and

influence must be viewed in their proper perspective, especially in
their impact on the men who used it—on President Roosevelt and
Secretary Hull, on General Marshall, Admiral Stark and Secretary
Stimson, and even on the middle-layer officials and officers in the
State, War and Navy departments such as Dr. Stanley K. Hornbeck, Mr. Hull's chief adviser in his negotiations with the Japanese, and Colonel Bratton in G-2.

The technicians who had produced the instrument after nineteen months of hard work were naturally proud of and pleased
with their achievement, and tended to view its value uncritically.*
Their enthusiasm then rubbed off on most of their clients. In
actual fact, however, "Magic" was not the perfect tool by any
means to grind out absolutely reliable, first-hand intelligence. The
diplomatic coverage it provided was substantially reduced by certain limitations which Dr. Hornbeck for one had recognized from
the outset. As he saw them, the "magics" were *diplomatic* messages written and sent by people who did not know much of what
the aggressive military clique in Tokyo was actually planning, and
who were, in fact, excluded from their secrets. Moreover, no
intercept of *military* significance was ever forwarded to State, and
therefore the American diplomats had no opportunity of project-
ing the diplomatic maneuvers against the military background of
Japanese intentions and, indeed, plans.

The intercepts State was receiving thus told only half the story
—in fact, only that particular half which was often deliberately so
designed in Tokyo as to camouflage military intentions and pending aggressive moves. The fabulous "Magic," which had been

* Zacharias tried to create a sense of proportion in this connection when he
cautioned that cryptanalysis is only part of the intelligence effort. "No one,"
he wrote, "can discover everything that is taking place within the enemy camp
by concentrating alone on the decoding and deciphering of his messages. . . .
Even the most comprehensive and efficient cryptanalysis leaves many gaps
unfilled and many of the problems unsolved." The messages which pass
between various agencies of countries are never comprehensive. They often
contain subcodes within the codes, oblique references to facts the knowledge
of which is presupposed, or short cuts to previously given oral instructions.
Thus, for example, the Germans found repeated references to something called
"Overlord" in the Allies' encoded dispatches of 1943–44, but did not know
that it was the code word for the Normandy invasion. "Cryptanalysis,"
Zacharias wrote, "is supplemental . . . part of the great and complex intelligence setup."

welcomed as an invaluable instrument of clarification, at times became an implement of obfuscation.

Unlike Yardley's translations during the Washington Conference of 1921–22, with their up-to-the-minute, unimpeachable, indispensable intelligence, the diplomatic "magics" produced little *original* or *definitive* information. Most of the material they yielded was actually available in the State Department from other sources—from the reports of American envoys and even from observations supplied by well-informed private individuals in the key areas of danger, such as Dr. John Leighton Stuart, president of Yenching University in Peking; the Reverend W. P. Mills and Dr. M. S. Bates, American missionaries in Nanking; and Dr. E. Stanley Jones, an eminent Methodist clergyman.*

For example, the dispatches of Admiral William D. Leahy from the American embassy in Vichy in 1940 and 1941 supplied as accurate and as timely information about Japan's underhanded dealings with the Pétain regime as could be obtained from the "magics." Ambassador Leahy's information was also first-hand. It was given him "under the counter" by Jean Chauvel, chief of the Vichy Foreign Office's Far Eastern Section.

Nothing obtained from the intercepts could surpass or supplement confidential information contained in the periodic reports of Horace B. Williams, the American commercial attaché in Tokyo; the pinpointed intelligence Willys R. Peck of the State Department's Far Eastern Division obtained from overt sources; and data Gerald Krentz, the American consul general in Mukden, procured from his secret contacts in Manchuria.

As a matter of fact, the reports of the American diplomats and observers had an important advantage which the "magics" lacked. They were far more succinct, direct and lucid than the pertinent texts of the intercepts. This was due partly to the innate obscurity of the Japanese diplomatic style, and partly to the frequently very poor translations of the decrypted messages by the Army's and

* Dr. Stuart was a confidant of Lieutenant General Seishiro Itagaki, chief of staff of the Japanese army in central China; Mills and Bates were close to high-ranking Japanese officials in the Nanking area; and Dr. Jones was in touch with Dr. Kagawa, a prominent Japanese publicist close to Premier Konoye's circle. Another writer in the Konoye group, Hotsumi Ozaki, was the main source of Dr. Richard Sorge, the exceptionally effective espionage agent working for the Soviet Union in Japan during this same period.

Navy's linguists. In addition, the American reports usually contained shrewd interpretations of the issues or events they were describing, while the Japanese telegrams left this burden to their readers in Washington.

In the last analysis, the "magics" produced really but one overwhelming piece of evidence. They showed that the Japanese were insincere; that they could not be trusted; that this whole business of seeking a peaceful solution of the problems was a sham as far as they were concerned. This impression created a deep-seated distrust of the Japanese in the minds of the American negotiators, and more than that—hostility and contempt.

In a different area "Magic" had a distinctly harmful effect on its highly placed clients. It filled them with a somewhat smug feeling of security, stemming from the belief that we had the Japanese "completely covered." Mr. Roosevelt and his associates in particular assumed that thanks to the "magics," they could learn well in advance everything the Japanese were planning, enabling them to apply whatever preventive or counter measures they deemed advisable or necessary. This reliance on "Magic" as an instrument of warning became partly responsible for the complacency with which the American authorities approached the final crisis in November and December 1941.

However, reservations, misgivings and misconceptions such as these were generally obscured and often glossed over by the fact that the coverage provided by "Magic" seemed to be both perfect and comprehensive. From a purely technical point of view, it actually was.

In 1940–41 the Japanese Foreign Ministry had five classes of telegraphic codes, rated according to the degree of their security, and a total of fourteen different systems in the five categories: two (A and B) in the top-security No. 1 class, two (TSU and OITE) in the second-class group, and ten so-called minor systems in the remaining three classes.

By 1941, when the Japanese stepped up their activities (by both negotiating for peace and preparing for war), the United States had succeeded in compromising five of these diplomatic cryptosystems—the machine-based A and B (RED and PURPLE), the TSU (J series), the OITE (P or PA series with a K code), and even "a piece of junk," as the Navy's cryptanalysts called it, a code labeled L which was used only to abbreviate the text of the messages in order to save money on the cable charges.

Moreover, no sooner were any changes made in these systems than the American cryptologists also managed to recover them. Thus, for instance, the Japanese made two changes in their TSU system within a five-month period in 1941, the first in March, a second in August. Both were solved promptly, within days in the first and within hours in the second instance. The TSU which the Honolulu consulate general used at the time of Pearl Harbor was the *nineteenth* version of this system in just five years, all of them recovered by the Americans.

The solution of PURPLE had brought considerable changes and improvements in the Army's and Navy's cryptological establishments. Both Safford's Communications Security Section and Friedman's Signal Intelligence Service expanded rapidly. Their monitoring and decrypting facilities were growing by leaps and bounds to enable them to cope with their great new responsibilities.

But the coverage of Japan was still not as complete as later events showed would have been desirable. Virtually no part of the Japanese army's crypto-system had been compromised. Unlike the Japanese navy, which was using mostly cipher in its secret communications, the Japanese army was using codes almost exclusively. It was, moreover, extremely security-minded in its cryptographic activities.

Even a modest attack on the army codes was hampered by several factors. It was considered absolutely impossible to procure the *code books* of the army in the manner which had enabled ONI to obtain the Japanese navy's fleet code in 1920. And SIS did not have a sufficient number of Japanese army intercepts on hand to enable its cryptanalysts to break the codes by the analytical method.

This created a major gap in the coverage—a significant one at that, for the army's messages contained vital information about the expansionist designs and arrangements of the military clique, much of it unknown to the Imperial Navy and the Foreign Ministry. But so slight was the United States Army's interest in the Japanese army at this time that the absence of this intelligence was not considered a really serious matter. Besides, SIS was too busy with its share in the "Magic" operation. It had neither the personnel nor the facilities to spare for the solution of the Japanese army's crypto-system.

On the other hand, the Navy's coverage was as complete as seemed possible under the circumstances.

The Japanese navy had innumerable ciphers, many of them with complicating code features. Op-20-G had succeeded in recovering three of its major systems, in addition to a minor one.

It had the twenty-fourth and twenty-fifth variants of the JN series of FLEET codes, a far cry from the primitive "Red Book" of 1920.

It had the so-called s or SA codes, a minor system used by the Japanese merchant marine.*

It had the naval attaché ciphers.

It had a comprehensive radio call signal list.

And above all else, it had the precious AD code of the Japanese admirals.

The task of keeping open these systems did not present any insurmountable difficulties. In June 1940, for example, the Japanese made rather radical changes in their FLEET code (JN-24), preventing Op-20-G from reading the Imperial Navy's messages in July and August. Work on the solution of the changes was given top priority by Safford. It was completed in September, coincident with the recovery of the PURPLE code by SIS. (The double triumph went far in persuading the American cryptanalysts that nothing in their craft was closed to them even if sometimes the impossible took them a little longer to accomplish.)

* Documents pertaining to this system were procured in their originals in another coup staged by the Office of Naval Intelligence. Around noon on May 29, 1941, naval intelligence agents posing as U.S. customs officials boarded the *Nichi Shin Maru*, a vessel of the Pacific Whaling Steamship Company, when she was about twenty miles off San Francisco, on the pretext that she was suspected of carrying contraband drugs. The boarding party searched the ship and found no illicit cargo, but seized the latest version of the SA code, secret naval documents the captain had in his custody, a code issued by the Central Meteorological Bureau, another used by the Planning Board, and the radio operator's classified wireless telegraphy instructions. The seizure of these documents naturally alerted the Japanese authorities, and the compromised codes were promptly changed. However, the confiscated papers yielded data of considerable research value to the men and women in Op-20-G.

This operation was deep under cover even within Op-20-G. No romantic cover name had been coined for it, but it was just as magical as the parallel "Magic." Supervised by Safford, it was managed as a separate Communications Intelligence Unit (C/I Unit B) * by Commander Joseph J. Rochefort, dean of the Navy's cryptanalysts. Working under him were what Safford described as Op-20-G's "best men as far as experience and all-round skill was concerned."

While the personnel processing "Magic" was relatively green— about 90 percent of them had been in service less than a year—the doubly secret Rochefort group included Thomas H. Dyer, Jack S. Holtwick, Thomas A. Huckins, Wesley Wright, all young cryptanalysts who had participated in the virtuoso "research" that resulted in the recovery of the RED machine. Most of them had been in communications intelligence since 1932, some of them even longer.

This activity was the Navy's own. The Army's Signal Intelligence had no part in it, and with the possible exception of Friedman, from whom Safford kept few secrets, had absolutely no knowledge of it. Nobody outside a few officers at the top in the Navy—not even President Roosevelt—was made its beneficiary. What went to the White House and the State Department was produced exclusively by the "Magic" operation. The value of the operation was diminished by this secrecy. As Admiral Morison put it: "The Navy Department laid such stress on security of communications that they sometimes failed of their essential purpose to communicate."

The AD code and the JN series supplied what the Navy regarded as more than adequate coverage of the Imperial Navy. And "Magic" produced what seemed to be perfect political and even some military intelligence. In actual fact, however, neither the naval codes nor the diplomatic ciphers provided comprehensive coverage by themselves.

Among the apparent diplomatic dispatches were those which

* By this time Op-20-G also had a Unit (C/I C) operating at Cavite on Luzon, Philippine Islands, handling most of the traffic of the old RED machine, guarding the Tokyo-Berlin and Tokyo-Moscow circuits, and processing their output on their own PURPLE machine. Neither at this time nor later was Hawaii given a PURPLE machine, not even when Rochefort's Unit was transferred to Oahu in the summer of 1941.

the Foreign Ministry's Cable Section was handling for the Third
Bureau in general and for Captain Ogawa's Section 5 in particular.
Op-20-G was badly misled about the parties involved in this traffic
by a confusing protocol the *denshin-ka* observed in the transmission of these messages. Since they had the highest security classification, they were handled as "Minister's Instructions" or as
"Chief of Mission Telegrams." They went out over the Foreign
Minister's signature when they originated in Tokyo, or in the
names of the various ambassadors, ministers and consul generals,
even though most of the time their signatories never saw these
dispatches and knew nothing about them.

A typical telegram handled by the *denshin-ka* for Naval Intelligence read:

To: Riyoji, Panama

August 18, 1941   No. 063

If possible, I would like you to report by telegram
English & American merchant ships transiting Canal

[signed] Toyoda

"Riyoji" was the cable address of Japanese consulates throughout the world, in this case of Consul General Akiyama in Panama
City. And "Toyoda" was Admiral Teijiro Toyoda, who was Foreign Minister in the summer of 1941.

In actual fact Toyoda never saw this telegram, did not send it
and did not have the slightest idea that it was ever sent. It was, as
its numbering indicated, a special signal to Akiyama from Captain
Ogawa, prepared in Section 5, and given to the *denshin-ka* solely
for transmission. Under Ogawa's arrangement with the Foreign
Ministry, messages of the Third Bureau were handled in utmost
secrecy within the Cable Section. A telegram like No. 063 was not
shown even to the young Foreign Service officer whose desk in the
American Affairs Bureau handled Panama.

No. 063 was an espionage message pure and simple, as was No.
008 of Panama City in which Akayima replied to Ogawa's inquiry.
Both went out in the guise of diplomatic dispatches. In a similar
manner, Ogawa's important telegrams of February 15, 1941, in
which he transmitted his "shopping list" to Consul Okuda in

Honolulu, went out as "Minister's Instructions" over the signature "Matsuoka"—Foreign Minister Yosuke Matsuoka—although he had absolutely nothing to do with it except for the purely technical fact that his Cable Section had taken care of its transmission.

Throughout 1941, all of Ogawa's espionage traffic was transmitted in this diplomatic guise, the Foreign Ministers (Japan had three during the year) lending their names to Ogawa's signals. The telegrams going to Tokyo were equally misleading. Thus, for instance, the messages Yoshikawa was sending from Honolulu via the Cable Section of the Foreign Ministry were all addressed to the Foreign Minister and signed "Kita," although the consul general did not send them and the Foreign Minister never got to see them.

The practice misled even the FBI. After the outbreak of the war, it assumed (and publicized the fact) that Consul General Nagao Kita had been the spy master of Japan in Hawaii whose activities had paved the way for Admiral Yamamoto's planes.*

Far more important, the practice confused Op-20-G. The espionage signals passing between Ogawa and Yoshikawa were accepted at face value as diplomatic messages passing between the Foreign Minister and the consul general. An occasional telegram in this category was presented to higher-ups. A few of them were forwarded to the "B" (Domestic) Branch in ONI for whatever clues they might have supplied to counterespionage. But they were dismissed as not representing any significance or value to positive intelligence. Most of them were destroyed.

Nobody in ONI was inclined to underrate the Japanese intelligence effort. "The Japanese for many years," said Captain Theodore S. Wilkinson, one of the four directors that Naval Intelligence had during this period, "had the reputation, and the facts bore out that reputation, of being meticulous seekers for every

* "Nagao Kita," wrote Don Whitehead in his officially endorsed book about the FBI. "It's a name to remember in the espionage of World War II. If any man can be named as the most effective enemy agent in the Pearl Harbor attack, it was Kita." On the other hand, the real "Pearl Harbor spy," Ensign Yoshikawa, was conspicuously unmentioned in Mr. Whitehead's book and, for that matter, in the FBI's own records, although there were passing references to a "Vice-Consul Tadashi Morimura" in reports compiled after the outbreak of hostilities. However, they still failed to identify him either by his true name or as the actual espionage agent Ogawa had in Hawaii in preparation for the attack.

scrap of information, whether by photography or by written report
or otherwise." However, the American intelligence specialists lost
some of their high regard for the *joho kyoku* when they assumed
from these intercepts that it had entrusted the collection of naval
intelligence in Hawaii to a bunch of amateur civilians.

Commander McCollum, an otherwise competent and shrewd
intelligence officer, concluded that these messages were of no value
even to the Japanese who received them, for they reflected merely
the efforts of dilettantes. Commander Kramer was condescending
in his appraisal of these dispatches, describing them merely as
attempts on the part of "the Japanese diplomatic service" to
dabble in naval intelligence.

And yet, it was in these pseudodiplomatic telegrams that the
Japanese showed their real purpose. Not one signal of the Imperial
Navy decrypted in Washington or Cavite contained even the
vaguest hint that Pearl Harbor was among the intended targets of
Japanese aggression. On the other hand, "Magic" produced this
evidence actually in abundance, from February 15, 1941, until the
morning of the attack.

It this segment of "Magic" never gained the prominence and
influence its significance would have warranted, it was due mainly
to the refusal of the American intelligence specialists to concede
that mere civilian consuls like Kita and Okuda could be capable of
producing naval intelligence of any real value.

As a result, the espionage messages of "Magic" were assigned
the lowest-priority schedule in decrypting and translations, even
when they were in the TSU system. This schedule had been agreed
upon in Op-20-G and SIS, at their own discretion. Two considerations were instrumental for the speed in processing. On the basis
of the class of cipher used, the B code (PURPLE) intercepts were
given the highest priority, messages in TSU (J series) came next,
while those in OITE (P or PA) were given a relatively low priority
rating.

As far as the apparent significance of the contents of the telegrams was concerned, three "important" priority categories were
established—"most important," "very important" and "important." * Two other categories were classed as "routine" or "nor-

* In an index of 193 intercepts, processed between March 1 and December
7, 1941, not a single one was marked "most important." Thirty-two were rated

mal," and "supplementary," and had no priorities assigned. They were supposed to be processed only after all other "magics" had been translated or whenever the cryptanalysts and translators had nothing else or better to do.

An ephemeral dispatch from Ambassador Nomura to Foreign Minister Matsuoka dated March 11, 1941, describing a talk with Secretary Hull on the day before, was rated "very important" and processed immediately, simply because it was in the CA version of the PURPLE code ("Chief of Mission Dispatch"). But a signal from Tokyo to Honolulu on March 22, instructing Kita to "secure intelligence even by bribing your informants," was marked "supplementary" and put aside. It took twenty-six days to process this particular dispatch. Okuda's first comprehensive intelligence report, of December 2, 1940, reposed in an incoming basket for forty-three days before Commander Kramer got around to translating it. The message reporting the withdrawal of the American ships from Lahaina, intercepted on December 20, 1940, was thirty-four days late in translation. Moreover, none of these particular telegrams was ever distributed outside the Office of Naval Intelligence. In ONI itself, they were filed by Kramer, and forgotten.

This system of priorities was unavoidable. The work load was growing far beyond what SIS and Op-20-G, with their still-limited personnel, could handle. A backlog was developing rapidly, especially in SIS, which was working only one shift of cryptanalysts and translators.

However, Kramer erred when he decided to assign "no priority" to the crucial espionage messages. Here, indeed, was one of the real causes of Pearl Harbor.

"important" and seventeen "very important." All espionage messages thus indexed were marked "supplementary." One of them carried the inferentially jeering notation: "This is why we do not worry too much over Japanese espionage."

14   "John Doe's" Secret Mission

Recalling the convulsive days of early 1941 with their budding war plots, Colonel Kenryo Sato, section chief in General Muto's Military Affairs Bureau in the War Ministry, protested: "Just because we slept in the same bed with Imperial Headquarters did not mean that we had the same dreams." What Sato meant to say was that despite all appearances to the contrary, not everybody in Tokyo, not even the politicking Military Affairs Bureau, was intent on total war with the United States.

The dominant view among many of Japan's top civilian leaders was still that conflicts of interest could be reconciled through negotiation. "There should still be," Marquis Kido, the Lord Keeper of the Privy Seal and closest adviser of the Throne, told Emperor Hirohito in February 1941, "various ways of bringing about an adjustment of relations with the United States. Persistent and constructive efforts should be made toward that end."

The Emperor did not have to be convinced. He had approved the Tripartite Pact and the thrust into Indochina under duress, only when his Prime Minister, Prince Konoye, warned him that the dynasty might not survive if he refused to sanction them. Konoye was convinced that the extremists had reached the point where they were prepared to assassinate even the Emperor if he stood in their way. The Emperor had capitulated but told Kido that "personally he did not like the idea of Japan's playing the thief at a fire."

While preparations for war were stealthily being made in the army and the navy, parallel efforts to preserve the peace were undertaken by the young Premier, Fumimaro Konoye, a hereditary prince with some of the melancholy traits of Hamlet. He headed a schizophrenic government split between members who favored adjustment of Japan's differences with the United States and his headstrong, voluble Foreign Minister, Yosuke Matsuoka, who had committed the country to all-out co-operation with Germany.*

Konoye commuted between the two groups, and since he was a man who wanted to be liked, he tried to please both factions. He was, as Admiral Nomura described him, a "refined gentleman and a man of popularity," a good talker and persuasive in his arguments. "But," Nomura added, "he had bitten off far more than he was able to digest." He tried to strike a balance between Japan's friendship with Germany on the one side and her dependence on the United States on the other. But while he knew exactly what the Germans wanted, he could not make out the purposes and intentions of the Americans.

Since September 1940, Washington regarded Japan as an ally of Hitler and the signatory of an alliance aimed at the United States. "We considered Japan's expansionist ambitions," wrote Secretary Hull, "an eventual danger to our own safety."

The United States had responded to the Tripartite Pact with economic measures that amounted to sanctions, and answered Japan's move into Indochina with a sharp increase in aid to China. Japan was now beginning to feel these pressures seriously both in her economy at home and in her hapless war in China. But Konoye, who could not or would not care to guess how much further the United States would be willing to go in applying pressures, still believed that he could come to terms with the United States.

This was a step he had to take cautiously if he wanted to escape

* Matsuoka's good intentions, Admiral Yonai once said, were the surest way for Japan to wind up in hell. A law graduate of the University of Oregon, Matsuoka's bitter anti-Americanism undermined his stability and judgment. On February 20, 1941, President Roosevelt remarked on a statement by Matsuoka that it seemed to be "the product of a mind which is deeply disturbed and unable to think quietly and logically." Listening to one of Matsuoka's harangues in a liaison conference on May 22, Navy Minister Admiral Koshiro Oikawa unknowingly agreed with the President when he told a colleague: "The Foreign Minister is insane."

the lethal censure of the extremists, who never hesitated to assassinate Premiers opposed to their reckless aspirations. Konoye therefore decided to negotiate a rapprochement with the United States on two different levels—one, the regular diplomatic channels; the other, under ground.

In November 1940 Konoye started a search for a prominent Japanese to go to Washington as his ambassador of good will and for a private intermediary who would clandestinely convey to the Americans his government's "proposal," as it was called, to "negotiate a peace agreement."

The diplomatic mission was eventually entrusted to Kichisaburo Nomura, a good-natured, bumbling man of sixty-two who had risen to prominence in the Imperial Navy and Japanese politics with the qualities of the admiral from H.M.S. *Pinafore.* He was regarded, however, as the ideal person for the job because he was a close friend of Admiral William W. Pratt's, former Chief of Naval Operations, and of other American naval officers'. Moreover, he had known the President when Mr. Roosevelt was Assistant Secretary of the Navy in the Wilson Administration and Nomura was naval attaché in Washington.

The clandestine prong of the drive was a different matter. It had to be conducted behind an *American* front, by men who had a stake of their own in a Japanese-American rapprochement, were prominent and forceful to make their influence felt, and discreet to assure the secrecy of the venture.

Several Americans came under consideration, among them Roy Howard, president of the Scripps-Howard chain of newspapers, and a New York businessman named Morris Kleiman. Howard was an old acquaintance of Konoye's, and Mr. Kleiman was even then working in Washington on efforts to improve Japanese-American relations, in association with a group that included Gracie Hall Roosevelt (a relative of the President's), Washington attorney Joseph C. Davies and a retired general named R. C. Marshall.

However, Howard was ruled out because his relations with Mr. Roosevelt were known to be rather strained. The Kleiman group was excluded, partly because Mr. Kleiman himself was not considered influential enough for such a mission and partly because Konoye feared that too many people in the plot might endanger its security.

In December, Tadeo Wikawa, a prominent financier, told the Prime Minister about two American Roman Catholic priests adrift in Tokyo who appeared to meet the qualifications Konoye had set for the confidential intermediary. They were Bishop James Edward Walsh and Father James M. Drought of the Catholic Foreign Mission (Maryknoll) Society, who had come to Tokyo to solicit the protection of the authorities for the Maryknoll missions at Kyoto in Japan, Pyengyang in Korea and Fushun in Manchuria. Wikawa had met them through an introduction from Lewis S. Strauss, senior partner in the banking house of Kuhn, Loeb & Company, who was a fiscal adviser of the Maryknoll Society and a friend of Wikawa's since the twenties, when Wikawa was Financial High Commissioner in New York.

Despite Wikawa's help and friendly support from other influential people, such as former Premier Wakatsuki, to whom Strauss had also introduced them, the Bishop and Father Drought did not fare well in Tokyo. Nobody in authority seemed to be willing to assure the protection they were seeking. When the failure of their mission became evident, the American clerics booked passage on the *Nitta Maru* for their return to the United States. They were to sail in the morning of December 28. But then their fortunes took an amazing turn. While previously they had been shunned, now they were suddenly catapulted to the highest echelon of the government.

A week before their scheduled departure they received a summons to the Foreign Minister's residence. They were cordially received by Foreign Minister Matsuoka himself, who told the missionaries in great confidence that he was working toward a rapprochement with the United States. He said he was planning to send a secret communication to Washington with the terms of a possible agreement, and he asked the Bishop to deliver the message.

Bishop Walsh was pleased but mystified. He asked Matsuoka why the message could not be sent through the American embassy.

"The embassy's telegrams are intercepted and decoded by other countries," the Foreign Minister replied. "We cannot, therefore, safely avail ourselves of such a precarious channel of communication."

The visit to Matsuoka broke the ice. A whirlwind of conferences now followed with some of Konoye's top-ranking advisers and associates both in and out of the government. Matsuoka himself had been somewhat vague and remote. He proposed no specific details for the agreement. But the others, posing as spokesmen for Konoye, offered an explicit "proposal" whose terms could not have been more sweeping and attractive: they agreed to "nullify" Japan's participation in the Axis pact and "guaranteed" to recall all Japanese forces from China and "restore to China its geographic and political integrity."

Bishop Walsh still had some reservations. He and Father Drought were talking to diplomats and politicians. Would the military go along with the proposal?

To demonstrate that Japan was united, as Wikawa put it, behind the "wish to bring about a reconciliation with the United States," meetings were arranged with the two top men in the army's and navy's political departments. Wikawa took Father Drought to Admiral Takasumi Oka, chief of the Navy Ministry's Military Affairs Bureau. And Bishop Walsh was introduced to General Muto himself, in his office at the War Ministry, over which Hideki Tojo already presided.

Both Oka and Muto assured the Americans that they and their associates were "wholeheartedly in accord" with the efforts to reach an "understanding" with America, and that they personally would do all in their power to assist them. "From this interview," Bishop Walsh later said, "Father Drought and I received the impression that General Muto was pledging himself—and as far as it lay in his power, the army he represented—to concurrence in the proposed undertaking."

More sophisticated men would probably have wondered about this strange turn. Why was the fiercely pro-Axis Matsuoka involved in an effort aimed at rapprochement with the United States he loathed? And what role was General Muto playing in this game? Why were two humble clergymen chosen for a venture of such intricacy and delicacy? Though venturesome, alert and effective as the guardian of Catholic missions precariously located in areas controlled by the Japanese militarists, Bishop Walsh was naïve in the ways of diplomacy and its especially devious Japanese course. Father Drought was a starry-eyed zealot. He now regarded himself as the reincarnation of St. Francis Xavier, undertaking the martyred Jesuit's mission in reverse.

Gratified and exhilarated by the unexpected results of their mission to Japan, Bishop Walsh and Father Drought sailed home on December 28, 1940. Upon their arrival in San Francisco they telephoned Mr. Strauss (who was serving with the Navy in Washington), acquainted him with the astounding proposal the Japanese had entrusted to their care, and asked him what to do next. "I suggested," Admiral Strauss recalled, "that before coming to Washington they might call to see [Herbert C.] Hoover and get his advice."

Mr. Hoover was then living in Palo Alto, only a short distance from San Francisco. The clerics called on the former President, who seemed to share their excitement and advised them to take the Japanese proposal directly to Mr. Roosevelt. But since Hoover himself was not on speaking terms with his successor in the White House, he suggested that they approach the President through a member of his Cabinet—perhaps Postmaster General Frank C. Walker. Although no expert in foreign affairs, Walker seemed the right man. He was very close to F.D.R. and was a Roman Catholic.

The two clergymen went on to Washington and arranged a meeting with the Postmaster General. Mr. Walker was "likewise impressed," called the President right away, and arranged an interview for the "volunteer peacemakers" to place the Japanese proposal before Mr. Roosevelt.

What the State Department came to call the "John Doe" operation was off to a promising start, far beyond, as it developed, the expectations of its Japanese authors.

The "John Doe" in the operation was Mr. Walker. Nothing in his past indicated that he might ever become the hero in an international mystery thriller. A Pennsylvanian by birth, he had gone west as a young man, obtained a law degree at Gonzaga University in Spokane, Washington, then settled in Montana. He served three years as district attorney of Silver Bow County, then moved into politics via the Montana Legislature.

He operated with mounting success in the real estate business, in newspaper publishing and as a motion picture exhibitor. But it was the New Deal that brought out the best in him. He went to Washington with F.D.R. in 1933, and served as presidential trouble-shooter in various executive agencies until 1940, when he was appointed to the Cabinet as Postmaster General.

On January 23, 1941, Mr. Walker took Bishop Walsh to President Roosevelt. The meeting in the oval study lasted for nearly three hours. The Bishop outlined the "proposal" he had brought from Tokyo and left a memorandum with Mr. Roosevelt recapitulating its salient points.

"The Japanese government cannot admit, through official channels," it read, "that American economic pressure and defense preparations under President Roosevelt have been so politically successful that the Japanese now would welcome an opportunity to change their international, and modify their China, positions.

"The domestic position of the present Japanese government is like that of the Brüning government in Germany in 1931. The Japanese would rather lose the war in China than lose the domestic war to their own Extremists. But, the loss of the China War and the imminence of an American War, would put the radical nationalists, civil and military, in complete control. If the Conservative authorities . . . can win, by diplomacy, a safe economic and international position, public opinion in Japan would restore the Conservatives to complete control.

"For such a reversal, the Japanese majority needs, no less than China, the help of the United States . . . They feel that if some constructive co-operation is not realized with the United States before March or April, the Fascist element will take control in both China and Japan, no matter whether England or Germany wins in the spring offensive."

Bishop Walsh urged the President to treat the matter with absolute secrecy. "If our efforts became known in Japan," he said, "the Konoye government would be toppled and war would immediately break out in the southwestern Pacific." He then suggested that Mr. Roosevelt name "a personal representative" to conduct the negotiations with the secret envoys Tokyo would send to the United States.

"The representative of the President," Bishop Walsh wrote, "should be someone whom he knows and trusts implicitly; someone who will be apprised fully of American aims in the Far East;

someone who is keenly aware that the Germans will attempt ruthlessly to prevent any American-Japanese agreement; and someone who will not attract attention as an official member of our State Department."

The President enjoyed this kind of personal diplomacy with melodramatic overtones. But Secretary Hull, who was present at the meeting, did not share Mr. Roosevelt's enthusiasm. And he was affronted by the Bishop's suggestion that the State Department be excluded from the affair. He did not like any of this amateur intrusion on the domain of the State Department, especially when a new Japanese ambassador would be coming to Washington, apparently to undertake an identical mission but through the proper channels. "I doubt the practicability of proceeding on any such line at this time," he wrote to the President. "We should not, I think, resort to other agents and channels before we have even talked with the Ambassador and while we can work through Mr. Grew in Tokyo."

However, Mr. Roosevelt liked the Walsh plan. Doing exactly as the Bishop had suggested, and overruling his Secretary of State, he delegated Postmaster General Walker to serve as his "presidential agent," as he called it, with a direct channel to him in the White House. Walker met two of Walsh's conditions—he was extremely close to the President and was not connected with the State Department. As far as his special qualifications as a key figure in a major maneuver of secret diplomacy were concerned, the question did not enter into any of the President's considerations at this time.

Walker was given his cover name and a budget from the President's unvouchered funds. Assistant Postmaster General Jesse Donaldson was instructed to take over running the Post Office Department while Mr. Walker was busy elsewhere, on "a special assignment personally for the President."

On February 6 Mr. Walker could thus advise Bishop Walsh (who had retired to the Maryknoll Society's headquarters at Ossining, New York, to await the President's decision) that "the operation was on" despite the State Department's objections. The Bishop immediately cabled his friends in Tokyo. The wheels began to turn. On February 8, only sixteen days after the first contact had been made in the White House, his associates in

Japan advised Walsh that "a plenipotentiary representative of the Japanese government" was being sent to the United States, "empowered to negotiate concrete terms for a settlement of all outstanding questions *vis-à-vis* the United States."

On February 14, after brief stopovers in Honolulu and San Francisco, Ambassador Nomura arrived in Washington. At the same time, the Japanese government's "plenipotentiary representative" was sailing on the *Tatsuta Maru* toward his secret mission. He was Tadao Wikawa.

Donald W. Smith, the assistant commercial attaché at the American embassy in Tokyo, happened to be going to the United States on the same ship. On the eve of his departure Ambassador Grew (who knew about Wikawa's trip to America but had not been apprised of the nature of his mission) asked Smith to cultivate Wikawa on the trip and size him up. "The visit of such an outstanding figure in Japanese politics," the ambassador told Smith, "could not fail to be of significance."

Aboard ship, Wikawa told Smith that he was, indeed, "the unofficial representative of a group of influential persons in Japan who desired to improve Japanese-American relations." Wikawa seemed to be hopeful that his efforts would lead to "a settlement of all differences." He had an extremely influential connection in Washington, he told Smith, adding cryptically: "The present administration [also] has its Colonel House." *

With the arrival of Ambassador Nomura in Washington and Mr. Wikawa in New York,** the management of American relations with Japan took a new turn. It moved under ground—from open confrontation to secret bartering by a mere handful of men. In the drift of events for which, as Mr. Roosevelt put it, "no hard and fast plans could be laid down," Washington and Tokyo agreed to make a try at negotiations "without any formal agenda."

---

* "Colonel" Edward House was a confidant of President Wilson during World War I, and helped to draft the Treaty of Versailles.
** It was decided on security grounds (and also to keep it as far as possible from the State Department) to establish the "John Doe" mission in New York rather than Washington. Mr. Wikawa moved into the elegant Hotel Berkshire, and camouflaged his true purposes in the United States by pretending that he was representing certain Japanese banks in a pending financial transaction with Wall Street.

President Roosevelt was fascinated by the secrecy of these talks. Yet, except for the "John Doe" operation, he preferred to remain in the background, for two major reasons.

First, he was so disturbed by the plight of Britain in the European war and so anxious to stop Hitler that he could not develop the interest and attention the deepening Japanese crisis fully warranted. In a letter to Ambassador Grew on January 21, 1941, he had conceded that he was weighing the problem of Japanese aggression in the light of its possible effects on "the chances of England's winning her struggle with Germany." * He was hoping that a head-on clash in the Pacific could be delayed until the United States had developed the physical strength of effective deterrence, and Japan could be contained with diplomatic and economic pressures.

Second, the technicalities of the Japanese-American negotiations either bored or exasperated him. He knew that Secretary Hull was jealously guarding his prerogatives in the State Department, resisting and resenting repeated Japanese attempts at by-passing him. The President was reluctant to antagonize Mr. Hull, who was conducting the negotiations in so personal a manner that he was holding most of his talks with Ambassador Nomura in his hotel suite rather than in his office in the Old State Building.

The diary of Prince Konoye has an interesting passage about the President's role in the negotiations, documenting Japanese disappointment that he was not more personally active in them. In a rueful description of one of the meetings the Japanese ambassador had in the White House, in which the possibility of a summit conference of Roosevelt and Konoye was reviewed, the Prime Minister wrote: "The President was in high spirits throughout this Nomura-Roosevelt conference," and even discussed various locations where such a meeting could be held. The Japanese government interpreted this as Roosevelt's acceptance of the proposal. However, Konoye added, "compared with the President's enthusiasm, Secretary Hull, who was present at the time, took an extremely cautious attitude."

---

* The President told Mr. Grew rather bluntly that "our strategy" was guided by our determination to give the British all the assistance they needed to win, doing nothing in the meantime that would deny them this help which, as he put it, was essential for "ensuring our own security."

A few days later Mr. Roosevelt summoned Ambassador Nomura back to the White House, but only to hand him a note rejecting the idea of the meeting. "In the light of the President's message," Konoye wrote wryly, "it became clear that the State Department's opinion had become the dominant opinion."

Mr. Hull thus emerged as the central figure in the negotiations, endowed with full discretionary powers. He determined not only the policies, but also the manner and tone of the talks, and molded the President's attitudes, even his sentiments, on this crucial topic. In other words, Mr. Hull was *the* arbiter of the United States. Whether the negotiations would succeed or fail was now dependent chiefly on his diplomatic acumen and negotiating skill, on his familiarity with the facts and issues, and on his personal attributes.

Judge Hull of Tennessee was somewhat miscast in this bravura role in the diplomatic drama. A strikingly handsome old man of great outward dignity, he looked like the classical diplomatist, but he did not know the intangible factors that lurked beneath the veneer of Japanese diplomacy—the Japanese character and the Japanese mind—and he made only a perfunctory effort to familiarize himself with them when those imponderables emerged as important factors in the negotiations. He was not cut out to treat his negotiating partners with any ethnic compassion. He was amused and irritated in turn by their constant bowing and hissing, and irked by their mysterious, frozen smiles. He was impatient with Ambassador Nomura's adequate but fumbling English, marred as it was by a horrid pronunciation that made it hard to listen to and difficult to understand.

The entire affair was a highly personal matter with Mr. Hull. And always he had to consider "Magic." Since his conversations with the Japanese were frequently based on material he had obtained from the intercepts, he had to be on his guard at all times. This placed a restriction upon this straightforward statesman that, as one of his closest associates said, "cramped his usually free-wheeling and candid style."

Another complicating factor was a human equation closer to home—the unevenly matched personalities of his advisers at the talks. Because of "Magic," the secrecy of the talks and his decision to make them as informal and personal as possible, he chose only

three officials of the State Department to aid him with the negotiations. They were Dr. Stanley K. Hornbeck, the adviser on
political relations; Maxwell M. Hamilton, chief of the Division of
Far Eastern Affairs; and Joseph W. Ballantine, the Department's
foremost "Japanologist."

Mr. Hamilton was an experienced and very competent career
diplomat but somewhat parochial in his outlook. He was not
exactly timid but neither was he bold. His knowledge of the issues
was broad, but his vision was limited. Plodding and punctilious,
he geared his mind to function in the stereotyped grooves of the
diplomatic bureaucracy.

Joe Ballantine was a serious, quiet, scholarly man whose vibrant
yet disciplined mind held a vast store of knowledge of Japan. But
he shied away from asserting himself. His innate modesty and
formal respect for higher authority made him self-effacing, even
humble, and forever reluctant to impose his ideas and conclusions
on his superiors.

Mr. Hull's chief adviser, Dr. Hornbeck (who was not a career
officer), was a different breed of man. Having been brought up in
China, and with his sympathies clearly defined, he brought to the
negotiations a subtle and subconscious antagonism to the Japanese. An extremely ethical man, he was inclined to place far too
much emphasis on the moral issues, quite oblivious to the fact
that morality was a relative matter representing one set of values
to an American and a different set to a Japanese.

Intellectually he towered over all the other members of the
group, including Mr. Hull. And since he was keenly conscious of
this fact, he possessed some of the arrogance, intolerance and
impatience that usually go with intellectual superiority. As a result
he was inclined to regard deprecatingly and with condescension
both his American associates and Japanese opposite numbers. It
was mostly upon his ideas and opinions, presented in innumerable
breezy, lucid and persuasive memoranda, which he turned out
with superb facility, that Mr. Hull built the American case.

It would be unfair to call Mr. Hull's group a "clique," for its
members were sincere men of lofty principles whose patriotism
and integrity were beyond the shadow of a doubt. It was a tightly
knit band dominated by a highly sophisticated, strong-willed, opin-
ionated and pedantic man, and led by a statesman whose intellec-

tual resources and ingrained personality traits were not ideally
suited to meet this historic challenge.*

The negotiations that had started out informally through two
different channels now became formal and official in both their
prongs. At Mr. Hull's insistence, Ambassador Nomura was drawn
into the Walker-Wikawa talks but only on a personal basis, without involving his embassy in the negotiations. The State Department, somewhat mollified by this partial shift into more conventional diplomatic channels, handled the talks with Nomura.
Walker continued in New York as the "John Doe" of the Wikawa
group.

Mr. Walker was enjoying himself in his new role as "presidential agent." He operated with all the familiar trimmings of secret
diplomacy, holding his meetings in out-of-the-way places where he
expected to remain unrecognized and sending all his communications to Washington in a special code he had devised. He had
set up headquarters on the eighteenth floor of the Hotel Berkshire
at 52nd Street on New York's East Side, where Wikawa was
staying, and advised Washington somewhat melodramatically that
he "could be reached only by phone number—Plaza 3–5800, extension 1812—and not by name."

As to Mr. Wikawa, he turned out to be a most pleasant partner
in these transactions and a man who seemed eminently qualified
for the delicate assignment. Though he impressed Mr. Hull as a
"slick politician type," he was not in politics at all, but was an
economist occupying a high position in the government-controlled
Co-operative Bank of Japan. A Christian married to an American
lady, he spoke English fluently, and seemed to be stanchly pro-
American. He had many influential friends in Wall Street, and

---

* This is not meant to say that Mr. Hull and his three principal aides
sought the solution to the crisis in war. Quite the opposite. Harry L. Hopkins
was undoubtedly right when, three weeks after Pearl Harbor, he commented
on the Roberts Commission report, which implied that from July 1941 on, the
State Department had abandoned all hope of an agreement with Japan: "Hull
wanted peace above everything, because he had set his heart on making an
adjustment with the Japanese and had worked on it night and day for weeks.
There was no question that up until the last ten days prior to the outbreak of
war he was in hopes that some adjustment could be worked out." The
objection is to some of the methods pursued by the Hull group, not to their
purposes, philosophy or judgment.

obviously enjoyed Prime Minister Konoye's complete confidence.

Thanks to Wikawa's prompt and congenial acquiescence in all the points raised, preliminary talks were completed quickly on the basis of the "draft proposal" Bishop Walsh had brought from Tokyo and Wikawa had with him. The time had come to compose the actual agreement that would, as Bishop Walsh had assured the President, clear up all misunderstandings between Japan and the United States.

It was an exciting moment for Mr. Walker, made auspicious by word from Prince Konoye that a distinguished military representative was being sent by the War Ministry to participate in the drafting of the "understanding," as the pact with the United States was to be called. The officer chosen for the mission was of exceptional stature, brilliance and influence. He was Colonel Hideo Iwakuro, a member of the General Staff, serving in the War Ministry as chief of the Military Administration Section. He was General Muto's principal assistant and personal confidant.

Mr. Walker was filled with great expectations, as reflected by his jubilant reports to Washington. "We have already begun the preparation of the draft agreement," he wired the President on March 10. On March 13 he wrote to him: "Judging from recent coded-cable communications from Tokyo, we are justified in having increasing confidence that agreement with Japan can be reached."

On the same day he advised Mr. Roosevelt: "This afternoon Wikawa also cabled Prince Konoye that every effort must be made to conclude a basic agreement on principles before the end of this month—since it is becoming increasingly difficult to maintain secrecy. Obviously," he added triumphantly, "the Premier is planning the American entente as a coup against the Axis groups in Japan—as well as Hitler."

Colonel Iwakuro (accompanied by Colonel Shinjo of Military Intelligence) joined Walker and Wikawa in New York on March 21. Mr. Hull, intrigued by the newcomer, sent Mr. Ballantine to New York to size him up in a meeting at the Berkshire. Mr. Ballantine's report was most flattering.

"Colonel Iwakuro appeared to be a person between 40 and 45 years of age," Ballantine wrote to Hull. "He has an attractive and vigorous personality. He did most of the talking. After a considerable amount of small talk, the Colonel abruptly remarked that he thought that a war between Japan and the United States would be a calamity, that it would be a prolonged affair lasting from three to five years, and that it would result in lowering of standards of living." Ballantine concluded his report: "The above conversation was carried on in Japanese and on an amicable plane. The Japanese did not bring up the subject of their mission."

At last the draft of the "understanding" was completed, and on April 5 it was submitted to the President. Postmaster General Walker confidently declared that "the 'Draft Document' is a proclamation of a revolution in Japanese 'ideology' and policy as well as a proof of the complete success of American statesmanship." *

It was so sweeping and so conciliatory that Mr. Walker urged the prompt and total acceptance of the draft and its immediate signing "as it was" or else, he wrote, "the Japanese leaders will possibly be assassinated." He told the President that "Mr. Wikawa and Colonel Iwakuro expect assassination in any event."

The "assassination" came on schedule, but not in Tokyo. It occurred in the form of a memorandum of Dr. Hornbeck. "Nothing that might be agreed upon between the American and the Japanese governments within the next few days or weeks," he wrote on April 11, "will substantially alter the world situation in its material aspects; a negotiation between Japan and the United States might have some effect as regards deliberation and discussion between and among the various Japanese factions, but it would not enable any group not now in control of Japan's affairs to oust those who are in control and gain control for itself; the decision of Japanese leaders whether to move or not to move southward will be made in the light of the physical situation in Europe as they view it and the physical situation in the Pacific as they view it."

---

* As written by Wikawa, Iwakuro and Walker, it consisted of a preamble; a section called "Rules for Nations," and another entitled "Aids to Peace." It dealt specifically with Japan's alliance with the Axis; mediation in the China-Japan conflict; naval forces; the merchant marine; export and import; gold credit; oil, rubber; the autonomous states in the southwestern Pacific area; the status of the Far Eastern states under what was proposed as a "joint Far Eastern Monroe Doctrine"; international conferences; and even such relative trivia as airline communications between Japan and the United States.

He concluded with a recommendation: "It is utterly desirable that, in our relations and our contacts with the Japanese at this time, we should avoid giving any indication of other than a firm attitude and firm intention on our part, we should do all that we can toward giving them an impression that we are both prepared and expecting to oppose by force any further moves southward if attempted by them."

Secretary Hull was valiantly plodding through cumbersome conversations with Ambassador Nomura during which both men tried as best they could merely to understand each other. Neither was willing to concede defeat, however. Mr. Hull pretended to understand the ambassador, when in fact he did not have a clear idea what the pathetic Nomura was trying to convey in his mournful singsong. And the ambassador politely gave the impression of comprehension by a smile or a nod of his head, when actually he was unable to follow Mr. Hull's drawl, aggravated by ill-fitting dentures.

The Secretary found in the "magics" Nomura's accounts of their conversations cabled to Tokyo, and most of the time was scandalized because the ambassador's reports bore little resemblance to what Mr. Hull thought he had actually said. It was quite hard on him not to be able to correct Nomura whenever they met next, but of course he could not do so lest he give away his source. Similarly, Nomura was often upset by the Secretary's failure to act upon matters which the ambassador thought had been clarified and agreed upon.

The "John Doe" operation was also continuing. Mr. Wikawa and Colonel Iwakuro remained in the United States, drafting and redrafting the "understanding" in the face of growing misunderstandings. By now the "operation" had been reduced to an almost personal bout between Postmaster General Walker, who was fighting in high spirits for the adoption of the agreement, and Dr. Hornbeck, who was doing his utmost to thwart it.

Walker, who was completely captivated by Wikawa's charm and Colonel Iwakuro's courtesy, was judging all Japanese by these men. He believed implicitly that their countries could get along as well as he did with the two emissaries. On the other hand, Dr. Hornbeck suffered from none of Mr. Walker's illusions. He was, as

Herbert Feis phrased it, "still dissecting every document which came from Tokyo with the scalpel of mistrust." There was ample intelligence at the State Department to shape his attitude and justify his uncompromising stand. "Magic" was producing more and more intercepts that convinced him of Japan's continuously aggressive designs while her envoys were talking of peace.

Dr. Hornbeck preferred to view the "John Doe" operation in the light of what the intercepts revealed. And he had come to regard the Postmaster General for what he probably was—merely a dupe. Hornbeck looked beyond him, at the fanatical Maryknoll missionary in the dim background of this peculiar "peace plan." "Father Drought," he wrote to Secretary Hull on June 10, "has taken upon himself and is playing the role of a promoter and salesman. My conjecture is that he first 'sold' the idea of a negotiation and if possible an agreement to certain Japanese and that he has been since and is doing his utmost to 'sell' the idea to you (and through you to the President): Drought is the pushing and the pulling agent in the matter."

It was hopeless and useless, Dr. Hornbeck was in effect telling Mr. Hull. "The proposed agreement is in my opinion," he wrote, "something which neither the Japanese nation nor the people of the United States want and which, if consummated, will be distasteful to both."

On July 12, when Mr. Walker and Father Drought showed up at the State Department for yet another "conversation," they were informed that "the general situation has now progressed to such a point that we feel that in the best interests of all concerned our conversations and any presentation of documents should be directly between the Japanese ambassador or his associates and the Secretary of State or his associates."

However tortuous the English of the statement was, it could not be misunderstood. As far as the Department was concerned, Father Drought was out in the cold and Mr. Walker had reverted to being the Postmaster General again. But Mr. Walker still did not think that his mission was completed. Under the spell of Father Drought, whose contagious enthusiasm and persuasive powers he found impossible to resist, the Postmaster General had opted for what basically was the Japanese side. He had set himself up in opposition, not only to the "State Department clique," but also to the official policies of his own government. Without actually realizing it, and motivated solely by his passionate desire to bring about a reconciliation with Japan to avert war, he had become a pawn in the game, an unwitting tool of the Japanese. He firmly believed that it was his duty as a patriot to persevere in his efforts, even though the State Department had disavowed him and all that he stood for.

But it was not only Father Drought who needed Mr. Walker in the "John Doe" operation—Colonel Iwakuro had become even more eager to retain his association with the Postmaster General. For all practical purposes the colonel's original mission had long since been accomplished. Yet, even as the State Department was wondering why he was staying on, he moved to Washington in May and established residence at the Wardman Park Hotel (where Secretary Knox was also living). He had been appointed assistant military attaché at the Japanese embassy, probably to gain diplomatic immunity.

Colonel Iwakuro no longer functioned as a mere parliamentarian of peace. He remained in the United States because he now had a new "project" whose potentialities seemed enormous and which he felt duty-bound to exploit. In the person of Mr. Walker, as he saw it, Japan had acquired an agent inside President Roosevelt's Cabinet.

Who was this suave and brilliant Japanese colonel whom General Muto had sent to the United States on a "peace" mission? Had Mr. Walker known the background of Iwakuro, he probably would have developed at least some doubts about his true purposes and shown greater reserve in his relations with him. But apparently neither the Postmaster General nor, for that matter, the State Department had thought it necessary to explore the past of this officer.

He had first come to the attention of the American authorities on February 27, when he visited Ambassador Grew in Tokyo to acquaint him with his impending mission to the United States, as "representative of the War Ministry, General Tojo himself." The colonel's ingratiating courtesy and straightforward talk captivated the ambassador. Iwakuro was disarmingly candid. Conceding that the problems dividing Japan and the United States could not be resolved permanently "at this time," he hoped, as he put it, to "contribute toward maintaining an equilibrium until prospects appeared of a basic solution being found."

In a brief telegram the ambassador alerted the State Department to the colonel's arrival, adding merely that Iwakuro was "one of the most important leaders of the young officers' group and [enjoyed] the complete confidence of the Minister of War." Perfunctory efforts were then made to probe the colonel's past, but no information could be obtained beyond some scanty biographical data, such as the fact that he was born in Hiroshima in 1897, and that he was a section chief in the War Ministry's Military Affairs Bureau.

There was ample reason in Tokyo to obscure Iwakuro's past. He was, in fact, one of the younger leaders of the military clique with a dubious record in Manchuria and China. In the summer of 1932, when the Japanese army began to suffer from the postoperational pangs of conquest, Iwakuro wrote a paper entitled "The Guiding Principle of Manchukuo," in which he proposed a drastic solution of the problems confronting the Kwantung Army. He recommended "the radical eradication of the bandits" who were preventing the Japanese from consolidating their conquest.

In August, Iwakuro was sent to Manchuria to practice what he had preached. It was also a kind of peace mission. He was expected to "pacify" the country by any means, fair or foul. In the Totaku Building, at Mukden headquarters of the Kwantung Army, Iwakuro met General Muto and became his closest associate. Iwakuro henceforth supplied Muto with some of the ideas and "projects" which resulted, after the war, in Muto's hanging as a war criminal, for "a campaign of massacre, torture and other atrocities . . . waged by the Japanese troops on the civilian population."

When in 1933 Japan decided to extend the war to China, Iwakuro helped Muto in plotting the advance beyond the Great Wall. In 1937, still at Muto's side, he participated in the rape of Nanking. When Muto took over the Military Affairs Bureau in Tokyo, he gave his protégé one of the key policy-making jobs in the War Ministry, by appointing him head of the War Affairs Section.

This was the dove of peace Tojo and Muto had sent to the

United States to aid Ambassador Nomura and Mr. Wikawa in their negotiations. It is unlikely that the colonel had changed overnight. His past rather suggests that his assignment in Washington was more to assay Japan's chances in a war with the United States than to work earnestly for a reconciliation.

The truth of the matter was that Colonel Iwakuro had been sent to this country on an intricate intelligence mission. He was chosen for it when it became known at the Military Affairs Bureau that President Roosevelt had accepted Bishop Walsh's proposal and commissioned a member of his Cabinet to work with the Japanese delegation. It was assumed that the "Cabinet member" could be used in two ways: first, to serve as a conduit for the Japanese peace feelers into the Cabinet room at the White House; and second, as a source of information on matters discussed in Cabinet sessions and in the privacy of the President's office. It was, undoubtedly, a brilliant scheme.

The full extent of Walker's indiscretion is not known. But one of the major coups Iwakuro scored was traceable directly to the Postmaster General. It proved of decisive importance, and had an eventual bearing on the Pearl Harbor attack.

Alarmed by the Japanese occupation of Indochina in July as a threat to his efforts, Mr. Walker discussed what he had evidently heard the President and his own colleagues say in Cabinet sessions and what, indeed, was the cornerstone of the American military policy. He warned Iwakuro that the American fleet in the Pacific, which would be built up to enormous strength in a war with Japan, would always be capable of checking the southward move, if only by cutting the life line between Japan's home islands and her forces at their overseas outposts.

Shortly after this conversation Colonel Iwakuro returned to Tokyo. He arrived in time to participate in the preparations for war which the imperial conference had authorized the army and navy to pursue in high gear.

15   Moment of Crisis

In the early spring of 1941, the tortuous prelude to Pearl Harbor passed through a totally unexpected crisis, and the entire "Magic" operation was put in jeopardy.

It began innocuously enough, even somewhat amusingly. On April 1 the Signal Intelligence Service had set up a top secret monitoring station, called MS-5, at Fort Shafter on Oahu, to improve "Magic's" spasmodic coverage of the Tokyo–Berlin circuit. One of the first dispatches intercepted by MS-5 was a triple-priority telegram from Berlin to Tokyo that raised both smiles and eyebrows in Op-20-G and SIS.

In the dispatch dated April 14,* the Japanese ambassador in Berlin, Hiroshi Oshima, expressed concern over the security of his embassy's code communications on which, it seemed, his German friends were trespassing. The Germans were as good as anybody at code-cracking. They had an elaborate cryptanalytical establishment that was intercepting and decoding much of the international dispatch traffic in the air.

The decrypted and translated intercepts were typed up on light-brown paper by the agencies which processed them, and circulated to a select group of high officials in the government and the *Wehrmacht*. One of the individuals on the *"Braun"* distribution list was Ernst Baron von Weizsäcker, the Undersecretary of the Foreign Office, an old-fashioned diplomat whose residue of moral

---

* All time references in this chapter are E.S.T. unless otherwise stated.

qualms were rather anachronistic considering his position in the Nazi regime.

He had no objection to tampering with the traffic of Germany's enemies. But he was so outraged when he found that the messages of her friends—including those of the Japanese—also came under this scrutiny that he decided to pass a warning hint to Ambassador Oshima. As Weizsäcker put it, he had reason to believe that the Japanese ciphers used in Egypt had been compromised by what he called "a foreign power."

In his telegram to Tokyo, Oshima suggested that stringent security measures be observed in the use of the Foreign Ministry's codes and ciphers, and that all "intelligence telegrams" emanating from Japanese missions in the Near East be paraphrased before they were sent on to him for his information. This was imperative, he wrote, "in order to avoid giving [the Germans] clues to solving our codes."

On April 16 MS-5 intercepted Tokyo's reaction to Oshima's warning. In a circular to Japanese missions in Europe and the Near East, Katsuji Kameyama, chief of the Cable Section, instructed the code-room personnel henceforth to encrypt all messages by machine or, where none was available, by TSU. "I want you," he added, "to use OITE only for messages of the lowest security rating."

Amused though they were by this evidence of a cryptological bout between the Germans and the Japanese, the Americans who read these intercepts followed developments with some apprehension. Any tightening of security in Japan's crypto-communications would be to American disadvantage as well. On the other hand, they were rather relieved by Kameyama's response to Oshima's warning. It was obvious from it that the security of the machines and of TSU was not questioned in the *denshin-ka*.

As a matter of fact, twice before during the year, brief flurries of excitement had been stirred up in Op-20-G and SIS by signs that Japan was becoming more than normally suspicious of some breach in her crypto-security. On January 24 the Foreign Ministry had raised "a very serious question of security" with Consul General Akiyama in Panama City, and reprimanded him for the "careless handling" of his codes that apparently had "resulted in leaks." On February 7 Consul General K. Ohmori in Chicago was suddenly and mysteriously ordered to "discontinue all secret communications" from his office, secure his codes and transfer them forthwith to the custody of the embassy in Washington.

No reasons were apparent for this measure. The excitement it stirred up in Washington soon waned, as did, indeed, the apprehension created by Oshima's warning.

Then a major crisis developed whose ramifications and consequences were impossible to foresee.

At two-twenty in the morning on April 29, monitors in England guarding the Washington–Berlin circuit intercepted a top-secret telegram from Dr. Hans Thomsen, the German chargé d'affaires in the United States, to Foreign Minister von Ribbentrop.

"As communicated to me by an absolutely reliable source," the telegram read, "the State Department is in possession of the key to the Japanese coding system and is, therefore, also able to decipher information telegrams from Tokyo to Ambassador Nomura here regarding Ambassador Oshima's reports from Berlin."

The ominous intercept was flashed from London to Washington that same morning. Safford and his colleagues at SIS were gripped by sudden panic. Their only hope was that the curtain of distrust between the Germans and the Japanese would keep Thomsen's information from Tokyo.

Weak to begin with, this hope was totally shattered in a few days. On May 3 the Navy's Station M at Cheltenham, Maryland, intercepted a PURPLE-CA telegram from Oshima in Berlin to Tokyo. It was marked by all sorts of panicky security specifications: "Chief of Missions Dispatch!" "Most Closely Guarded Secret!" "Foreign Office Secret!" "To Be Read By Foreign Minister Only!"

In the telegram Oshima told Foreign Minister Matsuoka that on the evening of May 2 he had received a visit from Dr. Heinrich Stahmer, ambassador-at-large in the Foreign Office in charge of Japanese-German affairs. "Stahmer told me," the ambassador wrote, "that Germany maintains a fairly efficient intelligence organization [in the United States] and, according to information obtained from the above-mentioned organization, it is fairly reliably established that the U.S. government is reading Ambassador Nomura's coded messages."

Oshima added the weight of his own experience to Stahmer's warning. "There are," he wrote, "at least two circumstances to substantiate the suspicion. One is that Germany is also reading our coded messages. And the other is that the Americans once before succeeded in compromising our codes, in 1922, during the Washington Conference."

The crisis sharpened on May 5 when Op-20-G translated a PURPLE message from Matsuoka to Nomura in Washington warning the ambassador that "it appears almost certain that the U.S. government is reading your code messages."

Matsuoka's answer to Oshima in Berlin was intercepted and translated the same day. The Foreign Minister asked the ambassador to find out the source of the information from Stahmer. But the Germans refused to divulge it.

Then Nomura's answer to Matsuoka was intercepted. It reflected the bafflement and consternation of the ambassador. The whole incident was a highly embarrassing personal matter for him. He remembered the Washington Conference only too well. Its aftermath was still rankling him, almost two decades later. As Director of Naval Intelligence and member of the Japanese delegation, he had been responsible for the security of Admiral Kato's communications.

He told Matsuoka in a "most guarded secret" telegram: "On our part, we are taking the most stringent precautions to protect our codes and ciphers, as well as our other classified documents. On this particular matter, I am at a loss for words. Pending an investigation at this end, please telegraph at once any concrete suspicions and details that may turn up."

Every American monitoring station, from Winter Harbor in Maine to the Philippine Islands, was alerted to watch for telegrams bearing on the crisis. Station S on Bainbridge Island in Puget Sound was ordered to teletype all pertinent intercepts as soon as they recorded them.

Safford, who sometimes became agitated even in routine snafus, could now barely control his nervousness. He dashed off to Cheltenham to kill time, and breathed down the neck of Chief Radioman Wingle as he was straining to pick up messages on any of the

Tokyo circuits that might have even the most tenuous connection with the emergency.

In Washington, top priority was assigned to the processing of such intercepts. There were no delays, no snafus. Never before did Op-20-G and SIS work with such dispatch and precision.

Japanese telegrams continued to indicate a crescendo of excitement. An urgent dispatch from Nomura asked for additional information, to aid him in his "investigations at the embassy."

In a top-priority circular Tokyo instructed all custodians of the machines to apply "the 1941 regulations until further notice." Known as the "Yu-Go" special directive, it enumerated the most stringent crypto-security measures to be applied in emergencies. News of this directive was received with grave misgivings in Op-20-G and SIS. With every passing hour "Magic" seemed more threatened.

But if there was tension in Washington, there was near-panic in Tokyo. Matsuoka held hasty conferences with Kameyama, Captain Inouye, chief of the Code Research Group, Chief Cryptographer Naoshi Ozeki, and Taro Terasaki, director of the Bureau of American Affairs. Kameyama assured him that it would be "humanly impossible" to compromise the machine ciphers by any conventional code-breaking methods. If the Americans really had the solutions, it could only mean that someone inside the embassy in Washington had betrayed them.

On May 7 the Foreign Ministry decided to act upon this suspicion. A telegram from Vice-Minister Chuichi Ohashi to Minister Kaname Wakasugi in Washington (a career man who was, therefore, trusted more in matters like these than Admiral Nomura) ordered the immediate quarantining of the Code Room.

Wakasugi was to transfer all code material and paraphernalia, including the embassy's A and B units, to the custody of Counselor Sadao Iguchi. Henceforth, Ohashi telegraphed, all coding would have to be done by Iguchi and the diplomatic staff. "No matter how long the communications may be," he wrote, "or how urgently the codes need to be used, there must be no occasion under any circumstances to call upon the services of your telegraphic clerks."

Ohashi's order created chaos at the embassy. Iguchi and his career colleagues did not know how to operate the machines or even how to handle the ordinary ciphers. Overnight, things became so confused that Ambassador Nomura had to ask Kameyama for a temporary relaxation of the emergency restrictions or else, he said, the embassy's crypto-communications would cease altogether.

He described to Kameyama how it had taken six hours for six members of Iguchi's staff to encrypt a simple message. He suggested, therefore, that three of "the implicitly trusted telegraph officials of the Code Room"—Horiuchi, Hori and Kajiwara—be allowed, for the time being, "to perform communication duties under strict supervision." And he recommended that a certain Kawabata, a code clerk at the Chicago consulate (where he was no longer needed) be transferred to Washington on temporary duty. At first the request was turned down, and Iguchi and his career aides were left to struggle with the codes.

By now the American authorities had "the leak" under frantic investigation. What Safford described as a "reign of terror" held both Op-20-G and SIS in its grip.

The FBI was called in on the case. Everybody even remotely connected with "Magic" was thoroughly questioned, and the files were combed to see whether any copies were missing. Even Colonel Bratton and Commander Kramer were shadowed by special agents from the FBI, ONI and the Army's Criminal Investigation Division. They were not suspected of any wrongdoing, but it was assumed that the leak had occurred somewhere along their routes —either in the White House or in the State Department.

Under the distribution agreement of January 23, the Army was to make deliveries to the State Department at all times and to the White House in January, March, May, July, September and November; the Navy was to have the responsibility during the other six months. Since these "outsiders" were still not trusted, only occasional distribution was made to them and none of the actual intercepts was delivered to the White House. They were shown to the President's naval aide in his office at the Navy Department; he memorized the more "interesting" ones, then reported them orally to Mr. Roosevelt. In addition, the aide was given "I.B. (Intelli-

gence Branch) Memos" and "GZ (Op-20-GZ) Summaries" prepared by Bratton and Kramer, with random excerpts from the
intercepts, for presentation to the President.

I.B. Memos were also left with Major General Edwin M.
("Pa") Watson, the President's genial military aide, to be shown
to Mr. Roosevelt and then returned to the files in G-2 or ONI. In
March, "Pa" Watson, who was notorious for keeping an untidy
office, had lost Memo No. 9, which Bratton had sent to the White
House. Then another Memo was lost, but Bratton recovered it
eventually—from Watson's unclassified wastepaper basket. These
were serious breaches of security, but the missing memo was not
considered likely to be the source of the leak.

It was different at the State Department, which had been
getting both the original intercepts and the Memos. Colonel
Bratton himself undertook an investigation and found that General Marshall's apprehension was justified. Mr. Hull had violated
the agreement by allowing at least seven of his associates access to
the intercepts. Moreover, he now discovered that State had copies
of several intercepts run off on a mimeograph machine by an
employee who had not been cleared even for restricted documents,
much less for the "magics." *

A recheck of the intercepts and Memos which Bratton had
taken to State (where they usually remained overnight and sometimes longer) now produced the first positive clue. One of the
mimeographed "circulation copies" of a Memo was missing. A
search led to its discovery in the files of Undersecretary of State
Sumner Welles.

This was the spring of 1941, when Germany and the Soviet
Union were still seemingly on the best of terms in the partnership
Hitler had forged with Stalin in August 1939. But the era of good
feeling was rapidly running out. The State Department had reliable information that Hitler was planning to attack the Soviet

---

* At one time or another, the "magics" were seen in the State Department
by Hull, Sumner Welles, Dr. Hornbeck, Hamilton and Ballantine on a
legitimate "need-to-know" basis, but also by Assistant Secretary of State
Adolf A. Berle, Jr., and James C. Dunn, Mr. Hull's adviser on European
affairs, who had no direct connection with the Japanese crisis. In addition,
several lower-ranking officials of the Far Eastern Division, including William R. Langdon, Max W. Schmidt, Joseph M. Jones and John P. Davies, Jr.,
had access to them.

Union and that preparations for the invasion, "Operation Barbarossa," had already been completed.

Mr. Welles was engaged in an ambitious project of his own—trying to wean the Russians from their German ally. In the process the Undersecretary used whatever data he could lay his hands on to persuade the Russians to change sides before it was too late. A survey of these efforts cleared up the mystery of how the Germans had succeeded in penetrating America's most closely guarded secrets.

Early in 1941 Welles had waged his campaign through secret conversations with Constantin Oumansky, the Soviet ambassador, most of the time in the Soviet embassy on 16th Street. At their meetings Welles fed intelligence material to Oumansky for transmission to Moscow, hoping to alert the Kremlin to the impending German treachery.

Then, in March and April, intelligence directly suited to his purpose came into Mr. Welles's hands. On March 19 SIS translated a telegram from the Japanese ambassador in Moscow to the Foreign Ministry in Tokyo describing an ominous change in Soviet-German relations. On March 22 SIS summarized in a special Memo all the intelligence it had collected from the "magics" on this topic and predicted in no uncertain terms "a German attack on the U.S.S.R. within two months." On April 3 and 4 two more pertinent intercepts were translated. They were telegrams of Ambassador Oshima outlining actual German "preparations for war with Russia." Later in April, Commander Kramer prepared a Memo (No. GZ-32) supporting SIS expectation of an "early intention of Germany to attack Russia."

This was exactly what Welles needed to dispel Oumansky's doubts. Imbued with the importance of his mission and disregarding all security risks, Welles decided to show his own circulation copies of the intercepts and the SIS Memo, with its many explicit references to "magics," to the Soviet ambassador.

Although similar intelligence was accumulating in the Kremlin from various sources, Stalin had stubbornly refused to accept the warnings as reliable. He preferred to regard them as part of the insidious propaganda campaign conducted by the British to break up the German-Soviet alliance. He not only threatened those who dared to talk to him about the possibility of a German attack, but went so far as to have several of his important intelligence experts arrested by the NKVD on charges of "spreading malicious information."

Oumansky knew what was good for him. He was strictly a Stalin man. He was taking the alliance with Germany seriously and was on friendly terms with Dr. Thomsen, with whom he frequently exchanged information. In the course of one of their conversations Oumansky told Thomsen that the Americans had some hard evidence of the German plans to attack the Soviet Union, and mentioned that the intelligence had been culled from Ambassador Oshima's telegrams to Tokyo.

German intelligence in Washington had a reliable agent in the Soviet embassy, one of Oumansky's aides. Thomsen now ordered this V-*Mann* (confidential informant) to find out all he could about the documentation Welles had produced for Oumansky. The agent reported back within twenty-four hours. He was certain that the Americans had succeeded in cracking the Japanese codes. The Germans did not go so far as to conclude that the United States had a direct coverage of Oshima's traffic. They assumed rather that the Americans had gained access to his dispatches from the copies of his reports which Tokyo was relaying regularly to Ambassador Nomura in Washington to keep him posted.

Dr. Thomsen immediately reported his findings to Berlin, where the authorities decided to relay the information to Oshima. The Germans had no solicitude for the security of Japanese crypto-communications, but they feared that information about their impending invasion of Russia was thus seeping to Moscow from the American intercepts of Oshima's telegrams. As a matter of fact, they acted promptly to tighten security in their relations with the Japanese ambassador. From April 30 on, Oshima could find out little if anything about "Barbarossa," no matter how he implored his German friends to take him into their confidence.

Among the American confidants of "Magic," the consternation turned into despair. This, they agreed, was the end of an era. "Magic" had collapsed as a result of Mr. Welles's well-meant but inexcusable indiscretion.

For several days Commander Safford and his colleagues at SIS watched in puzzled amazement as the Japanese continued to keep the B machine in operation in the face of apparently conclusive evidence that it had been compromised. Moreover, they used it even to encode telegrams dealing with the crucial issue of its own security.

The explanation was as simple as it was incredible.

In Tokyo and Washington the Japanese completed their investigations, and on May 19—only a fortnight after the first warning—Kameyama reported his findings to the Foreign Minister. Both investigations, he told Matsuoka, had produced nothing but gratifying results. It was known that the Americans had an active cryptanalytical establishment—what country did not have one? And it was taken for granted that several codes and ciphers of the Japanese crypto-system had been compromised—not only by the Americans but also by the British and Russians, the Germans and even the Italians. This had been anticipated by the *denshin-ka*, he said. No truly secret and important communications were ever encrypted in those low-grade codes.

However, Kameyama assured the Foreign Minister, the ciphers based on the A and B machines remained absolutely safe. As he put it: "Our ciphers were known to the American government during the Washington Conference. But this time they are all right." * Thus, as abruptly as it had broken, the crisis passed.

May 20 was a strange day in this emergency. There was one final but brief flurry of telegrams on the subject. Two dispatches crossed each other's path with diametrically opposite messages. Ambassador Nomura, thinking that he had new information, sent a frantic telegram to Tokyo, now confirming independently that the "United States is reading some of our codes." ** At the same

* Referring to the "Magic" operation, Togo Shigenori, Foreign Minister in General Tojo's first war Cabinet and again in 1945, placed the blame for this monumental blunder squarely on Kameyama's shoulders. "After the war," he wrote, "when I learned of the disclosure by the Congressional investigation [in the United States], I called upon Mr. Kameyama . . . to investigate. He told me that such deciphering could have been possible only by acquisition of the secret of the sending-and-receiving machines." At one point Kameyama toyed with the idea of committing suicide to atone for his blind faith in his cipher machines.

** This telegram was sent over Nomura's signature by First Secretary Hidenari Terasaki, younger brother of Taro Terasaki and chief of the Japanese secret intelligence service in the Western Hemisphere. However, the embassy's investigation confined itself to finding out whether any member of the Code Room staff was guilty of treason or indiscretion. When no evidence to this time Foreign Minister Matsuoka assured Nomura that the whole matter had been cleared up to his complete satisfaction. Several of the minor cipher systems had been compromised, he wrote to the ambassador, and cautioned him against using them for high-security communications. However, he added, the top-secret cipher based on the machines remained absolutely safe.

In another telegram, to Berlin, the Foreign Minister reprimanded Ambassador Oshima for even doubting the invincibility of the *denshin-ka*'s machine system.

What was behind Matsuoka's abiding faith in the security of the B machine? There are two possible explanations, and while neither is conclusive, either may be adequate to answer the question.

In the first place Kameyama, who was not a cryptologist, was entirely dependent on experts like Captain Inouye and Chief Cryptographer Ozeki in assessing the crisis and judging the security of the Foreign Ministry's crypto-systems. And they were emphatic in assuring him that it was absolutely impossible to crack the machine-based ciphers.

The second explanation has its own element of mystery, for it stems from the patently untenable nature of Kameyama's conclusions. He knew that none of his low-grade ciphers had been involved in this particular commotion. The Oshima telegrams mentioned in the document Sumner Welles had shown the Soviet ambassador were in the B code—proof positive that the Americans were somehow reading dispatches encrypted on the B machine.

Why, then, did Kameyama persist in his stand that the B unit continued to be safe? According to the skeptics who view the prehistory of Pearl Harbor and cryptology's part in it with a great deal of misgivings and suspicion, there was more behind Kameyama's attitude than met the eye. They are inclined to believe that the B machine had been retained because the Japanese decided to use it as a channel for misleading information.

Whatever the explanation, the final telegrams of the crisis were greeted jubilantly in Op-20-G and SIS. What threatened to end the "Magic" operation produced the unexpected reassurance that PURPLE was as safe as ever.

---

effect was produced, everything was allowed to return to normal, despite Terasaki's warning.

But while nothing was changed in Japan, the incident resulted in certain rearrangements in the United States which were not exactly conducive to enhancing the overall effectiveness of "Magic."

By every instrument of authority, the President of the United States sits at the apex of the American governmental pyramid. He is Chief Executive, Chief Magistrate, Commander-in-Chief, and chief of his ambassadors stationed abroad, who serve as his personal representatives. Under the Constitution, he may make treaties, reprieve doomed criminals, nominate the diplomatic corps, call men and women into the armed forces, name judges, commission officers, convene or adjourn Congress. Yet from May to November in 1941 the President was not allowed to see the "magics." This incredible situation was the direct result of Sumner Welles's indiscretion, the only lasting repercussion of the emergency.

The White House was "serviced," but grudgingly and perfunctorily, because the custodians of the "magics" viewed the "long-hair New Dealers" in the Executive Office with jaundiced eyes if not contempt. They did not consider them either properly "cleared" or innately prudent to rate access to "Magic's" momentous secret.

Even after they had agreed in January 1941 to open up "Magic" to the White House and the State Department, Bratton and Kramer tried to keep this channel as narrow as possible. Whenever they could they withheld material, especially from the White House, even in the few instances when the President demanded to be shown certain intercepts "in the raw."

In May another one of Bratton's Memos got lost somewhere in the White House, and Bratton again discovered it in "Pa" Watson's trash basket. That did it. In the heat of the emergency he persuaded General Miles to withdraw the Army from the January agreement. He justified the preposterous decision—which removed the White House from the Army's "Magic" distribution list—with the argument that "the subject of the traffic" involved mainly the State Department, and therefore it was really Mr. Hull's responsibility to brief the President about anything important contained in the intercepts. From the end of May not a single "magic" or I.B. Memo was forwarded to the White House by the Army.

Captain Alan Goodrich Kirk, who was Director of Naval Intelligence at this time, refused to join General Miles in this boycott of the White House. Kramer therefore continued to service the White House, but Kirk instructed him to take care to observe all of "Magic's" special security rules. Kramer heeded Kirk's admonition too literally.

In May Captain John R. Beardall was transferred from the U.S.S. *Vincennes* to serve as naval aide to the President. But since the overcrowded White House could not spare even a desk for him, he occupied an office on the second deck of the Navy Building, a five- to ten-minute walk from the White House. This suited Kramer. He could make an arrangement with Beardall whereby the President could be told about at least some of the "magics" without any of them actually leaving the premises of the Navy Department.

June was the first month after the crisis when the Navy was again responsible for deliveries to the White House. It was also a rather significant period in the "Magic" operation. Since March 19, when SIS had intercepted the message on the Moscow–Tokyo circuit about "a radical change" in Soviet-German relations, the "magics" furnished mounting documentation that war between the Germans and the Russians was imminent.

The evidence had become conclusive. On June 3 SIS translated a dispatch on the Rome–Tokyo circuit in which the Japanese ambassador to Italy informed the Foreign Ministry that "Germany had completed all preparations for attacking Soviet Russia." On June 14, 16 and 17 Kramer summarized the pertinent intercepts in three of his Memos. One presented all the direct intelligence culled from the "magics" that "Germany was planning to attack Russia"; the second documented "the crisis in German-Soviet relations"; and the third stated categorically that the "surprise attack [was] imminent." (It came exactly as Kramer had predicted, on June 22.)

But none of this material—not even the Summaries—went directly to the White House. Kramer chose the intercepts that he thought had information of interest to the President, and together with his GZ Summaries, took them down the corridor to Beardall's office. He let the captain read them while he waited, then took everything back to his own files. He did not permit Beardall to keep any of the material or even take notes. The captain was supposed to relate orally to the President whatever he could remember from the intercepts and Summaries.

It is impossible to say whether the course of history would have been different had the President been granted the privilege of seeing the "magics" personally and regularly—all the "magics" of importance and not only those which Kramer selected; if he had been allowed to keep them in his own files, to re-examine them when he felt it necessary in the light of the rapidly changing situation; if he could have obtained a wider perspective of the Japanese maneuvers from all of the pertinent "magics" instead of getting his information second and third hand, and piecemeal.

16   "Magic's" Finest Hour

On June 30 Unit 82 had submitted its master plan for the campaigns in the south, and on July 2 the imperial conference authorized the army to start measures for its implementation.

But at Taipeh, in the isolation of their makeshift headquarters, the chief architects of the war plan—Colonel Hayashi and Lieutenant Colonel Tsuji—felt like forgotten men. Ten days had passed without a word from Tokyo, nothing either commending or reprimanding them for their efforts; not even an acknowledgment that their final report had been received.

Then, on July 11, a radiogram signed by Major General Shinichi Tanaka, chief of the Operations Bureau of the General Staff, ordered Tsuji to report at once to General Staff headquarters with all the "research material" the unit had assembled.

Three days later he was in Tokyo. But if he had expected a warm reception he was sorely disappointed. His mentor in the War Ministry, General Muto, seemed to be too busy to receive him. In the Operations Bureau, General Tanaka and section chiefs Arisue, Hattori and Karakawa were friendly but remained noncommittal when Tsuji tried to draw them out about the prospects of the southern advance.

"I did not know," Tsuji wrote later, "why I, who had previously been reproved by General Tojo, had been recalled to Tokyo. Presumably I would be required to participate in preparations for fighting either in the north or the south—I had no idea which."

In his quest for congenial company, he sought out an old acquaintance from his days in China, Lieutenant Colonel Aribumi Kumon, air operations officer of the General Staff. Kumon at least seemed willing to talk.

In June, he explained, when the advance reports of the unit had reached Tokyo, the idea of the southward advance was gaining popularity and, consequently, the work of the unit was much appreciated. In the War Ministry, General Muto studied the reports and liked what he read. In the Operations Bureau, General Tanaka lavished praise on them, and Hattori told Kumon: "This is exactly what I have been waiting for."

Then, abruptly, everything changed. Hitler had plunged into war with Russia without giving his Japanese allies any advance warning. ("The outbreak of the Soviet-German war," Hattori wrote wryly, "following the conclusion of the Soviet-German Non-Aggression Pact of the summer of 1939, strongly impressed upon us the fact that the course of history is unknown and unpredictable.")

The war in Russia threw the government into confusion. On the one hand, Japan was committed by the Tripartite Pact to follow Germany's lead. On the other, she could not "morally" justify an attack on Russia because she had just concluded a neutrality pact with the Soviet Union. The China Incident was nowhere near settlement. Negotiations with the Netherlands East Indies for oil had failed. Japan's relations with the United States were growing steadily worse.

The imperial conference of July 2 devised the way out of the confusion. It resolved to move southward, after all—even at the risk of war with Britain, and the United States.

"In order to achieve her objectives [the establishment of a Greater East Asia co-prosperity sphere] Japan will not decline a war with England and the United States." This was the exact wording of the resolution, which typically accentuated the negative. It had been demanded by the army, was proposed by Foreign Minister Matsuoka and sanctioned by the Emperor. The conference authorized the armed forces "to carry out the preparations necessary for fighting these powers."

Then the situation underwent another change. Disliked and distrusted though the Germans were in Japanese military circles, they had gained a dominant influence on Tokyo's policies and thinking by the force of their triumphs in Europe and North Africa. On July 10 Japan almost decided to join Germany in the liquidation of the Soviet Union. The north again loomed as the most enticing plum.* The southern advance receded into the background.

This was the picture Colonel Kumon painted for his friend Tsuji. "He told me," Tsuji recalled later, "there . . . were many who believed Hitler would force a decision in Russia in the late autumn, and that we should miss the bus if we did not hurry to get into the war, and that consequently our share of the spoils of victory would be decreased."

But Colonel Tsuji remained undaunted. At dinner the next night with officers of the General Staff, he suddenly jumped to his feet, and like a man possessed, burst into an impassioned speech. He argued vehemently against war with Russia, and pleaded for an attack in the south instead. In the middle of his harangue Colonel Kumon seized him by the arm and took him to an adjoining room. "Are you again trying to dig your own grave?" Kumon asked. "You've been here only two days, so you cannot possibly know the situation! . . . You better keep quiet, if you know what is good for you, or you'll be fired again, this time for good."

But then the urge to wage war in the north subsided again—as abruptly as it had risen a few weeks before. And as it waned, the prospect of war in the south returned to prominence.

Now at last Colonel Tsuji received the call he had been waiting for. He was ordered by General Tanaka to present himself to the General Staff on July 24, at a conference summoned especially for Colonel Tsuji to present his report. For two days Tsuji demonstrated to the army high command, in miniaturized exercises staged on specially equipped tables, the plan his unit had evolved and tested. He outlined in detail all that was needed in logistics and collateral support to make the operation a success.

---

* During these few days of "vacillation," Japan even moved to implement its stillborn venture in the north. The Kwantung Army was alerted, then rapidly reinforced from 400,000 to 700,000 men, and ordered to go into *kantokuen* ("deceptive special maneuvers"), from which it could launch a full-scale offensive operation on a moment's notice. The navy organized a special force, called the Fifth Fleet, for the campaign, and 1,000,000,000 yen was hastily appropriated to finance the war against the Soviet Union.

War Minister Tojo was present as an observer, puffing on his cigarette in a long holder. The General Staff was represented by all its leading men, of whom General Sugiyama was the first to rise and congratulate Tsuji. "You have done well," he said, "and deserve the gratitude of the nation." Then he asked: "What is your estimate of the rate at which the operations you demonstrated can progress?"

"If we commence on *Meiji Setsu*," Tsuji replied, "we will be able to capture Manila by New Year, Singapore by *Kigensetsu*, Java on Army Commemoration Day, and Rangoon on the Emperor's birthday."

The answer brought gasps from the audience. According to his schedule, if operations began on November 3 (*Meiji Setsu*), Manila would fall in 59 days, by January 1. Singapore and Malaya would be conquered in 101 days, by February 11 (*Kigensetsu*). Java would be secured in 128 days, by March 10 (Army Day), and Burma in 168 days, by April 19, the Emperor's birthday. The whole war in the south would be concluded in a little more than five months.

General Tojo was silent throughout the meeting, but now he asked: "How do you believe this war against Britain and America will end?"

"We hope," Tsuji said, "the war will be brought to a conclusion as rapidly as possibly by a co-ordination of political and military strategy."

Though the exercises were held and the great decisions reached behind closed doors, word about them leaked out nevertheless, to the Germans and the Russians, and, thanks to "Magic," to the Americans.

The Kremlin had an enormous stake in the decision of the imperial conference. Despite oppressive need for reinforcements to bolster its fronts in Europe, the U.S.S.R. had to leave some of its best-trained and best-equipped troops in Siberia and along the Amur River. Russia could draw on them only if it were absolutely certain that Japan would not attack.

The Germans, who had not previously showed any great interest in Japanese plans, now became intensely curious. Berlin was split in its design for Japan: the Ribbentrop coterie, still mesmerized by its hatred of England, was pushing for the Japanese to move against Singapore; one group in the *Wehrmacht* hoped Japan would attack in the north and hasten Russia's defeat, and another group wanted her to sit tight, thus pinning down at least twenty-three Red Army divisions and immobilizing a thousand Russian planes without the slightest drain on her own resources.

Both Germany and the Soviet Union had excellent listening posts in Japan: Germany through competent and well-connected service attachés, the Russians through a superb espionage organization. As usual, the spies were quicker than the attachés in procuring the information.

The Soviet Union's ranking secret agent in Japan was a remarkable German intellectual, Dr. Richard Sorge. He maintained intimate contacts with the German embassy, but he was getting what he wanted most—first-hand intelligence—direct from Hotsumi Ozaki, a noted Japanese publicist who was one of Prime Minister Konoye's closest confidants.

On July 31 Ozaki—who was a Communist himself and a full-fledged member of the Soviet spy ring—began to furnish Sorge with a running commentary of the rapidly developing situation, including details of decisions reached in the closed council meetings.

Frequently Ozaki was able to give Sorge the very documents in which the decisions had been formalized. On August 1 he gave Sorge a paper dated July 31 in which the Army General Staff explained the decision to scrap all plans for war in the north. On August 4 Sorge received written confirmation of the decision from Ozaki, in a paper entitled "Basic Concepts of the Final Solution of the Northern Flank Problem." Before long he was also getting positive evidence that Japan was preparing for war against Britain and the United States.

Sorge radioed the information to Soviet Military Intelligence in Moscow. At the same time Rear Admiral Paul M. Wenneker, the German naval attaché in Tokyo, was getting similar intelligence from Admiral Nobutake Kondo, the Vice-Chief of the Naval General Staff, who was one of the three naval officers permitted to attend the imperial conferences.

On August 22 Wenneker was able to teletype to the Admiralty in Berlin: "Japan will not attack Russia." He concluded his report with an equally categorical statement: "The next steps planned are occupation of Dutch oil fields simultaneously with an attack on Manila, and the blockading of Singapore by cutting off all access routes." In another dispatch Wenneker even timed these moves. The situation, he teletyped, was not expected to become "acute for about six months." He was mistaken by only a few weeks, but he was right in everything else.

These feats of German and Soviet intelligence in Japan on the eve of the Pacific war seemed to be in contrast to the efforts of Japan's intended victims to obtain such intelligence on the spot. The reports the War Office was getting in London from Major General F. S. G. Piggott, the veteran British military attaché in Tokyo, were remarkable for their lack of information or, indeed, for their misinformation. General Piggott was an old "Japan hand." Filled with an abiding passion for all things Japanese, he simply could not visualize that the people he so loved would go to war against his own country.

The American attachés showed little sophistication in their attempts to penetrate to the core of Japanese military secrets. The United States had every reason at this acute stage of the crisis to station its most experienced and resourceful attachés in Tokyo, with the seniority in rank that the situation and importance of the mission required. But the American military attaché, Harry I. Creswell, was only a lieutenant colonel; and the naval attaché, Henri H. Smith-Hutton, a lieutenant commander. Both were gallant officers and able men. But they lacked both the rank and the acuity their jobs demanded at this critical juncture.

Colonel Creswell and Commander Smith-Hutton had no inkling of the historic decision reached at the imperial conference to risk war with the United States. On the contrary, their reports tended to reassure Washington that Japan would think twice before challenging America in a head-on clash. On July 17, fifteen days after the momentous conference, Ambassador Grew forwarded to Washington a lengthy estimate of the situation which Creswell and Smith-Hutton had prepared. It revealed that the attachés had evidence of "apparent preparation for some impending event"—such as spreading mobilization, the calling-up of reserves, the recall of Japanese merchant vessels from abroad.

But how did they interpret this evidence? According to their deductions, Japan was planning to make one of three moves: attack the Soviet Union in the Maritime Territory; pounce upon Yunnan via Indochina; or intensify operations on the Chinese fronts. The estimate concluded that "the last of these possible developments"—the stepping-up of the war in China—was "the most likely explanation of the factual evidence."

As a matter of fact, the estimate stated that "no evidence has as yet been brought to [their] knowledge which would support the view that Japan will resort to initiatives risking conflict with the United States." The attachés strongly advised Washington not to attach undue importance to "dates specified for future Japanese military operations." They concluded by saying that in their opinion, Japan's far-flung commitments and steadily diminishing resources made involvement in a large-scale war unlikely.

When Colonel Hayes A. Kroner took over the Intelligence Branch of G-2 in the spring of 1941, the first gripe he heard was a complaint about Creswell: Bratton was disturbed because he was getting "practically no information from our military attaché in Tokyo."

But no efforts were made to replace him. At this time the prestige of G-2 was at its lowest ebb throughout the military establishment as well as in the White House. President Roosevelt was wont to describe the G-2 officers, especially the military attachés, as "doughheads." And General Eisenhower expressed the consensus of the Operations Division, which he headed, when he spoke of "the shocking deficiency" of G-2. "Initially," he said, "the Intelligence Division could not even develop a clear plan for its own organization nor could it classify the type of information it deemed essential in determining the purposes and capabilities of our enemies." Eisenhower also had a very low opinion of the military attachés. "Usually they were estimable, socially acceptable gentlemen," he said. But as far as their special qualifications were concerned, "few knew the essentials of intelligence work."

So fuzzy was the coverage of Colonel William Meyer, military attaché in China, and so contradictory was his prognostication of "the next Japanese moves," that Secretary Hull felt called upon to complain in a sarcastic letter to Ambassador Clarence Gauss. "Our military attaché in Chungking reports on October 21," he wrote, "that 'the official Chinese view' is that the Japanese will begin an offensive in eastern Siberia within 2 weeks . . . and reports on October 23 that the 'official view' in Indochina is that the Japanese intend to attack Thailand about November 15. [On October 30 Meyer reported that "definite information" had reached him that the Japanese intended to make an attack on Yunnan in November.]

"There seems to be a good deal of variety in 'the official views' which prevail in the Far East. We would like to have an estimate on your part, in consultation with the military and naval attachés, and General [John B.] Magruder, as to which and how many of these anticipated attacks the Japanese may be about to make." Hull wrote a similar note to Grew in Tokyo, on November 3, 1941.

Our neglect of the conventional intelligence function at this critical time was not due to any lack of interest in what Japan was doing. It was rather a sign of surfeit. We had "Magic" and there seemed to be little that either Smith-Hutton or Creswell could find out that could not be learned in Washington from the intercepts. Indeed, "Magic" was about to prove what its adherents claimed for it. In July Op-20-G scored one of its most remarkable triumphs by producing intelligence of inestimable potential value culled entirely from the "magics."

At three o'clock in the afternoon on July 2, Ambassador Grew advised Washington that the imperial conference had been held in the morning, and cabled the official communiqué issued an hour and a half before. "At the imperial conference held today," it read in full, "the fundamental national policy to be taken toward the present situation was decided."

Nothing in the record indicates that Grew had any knowledge of what those decisions were and what turn "the fundamental national policy" had taken. Creswell certainly did not know that the army had been authorized to occupy the southern part of Indochina. Smith-Hutton did not know that the navy had received orders to intensify preparations for war with the United States.

July 2 in Tokyo was July 1 in Washington. It was a Tuesday. Within hours after the announcement that the imperial conference had been held, Op-20-G put a special watch on the Tokyo circuits to monitor whatever information could be picked up about it.

At the same time the Japanese made a rather elaborate effort to throw us off the scent. On Friday afternoon, July 4, Ambassador Nomura sent for Joseph W. Ballantine of the State Department and handed him, in an unsealed envelope, a personal letter for Secretary Hull. "I am glad to inform you," it read, "that I am now authorized by the Foreign Minister to assure you that there is no divergence of views in the Government regarding its fundamental policy of adjusting Japanese-American relations on a fair basis." The letter survives as a major document in Tokyo's campaign to camouflage its true intentions. It was the sort of deception that later compelled Nomura to beg in tears for reprieve from the kind of cunning diplomacy he was forced to practice at his post in Washington.

But it was a vain effort. Already a number of intercepts were on hand to belie Nomura's assurance. They were beginning to illuminate the mysteries of the imperial conference. Commander Kramer had taken upon himself to expose its secrets through a concentrated analysis of the pertinent intercepts. By Saturday morning, he had three items on the conference's agenda clearly established:

(1) Germany had asked the Japanese to move in force against the Soviet Union in the Far East, but the Japanese decided not to comply.

(2) The Japanese decided rather to "proceed with operations calculated to strengthen their military position in French Indochina."

(3) The Japanese resolved to intensify their air operations in China.

It was, even at this early stage of Kramer's efforts, an uncanny reconstruction of decisions which had been made by twelve of the highest-ranking officials of the Japanese government, behind closed doors of the imperial palace, thirteen thousand miles from Washington.

Kramer pursued the matter throughout the month, and by early August he had the imperial conference completely revealed.

He described his findings in two special memoranda (GZ-1,

dated August 4, and GZ-4, dated August 9). They presented the following conclusions in categorical terms:

- Japan will not go to war against the U.S.S.R. in the north.
- She will intensify preparations for "the southward move."
- She will immediately begin to "arm for all-out war against Britain and the United States to break," as Kramer quoted from one of the actual intercepts, "the British-American encirclement."

This was "Magic's" finest hour.*

* The Kramer survey made a deep impression in the State Department. Even Dr. Hornbeck, who was usually reserved in his praise of Bratton's Memos and Kramer's GZ's, described it as "excellent."

PART IV

On the Collision Course

Games of War

For all his exquisite manners and the fine personal qualities of a nobleman, Prince Konoye was the worst possible person to lead his restive country at this juncture of history. A novice in the complex ways of international politics and rash in his acts, he was unable to perceive the inherent contradictions in his maneuvers—such as the incompatability between the Tripartite Pact and the rapprochement with America, both of which he promoted.

"Just as the maxim puts it," Nomura later wrote, " 'no man can wear two pairs of shoes at the same time.'" But Konoye tried. Trapped by his impetuous acts and prone to outsmarting himself, he no longer knew how to escape from his predicaments. Even by the time he presented the Axis pact to the Emperor in the fall of 1940, he regretted that he had ever become involved in it. The Emperor, a much less impressive but far more stable and wise man, had consoled his distressed Premier. "Well," he said, "you and I will have to stand or fall together."

In actual fact, the decision to join the southern venture had been reached even before the American oil embargo of July 26 (imposed in retaliation for the occupation of the southern provinces of Indochina) threatened to throttle the navy's already diminished fuel supply. On April 17 a "tentative plan" entitled "Outline of Measures to be Taken toward the Southern Areas" had been adopted by the Navy Ministry and the Naval General Staff. On June 22 a meeting of the combined army-navy high commands (to which Yamamoto had sailed in the *Nagato*) had resolved specifically to "intensify preparations against the United States."

By August 15 the Naval General Staff had completed the drafting of tentative operations plans for "the naval aspects of the occupation of the Philippines, Malaya, the Netherlands East Indies, Burma and the South Pacific islands." And the finishing touches had been put to Yamamoto's draft of "Plan Z."

To calm the generals and to gain time, Konoye had agreed to the occupation of the southern part of Indochina in July. But this only made things worse by further antagonizing the United States. And it did not satisfy the generals.

Now, in the late summer of 1941, Konoye was again frightened, this time by the shadows he had conjured up at the imperial conference of July 2. And when he was informed that the army and the navy had agreed at last to take Japan into war along the southern route, he again went to the Emperor in despair. The Premier realized that he himself was powerless to change the military minds, but hoped that the Emperor could reverse their decisions, even if it meant issuing a direct order to them, an act without precedent.

On September 5 the Premier had his private audience with the Emperor and showed him the General Staff's master plan. Hirohito recoiled as he studied it. "Judging by this plan," he said, "preparations for war are placed first and diplomatic negotiations second."

Konoye said that this was exactly why he had sought the audience, and hoped that the Throne would intervene to halt the generals. The Emperor said he would talk to General Sugiyama at the imperial conference scheduled for the 6th. But Konoye thought that even a day's delay might be too late. He pleaded with the Emperor to talk to General Sugiyama, and also to Admiral Nagano, right away, in a private audience rather than at the plenary session of the conference. The Emperor ordered his aide-de-camp to summon the chiefs of the Army and Navy General Staffs. They came promptly, flushed and apprehensive as usual when called to the palace. It was an extraordinary meeting.

Turning his plaintive yet scolding glance on Sugiyama, Hirohito asked the Chief of Staff: "How long, in the Army's opinion, would hostilities last in a war with the United States?"

"We believe," Sugiyama replied, "that operations in the South Pacific could be disposed of in about three months."

The Emperor stiffened, then said in an icy voice: "We recall that you, Sugiyama, were Minister of War at the time the China Incident started, and then assured us that it would be disposed of in about a month. Yet, in spite of your advice and assurance, the war with China is still not concluded after four long years of hard fighting."

In "trepidation," as Konoye later put it, the Chief of Staff went to great lengths to explain that "the extensive hinterland of China prevented the consummation of operations according to the scheduled plan." The Emperor looked at him sternly. "If the Chinese hinterland is extensive," he said, "the Pacific is boundless. How, then, can you be so certain of your calculations and schedules this time?"

The Chief of Staff, Konoye wrote, "hung his head, unable to answer."

Then something happened that the Emperor and Konoye least expected. Admiral Nagano came to the aid of the old general. "Japan is like a patient suffering from a serious illness," he said. "His case is so critical that the question of whether or not to operate has to be determined without delay. Should he be let alone without an operation, there is danger of gradual decline. An operation, while it might be extremely dangerous, might still offer some hope of saving his life." Both he and General Sugiyama, the admiral said, were in favor of negotiations. Yet it was their duty to be ready for the worst.

The Emperor asked him firmly: "You mean, therefore, that the high command is, now as before, giving precedence to diplomacy."

This time both Sugiyama and Nagano spoke up, assuring His Majesty that, indeed, they were.

At the imperial conference Yoshimichi Hara, president of the Privy Council, set himself up as the devil's advocate. "The proposal before this conference," he said earnestly, "gives the impression that all hopes of peace have now been abandoned, and the emphasis is placed on war rather than diplomacy in Japan's future course. I desire clarification of this point, both from the government and the high command."

Navy Minister Oikawa reassured Hara that diplomacy still had priority over war. But Sugiyama and Nagano remained silent. The Emperor looked at them, waiting for their comment, but when none was forthcoming he decided to speak up, for the first time in an imperial conference.

"We regret deeply," he said, "that the high command has not seen fit to clarify the question before us." He took from his pocket a small piece of paper, glanced at it, then said: "Our august ancestor, Meiji Tenno, once wrote a poem which we are going to read to you now: *'Since we are all brothers in this world, why is there such constant turmoil?'* We have read this poem over and over again, and we are determined to make the Meiji ideal of peace prevail in the world."

"Everyone present was struck with awe," Konoye later recorded, "and there was silence throughout the hall. Soon the Chief of the Navy General Staff rose and said that he was filled with trepidation at the prospect of the Emperor's displeasure with the Supreme Command." Admiral Nagano assured the Throne that the chiefs of the high command wholeheartedly concurred with the Navy Minister's answer and that they, too, were fully convinced of the overriding importance of diplomacy in the crisis, contemplating the use of arms only as a last resort.

"The meeting adjourned," Konoye wrote, "in an atmosphere of unprecedented tenseness."

For all their "trepidation" and "awe," Sugiyama and Nagano were deceiving the Emperor. The army staffs were busy even then drafting the final plans for war in the south. And Admiral Nagano's unexpected intervention was much more than just a Samaritan gesture to help out old Sugiyama in a moment of embarrassment. The navy had stopped hedging and stalling. After the war, in a rueful book about lost battles, Vice-Admiral Koyanagi Tomoji wrote: "Reluctantly we in the navy were gradually dragged to war." Reluctance had become determination. The navy no longer had to be "dragged" to war.

The naval forces slated to participate in the southern operations had begun to assemble at Sukumo, Sueki, Kagoshima and Kanoya. They were in combat readiness and underwent realistic exercises under combat conditions, practicing support in landing operations.

On August 28 a signal sent jointly by the Chief of the Naval General Staff and the commander-in-chief of the Combined Fleet had ordered the fleet commanders and their key staffs to assemble at the Naval General Staff building in Tokyo for a series of indoor war games, to last four or five days.

Three admirals, seven vice-admirals, six rear admirals, seven captains and twenty commanders reported for the games led by Nagano and Yamamoto. The Naval Staff's cramped quarters proved inadequate to accommodate them, so the exercises were transferred to the more spacious facilities of the Naval War College, where they began on September 2—three days before Nagano's audience with the Emperor.

The party split up in teams—an N-team led by Yamamoto representing Japan, an A-team the Americans, and an E-team the English. For three days the games rehearsed the support operations to be mounted in co-operation with the army. Some faults and deficiencies were exposed, but the plan the General Staff had drafted was found to be sound. Finally, on September 5, Admiral Yamamoto presented his "Plan Z" for the attack on Pearl Harbor.*

By the end of the day it was all over. The games had confirmed Commander Genda's conclusion that the attack was perfectly feasible. But though the bold sweep of the plan impressed and exhilarated the assembled officers, nobody outside Yamamoto's own circle expressed himself completely in favor of it. The principal objection was not that it was too risky or too costly or too vague, but that it was "radically opposed to the well-established concepts of Japanese naval strategy."

The games adjourned on September 13 without producing a

* The plan was outlined by Commander Yasuji Watanabe, then the games got under way under the direction of Rear Admiral Jinsaburo Ito, the Combined Fleet chief of staff. A heated controversy developed between Ito and Captain Kameto Kurojima, the Deputy Chief of Staff, over the advisability of "following up the initial air attack by a landing force" to occupy the Hawaiian Islands. In the end Kurojima, who opposed such a follow-up landing, prevailed, and the possibility of occupying Hawaii was never discussed again.

definitive decision on "Plan Z." Neither rejected nor accepted, it was discussed throughout September. Yamamoto countered the objections of the General Staff with a passion rare for this man. His major argument was his familiar thesis that "as long as the United States had a powerful fleet in being, there was a constant danger that they would be able to . . . cut Japan's all-important lines of sea communications." His arguments failed to convince his opponents, however, and Yamamoto grew bitter and adamant. Eventually he threatened to resign from the navy unless "Plan Z" was adopted. But then support for his cause showed up from an unexpected quarter. Colonel Iwakuro had returned from Washington and was lecturing to the Army General Staff on his findings in the United States. When he related what Postmaster General Frank C. Walker had told him about the American idea of using the Pacific Fleet, he was sent over to the Naval General Staff to acquaint them with his information.

Objections to the Pearl Harbor attack began to weaken. In October they collapsed altogether and "Plan Z" was adopted. The basic operations plan was drawn up, and the First Air Fleet started to train for the attack in earnest.

By now Konoye was almost penitent about his past mistakes and committed himself in a last major endeavor to placate the United States. He offered to meet President Roosevelt almost anywhere to straighten things out. He had, somewhat like F.D.R., boundless faith in his own charismatic powers. By explaining Japan's cause to the President and acquainting him with his difficulties at home, he hoped they could work out a *modus vivendi*.

But the President sent word that he was not ready for such a meeting. And Konoye was on notice from the high command that their patience with diplomacy was wearing thin: they would go to war in the south if the negotiations failed to produce a settlement by October 19 at the latest. They showed Konoye their master plan, which Colonel Hattori called "Scope of Operations in the South and the Scheme of Attack."

The army held its conclusive indoor war games from October 1 to 5 at the Army War College under the direction of General Osamu Tsukada, the Vice-Chief of Staff. Present were the entire

General Staff, the key staffs of the various armies chosen to participate in the campaign, and observers from the navy. Agreement was promptly reached on all aspects of the projected operations. As soon as the exercises ended, the field staffs dispersed, and physical preparations for the multiple campaign got under way.

There was, however, still apprehension among the sponsors of the southward advance that negotiations in Washington might thwart their designs. The extremists among them singled out the pathetic Prime Minister as the one man who could still deprive them of the glory of conquest. They decided to resolve the problem once and for all with a single act of their familiar terrorism.* In the midst of what Konoye so aptly characterized as "unprecedented tenseness," an attempt had been made to assassinate him.

On the morning of September 18 four men armed with guns, daggers and short ceremonial swords attacked the Premier as he was leaving Tekigaiso Villa, his private residence, to go to his office by car. They fired at him wildly, one of the shots missing him by only eighteen inches. The assailants were overcome and arrested by Konoye's police guard, so no harm came to the Premier, but the warning was unmistakable.

For all his consummate optimism and talent for self-deception, Konoye began to realize, even aside from the eloquent message of the assassination attempt, that his cause was lost. It was confirmed beyond the shadow of a doubt on October 3, when he received a cable from Nomura reporting an "oral statement" Secretary Hull had given him the day before. It was a polite communication, still holding out the prospect of reconciliation at some future date. But Konoye had no time left to wait for future panaceas. He needed immediate results to survive, and Hull's statement made it clear that he could expect none within the time left for his maneuvers.

Hull was questioning the sincerity of the Japanese efforts and

---

* Assassination was a favorite means of persuasion of Japanese extremists. In November 1921 Prime Minister Takashi Hara, the first commoner to head the government, was stabbed to death by a young fanatic. In November 1930 Premier Yuko Hamaguchi was shot and seriously wounded by a "patriot" for his acquiescence in the London naval disarmament agreement. On February 26, 1936, army extremists went on the rampage and massacred two former Premiers; the army's Inspector General; the brother-in-law of Admiral Okada; and seriously injured Admiral Suzuki, the aged Grand Chamberlain (who survived, however, to become Japan's last wartime Premier nine years later).

was insisting upon Japan's departure from China and Indochina before the meeting, a condition Konoye could not possibly fulfill. Bishop Walsh, who had returned to Tokyo for a final attempt at his missionary efforts, described the Premier's reaction to Hull's statement in a memorandum that succinctly summarized the whole tortuous course of these strange negotiations as the Japanese viewed it: "With some difficulty, the protagonists of peace in the Japanese government . . . had held Cabinet, army, navy and all the other elements in line, or at least in quiescence, pending the conclusion of the negotiations. . . . Many, both in the civil government and the army, now think that the deception goes back to the beginning, that is to say, that the American government wanted only to draw them out in order to gain time, and to get a statement of their policy in order to condemn it. . . . After the receipt of the [October 2] message it was very difficult to make any one in the Japanese government believe in the sincerity of the American government."

As a last resort, Konoye asked Bishop Walsh to intervene again by returning to Washington at once, on a *laissez passer* General Muto was to provide for him, to explain to the President and Hull "the present situation of the Japanese government together with their desires and hopes and fears in regard to the proposed agreement." The Bishop had had his quota of rebuffs and was at first reluctant to return to the picture. But he talked things over with Ambassador Grew and Counselor Eugene Dooman at the embassy, and was persuaded by them to undertake the mission.

In the evening of October 14 he visited Prince Konoye at his villa and received from the Premier a personal message he was to convey to the President. It was the blunt warning that "unless some substantial sign of serious intention on the part of the American government promptly [materialized], the existing Japanese government would not be able to hold the position any longer."

The next morning, with General Muto's pass to expedite his departure, Walsh left Tokyo for Washington. But it was too late. While he was en route to Hong Kong in a Japanese plane (a seat on which had been secured for him at the last minute through the Premier's intervention), the situation took a turn for the worse. Konoye could stem the tide no longer. On October 16—just seventy-two hours before the expiration of the time limit the military clique had granted him for the conclusion of the negotiations—he resigned with his entire Cabinet.

The Emperor named General Hideki Tojo, the fifty-seven-year-old son of a *samurai* and veteran of the Manchurian Incident, to succeed him. Tojo's mandate was either to bring the negotiations to a satisfactory conclusion or to take the nation to war.

The fate of Japan passed into the hands of the generals.

As a final concession, General Tojo extended the deadline to November 25, and then to November 29. But under him the negotiations slackened while preparations for war accelerated.

Japan's course was now clear.

⁄8   The Missed Clue

Shortly after eight o'clock in the evening of September 24, 1941, Yoshimichi (Joe) Hashida, a new "Jap boy" at the Mackay cable office in downtown Honolulu, rode his bike up Nuuanu Avenue to the Japanese consulate general at No. 1742, to deliver a radiogram. Nothing was stirring at the five buildings of the compound, although two cars with nondiplomatic license plates stood in front of a handsome villa on the *makai* (seaward) side of the grounds.

Young Hashida stopped at the office nearest to the Nuuanu Avenue gate, but found its door locked. Yokichi Seki, the senior consular secretary who lived upstairs, was out. Joe then tried the villa where the cars stood, rang the bell, and was let in by a pretty girl. She was Kimika Asakuru, a Nisei like Joe, the consul general's personal maid—this was his house. "It's for Kita-*san*," the messenger said to the young woman

Nagao Kita was in the dining room entertaining three prominent members of Honolulu's Japanese colony. When he heard voices downstairs, he went into the hall to see what was going on. He took the envelope from Kimika, ripped it open and glanced at the radiogram. Though it was signed "Toyoda"—for Foreign Minister Teijiro Toyoda—Kita recognized by the marking "SIKYU 00830" that it was actually from Captain Ogawa of Naval Intelligence, and that it was "very urgent." * Since he always gave his

---

* The Kita–Ogawa telegrams, sent in the KANOHO FOGO (Chief of Consulate code), had their own separate serial numbers and prearranged priority "indicators." The word KINQU (for *kinkyu*) was written next to the serial

immediate attention to such dispatches, he told the maid: "Find Tsukikawa-*san*. Tell him I want to see him right away." When the girl came back with the code clerk, Kita asked him to decrypt it at once and bring the plain-text copy back to him.

In Tsukikawa's transcript the message read:

Henceforth please make your reports concerning the ships (in Pearl Harbor) as follows as far as possible:
(1) The waters are to be divided roughly into five subareas. (We have no objection to your abbreviating as much as you like.) Area A: The waters between Ford Island and the Arsenal. Area B: Waters adjacent to but south and west of Ford Island. (This is on the opposite side from Area A.) Area C: East Loch. Area D: Middle Loch. Area E: West Loch and the Channel.
(2) With regard to battleships and aircraft carriers, please report those at anchor separately from those tied up at the wharves, buoys and in the docks (but the latter are not too important). Designate types and classes briefly. If possible, we would like to have you mention whenever there are two or more vessels tied up alongside the same wharf.*

When his guests had left, Kita sent Kimika for Vice-Consul Tadashi Morimura, who lived in one of the villas along Kuakini Street. "Morimura" was, of course, Ensign Takeo Yoshikawa, the young intelligence expert the Third Bureau had sent to Hawaii in March. He had been out on the town and returned only at two o'clock. When he found Kimika's note summoning him to the consul general, he went immediately over and was shown Ogawa's telegram.

Yoshikawa told Kita that Ogawa was a great believer in the statistical method of intelligence and that by setting up a grid system for Pearl Harbor, he wanted them to pinpoint the exact locations of the ships so that he could establish their berthing pattern with perfect accuracy. But there seemed to be no special

---

number at the head of the encoded text to indicate that it was "an emergency wire requiring immediate disposition no matter how late at night." The words DAIQU (for *daikyu*) or SIKYU (for *shikyu*) were used for "very urgent dispatches to be taken care of as soon as possible." After October 1 Kita and Ogawa used KONGO for the *kinkyu* telegrams and HYUGA for routine dispatches.
  * The battleships were in Area A, the cruisers and carriers in Area B, the destroyers in Area C, the minecraft in Area D. The submarines had their own base in the Southeast Loch, near the dry dock and wharves, in Area A.

urgency behind the telegram. They were now sending one report a week about the movements of the fleet and Ogawa was not asking them to increase the number of reports they were sending each Monday. Nothing in the message seemed to indicate a significant broadening of the Third Bureau's normal curiosity.

Yoshikawa had sent off his last report on September 22. The next one would not be due until Monday, the 29th, so he had four days to collect fresh data.

In the morning he called Johnny Mikami, the cabbie, who drove him to Aiea. Just below the Chester Clarke residence on the Heights he asked Johnny to stop the car. Yoshikawa got out and walked a few steps back, then looked down on what Captain Ogawa had designated as Area A—on Battleship Row, on the docks and wharves below, on the Signal Tower and the Tank Farm with its twenty-seven huge fuel tanks. Then, skirting Area C, he rode around the northern perimeter of Pearl Harbor to the tip of the peninsula. He let Mikami go, then sat down on a pile of leftover lumber near the Pan American Clipper Landing in Pearl City. There, in the imaginary grids B and D, he saw four cruisers and a few smaller vessels at their moorings a little farther to the west. The Middle Loch was nearly deserted.

He repeated the tour several times during the next three days, and in a game of his own memorized the grids, etching the main features of the harbor on his mind.

In the evening of September 28 Yoshikawa drafted two telegrams for transmission to Tokyo. In the first he proposed a simple two-letter code he had devised to improve Ogawa's area code and make it possible to pinpoint the ships in the harbor:

The following codes will be used hereafter to designate the locations of the vessels:
(1) Repair Dock in Navy Yard: KS.
(2) Dock in the Navy Yard (the Ten-Ten Pier): KT.
(3) Moorings in the vicinity of Ford Island: FV.
(4) Alongside Ford Island: FG. (East and west sides will be differentiated by A and B respectively.)

Then he wrote up the week's ship-movement report, using Ogawa's grid and his own code for the first time. It read:

The warships at anchor on the 28th were as follows:
(1) FGA—one *Texas*-class battleship, total one.

(2) FGB—one *Indianapolis*-class, one unidentified-type heavy cruiser, total two.

(3) FVBC—seven light cruisers of *Honolulu*- and *Omaha*-class, 26 destroyers.

(4) KS—one *Omaha*-class light cruiser.

(5) Also, six submarines, one troopship, and two destroyers off Waikiki.

It was Yoshikawa's 179th report in six months.

Captain Ogawa's radiogram setting up the grid system was intercepted on September 24 by MS-5, the new monitoring station the Army had established on Oahu earlier in the year. Unlike the other Army stations, which performed only collateral services for SIS, this one was an integral part of "Magic" and was therefore subject to all the ultra-security rules and regulations of the operation. Since General Walter C. Short, who commanded the Hawaiian Department of the Army, had not been cleared for "Magic," he was not apprised of the existence of the station at his own Fort Shafter.

MS-5's "assigned mission" was to "guard" the Tokyo–Berlin and Tokyo–Moscow circuits because the Stateside monitors were experiencing recurrent reception difficulties with this important traffic. It was also supposed to monitor the messages passing between the Japanese consulate general in Honolulu and the Foreign Ministry in Tokyo. Coverage of the consular traffic was incomplete by necessity, confined as it was to messages transmitted by radio. The district managers of the cable companies in Honolulu had steadfastly refused to heed repeated "suggestions" of the American counterintelligence authorities in Hawaii that copies of Japanese messages going by the cable be delivered to them.

Major Carroll A. Powell, who was in charge of the station, was supposed to pick out of the mass of intercepts those which seemed important, and radio them to the Army station at Fort Hunt in Virginia, just outside of Washington, for immediate processing by SIS. But since the station had not been given decrypting facilities, Powell had no way of knowing what the intercepts contained and which among them were "important." As a result the entire "raw schedule" of intercepts had to be sent by air mail to Washington in their original, encoded form. At this time there was one Pan

American Clipper a week from Honolulu to San Francisco, leaving on Fridays. When the weather was poor the flights could be delayed as long as a week or more.

The next Clipper was scheduled to leave on September 26, but the flight had to be canceled because the weather was bad. The "lot" of accumulated intercepts, which included the transcript of Captain Ogawa's telegram, was, therefore, sent by surface mail on September 28, arriving in San Francisco on October 3. It was held there for two days, was then sent off by air mail and finally reached SIS in Washington on October 6.

The usual spot check indicated that the Ogawa telegram was in the deferred category of routine intercepts, and it was therefore put aside to await its turn. It was October 9 when it was processed at last—decrypted, translated and sent to Colonel Bratton in G-2—fifteen days after it had been picked up by MS-5 at Fort Shafter.

Neither the Army's nor the Navy's monitoring stations had picked up Ensign Yoshikawa's two telegrams of September 29. A copy of his No. 178, however (the first, in which he improved Ogawa's grid scheme with an abbreviating system of his own), reached OP-20-G nevertheless. Kita had sent duplicates of the dispatch to the embassy in Washington and the consulate general in San Francisco, and Commander Safford's Section managed to obtain a photocopy of it by the X process, presumably from the Mackay office which handled the telegram.

The X copy of Yoshikawa's No. 178 arrived in OP-20-G at a time when an apparently far more interesting traffic pre-empted the attention of the Section and the "Magic" people in ONI. It was, in a sense, great fun to eavesdrop on secret correspondence, especially its lighter side. This time the attention of the "Magic" operatives was almost monopolized by a lively quarrel between Prime Minister Konoye and Ambassador Nomura. The whole controversy, it turned out, was produced by the caprices of cryptology.

Ambassador Nomura had been pressing Secretary Hull to agree to a Roosevelt-Konoye meeting in Juneau, Alaska, even if only, as he put it, "in principle." In support of his plea the ambassador assured the Secretary of State that "in contrast to some people in Tokyo," Konoye was sincerely anxious to see his, Nomura's, efforts for a rapprochement succeed. A long memorandum describing Nomura's efforts was given by the State Department to Lord Halifax, the British ambassador, who sent it on to the Foreign Office in London in his own cipher.

The telegram was intercepted and decoded by the Germans, who promptly forwarded copies to the Japanese, causing considerable embarrassment in Tokyo. Something had to be done to reassure the Germans that Konoye was not trying to stab them in the back. Nomura became the whipping boy in Konoye's attempt to extricate himself from another one of his predicaments.

In a strongly worded telegram the Prime Minister rebuked the ambassador and demanded that he correct "the wrong impression" he must have created in Secretary Hull's mind. Badly shaken, Nomura radioed back abject apologies for the "misunderstanding." *

These telegrams were in turn intercepted by the Americans, were processed at once, and distributed under the captions "Nomura Bawled Out" and "Nomura Apologizes." They were important, to be sure, if only because they produced further evidence of Japanese duplicity in the negotiations. But their chief appeal, while they lasted, was the "incidental intelligence" they yielded on these bickerings within the Japanese camp. In the meantime the Ogawa-Yoshikawa spy messages had to await their turn. Finally, on October 10—eight days after the X copy of the Yoshikawa telegram had been logged in and decrypted—Commander Kramer got around to translating it. But the Ogawa message that triggered it had not yet been sent over from SIS.

If Kramer had seen the Ogawa dispatch before he read the telegram with Yoshikawa's supplementary code, he probably would have taken notice of it. But by itself, No. 178 did not strike him as being unusual. He had repeatedly noticed that the Japanese were sending out abbreviations to be used in conjunction with their codes, presumably to cut down on the cost of the

* Nomura followed up his apologies with four telegrams, pleading for some such concessions as "the evacuation of our troops from China," and warning against "further aggression."

telegrams. He assumed that this dispatch, too, was merely "an attempt on the part of the Japanese diplomatic service to simplify communications."

He decided to file Yoshikawa's dispatch containing his abbreviating code without showing it to anyone. He never as much as looked at it again, not even when the Ogawa telegram at last came into his hands and attracted some interest for a short time.

Bratton had concluded in the meantime that the setting-up of a grid for Pearl Harbor deserved more than the perfunctory attention the espionage messages had been receiving. He had seen these "normal"-rated intercepts from time to time and paid no more attention to them than anyone else. When, for instance, Ogawa had sent his "shopping list" to Honolulu on February 15, identical telegrams went to the embassy in Washington and to the consulates in Panama, Los Angeles, San Francisco, Vancouver and even Havana (which was watching the Guantánamo naval base). The Third Bureau seemed to be interested in anything and everything: tankers passing through the Panama Canal, the number of Negroes being drafted, the warships undergoing repair at the Bremerton Navy Yard, the size of the air force General MacArthur had in the Philippines, "conditions" in Vladivostok, the movements of ships in Singapore—as well as Pearl Harbor.

Since no special cumulative study was ever made of the espionage messages, Bratton could not have discovered that the Honolulu–Tokyo traffic was different—and heavier in its emphasis on ship movements—than similar reports on any of the other circuits. It had also gone unnoticed that between January 1 and the end of September 1941, Panama had received only 63 queries from Tokyo, and Los Angeles less than 50, while Honolulu was up to 83 —the number of the telegram in which Ogawa had sent his grid code.

But now Bratton needed no statistical appraisal of old dispatches to realize that No. 83 was different from all the others in this particular category of messages. No other outlet—not even Seattle, Panama or Manila—had ever been asked to report in such detail, and no other region was assigned a grid system like the one the Third Bureau had devised for Pearl Harbor. He concluded therefore that this was an important intercept—the first evidence ever produced by "Magic" that the Japanese had a special interest in Pearl Harbor.

Bratton took the telegram to General Miles, head of the Military Intelligence Division, and tried to impress upon him the possible significance of Ogawa's message. But Miles could not see anything extraordinary in it. Moreover, he said, the dispatch was of strictly naval character and therefore of no interest to Military Intelligence.

"There was no way of studying these messages," Miles later said, "except to look at what they said, and since they said much the same thing about all the places involved, they simply added up to the picture of a detailed and efficient Japanese espionage agency."

Bratton did not think so. On the supposition that the Navy might find it more interesting, he decided to deliver it to ONI personally, on October 12. A new director, Captain Theodore Wilkinson, was coming in on October 15. He was already around, "learning the ropes," as he himself put it, for he had no previous experience in intelligence. Bratton found him with McCollum and Kramer in McCollum's office, and the four of them discussed the possible implications of the Ogawa telegram for some time.

Captain Wilkinson, speaking from his experience as a line officer at Pearl Harbor, interpreted the message as essentially defensive in character. The Japanese had set up the grid, he said, to aid themselves in figuring out how quickly the American fleet could sortie, and not because they were planning to attack the ships at their moorings. He was impressed by Ogawa's pedantic arrangement, but only because, as he later put it, it reflected "the nicety of their intelligence."

Commander McCollum, who had unbounded confidence in Admiral Kimmel's acumen as a fleet commander, also doubted that the Japanese had any aggressive designs on Pearl Harbor. It did not seem to make any sense to him. "They know," he told Bratton, "as well as you and I do that the fleet would not be just sitting there waiting to be attacked."

Commander Kramer did not share Bratton's excitement and apprehension, but neither did he go along with Wilkinson's interpretation and McCollum's optimism. He clamped a paper clip on the intercept, his way of indicating that the message was "interesting"; put an asterisk next to its caption in the distribution sheet to call attention to it; and prepared a "gist," a brief recapitulation of its salient points, for those who rarely went to the trouble of reading through the "magics." "Tokyo directs special reports on ships in Pearl Harbor," he wrote matter-of-factly, "which is divided into five areas for the purpose of showing exact locations."

He showed the intercept only to a few people even within the limited circle of Ultras—Admiral Stark, for example, could not recall that he had ever been shown this particular dispatch. The others who did glance at it did not think it had any special significance. "I do not believe," Kramer later said, "it was interpreted by any of those persons as being materially different than other messages concerning ship movements being reported by the Japanese diplomatic service."

Kramer's description of the intercept as a message of "the Japanese diplomatic service" was rather strange. There could be no mistaking this series of dispatches for "diplomatic" reports. Even if their different serial numbers had not set them apart from the consulates' regular dispatch traffic—a humdrum flow of telegrams about visa applications, so-called protection cases, commercial matters, and other routine consular problems—the added line "For Chief of Third Bureau, Naval General Staff" included in the address of each of these telegrams placed this traffic in a distinctly different category. Moreover, many of the dispatches were clearly labeled "Intelligence Message" or occasionally "Secret Intelligence Message."

The mild interest Ogawa's grid had provoked in ONI quickly vanished. The telegram was filed and forgotten. No effort was made to probe the possible reasons for Ogawa's new arrangements. Nothing was done to monitor for a follow-up or to subject this sensitive traffic to special attention. The espionage messages were left in the deferred category of intercepts with the lowest priority assigned to their processing. They were still there on the day of Pearl Harbor.*

* The Ogawa telegram was sent with a batch of other intercepts to Admiral Thomas C. Hart, commander-in-chief of the Asiatic Fleet, in Manila. Kramer "assumed" that Hart would send a copy to the Pacific Fleet. However, this particular intercept was never forwarded to Admiral Kimmel or anybody else at Pearl Harbor.

This was a turning point nevertheless, even if only in Colonel Bratton's evaluation of the situation. Up to this moment he, too, had been inclined to doubt that the Japanese had any warlike intentions toward the United States, but now he came to regard an attack on some American territory—even on Pearl Harbor—as a distinct possibility. He conceived the idea of plotting Japan's gradual march to war day by day, from data he was collecting from the "magics" and his other scattered intelligence sources.

He got himself a couple of maps published by the Cartographic Section of the National Geographic Society—a 1:8,000,000-scale transverse Mercator's projection of Southeast Asia, and another of the Pacific Ocean, scale 1:27,500,000—and began marking on them every Japanese move that even remotely hinted at some deployment for war.

On October 13 he stuck a marker on the map where Pearl Harbor was.

19 The Pearl Harbor Spy

A single spy at large is like the pro-verbial needle in a haystack—he is very difficult to find. Ensign Yoshikawa was such an elusive loner in espionage.

At the consulate, only Kita and Okuda were aware of his true identity, and even they knew nothing of his background and very little about the exact nature of his work. To all others, he was a brash, indolent probationary consul of the eighth rank, the lowest man in the hierarchy, who was falling down badly on his job.

His associates considered him an upstart, the worthless protegé of someone influential at the Foreign Ministry. To Yoshie Kik-kawa, his personal maid, he was something of a mystery man whom she knew only as Vice-Consul Morimura. He kept one of his rooms at his quarters permanently locked and would not even let her in to clean it.

His behavior naturally caused much comment among the consu-late's secretaries and clerks. Some of them suspected that Yoshi-kawa was an officer of the Imperial Navy on a secret mission. But Yokichi Seki, who had had a year in the navy and fancied himself an expert in naval matters, doubted this. "I know how our naval officers behave," he told the others, "and Morimura definitely doesn't conduct himself as an officer. As a matter of fact," he added, for he resented the new man who had replaced him at his clandestine side line, "he doesn't really know what he's doing."

As for Yoshikawa himself, he seemed to be enjoying himself hugely, playing much harder than he worked. A handsome, outgo-ing man of twenty-eight with a good sense of humor and a certain rough charm, he was, as consumptive people often are, highly sensuous and a lover of life. The budget of his mission was by no means generous—the *joho kyoku* kept a very thrifty house—but it enabled him to indulge in certain of the luxuries he had had to forgo before. And apparently he was determined to make the most of this windfall.

He had made many friends in Honolulu even in this short time, and had become a fixture at the Venice Café and the Seaview Inn, and especially at the tea houses where the service was enhanced by accommodating geisha girls. He taught *kendo* fencing at the Dai Nippon athletic club, which had a sprinkling of American servicemen among its members; took his girl friends on sightseeing trips to Kaneohe Bay in the glass-bottom boat, and over Pearl Harbor in a Piper Cub he rented at John Rodgers Airport; played golf (badly but dutifully with the consul general) and baseball on the consulate grounds; gossiped in the City Room of the *Nippu Ji Ji,* a local Japanese–English newspaper; joked easily, drank heavily, stayed up late at night; courted a prim little schoolteacher from Wahiawa and wrote sentimental poems to Tomoyoka, a lovely geisha at the Muchizoki tea house.

In between he put in brief appearances at the office (where he had a desk in Okuda's room) but spent most of his time roaming about Oahu or going on tours to Maui or Kauai islands. He bought picture postcards of volcanos and exotic plants, like any proper tourist captivated by the scenic splendor of the islands.

On the rare nights when he stayed home, he gave *sake* parties to the girls from the tea houses or tried to learn English (which he understood but could not speak well) by listening to the radio for hours or struggling with such books as Beth Proun's *For Men Only* and *Wife for Sale* by Kathleen Norris. He kept a notebook in which he jotted down idiomatic phrases that happened to strike his fancy—such as "boisterous merrymaking" and "both my feet had gone to sleep"*—but he had no intellectual pretenses. He did not strike people as being very bright.

---

* A few entries in the notebook were more suggestive of other interests. He once jotted down the word "observe" and underlined it four times. On another occasion he put down the sentence: "If there is any problem that you like to have explained, please feel free to call upon us." But the next entry was: "The man has committed single adultery, double adultery."

Actually, Yoshikawa was neither the simpleton nor the sybarite he appeared to be. His casual approach to espionage was calculated—in fact, it was his own shrewdly chosen cover. The man who could be exasperatingly indiscreet in his private affairs was a paragon of discretion in his professional pursuits.

Technically competent both as a naval officer and a secret agent, he was indefatigable, conscientious, and an excellent judge of men. He suffered from none of the usual delusions of espionage operatives and eschewed the hoary melodrama of their craft. He regarded his mission fatalistically, with the stoic submission of an officer doing his duty. As he himself later put it, "I, who was reared as a naval officer, never came to serve in action, but look back on my single top-secret assignment as the *raison d'être* of the long years of training in my youth and early manhood."

Yoshikawa once said that when he first arrived in Honolulu the only useful information he had about the place was that the Seaview Inn served an excellent balloon-fish soup. In only a few months, however, he learned everything one could find out about Hawaii—from trivial rumors abroad in the taverns and barber shops to such crucial details of Pearl Harbor's defenses as underwater obstructions, beach gradients, the protective net in the entrance channel, and the exact schedule and range of the American patrol planes.

He thoroughly familiarized himself with the topography of Oahu during his first fortnight in Hawaii, pinpointed the places of special interest to him and chose vantage points from which they could be observed best. He returned to these spots again and again, sometimes driven by Mikami or Kotoshirodo, but often by himself, covering enormous distances on foot.

On one of his set tours (which usually lasted from two to four hours) he would board a jitney bus at the Kalihi junction, get off at Aiea just below the sugar refinery, look down on Pearl Harbor, then walk back all the way to the gate of the Submarine Base in the Southeast Loch. On the return hike he would observe the submarines from a favored spot between Aiea and Makalapa. Sometimes he would ride with Mikami around Diamond Head and Koko Head, passing Hanauma and Waimanalo beaches on the windward side of the island, to the Kailua Beach Pavillon, dismiss the driver and walk along the road past the Kaneohe Naval

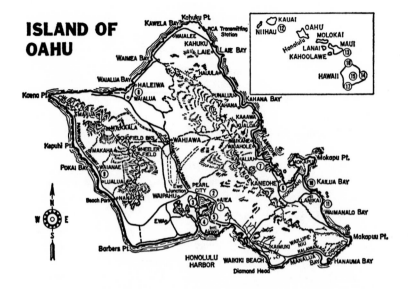

ISLAND OF OAHU

Major vantage points of Ensign Yoshikawa's surveillance of the islands of Oahu, Kauai, Maui and Hawaii, shown on a map similar to the one Yoshikawa himself used on his wanderings in Hawaii.

(1) Aiea Heights, best view of the ships in Pearl Harbor
(2) Naval Radio Station
(3) Pan American Clipper Landing on Pearl City Peninsula
(4) Main Gate of Navy Yard (Eto's soft-drink stand)
(5) Gate of Submarine Base
(6) Kaneohe Naval Air Station
(7) Best view of Kaneohe Bay, with U.S. Marine Corps camp
(8) Haleiwa Beach ⎫ potential landing beaches
(9) Waianae Beach ⎭
(10) Otto Kühn's residence at Kalama
(11) Otto Kühn's beach house at Lanikai
(12) Island of Kauai
(13) Island of Maui (Lahaina Anchorage is on the west coast)
(14) Hilo Harbor on the island of Hawaii
(15) Hawaii National Guard camp
(16) Airstrip at Upolu Point
(17) New airfield under construction at South Point

Air Station. He went bathing at the Haleiwa and Waianae beaches on the west side of Oahu, potential landing spots for invasion forces, or walked to Wailupe for a look at the Naval Radio Station.

He never spent more than a few minutes at any one point, but would rather return a next time for another look. There was a certain spot on Aiea Heights which he visited thirty times in a two-month period because it was what he considered the best spot from which to view Pearl Harbor.

Yoshikawa carried out his mission with remarkable decorum. Except for having entered Hawaii under assumed name and diplomatic cover, he did all his spying without violating any American laws. His primary rule was "not to get caught." He never went out of his way to get information. Even when he could not see his objective from a nearby highway he never asked questions about it, nor did he ever leave the road to get a better view.

He carried a cheap little camera hanging from his shoulder on his sightseeing excursions, but mainly as a "prop" to aid his pose as a tourist, for he would have been conspicuous without it. Only once did he take pictures. The maps he used during his tours were issued by the Hawaii Visitors Bureau. He never made any notes or sketches on his wanderings; he had trained himself to memorize the things in which he was interested. Once in a while he took a pair of field glasses along, but nobody ever saw him using them. And though he had several acquaintances who could have been developed as intelligence sources (including the chief yeoman in the office of the Navy's Cable Censor and two young draftsmen at the Navy Yard to whom he gave *kendo* lessons), he never pumped them for any information.

Not a single individual was later found by the FBI or the Navy's District Intelligence Office whom Yoshikawa had involved in his clandestine activities—except for the two men the consulate had enlisted prior to his arrival—Dick Kotoshirodo and Johnny Mikami. Yoshikawa needed them to chauffeur him around on Oahu; this remarkable secret agent did not know how to drive an automobile.

For all his informality, however, and his smart security precautions, Yoshikawa's existence in Hawaii was precarious. The special nature of his mission projected him more than any other member of the consular staff into a strange and highly distrustful environment, and made him a fifth wheel even within the consulate (where he was supposed to handle repatriation cases).

The American counterintelligence agencies—of which there was no shortage in Hawaii *—kept elaborate suspect lists in which people were graded "A," "B" and "C," according to the degree of danger they were presumed to represent. Otto Kühn, the "sleeper spy" Captain Ogawa had planted on Oahu in 1936, was an "A" suspect on the FBI's list, as was the intelligence officer who posed as a chemist at the Honolulu Sake Brewery. But Yoshikawa was on none of the lists.

The Japanese consulate general was under close surveillance. Both the FBI and the DIO had several "contacts" who reported periodically on most of the goings-on in its offices, including Consul General Kita's visitors. Since 1940 the DIO had taps on six of the consulate's business phones, another on Okuda's private line, and still another on the phone in Kita's residence. An average of sixty conversations were recorded daily by Chief Ships Clerk Theodore Emanual in the DIO's office. They were translated by Lieutenant Commander Denzel Carr, and circulated to Colonel Bicknell's Contact Office and the FBI. Okuda was thus overheard in December 1940, when he asked the Reverend Unji Hirayama to observe the ships at Lahaina and found out from him that they had abandoned this anchorage.

But no amount of tapping developed even a scintilla of derogatory information about Yoshikawa. He was, in fact, the only Japanese official at the consulate who was never as much as suspected of espionage activities by the American authorities. They accepted him implicitly for what he pretended to be—a

---

* Counterespionage in Hawaii was split three ways: (1) the Navy (the District Intelligence Office of the 14th Naval District headed by Captain Mayfield); (2) the Army (the so-called Contact Office of the Hawaiian Department G-2 under Lieutenant Colonel George W. Bicknell, the Criminal Investigation Division at Fort Shafter headed by Lieutenant Colonel Byron M. Meurlott, and the G-2 of the Hawaiian Air Force under Lieutenant Colonel Edward W. Raley); and (3) the FBI Field Office, with Special Agent Robert L. Shivers in charge. Together, they had a personnel of about a hundred officers and full-time investigators, and several hundred "special agents" and "confidential informants" in a dense web that covered the Islands.

mere vice-consul who was having a corking good time in Hawaii. Nobody among the American counterspies was prepared to believe that the Japanese intelligence service would entrust as important a spot as Hawaii to the care of a single bibulous spy.*

Ensign Yoshikawa had come to Hawaii on a crucial mission, but was accomplishing it with very little fuss. In September, however, the pace had quickened; it was his busiest month.

Fifty American pilots had passed through Oahu en route to China, to join Major General Claire L. Chennault's Flying Tigers. Brigadier General John Magruder of the War Department had been in town on his way to Chungking on some secret mission. A French warship was in port for three days, taking a new high commissioner to the Free French islands in the Pacific. According to a dispatch in the *Star-Bulletin,* the United States Navy was constructing a new dock at Pago Pago on Samoa.

These items necessitated seven special dispatches in addition to Yoshikawa's regular weekly reports about the movements of the fleet in Pearl Harbor. But then activities slackened off. He sent a

* It was only on February 15, 1942—seventy days after Pearl Harbor, in an Investigation Report prepared by the 14th Naval District—that "Secretary Tadasi [sic] Morimura" was first mentioned at all. And it was not until June 15, 1942, that "Morimura" was identified as "the chief collector of facts for the consulate concerning the movements of U.S. Navy vessels in and out of Pearl Harbor." His true identity was never established by any of the American counterintelligence agencies.

In December 1953 the *Ehime Shimbun,* a provincial Japanese newspaper, published an interview with a former officer of the Imperial Navy who stated that "an ensign named Takeo Yoshikawa" had been "assigned as intelligence officer to the Japanese consulate at Honolulu prior to the Pearl Harbor attack on December 7, 1941." The interview was reprinted in the *New York Times* on December 9, 1953. In the wake of this publicity, Yoshikawa received several offers from newspapers and magazines to tell his own story. He did not accept these invitations.

However, in the summer of 1960 Lieutenant Colonel Norman Stanford, USMC, the American assistant naval attaché in Tokyo, managed to track him down at Matsuyama on Shikoku Island, where Yoshikawa was managing a gasoline station. The Japanese, who are still anxious to hide their espionage effort before Pearl Harbor, never rewarded him with a promotion or decoration for his extraordinary service.

Yoshikawa himself views his fate philosophically.

"I am older now," he told Colonel Stanford, "and dwelling more in the past as the years go by. Some things are certainly ordained. . . . In truth, if only for a moment in time, I held history in the palm of my hand."

report to Ogawa on October 2 about British soldiers being transported to Singapore in American ships, and filed another two days later describing the emergency defense measures the Territorial Legislature had just adopted to go into effect in case of war. He sent in his first ship-movement report of the month when it was normally due, on Monday, October 6, and followed it up with another on the 10th.

On the 13th he found time to go on a three-day excursion to Hawaii, the largest island of the group, whose four thousand square miles are filled with an endless variety of tropical beaches and lush jungle growth, ginger-bordered highways and enormous lava vastes—much to attract a carefree tourist but little, it would seem, to interest a spy.

His trip to the island was an illustration of the skill with which Yoshikawa masked his business behind his pleasures. Although there were a number of good Japanese hotels on the island, he stayed at the Naniloa in Hilo, a new and expensive hotel catering to the tourist trade. He visited the Volcano Photo Shop at Kilauea, but only to buy picture post cards of the volcano in eruption and of the *lehua*, the native flower of the Island.

He visited only such innocuous places as the immense Parker Ranch at Kawaihae to watch the cattle swimming out to the ships, the county fair at the Hilo high school, the Akaka and Rainbow falls, the Puumaile hospital for tubercular patients, and the golf course at the country club.

He spent his evenings watching movies in the company of two pretty Nisei girls and participating in wild drinking parties at the Kona Inn, staying up until four o'clock every morning.

But at the end of the journey, he had what he had come to get in the first place: a good mental picture of the Hilo harbor and information about a new airport under construction at the Kapu Military Reservation and about an old airstrip at Upolu Point. He had gone to the Kilauea Volcano, apparently because he was interested in its craters, but actually for a good view of the nearby camp of the Hawaii National Guard. On October 20, back in Honolulu, he skipped his weekly fleet-movement report and mailed one instead in which he described his findings on the trip.

Three days later the liner *Tatsuta Maru* arrived in Honolulu with two visitors from Japan who went straight to the consulate.

One was a Foreign Ministry official traveling on a diplomatic passport made out to "Inspector Kuniaki Maeda." The other was Seiichi Tsuchiya, the regular courier of the Foreign Ministry, bringing the pouch.

The man with the diplomatic passport was neither a diplomat nor was his real name Maeda. He was, in fact, Lieutenant Commander Minato Nakajima, from the America Section of the Third Bureau, stopping in Honolulu (before going on to the West Coast) to liquidate the "outside system" of secret agents who were still at large. In Honolulu (where he spent only a day) he passed word to the spurious chemist at the *sake* brewery to wind up his affairs at once, see to it that the other "outsiders" did the same, and depart for Tokyo on the *Taiyo Maru*, due in Honolulu on November 1.

The pouch Tsuchiya had brought contained a little canvas bag of the Yokohama Specie Bank with 140 crisp new $100 bills in it; a sealed envelope addressed to "Friedel"; and instructions for Kita to deliver both envelopes to Otto Kühn, the dormant agent at Kalama who was supposed to become active only in what Ogawa had called "the ultimate emergency." *

Kita immediately made arrangements to have the money and the sealed envelope turned over to Kühn. Since a substantial sum was involved, he was reluctant to entrust it to Yoshikawa alone. Instead he decided to send it by a three-man delegation consisting of Okuda, Yoshikawa and Kotoshirodo. Delivery was to be made on Saturday, October 28, when the trip to Kühn could be camouflaged as an outing to one of the popular beaches of Kaneohe Bay.

For a few hours on this pleasant weekend afternoon Captain Ogawa's entire "inside system" in Hawaii emerged from its clandestine existence as Yoshikawa, accompanied by Okuda and Kotoshirodo, now converged on Kühn at his home. Two members of the group figured prominently on the suspect lists—Kühn since July 1940, Okuda since December 1940. Had they been under surveillance, this strange encounter could have been observed, and Yoshikawa and Kotoshirodo would also have been exposed as spies. But this was a weekend when vigilance was relaxed, just as Kita expected it would.

* Commander Nakajima was taking a similar envelope to Los Angeles, for one William L. Rutland, another "sleeper spy" Ogawa had under contract.

The trip to Kühn was the only truly melodramatic episode in Yoshikawa's whole career as a Pearl Harbor spy. He left the consulate with Okuda in Kotoshirodo's car at half past three in the afternoon; they were dressed in white slacks and *aloha* shirts for the "outing."

Okuda, who was keenly conscious of the potential perils of the venture and apprehensive about his own participation in it, was "very nervous" throughout the trip. He did not tell Kotoshirodo where they were going but merely instructed him to "keep on driving." Kotoshirodo took them up the Nuuanu Pali. When they reached the Kailua Tavern, Okuda told Kotoshirodo to drive on toward the ocean and stop at the second intersection. Yoshikawa got out there. Okuda handed the canvas bag and the envelope to Yoshikawa, and instructed Kotoshirodo to drive him down to the junction of Kalama Road and wait there.

It was now four o'clock. Yoshikawa walked half a mile to Kühn's house, where he found young Eberhard out in front puttering with his bicycle. Kühn was in the back working in his garden. He came out front to meet his unexpected caller.

"Are you Otto Kühn?" Yoshikawa asked "very brusquely."

"Yes," Kühn said. He was noticeably alarmed. He knew Yoshikawa as Morimura and did not like the idea of anybody connected with the consulate calling on him at his home.

"I have something for you from Dr. Homberg," Yoshikawa said. This was the password. "Dr. Homberg" was the German in Tokyo in whose name the *joho kyoku* was forwarding funds to Kühn.*

Kühn took Yoshikawa back to his little garden shed, where the ensign gave him the bag and the envelope. Kühn opened the envelope first and pulled out an unsigned letter typewritten in English on a single sheet of paper. "The letter asked me," Kühn later recalled, "to make a test with my short-wave transmitter at a certain time which was on a night several nights later, on a certain wave length." **

Yoshikawa then handed him a blank sheet of paper and an envelope, and Kühn, who was becoming increasingly jittery,

* In September 1940, $10,000 had been delivered to Kühn from "Dr. Homberg" by a man named Kai, the purser of the *Kamakura Maru*, another NYK liner. Kai served as an occasional courier for the Third Bureau.
** The call letter Kühn was supposed to use was EXEX, the frequency 11980. He was to contact Station JHP, at 0100 Pacific Standard Time on November 3, and 0530 P.S.T. on November 5.

scribbled a brief reply that he would be unable to make the test. "I was quite nervous," Kühn later said, "and put the note in the envelope and gave it to him. I asked him if he knew what was in the package and he said no. I asked him if he wanted a receipt for the package and he said no. When he left, I opened the package and counted the money. . . . I think," Kühn hedged (understandably, for he was talking to the FBI after the outbreak of the war), "that this was a contact the *joho kyoku* was trying to make with me through this letter." But of course it was much more than a contact. Otto Kühn had just been "activated."

Ogawa's message gave Kühn the shock of his life. When he had last seen the captain during his stopover in Honolulu in the late fall of 1940, Kühn boasted that he had assembled a powerful short-wave transmitter "for direct communications with Japan in an emergency." He had also outlined to Ogawa an intricate number code he had designed to conceal ship-movement information, as well as a scheme for the transmission of this intelligence. He proposed to signal Japanese ships in the Kawai Channel by lights in the dormer windows of his house at Kamala; by hanging out linen on the clothes line of his Lanikai beach house; by changing the position of the star and the number on the sail of his boat; by buying time on Station KGMB for want ads which would be coded messages; and in case everything else failed, by burning garbage "in certain localities at certain hours."

His plan had made a lasting impression on Ogawa. The captain was now ordering Kühn to develop his code and signal systems in explicit detail, and submit them "as soon as possible" to Tokyo via the consulate. He also assigned him a new cover name—"Jimmie"—to replace "Friedel," and instructed him to rent a box at the Honolulu post office to which the consulate could send mail for him.

Kühn already had a box—No. 1476—at the main post office in the city. He also had his house at Kalama, and plenty of garbage to burn. But otherwise, Ogawa's instructions proved most awkward. He had treated Ogawa to a pack of lies. He had neither a short-wave set nor a sailboat. Moreover, hard up as he was for cash, he had just rented his beach house at Lanikai to a couple of Army lieutenants attached to Schofield Hospital.

However, Kühn had to do as he was told. He went to work at

once to compile a complicated code and devise a system of signals based on his Kalama house, the want-ad program and the garbage cans. The dispatch in which his scheme was later submitted to Tokyo for Ogawa's approval could have become the conclusive warning sign to alert Washington. It became, as we shall see, just another clue that was missed.

At nine o'clock in the morning on November 1 the *Taiyo Maru* docked at Pier 8 in Honolulu Harbor. This voyage reflected the deepening crisis. Since all Japanese shipping to America had been suspended, the *Taiyo Maru* had been especially chartered to make the trip so that people who had been stranded in Japan or in Hawaii could go home under the gathering war clouds.

A little army of immigration and customs officials greeted the passengers instead of the usual hula troops and carnival atmosphere. Mingling among them were all of Colonel Bicknell's Contact agents and Shivers' G-men. Passports and baggage were thoroughly inspected, but no suspicious persons were found among the passengers, and no papers of any importance from the standpoint of national security were discovered in the suitcases.

And yet, the *Taiyo Maru* was on a crucial secret mission. Disguised as stewards in her crew were two young men whose presence on the trip made this a momentous voyage—nothing less than a test cruise to chart the course of Admiral Yamamoto's striking force to Hawaiian waters. One of them was Suguru Suzuki, the youngest lieutenant commander in the Imperial Navy, now serving on the staff of Admiral Chuichi Nagumo's air fleet getting ready for "Operation Z." The other was Lieutenant Commander Toshihide Maejima, staff officer of Vice-Admiral Gunichi Mikawa's support force of battleships, cruisers and submarines.

On instructions from the Naval General Staff, the *Taiyo Maru* had altered her regular course outward bound and taken a northern route, crossing over between Midway and the Aleutians, then cutting south to Honolulu. Suzuki and Maejima had been assigned to check the winds and atmospheric pressures during the crossing, observe how the liner behaved in heavy weather, and record how many ships they encountered. Not a single one was sighted during the entire voyage.

On November 2, when the crew was allowed to go ashore,

Suzuki drove to the consulate compound and demanded to be taken to Kita, who had been alerted to his arrival in a telegram from Ogawa on October 19. Closeted with the consul general, he revealed his identity and told Kita that "the day is rapidly approaching." He asked him in Captain Ogawa's name to instruct Ensign Yoshikawa to intensify his surveillance of Pearl Harbor.

During the meeting Suzuki gave Kita a ball of crumpled rice paper. It was a list with ninety-seven specific questions about the defenses of Pearl Harbor. When Suzuki had left, Kita called in Yoshikawa and passed the list to him. That same day Kita boarded the *Taiyo Maru*, going in his official capacity as consul general and pretending to supervise the repatriation cases. He sought out Suzuki and handed him Yoshikawa's answers to most of the questions, including the one that topped the list:

"This is the most important question: On what day of the week would the most ships be in Pearl Harbor on normal occasions?"

"Sunday" was Yoshikawa's reply.

He also smuggled a package to Suzuki containing a collection of intelligence documents which Yoshikawa had assembled—sketches, a map he had drawn of Pearl Harbor with the berthing plan and another on which he had marked the airfields on Oahu, with a special report describing the structural details of the hangars at Hickam and Wheeler fields. Included in the package was a set of aerial photographs—the only such pictures Yoshikawa had taken with his little "prop" camera during his mission. He had made them only twelve days before, on October 21, on a flight in a small plane he had chartered at John Rodgers.

"We knew then," he later wrote, "that things were building to a climax and that my work was almost done."

The ship was held in Honolulu for five days to give the American authorities ample time to make a thorough inspection of the departing passengers. Suzuki and Maejima used the long stopover to advantage. From information they picked up by interviewing certain visitors, they corroborated Okuda's previous intelligence that the Pacific Fleet was no longer using the Lahaina Anchorage as an assembly point. They picked up some additional data about the hangars at Hickam and Wheeler, and purchased picture post cards of Oahu and Pearl Harbor.

In one of the gift shops in downtown Honolulu they discovered a Laporello set of post cards showing a panoramic view of Pearl Harbor from the air. It sold for one dollar a set, and Suzuki purchased several sets. (Less then five weeks later, photo copies of the set were in the cockpits of the Japanese planes attacking Pearl Harbor. The panorama of the harbor was divided into numbered squares. Each bombardier knew which square was his target and what ships he would find there.)

From seven in the morning until seven in the evening each day on November 3, 4 and 5, the departing passengers—238 alien Japanese and 210 AJA's (Americans of Japanese ancestry)—were questioned, their baggage searched, their papers and funds checked. The painstaking inspection uncovered a number of items Colonel Bicknell regarded as sufficiently quaint or interesting to warrant mention in his report to Washington about "Operation *Taiyo Maru*." For instance, the diary of young Shoyei Komiya showed that he was planning to join the Imperial Army as soon as he reached Japan. The Reverend Katsuto Takumyo, a Buddhist priest, was discovered concealing a collection of obscene pictures in his battered suitcase. But none of the departing agents of Ogawa's "outside system" was exposed during the search; neither were "stewards" Suzuki and Maejima.

Finally, at seven-thirty on November 5, with Suzuki and Maejima on board, the *Taiyo Maru* sailed from Honolulu. "As soon as the final inspection was finished," Colonel Bicknell wrote in his report, "the people were taken aboard and were not allowed to come ashore. Hence, customary good-byes were exchanged out in the street and in the park in front of the pier hours before the actual sailing of the ship.

"The Royal Hawaiian Band played 'Aloha' at least three hours before the ship sailed. In other words, all the color and gaiety of the past was missing when the *Taiyo Maru* actually slid away from the pier."

"I May Make War"— A Secret Alliance

"Magic" was mentioned only once, and then merely in passing, in Winston S. Churchill's six-volume memoirs of World War II. On page 504 of *The Grand Alliance*, in which he managed to do justice to 349 years of Japanese history in a single chapter, he wrote:

"From the end of 1940 the Americans had pierced the vital Japanese ciphers, and were decoding large numbers of their military and diplomatic telegrams. In the secret American circles these were referred to as 'Magics.' The 'Magics' were repeated to us, but there was an inevitable delay—sometimes of two or three days—before we got them. We did not know therefore at any given moment all that the President or Mr. Hull knew. I make no complaint of this."

This was no magnanimity on Mr. Churchill's part. He did not have the slightest reason to complain. The British were, in fact, reading the Japanese dispatches as promptly and fully as the Americans did, simply because the Americans had given them the machines and all the cryptographic paraphernalia needed to read them.

This was part of a secret arrangement President Roosevelt had made on his own—quite properly and wisely, one must add—to broaden his sources of information when knowledge of Japan's intentions and plans became essential to guide him in his policies and decisions.

The British, of course, had an even greater stake in the areas threatened by Japan. These contained some of the major bastions and treasure chests of their beleaguered empire. Yet Mr. Churchill decided to remain the minor and, most of the time, silent partner in the guardianship of the strategic area, leaving the solution of the thorny problem to the wisdom of Mr. Roosevelt and the skill of American diplomacy.

To be sure, he had his doubts about both. But there was little else he could do. "Our major interest is: no further encroachments and no war, as we have already enough of this latter," he wrote to his Foreign Secretary during this fateful autumn.

The question of what to do with Japan was high on the agenda of the Atlantic Conference the Prime Minister and the President had held in August on board their warships anchored in Placentia Bay. Churchill had risked the perilous crossing to Newfoundland in bold spirit and with high hopes. Though he did not dare to put it directly to Roosevelt, he told his circle, hoping that it would be repeated to the President: "I would rather have an American declaration of war now and no supplies for six months than double the supplies and no declaration of war."

When the statement was indeed repeated, Mr. Roosevelt thought it was "a hard saying." But he told the Prime Minister: "I may never declare war; I may make war."

It was a startling statement for an American President to make, but essentially it was vague and tantalizing. Nevertheless Churchill subsisted on it. He wanted the United States in the war, and wanted it very badly. But he knew that "the wretched Hitler" (who had nothing but contempt for the United States and loathed Roosevelt even more than he despised Churchill) did not desire a head-on clash with the Americans, and that the United States would not be drawn into the European war except by an act of God or a folly of the Führer.

But there was another avenue to intervention in Europe—a detour to war via Japan. "I confess," Churchill wrote, "that in my mind the whole Japanese menace lay in a sinister twilight, compared with our other needs." He felt that if Japan attacked any part of the British Empire, one of two things might happen: America would either go to war or still remain aloof. "If the United States did not come in," he wrote, "we had no means of defending the Dutch East Indies, or indeed our own Empire in the East. If, on the other hand, Japanese aggression drew in America I would be content to have it. On this I rested."

But he did not rest on that. He promoted a long series of staff conferences, first with the Dutch, and then, from December 1940 on, also with the Americans.

The British-Dutch talks concluded that "the only practicable form of cooperation was a scheme for mutual assistance and combined operations." The two staffs proceeded promptly to implement the "scheme." Agreement was reached in these talks to draw the geographical bounds of Japanese aggression: "The crossing of a line such as the parallel of 6° north between Malaya and Borneo by a formation of Japanese warships, or a convoy of merchant ships escorted by warships, should be deemed an act of war."

The British and American staff conversations produced "a joint basic war plan," known as ABC-1. It re-emphasized that the defeat of Germany was the primary strategic objective, and set forth that the United States would increase its naval forces in the Atlantic and Mediterranean so that major elements of the British fleet could be released for Asian waters to guard them against the Japanese.

But the United States neither accepted an obligation to enter the war nor even specified any of the circumstances under which it might do so. In April 1941 the British sought American co-operation in a plan prepared with the Dutch—the so-called ADB Agreement—providing for combined operations in the Far East in the event of war. An American mission was present at the ADB Conference. But the United States refused to adopt its resolutions.

Efforts were then made to persuade the United States to join Britain and the Netherlands East Indies in a mere declaration that "the British Commonwealth, the Netherlands East Indies, and the United States had prepared a combined strategic plan with which to meet any act of open Japanese aggression." Churchill expected much from the deterrent effect of such a statement, but no amount of eloquent pleading or indeed pressure succeeded in obtaining American participation in the declaration. Washington held that it would be incompatible with the Japanese-American negotiations.

While military co-operation in the Far East was thus thwarted, mainly by the opposition of the American naval high command, close ties had been forged in great secrecy in two extremely sensitive areas under direct presidential jurisdiction. The United States had agreed to share its vast store of cryptological information and equipment with the British. And a channel of intelligence had been opened up—a kind of early hot line—directly between President Roosevelt and Prime Minister Churchill.

The origins of this secret alliance went back to the uncertain summer of 1940, following France's collapse. On July 8 Lord Lothian, the British ambassador in Washington, told Mr. Roosevelt that His Majesty's Government "would greatly appreciate it" if the United States, given "the full details of any [British] equipment or devices . . . would reciprocate by discussing certain secret information of a technical nature which [the British] are anxious to have urgently."

This was to be an enormously confidential arrangement. "Should you approve the exchange of information," Lothian wrote to the President, "it has been suggested by my government that, in order to avoid any risk of the information reaching our enemy, a small secret British mission consisting of two or three service officers and civilian scientists should be despatched immediately to this country to enter into discussions with [American] Army and Navy experts."

There was some bitter and occasionally rancorous opposition to the exchange both in Britain and the United States. Intoxicated by their successes in what Mr. Churchill had called "the wizards' war," British scientists and electronic ordnance experts thought that this would be an uneven barter in which England had too much and the United States too little to offer.

Some on the American side, suspicious of Britons bearing gifts and wary of what they regarded as an "encroachment upon our secrets," lobbied vigorously against the proposal, arguing that an exchange of such technical information would mean a "surrender of national advantage." A memorandum prepared on July 19 in the War Plans Division for the Chief of Staff asserted that the whole proposal was inspired by the British desire to get "full information in regard to our airplane detector, which apparently is very much more efficient than anything the British have."

Impressed by these arguments, even General Marshall and Admiral Stark held back their concurrence. But the air was, as

Dulany Terret put it, electric with peril. The President overrode all objections, approved the plan, and issued orders to make the exchange comprehensive, wholehearted and prompt.*

A British mission, headed by Sir Henry Tizard, adviser to the Ministry of Aircraft Production, came to the United States in the fall to arrange for the exchange of radar and all kinds of airborne interception equipment, RCM (radar countermeasures), sonar, gunnery and certain explosives.

In September Major General George V. Strong was in London as General Marshall's representative to study the military intelligence organization with a view toward revamping G-2 on the British pattern. In his excitement over the recent triumph of the American cryptologists, he revealed at the War Office that the United States had broken the major Japanese diplomatic code and succeeded in reconstructing its machine. In October Vice-Admiral Robert L. Ghormley, who represented Admiral Stark in London, told Admiral John H. Godfrey, the director of British Naval Intelligence, about PURPLE.

Before long, upon instructions from Whitehall, Sir Henry Tizard asked the President to include cryptological data and equipment in the technical exchange program. The request was met with vehement opposition, especially in the United States Navy. The "working echelons"—those around Safford in Op-20-G, that is—were, as one of them put it, "absolutely stunned by the British proposition." And Captain Leigh Noyes, the Director of Naval Communications, adamantly refused to approve the exchange.

Noyes, fresh from the *Saratoga* (where he had been chief of staff and aide to the air commander of the Pacific Fleet's battle force), had found the mystery-shrouded "Magic" among his baffling new responsibilities, and became overawed by its oppressive security features. Afraid of a possible leak, he was inclined to exaggerate these aspects of the operation, and introduced measures which were even more stringent than those originally devised by General Marshall. Under his policy, nobody in Naval Communi-

---

* "Both sides had more to learn about the other than they realized," Terret wrote in the official history of the Signal Corps. "The truth was that probably neither would have brought electronics to the maturity it quickly reached had they not got together. And had electronics lagged . . . the effect upon the war would have been grave."

cations was supposed "to tell anyone else anything, anywhere, at any time." Exchange of data was to be held to a minimum within the Navy and even in Op-20-G's relations with the Signal Intelligence Service. He was therefore mortified and scandalized when told that he would have to disclose *everything* to the British, including secrets he would not share even with the Army. With the support of Rear Admiral Walter S. Anderson, the Director of Naval Intelligence, he undertook a somewhat insiduous campaign against the proposed exchange.

But Noyes and Anderson were overruled rather curtly by the President. Emphatic orders came down from the White House to deliver to the British everything Op-20-G and SIS had accumulated in two decades of code-cracking, in exchange for British information about the German and Italian crypto-systems, as well as radio direction finders.

The ruffled feelings were soothed when it developed that the United States would profit considerably from such an exchange. The British had several working models of the Enigma, the German cipher machine—one captured in North Africa, another salvaged from a surrendered U-boat, and a third the Commandos had brought back from a raid on Lofoten, an island group in the Norwegian Sea. The Americans also hoped to obtain the German so-called Contact Report Code used by the U-boats in tracking down the transatlantic convoys, and other cryptological information believed to be substantial.

A written agreement was signed in late November 1940, providing for "a full exchange of cryptographic systems, cryptanalytical techniques, direction finding, radio interception and other technical communication matters pertaining to the diplomatic, military, naval and air services of Germany, Japan and Italy." Colonel Friedman was chosen to head a joint Army-Navy mission that would take all the paraphernalia to England, but just before his scheduled departure he suffered his breakdown. In his place went a four-man delegation of younger officers: Major Abraham Sinkow and Captain Leo Rosen, representing the Army Signal Corps, and Lieutenant Robert H. Weeks and Ensign Prescott H. Currier, on behalf of Naval Communications.

They took along two PURPLE machines with keys (plus the three-letter code and techniques of solution), two RED machines with keys and techniques, two j-series consular codes and keys, and two sets of the minor diplomatic systems. Also going in duplicate were the JN (FLEET) codes, merchant-ship codes, naval attaché ciphers, radio call signal lists, German consular codes (from the FBI), the radio intelligence manuals of the U.S. Navy, an American manual on Japanese communications systems, the Intercept Operators Training Course, and whatever work the Americans were doing on German and Italian systems.*

The Admiralty immediately sent one each of its PURPLE and RED machines to Singapore, as well as other American equipment. Close and friendly co-operation ensued, and henceforth the British made a material contribution to the "Magic" operation.

As a result of the exchange, Britain had the opportunity to know as much as the United States of the secret background of the crisis, not only because they were now reading the Japanese dispatches, but because they had also cracked the American codes, and had thus gained an insight into the policies and maneuvers of the Roosevelt Administration.

The Singapore intercepts were used locally and in co-operation with the American establishment at Cavite which was operating both the PURPLE and RED machines. However, translations of the Japanese dispatches prepared in London by the Admiralty's cryptologists poured daily into Whitehall and were in Mr. Churchill's hands for keeps—a better arrangement, as we shall see, than even Mr. Roosevelt had for the "magics."

At the same time, intercepts of the decoded American dispatches were rushed to the Prime Minister from Blandford in Blenchley Park, a secluded spot near London, where the Admiralty and the Foreign Office had their cryptographic branch under Captain Edward Hastings. The intelligence culled from this mate-

---

* The exchange did not work out as well as the Americans had hoped. The Sinkow mission, coming home in reduced style in a battered destroyer rather than on the *Queen Mary*, returned with the Admiralty's Marconi-Acock high-frequency direction finder, which was superior to anything the United States Navy had, and other valuable crypto-equipment. But the Enigma was not included, nor as yet the coveted contact report code. The delivery of the German machine and the U-boat code had been vetoed by the Foreign Office at Lord Halifax's direction, on the ground that it had supervisory powers over all intelligence and cryptological matters. The Foreign Office explained that it was contrary to British policy to surrender any of Britain's cryptological secrets under any circumstances, to anyone.

rial was cabled to several British outposts involved in the crisis, and especially to a mysterious British agent in New York, to guide him in his manipulation of the American government.

The man the British chose in June 1940 for the job of passport control officer in New York had little experience with passport control, except perhaps his own well-worn travel document. The newcomer was William Stephenson, a Canadian fighter pilot in World War I who had become a millionaire industrialist before he was thirty years old, through his invention of the device for transmitting photographs by wireless.

He had been recruited for the P.C.O. job in New York by Mr. Churchill himself. "Your duty lies there," the P.M. told him. "You must go!"

Obviously Stephenson was not expected to spend his time controlling passports. But "Little Bill," as the diminutive Canadian was called by his many friends, had to be "processed" for his new job by M.I.6, the vastly enlarged British secret intelligence service. And the only slot Colonel Stewart Menzies, Britain's top-ranking spy master in World War II, had available for him in the intelligence bureaucracy was in the bogus passport control office in New York.

Stephenson moved briskly into the stuffy single room reserved for the P.C.O. on the premises of the British consul general at 25 Broadway in New York, determined to burst the walls of his tiny office and make his mark in secret intelligence. Very soon he blossomed out as director of a new agency called British Security Co-ordination, set up to bring all British espionage and sabotage operations in the Western Hemisphere under his command. He moved uptown, into a suite of offices on the thirty-sixth floor at 630 Fifth Avenue, in Rockefeller Center, where a new Japanese consul general, Morito Morishima, also had established himself upon his recent arrival in New York.

Stephenson had come on a momentous mission that was similar to the assignment of the banker Sir William Wiseman in 1917. It had been imperative then, as it was in 1941, for the survival of Britain, to pull or push the United States into the war on England's side. It had been accomplished by Wiseman twenty-four years before, with the help of Admiral Reginald Hall, whose O.B.

40, the Admiralty's cryptanalytical establishment, produced the "Zimmerman telegram" that persuaded the America of Woodrow Wilson to join Britain in the war against Germany.*

Churchill's instructions to Stephenson were explicit: to get as much in aid from America as possible and to "bring them in." He went to work with his characteristic élan, on an impressive scale. He lined up allies wherever he could—in the highest American circles, among the fence sitters, in the offices of influential columnists, but also inside the Washington missions of His Majesty's actual and potential enemies.

In order to gain his ultimate goal, he had to establish a direct line to the President. He therefore enlisted the aid of a remarkable American who was very much like himself—a successful self-made man with a lively imagination and an adventurous turn of mind. Stephenson's new friend was the ebullient New York lawyer William Joseph Donovan, a Reserve colonel on the retired list and a Republican politician, but with excellent standing in the Democratic Administration.

It was one of "Little Bill's" master strokes to pick Donovan for the job of selling the idea of an Anglo-American spy alliance to the President. Sticking his neck out and paying his own expenses as he went, the venturesome, romantic "Wild Bill," as Donovan was familiarly called from his fast-football-playing days at Columbia University and wartime heroism in France, had carried out several secret missions for Secretary Knox. He had won the President's admiration for his skill in accomplishing what the professional American intelligence officers apparently could not—getting reliable secret intelligence about the Germans and creating trouble in the Balkans and the Middle East through his adroit "special operations." Stephenson described his friend's qualifications to his superiors in London:

"Donovan exercises controlling influences over Knox, strong influence over Stimson, friendly advisory influence over President and Hull. There is no doubt that we can achieve infinitely more

---

* Herr Zimmerman was the Kaiser's Foreign Minister in 1917. The telegram contained a proposal to Mexico (cabled via the German ambassador in the United States and intercepted by Hall's bureau) "to enter the war on the German side, and to persuade Japan to leave the Allies and join in an attack on the United States, which would recover Mexico's lost lands."

through Donovan than through any other individual . . . He is very receptive and should be made fully aware of our requirements and deficiencies and can be trusted to represent our needs in the right quarters and in the right way in the U.S.A."

The idea of the "marriage" of the British and American secret services was broached to the President through "Wild Bill," and Mr. Roosevelt readily agreed because, as he told Donovan, "We have no intelligence service!" The link was established along two avenues. As far as counterespionage was concerned, Stephenson was to work with J. Edgar Hoover's Federal Bureau of Investigation. Positive intelligence was to be handled on the very highest echelons, on a direct line between Roosevelt and Churchill. Stephenson and Donovan were chosen to serve as their go-betweens, handling the lines of communications and processing the top-secret intelligence for them.

The arrangement was to be kept the personal secret of these men. Not even Mr. Hull at the State Department or Anthony Eden, the Foreign Secretary, were to find out about it. Under the circumstances it is not improper to say that President Roosevelt had become Stephenson's foremost American undercover contact. So carefully shrouded was this connection that the President used his son James, then serving as one of his aides in the White House, as the courier for his personal communications with Churchill via Stephenson.

But this was a two-way street. Mr. Roosevelt was not only Stephenson's "hottest" source but also the beneficiary of his phenomenal intelligence service. Stephenson saw to it that a steady stream of intelligence flowed to the President's desk. It was of the highest quality, even though some of it was flavored by "Little Bill's" too fertile imagination and unbridled enthusiasm for the British cause.

Stephenson was, of course, primarily interested in the Germans in the Western Hemisphere, but he extended his coverage to the Japanese, in a *quid pro quo*. He was eager to furnish intelligence of acute interest to the President in exchange for the information and help he expected to receive in turn from the White House. He was neither inhibited by qualms of his own nor restricted by American laws governing civil rights or privacy, not even by international covenants guaranteeing diplomatic immunity. With the help of a stable of intrepid secret agents he infiltrated offices and homes, stealing confidential documents, intercepting mail, collecting and disseminating derogatory information about Americans whose sympathies for Britain were less ardent than Stephenson would have liked. These agents also penetrated the diplomatic missions of Germany, Italy, Spain and Vichy-France, removing code books and classified papers. On another line, Stephenson established contacts inside the Japanese embassy in Washington, and in the consulates general in New York and San Francisco.

He scored his first coup over the Japanese in July, barely a month after he had set up shop in New York. A British agent in Buenos Aires had reported that the Japanese were about to reorganize their secret service in the Western Hemisphere. While previously Washington was the center for these activities, now Buenos Aires was to replace it. The prospect of conflict with the United States made this necessary, for an America-based espionage network would automatically collapse in the event of war.

The chief of the Washington organization was identified. He was a certain Hirasawa, carried in the diplomatic *Blue Book* as a secretary at the Washington embassy. According to the report from Buenos Aires, a request for Hirasawa's accreditation had been received by the Argentine Foreign Ministry, and the man himself was expected in Buenos Aires momentarily. In Washington, Hirasawa would be replaced by First Secretary Hidenari Terasaki, who was married to an American woman, had excellent connections in New York and Washington, and was well liked in the State Department.

This was important news and Stephenson decided to make the most of it. His contacts in the Japanese embassy advised him that Hirasawa would depart for Buenos Aires in late July. Arrangements were then made to intercept the man when his ship called at Barbados. On Stephenson's instructions Hirasawa, his wife and their party were removed from the ship and flown to Trinidad, where a "reception committee" sent from New York was awaiting them. He was thoroughly interrogated, even photographed and fingerprinted. A search of his belongings produced considerable evidence that Hirasawa was, indeed, a secret agent. In double-bottom suitcases he was carrying maps on which British and

American naval bases had been marked. He also had with him publications of intelligence value and $40,000 in cash ($15,000 of which was sewn into Mme. Hirasawa's handbag).

Considerable intelligence was produced by this coup. Above all else, Hirasawa's transfer and the information his interrogation had produced convinced Stephenson firmly that "the militarists in Tokyo were bent upon war." He intensified his coverage of the Japanese in the United States. By November this British outpost, freebooting in America, had better contacts inside the Japanese embassy than any of the American intelligence agencies. Stephenson was getting information which, if it was not actually superior to the intelligence we were gaining from the "magics," certainly supplemented and broadened it.

Shortly before midnight on November 3, Maxwell Hamilton, chief of the State Department's Far Eastern Division, was awakened by the persistent ringing of the telephone in his bedroom. It was Counselor Eugene Dooman of the American embassy calling from Tokyo with word that the Japanese government had decided to send "a person to the United States . . . to co-operate with Ambassador Nomura in connection with the current conversation.

"They wish," Dooman said, "to send Saburo Kurusu."

Both the decision and the choice of the emissary astonished Hamilton. Kurusu had been Japanese ambassador in Germany at the time of the conclusion of the Tripartite Pact—in fact, it was he who had signed it on behalf of Japan. Why would he now be sent to the United States? True, Nomura seemed to need help. He was becoming increasingly confused and desperate. Only a few days before, "Magic" had produced a telegram of his which showed that the admiral was losing his nerve. In it he begged Shigenori Togo, Foreign Minister in the new Tojo Cabinet, to permit him to return to Japan, for he could no longer bear up under the strain of "all this deception." But was Kurusu the right man to replace him or to bolster him in negotiations aimed at a rapprochement?

Anyway, he was coming. Dooman advised Hamilton to expedite Kurusu's trip, quoting what Togo had told him earlier in the afternoon: "Delay in bringing the conversations to a speedy and satisfactory conclusion will only aggravate the situation which is already tense. Please accept this as though it were a message communicated by [me] to Mr. Hull in person."

Arrangements were made for Kurusu to board the China Clipper in Hong Kong in the morning of November 5, fly to Saipan in the Marianas, proceed to Guam in a Japanese destroyer and transfer to the Clipper for San Francisco by way of Hawaii. He arrived in Honolulu at four thirty-five on November 12, getting a good view of the warships in the harbor as the Clipper came down at the Pearl City Landing. He spent all of the next day with Consul General Kita at the consulate, then left at three o'clock on November 13, arriving in Washington two days later.

Kurusu was accompanied on his mission to Washington by a young diplomatist named Shiroji Yuki. In the Foreign Ministry since 1927, Yuki had been made chief of the United States Section of the Bureau of American Affairs in December 1940. On November 1, 1941, he was named senior secretary and chosen to accompany Ambassador Kurusu on his mission to Washington. His job would be to manage the general business of the negotiations. As Yuki himself later put it, he had intimate knowledge of all that was going on during the Japanese-American talks in their terminal stage.

Stephenson was keenly interested in the Kurusu mission because he had misgivings about their true purpose. He sensed, in fact, that Kurusu was being sent to Washington either to "try to push the United States into accepting Japan's overlordship in the Orient" or, if and when that failed, to "lull the Americans into a false sense of security with peace talks until her military masters were ready to strike." He immediately made arrangements to penetrate the Kurusu mission with one of his own agents who, thanks to Yuki's presence in Washington, seemed to be eminently qualified for the job. The "agent" was a distinguished British scholar who had spent fifty years in Japan, and who had taught at Tokyo University, where Yuki was one of his students.

The scholar made contact with the young diplomatist and Yuki gladly accepted an invitation to a reunion with his old teacher. Several meetings then took place in the presumed privacy of a Washington apartment which, however, Stephenson had had wired for sound. At these genial meetings the Englishman assured

Yuki of his enduring "love for the Japanese" and suggested that he could use his influence with Ambassador Lord Halifax—and through him, with the British government—to "prevail upon the United States to appease the Japanese war lords."

Yuki opened up completely. Presently he was telling his friend details of the talks and of the deteriorating situation; he even admitted in so many words that Japan was moving toward war. He also revealed information that Kurusu had brought to Washington, and other intelligence of acute importance that never showed up in the intercepts. Every bit of these conversations were recorded.

Each day, then, translated transcripts of the conversations were taken to President Roosevelt by Stephenson, who had moved to Washington for the duration of this crucial operation.

The transcripts furnished additional intelligence for Mr. Roosevelt and confirmation of information he was getting from the "magics." This source, as Stephenson phrased it, "supplemented the Japanese telegrams between Tokyo and Washington, which had been known to the American authorities for some time through the skill of the American cryptographers in breaking the Japanese codes and ciphers."

21 How the Japanese Fleet Was "Lost"

The Cabinet change in Japan was getting a bad press in America, and Ambassador Grew sent a long telegram to the Secretary of State to place the emergence of General Tojo as Japan's new strong man in what he called "accurate perspective."

"As . . . American radio broadcasts and reports of American press comment indicate," he wrote on October 20 in rather convoluted diplomatese, "that the Cabinet change is almost universally interpreted by the American public as an adjustment preliminary to attack by Japan on Russia or to some other drastic action which must inevitably lead to war between the United States and Japan, I submit certain considerations, some of which rest on fact and some on reasonable assumption, that suggest that the view which seems to have been taken by the public at home with regard to the significance of the Cabinet change may not be in accurate perspective."

Grew described Konoye's successor as a man "who would endeavor to follow the course laid down by the previous Cabinet toward adjusting relations with the United States and settlement of the China conflict." * As a matter of fact, this, too, was the

* In another long telegram, on November 3, Grew castigated the State Department for "misconceptions" in gauging Japan's dangerous mood, and warned that American inflexibility "might render unavoidable an armed conflict with the United States" that may come, as he phrased it, "with dangerous and dramatic suddenness." In recording this telegram in his diary, Grew voiced the hope that history would not overlook it. This is now widely

consensus of the State Department's own experts at home. William R. Langdon of the Far Eastern Division thus wrote in his estimate of Tojo and the Cabinet change: "It is believed that his designation as Premier signifies a continuation of Prince Konoye's policies including continuation of conversations with the United States."

Mr. Hamilton, the chief of the Division, concurred in Langdon's opinion with some qualification. "[Tojo's] appointment," he wrote, "does not rule out hostilities between Japan and Russia and/or the United States, but at the same time it would appear to indicate that the Japanese government may have in mind continued efforts towards a negotiated settlement with the United States and with Russia." How Tojo could make both peace and war "at the same time" Mr. Hamilton did not explain.

From Peking, President Stuart of Yenching University assured the State Department that "all Japan wishes is to end the China affair and from the Japanese point of view the Tojo Cabinet, like the Konoye Cabinet, is organized for peace rather than war."

Even as the experts labored on their oracular memoranda, signs multiplied that Japan under Tojo had abandoned all hope for a reconciliation with the United States and accepted war as inevitable. The new government in Tokyo was no longer seeking a way out of the awesome impasse but was engaged merely in preparing Japan's case for some posterior court. It was exhausting itself in the drafting of "final proposals" that could not possibly solve the problems but would make Japan's case "look good" before history.

"Magic" was scoring the crescendo of events against a background of pretense and hypocrisy. On October 23 an intercepted telegram from Nomura to Togo showed how badly negotiations had deteriorated and how patently pretextuous they had become. In what survives as one of the quaintest, most pathetic documents in diplomatic history, the hapless ambassador begged Togo to let him go out with the defunct Konoye Cabinet. He wrote:

---

regarded as a testimonial to the ambassador's prescience as contrasted by the "shortsightedness" of what he called "certain quarters" in Washington. In actual fact, it proves only that Mr. Grew's faith in the sincerity and good will of the Japanese statesmen remained steadfast, blaming, as he did, his colleagues in the State Department for the perilous turn the negotiations were taking.

"There are some Americans who trust this poor novice and say that things will get better for me, but, alas, their encouragement is no solace for me. Among my colleagues here there are those who profess compassion for me but, alas, they are but deluded souls. . . . I do not want to be the bones of a dead horse. I don't want to go on with this hypocrisy, deceiving other people. No, please do not think that I am trying to flee from the field of battle, but as a man of honor this is the only way that is left for me to tread. Kindly allow me to return to Japan. Most humbly do I beseech your forgiveness if I have injured your dignity and I prostrate myself before Your Excellency in the depth of my rudeness."

Saburo Kurusu was presumably sent to Washington to steady Nomura's frayed nerves and bring to the negotiations the savvy of the professional diplomat. In actual fact, his mission was but part of the subterfuge, and its ulterior purpose could not remain concealed from those who read the "magics." In a telegram intercepted and translated on November 5, Togo told Nomura that Ambassador Kurusu was being sent to Washington merely "to make a show of our Empire's sincerity"—to make Japan's case "sound good."

The Tojo clique had approved Kurusu's mission because it served their purpose. It enabled them to complete their preparations and deploy their forces while leaving the American government under the impression that a military confrontation in the Pacific could be delayed if not altogether averted.

The envoy's departure was accompanied by a shrewd campaign of deception, designed to divert attention from the Japanese-American crisis and lull the United States into a feeling of complacency. Agents in Japan and China planted "inside information" indicating that Japan was poised to "begin an offensive in eastern Siberia within two weeks," that the Japanese forces in Indochina were "not believed to be sufficiently strong to permit an immediate attack in any direction," and that "the logical objective" of a Japanese attack would be Yunnan in China.

Between October 21 and November 15 such "plants" reached Washington in a steady flow from Ambassador Clarence Gauss in Chungking, from Colonel William Meyer, his military attaché, and from President Stuart, who went so far as to write: "There never has been any serious threat of war between Japan and the United States."

On November 11 Counselor Richard P. Butrick of the American embassy in Chungking sent to Washington what purported to be the "secret agenda" of Kurusu's mission. According to Butrick, the envoy was taking the following program to the United States: "(1) Japan abandons Tripartite Pact; (2) Manchukuo for future discussion; (3) distribution Pacific spheres of influence; (4) Japan ceases political, military, but not [economic] southward expansion; (5) China returns to *status quo ante* prior China Incident." This piece of "intelligence" had been obtained by the Associated Press correspondent in China "from different, fairly reliable contacts."

At the same time, Toshi Tanaka, editor of the violently anti-American *Nichi-Nichi* newspaper, sought out the United Press correspondent in Tokyo and assured him that "Japan had no intention of going to war, being unable in the present situation even adequately to supply its troops." The Tanaka "plant" was promptly forwarded to Washington by Ambassador Grew.

All this was but the smoke screen behind which the Japanese advanced with growing momentum on two different tracks. Saburo Kurusu traveled on one of them; the Japanese war machine had begun to move on the other.

On October 5 about a hundred officer pilots, assembled on board the *Akagi* in Ariake Bay, were addressed by Admiral Yamamoto, who told them "under the seal of high secrecy" that they had been "chosen to destroy the American fleet at Hawaii on or about December 8." Two weeks later Yamamoto sailed in the *Nagato* to a meeting with Admiral Nagano and General Sugiyama, Chiefs of their respective General Staffs, to review the "final plan for war with the British, the Dutch and the Americans." *

After that, events moved faster. By November 1 Yamamoto was so certain that war with the West had become inevitable that he

---

* The plan provided for a five-pronged drive in three operational phases, the first phase to include "the attack on the American fleet at Hawaii" and "the seizure of the Philippines." The second phase would consolidate the conquests, and during the third phase "any forces attempting to penetrate the defensive ring . . . [would be] intercepted and destroyed."

ordered his "Top-Secret Operations Order No. 1" printed in seven hundred copies. "The Japanese Empire will declare war on the United States, Great Britain and The Netherlands," its opening part read. "War will be declared on X-Day. This order will become effective on Y-Day."

On November 5 an imperial conference was held in Tokyo. In a brief and muted session it approved two "proposals" containing Japan's "final terms," to be placed before the American government by Nomura and Kurusu. Not a single man at the conference expected these proposals to be acceptable to the Americans or the crisis to be resolved on Japanese terms. The actual purpose of the conference was to issue orders to the army and the navy "to be ready to fight in the beginning of December."

As soon as the conference broke up, Yamamoto had his "Operations Order No. 1" distributed to the Combined Fleet. It began with the sentence: "In the east the American fleet will be destroyed, and American lines of communications and supplies to the Orient will be cut." Then Yamamoto called in Commander Kanai Ota, a meteorologist attached to his staff, to discuss a tentative day for the Pearl Harbor attack. In setting the date, they had to consider the phase of the moon as well as the day of the week. Commander Ota suggested that Y-Day be December 10, "when the dark of the moon would fall."

But December 10 would be December 9 in Hawaii, a Tuesday. Yamamoto knew that the American fleet customarily returned from exercises on Fridays and left again on the following Mondays. It was unlikely that it would be in Pearl Harbor on a Tuesday.

Yamamoto chose the Sunday nearest to December 10. On November 7 he issued "Top-Secret Operations Order No. 2" to the Combined Fleet, setting the day of the attack tentatively as "December 8, 1941"—Sunday, December 7, in Hawaii.

On November 10 Admiral Chuichi Nagumo, commander of the striking force, issued his first order from his flagship, the *Akagi*, to the units chosen for the Pearl Harbor attack. He directed all ships in his force to "complete battle preparations by November 20" and to rendezvous in Hitokappu Bay at Etorofu Island in the Kuriles.

The next day Isoroku Yamamoto wrote a pensive, almost remorseful letter to his old friend Teikichi Hori, a retired admiral:

"My family I leave to your guidance while I am away." And further down he added: "What a strange position I find myself in now—having to make a decision diametrically opposed to my own personal opinion, with no choice but to push full speed in pursuance of that decision."

But on this same day Rear Admiral Matoi Ugaki, his chief of staff, gave the flag officers of the striking force an impassioned "explanation" of the operation. "A gigantic fleet . . . has massed at Pearl Harbor," he said. "This fleet will be utterly crushed with one blow at the very beginning of hostilities. . . . The success of our surprise attack on Pearl Harbor will prove to be the Waterloo of the war to follow." Then he bowed ceremoniously and said: "Heaven will bear witness to the righteousness of our struggle."

On November 15 General Sugiyama and Admiral Nagano went to the palace with their staffs and rehearsed the operations in the Imperial Presence. From his flagship, anchored in Saeki Bay on the eastern coast of Kyushu, Yamamoto watched the units of the Pearl Harbor striking force assembling. Five of the six carriers steamed in, one after another.* Then came the battleships *Hiei* and *Kirishima,* followed by the cruisers *Tone* and *Chikuma,* the nine destroyers of the screen, and the supply ships of the train. By November 16 the task force was assembled. At dawn on the next morning it sailed down Bungo Strait, and turning north just below Cape Ashizuri, vanished in the fog of the Pacific Ocean.

The units assigned to the Pearl Harbor attack now operated on Yamamoto's exact timetable. The advance expeditionary force of submarines sortied from Yokosuka and Kure on November 18 to 20. Its schedule called for arrival in Hawaiian waters on December 5 in pre-arranged scouting and patrolling sectors, one of which was only eight miles from the mouth of Pearl Harbor's entrance channel. The main striking force sailed north to the Kuriles, where Yamamoto hoped it could remain unobserved until its departure for Hawaii on November 26.

Secrecy was now of the essence. Elaborate measures were taken to make it ironclad. All ships of the "Z" forces had orders to maintain radio silence. But Yokosuka, Kure and Sasebo kept up a

---

* The *Akagi* was at the Yokosuka naval base awaiting delivery of the new torpedoes which the Ordnance Department of the Naval General Staff had built at Yamamoto's request for the attack in Pearl Harbor's shallow waters.

large volume of radio traffic to compensate for the sudden diminution of communications from Japanese home waters.

More important, the Japanese had begun to camouflage their fleets. Promptly at 0000 hours on November 1, all radio call signs of the forces afloat were changed. This was unusual. Service calls were normally revised only every six months, but this change occurred a whole month before the end of the current period. The Japanese sought to conceal the purport of the change by leaving shore-station calls, shore addresses and some of their tactical calls unaltered, and using their old garble tables, to give the impression that the revision amounted merely to a re-assignment of old calls. In the immediate wake of the change, moreover, they held traffic volume below normal to make it more difficult for American radio intelligence to "line up" the new calls.*

This was a severe blow to the American intelligence effort at this crucial juncture. Fleets are usually kept under surveillance either by so-called naval observers or by radio intelligence. In Japan, the United States Navy had only a tiny group of "fleet watchers," partly because the maintenance of observers on the scale which the surveillance of Yamamoto's mercurial fleet needed would have been too difficult and costly, but mainly because it was not deemed necessary. Communications intelligence had proved more than adequate to ascertain the missions and positions of Japanese fleets and ships.

For a long time the compromised FLAG OFFICERS code had supplied most of the intelligence the United States Navy needed about its Japanese adversary. In addition, a relatively well staffed and well endowed radio intelligence organization was maintained in Washington, Hawaii and the Philippines.** By the late fall of 1941, however, huge gaps had developed in this coverage. The

---

* In the scheme of naval communications, each facility, command, authority or unit is assigned a call sign of its own. One of the functions of radio intelligence is "traffic analysis"—the recovery ("line-up") of these calls to identify the agencies or units which use them. The location of the sender is established by means of goniometric direction finding.

** In Hawaii, Commander Rochefort's Communications Intelligence Unit was composed of a decryption section, an interception section, a traffic intelligence section and the mid-Pacific direction-finder net, with stations at Dutch Harbor in Alaska, Samoa, Pearl Harbor and Midway. Rochefort had a total of twenty officers and about eighty enlisted men working in his C/I Unit on various "missions," one of which was traffic analysis.

FLAG OFFICERS code was lost and Rochefort's team of cryptanalysts was making no headway whatsoever in its effort to solve its replacement. Op-20-G did succeed in keeping the old JN series open and was, in fact, using its twenty-fifth variant, solved a few months before. But it was yielding only routine information, mostly of an administrative nature, with very little operational or tactical intelligence.

Under these circumstances, dependence on traffic intelligence had become crucial. At about this time Lieutenant Commander Wilfred J. Holmes, a communications expert specializing in traffic intelligence, joined Rochefort's staff in Hawaii to plot the movements of Japanese ships by sifting and collating their radio calls. He was confronted with a major emergency even before he could settle down in his new job.

"Greatest effort is being made," he wrote on November 7 in the Unit's daily Communication Intelligence Summary, "to increase the number of identified calls to facilitate analysis of the traffic but Orange changes in methods of handling fleet traffic renders this more difficult than had been hoped." Even a week later he had to concede that "the large number of alternate calls used by major forces renders analysis of traffic headings very slow and difficult."

For a brief moment in this race it seemed, nevertheless, that Holmes had stumbled upon Yamamoto's big secret. On November 3 he discovered what he described as "an entirely new organization of the naval air force" and identified it as "the First Air Fleet." It was, indeed, Nagumo's task force, exercising at Saeki Bay for the Pearl Harbor attack. But no sooner was it spotted and identified than it was lost again.

Most of the intelligence that traffic analysis produced during these weeks proved not only woefully erroneous but fatally misleading. Thus, on November 17—when Admiral Nagumo's fleet was at sea, en route to Tankan Bay in the Kuriles—Holmes reported that "the carriers are mostly in the Kure-Sasebo area." On November 27—when the striking force with its six carriers was a day out of Etorofu, steaming toward Hawaii—traffic analysis located the carriers "in home waters" and the submarines "in Chichijima area."

After that Commander Holmes gave up this guessing game. He

admitted that he had lost both groups. From then on to the bitter end, the refrain of his Communication Intelligence Summaries was: "No information on submarines or carriers."

Yet, Admiral Yamamoto's supposedly ironclad communications security had a "leak" after all. Through a narrow opening his aides had overlooked, a channel to his big secret had opened up. This channel was the Foreign Ministry's line of confidential communications. It had been used for some time by the Third Bureau of the Naval General Staff, but the intelligence reports this circuit carried until the middle of November were neither important nor urgent. Now, however, it suddenly became the main link in Japan's most vital intelligence operation—Ensign Yoshikawa's watch at Pearl Harbor.

During the whole first half of November, Yoshikawa had sent only two ship-movement reports to Captain Ogawa in the Third Bureau—one on the 10th, the other on the 14th. But he knew from Commander Suzuki's mission to Hawaii that "things were building to a climax," and was awaiting direct word from Tokyo to accelerate his espionage effort.

It came on November 15, in a radiogram from Ogawa. "As relations between Japan and the United States are most critical," it read, "make your 'ships-in-harbor' reports irregularly but at a rate of twice a week. Although you already are no doubt aware, please take extra care to observe secrecy."

This was Y-Day for Yoshikawa's operation in Hawaii. The cadre of "inside agents" at the consulate received its own call to action. Dick Kotoshirodo was now given the assignment of "counting" the destroyers in Pearl Harbor. He motored daily to the harbor area, driving at a speed of 25 miles an hour on Kamehameha Highway along the perimeter of the Navy Yard, observing the destroyers as he drove. Secretary Seki, back in the secret fold, was to report on the cruisers. He became a regular customer at old Eto's soft-drink stand and a daily visitor at the Pan American Landing in Pearl City, whence the cruisers could be seen best. Johnny Mikami was asked to obtain whatever information he could about the defenses of the harbor. Otto Kühn was told to complete his visual signal system and submit it as soon as possible so that it could be forwarded to Ogawa.

Ensign Yoshikawa observed the battleships and carriers, and co-ordinated the effort. On November 18 he filed his first report under the new schedule. No. 222 in the series of intelligence dispatches sent in the consulate's code, it read:

(1) The warships at anchor in the Harbor on [Saturday] the 15th were as I told you in my No. 219 on that day:
Area A—A battleship of the *Oklahoma*-class entered and one tanker left port.
Area C—3 warships of the heavy-cruiser class were at anchor.
(2) On the 17th, the *Saratoga* was not in the Harbor. The carrier *Enterprise* (or some other vessel) was in Area C. Two heavy cruisers of the *Chicago*-class, one of the *Pensacola*-class were tied up at docks KS. Four merchant vessels were at anchor in Area D.
(3) At 1000 on the 17th, 8 destroyers were observed entering the Harbor. Their course was as follows: In a single file at a distance of 1000 meters apart at a speed of 3 knots, they moved into Pearl Harbor. From the entrance of the Harbor through Area B to the buoys in Area C, to which they were moored, they changed course five times, each time roughly 30 degrees. The elapsed time was one hour. However, one of these destroyers entered Area A after passing the water reservoir on the eastern side.

For the next eighteen days, until the night of December 6, Yoshikawa filed twenty-four telegrams, a list of which will show by itself the intensity and scope of his effort in this final phase of his secret mission:

NOVEMBER
18th—ship-movement report
    report that the customary announcements of ship sailings had been suspended
    arrival in Honolulu of American technicians en route to the Burma Road
19th—two ship-movement reports
22nd—departure of an American convoy bound for Singapore
    two ship-movement reports
23rd—ship-movement report *
24th—report on the Pacific Fleet's training areas

* It was on this day that Yoshikawa entered in his diary the word "observe," underlining it four times.

25th—ship-movement report
26th—ship-movement report
28th—miscellaneous military information
29th—two ship-movement reports

DECEMBER
1st—ship-movement report
2nd—ship-movement report
3rd—three ship-movement reports
    submission of Kühn's signal system
4th—two ship-movement reports
5th—ship-movement report
6th—the last two ship-movement reports

In the meantime Captain Ogawa sent a number of triple-priority telegrams to Yoshikawa asking him to report on specific features of Pearl Harbor's defenses. On November 18, for instance, he asked the ensign to report on vessels in Honolulu's Mamala Bay and "the areas adjacent thereto"; on the 20th he instructed Yoshikawa to "investigate thoroughly the fleet air bases in the vicinity of the Hawaiian military reservation"; on the 29th he asked him to report henceforth "even when there are no movements of ships." And he repeated the admonition: "Make your investigations with great secrecy."

At the diplomatic end, the Foreign Ministry was now liquidating the peace and preparing the war, and this whole hectic business was reflected fully in the telegrams. Foreign Minister Shigenori Togo's dispatches to Ambassadors Nomura in Washington, Oshima in Berlin and Horikiri in Rome resounded with impatience, exasperation and alarm. The telegrams carried increasingly broader hints that the critical moment of the crisis was at hand. The Foreign Ministry's dispatches to Japanese missions abroad had the unmistakable tone of a supreme emergency.

A sequence of urgent dispatches to Washington in particular made clear that Japan had set a time limit on the negotiations and would take "drastic action" after that. The series began with three telegrams on November 4—the eve of the imperial conference—in which Togo told Nomura bluntly that the Empire had reached the crossroads. "Conditions both within and without Japan are so tense," Togo wrote in the first telegram of this day, "that no longer is procrastination possible. This is our last effort. The success or failure of the pending discussions will have an immense effect on the destiny of our Empire."

His second and third telegrams of the day re-emphasized this theme. "Our internal situation makes it impossible for us to make any further compromise," he wrote in one; then added in the other, as a footnote to the Tojo government's "final proposals" for a "truce" sent to Nomura in the same dispatch: "This is the last effort to prevent something from happening."

On November 5 Togo advised Nomura of the ominous decision of the imperial conference. "Because of various circumstances," he wrote, "it is imperative that all arrangements for the signing of this agreement be completed by the 25th of this month. I realize that this is a difficult order, but it is unavoidable under the circumtances. Please understand this fully and do your utmost to save Japanese-American relations from falling into a chaotic condition. Do so with great resolve and with unstinted labor, I beg of you. This information is to be kept strictly to yourself only."

For the first time a deadline was explicitly set and Nomura, who apparently regained some of his equilibrium, responded by advising the Foreign Minister to be more circumspect and discreet in his telegrams. "There is danger," he wrote, "that America will see through our proposals. If we have made up our minds on a final course of action, it would be the part of wisdom to keep quiet about it."

But Togo had implicit faith in the absolute security of his communications. In his next telegram he spoke of "the exceeding seriousness of the moment," and told Nomura: "The situation is nearing the climax. Time is indeed becoming short."

On November 14 Nomura sent a long dispatch to Tokyo, which Commander Safford aptly described as the ambassador's swan song. The policy of the American government in the Pacific, he told the Foreign Minister, is to stop any further move on Japan's part, "either southward or northward." The Americans, he wrote, "are contriving by every possible means" to prepare for war if need be; it was not Washington's intention to see Munich repeated. The United States would never grant Japan preferential treatment over China. A war resulting from the crisis would be a long one.

Whoever had the power to hold out would win. "I would like to counsel patience for one or two months," Nomura concluded his passionate plea, "to get a clear view of the world situation. This would be our best plan."

Togo's answer was curt. The fate of the Empire hangs by the slender thread of a few days, he wrote. I set the deadline, not you! There will be no change in our policies!

The threat had become explicit. On November 22 Togo wrote to Nomura as bluntly as he could afford: "There are reasons beyond your ability to guess why we want to settle Japanese-American relations by November 25, but if the signing [of an agreement] could be completed by the 29th, we would be willing to wait until that date."

Then he added: "This time we mean it that the deadline absolutely cannot be changed. After that things are automatically going to happen."

Like a man condemned to be hanged in the morning, Nomura was now fighting for every precious hour. Togo had set the new deadline as November 29. But the 29th in Tokyo would only be the 28th in Washington. Perhaps Togo had meant Washington time. Here was the prospect of gaining a whole day's reprieve. Nomura eagerly queried the Foreign Minister, only to have his last hope promptly squashed. "The time limit set in my telegram No. 812," Togo wrote back, "is in Tokyo time."

Simultaneously Admiral Yamamoto sent another "Top-Secret Operations Order," this one to Admiral Nagumo with the striking force at Tankan Bay. "The task force will depart Hitokappu Wan [Bay] on November 26," he wrote, "and proceed without being detected to rendezvous set for December 3.

"X-Day will be December 8."

Yamamoto's signal went out in the impregnable new code on a masked circuit and was completely missed by "Magic." But the Togo–Nomura exchange was in the B system (PURPLE) and moved in the usual way, by radio via the commercial cable companies. Togo had betrayed the hidden hand of Japan, and "Magic" caught him in the act.

Every single one in the Togo–Nomura exchange of telegrams was intercepted and processed promptly and fully. The dispatches

—all of them in translations whose English even exaggerated the furor of their tone—were before the American policy makers by the morning of November 25.

Mr. Hull recognized them for what they were. He concluded from their tone and contents that the military in Japan were chafing at the passage of time and that Tokyo regarded the "proposals" as the last bargain—"the hinge on the breach of the cannon." He knew that the alternative was war.

At this time the President, too, was getting the intercepts. He was no longer denied access to the " 'magics' in the raw," but it had taken a presidential order issued in no uncertain terms to bring this about. From June to the end of September, no intercept had been shown to Mr. Roosevelt: Bratton had simply ignored the procedure during the months when the Army was supposed to service the White House, and when it was the Navy's responsibility, Commander Kramer picked the "magics" which he thought might be of special interest to the President. He would then show them to Captain Beardall, who related those items to Mr. Roosevelt that stuck in his mind.

When, however, the situation sharpened and the intercepts became more explicit in their revelation of Japan's intentions, the President began to feel that he needed this intelligence in its original form. He therefore suggested that actual copies of the translated intercepts be presented to him instead of being merely briefed about them by Mr. Hull or getting only their "gist" from the memoranda Kramer was preparing and occasionally leaving with the naval aide for transmission to the President.

This created a crisis within the crisis. In some consternation Kramer took the matter up with the Director of Naval Intelligence, explaining that he needed G-2's approval before he could deliver any raw intercepts to the White House. The DNI told Kramer to "clear it" with Bratton, and Bratton then carried the problem to General Miles. After some wrangling and under pressure from Captain Beardall, G-2 granted the permission, as it was called, to show some of the intercepts to Mr. Roosevelt.

On November 1 it became the Army's turn again to service the White House, but Bratton chose to ignore the new arrangement. When no deliveries had been made by the 7th, the President instructed Captain Beardall to settle "this ridiculous thing" once and for all, by picking up "the original material" and presenting it to him each day.

Beardall reopened the controversy in ONI, but now Kramer balked. Using the argument that this was November, "the Army's month for dissemination," he told the naval aide there was nothing he could do to get the intercepts for the President. For three days the issue was debated in G-2 and ONI, without producing a solution. But when Beardall informed the President of this hassle, Mr. Roosevelt directed the naval aide "to pay no attention to those dunderheads in the Army and Navy" and bring him the intercepts each day as soon as they were processed. An emergency meeting was called in General Miles's office, and G-2 finally agreed to letting Beardall handle the *original* material for the President.*

It required no exceptional imagination, no reading between the lines to gauge the portent of these intercepts. Yet for all their clear understanding of the ominous message which the intercepts carried, both the President and Mr. Hull decided to bide their time. They undertook nothing to advise the nation of the utmost seriousness of the situation or to alert the Army and the Navy for the showdown. While the pall of war thus hung heavily over the Pacific, Mr. Hull preferred to continue the talks—"for the purpose," as he wrote on November 29, "of making a record."

His three major advisers—Hornbeck, Hamilton and Ballantine —were caught in the forms rather than the substance of crisis diplomacy, and paid but passing attention to the feverish "magics." They were too busy drafting a note in which the United States would answer the Japanese "proposals" (that Nomura and Kurusu had got around to submitting only on November 20). It was to set forth the "principles" on which Washington would be willing to agree to a "truce."

---

* It was, therefore, only from November 12 on (when "Magic" had already been operating for about fourteen months) that the President was allowed to see the intercepts—but even then only those which Commander Kramer chose to give to Beardall for delivery to the White House. The President was thus granted the privilege of seeing the actual "magics" for only twenty-five days immediately prior to Pearl Harbor. The total number of intercepts he was finally permitted to read between November 12 (when the originals started going to him) and December 7 (up to two hours before the attack) totaled sixty-four out of some eighteen hundred processed during this same period.

They worked under enormous pressure. The Chinese objected vehemently to a *modus vivendi.* The British and the Dutch beseeched Mr. Hull to make the occasion of his note a demonstration of American determination. Mr. Churchill voiced his opposition from behind Chinese backs. "What about Chiang Kaishek?" he wrote to the President. "Is he not having a very thin diet?"

If the dispatches passing between Togo and Nomura made it unmistakably clear that Japan was accelerating its move to war, the Ogawa–Yoshikawa exchange of telegrams pinpointed Pearl Harbor as an objective in the coming conflict. And since they were sent through the facilities of the Foreign Ministry in a diplomatic code which the Americans had cracked, "Magic" had them completely covered. It had become more than just a source of diplomatic intelligence. Suddenly it began to carry at least some of the information the United States Navy had lost with the collapse of its traffic analysis and the change of the FLAG OFFICERS code.

Most of Ogawa's telegrams to Honolulu and Yoshikawa's reports to the Third Bureau were intercepted by at least three of the "Magic" monitoring stations—by the Navy's Station S in Puget Sound or by the Army's MS-2 in San Francisco and MS-5 in Hawaii. Moreover, Ogawa's telegram of November 15 and Yoshikawa's report three days later had been fully processed by December 3 and 6, respectively. Three other Ogawa dispatches—those of November 18, 20 and 29—were also translated before December 7. But this particular coverage went no further. At this stage of "Magic," the operation was startlingly similar to Yardley's activities, especially during the Washington Conference when the War Department conducted the venture not to satisfy its own intelligence requirements but solely for the benefit of the State Department.

The "magics" were, of course, avidly read in the War and Navy departments by the handful of Ultras who had access to them. But as they saw it, "Magic" was merely a collection of broken *diplomatic* codes—important to the White House and the State Department, to be sure, but yielding only a trickle of hard intelligence of any "operational or tactical value" to the Army and the Navy.

In the preoccupation with "Magic's" importance as a source of diplomatic intelligence it was overlooked that now it also carried information of inestimable military and naval significance. The consular traffic between Honolulu and Tokyo was still deprecated as reflecting merely the haphazard intelligence effort of a band of amateurs. It was left, now as before, in the "deferred" category of intercepts that deserved no special consideration and whose processing required no particular haste. The sudden increase of Yoshikawa's reports, and the tone and urgency of Ogawa's telegrams to Honolulu, did not impress any of the men who processed these "magics" as being unduly significant.

Most of these intercepts were decrypted by SIS and Op-20-G as soon as they arrived in Washington from the interception stations. There, however, their processing ended. They were sent to Commander Kramer for translation and distribution, but his section was now overburdened with the more important "magics" it had to handle. The PURPLE messages of high-priority rating were flowing in a steady stream as the Tokyo–Washington traffic was reaching peak volume.

Yoshikawa's espionage messages piled up in the incoming baskets of the translators in Op-20-GZ. They were left there, unattended, to await their turn—until it was too late.

PART V

Prelude to Disaster

Bratton's Last Stand

There was at least one man in the American government—in actual fact only a single Army officer—to whom Foreign Minister Togo's recent telegrams signified a clear intention to go to war against the United States. He was Colonel Rufus S. Bratton, chief of the Military Intelligence Division's Far Eastern Section and custodian of the "magics" in the War Department.

"Rufe" (or "Togo") Bratton, a dour-faced native of South Carolina, was a Regular Army officer in more ways than one. He had risen to the rank of full colonel in thirty years of service, not by any exceptional personal traits or spectacular achievements, but by his admirable regularity.

After graduation from West Point in 1914 he spent World War I in Hawaii and in the mushrooming new Army camps in the continental United States. Three times in his career he had long tours of duty in Japan to study the language, attend courses at the Army War College and serve as military attaché. His daughter Leslie was born in Tokyo.

He was an earnest and meticulous, competent and hard-working officer ideally suited for one of the middle-layer desk jobs in the peacetime General Staff. In 1935 he was taken out of circulation and placed in the Military Intelligence Division's Far Eastern Section. By 1937 he was its chief, personally handling all matters involving Japan. For several years this was a humdrum task. He kept the Japanese army's order of battle, updated its senior officers' biographical file, and tried as best he could to stay abreast of developments in its doctrines, tactics and arms.

Now this inconspicuous man, who cherished the seclusion of his post, was catapulted into a certain faceless prominence. He had become charter member of the secret little fraternity of intelligence and communications experts who processed the "magics" for the policy makers and their aides. Other members of the tight little group were Colonel Otis K. Sadtler of the Signal Corps, and Commanders McCollum, Safford and Kramer of the Navy. They moved ominously and officiously behind the scenes, convinced that they were more familiar with the awesome facts of the emergency and had a better appreciation of the Japanese threat than the superiors they served.

When Bratton arrived at his office in the Munitions Building on November 26—a dull Wednesday morning under cloudy skies —he was a lot more tense than usual. It was his job to know what was going on, and as he himself put it, he now had the picture. "It was a picture," he later said, "that was being painted over a period of weeks if not months"—the picture of "frantic Japanese preparations to wage offensive war against Great Britain and the United States."

For six weeks, on a day-by-day basis, Bratton had plotted what he was certain was the Japanese deployment for war. The first thing he did on this murky late-fall day was to bring out his secret "war maps," which now had enough pins in them to show graphically, even at a glance, the pattern of the scattered moves and reveal it as a *systematic* deployment of the Japanese forces. The "magics" hardened whatever information he had from his own meager sources and from his friends in ONI. McCollum was "smuggling" over to him an increasing number of intelligence reports that ONI was receiving from its own outlets in the Far East and from British Intelligence in Singapore.

Since November 22, Bratton was viewing the contours of the Japanese deployment in the light of the intercepted dispatch from Tokyo in which Foreign Minister Togo had told Ambassador Nomura that "things are automatically going to happen [by November 29]" unless he managed to squeeze an agreement out of his negotiations. His map furnished dramatic confirmation of Togo's warning. The Japanese were on the move everywhere. One of their expeditionary forces was embarking in Shanghai on as many as forty or fifty ships. Another was proceeding along the China coast, south of Formosa. Major units of the Japanese fleet had left their home ports and were steaming toward the Pescadores.

The picture Bratton had developed on the maps convinced him that war with Japan was a foregone conclusion. And from what Togo had told Nomura, he became absolutely certain that it would break out the following Sunday, November 30.

Bratton was examining his "morning mail" when McCollum called to say that ONI had just received a couple of signals which seemed a lot more specific than anything he had seen before. According to one message, a cruiser division, a destroyer squadron and a score of transports had been spotted in the harbor of Samah on Hainan Island, waiting to take aboard and escort a division of the Japanese 25th Army which British Intelligence had previously identified. Activities in Indochina indicated that General Tomoyuki Yamashita's forces would be moving out in a matter of days, if not hours.

The other report was from the American naval attaché in Shanghai. "At Woosung military supply base," he wrote, "intense activity since 15th. Unusual number ships present including former merchant craft averaging 10,000 tons and up. Wednesday 10 transports sailed 8 of which carried troops. . . . Landing boats continue part of outgoing equipment. . . . 1,000 troops departed from Swatow last Saturday."

Bratton took the reports to General Miles, and Miles told him to show them to the Chief of Staff. But General Marshall was out of town; he had left the night before to attend maneuvers in North Carolina. Bursting to show the intelligence to somebody at the top, Bratton carried the reports to Colonel F. L. Harrison, the Secretary's aide, for presentation to Mr. Stimson. Bratton sensed that he had an ally in the elderly Secretary of War, the only member of the President's War Council who expected the worst and appeared to be reconciled to it as well. This crisis was nothing new to Stimson. He had first tangled with the Japanese in 1931 when the Imperial Army unleashed the "incident" in Manchuria.

Stimson had lived with the Japanese threat for ten years, and regarded the emergency as the culmination of all the mischief Japan had perpetrated with impunity for far too long.

This was the day when Secretary Hull was going to deliver his stiff rebuttal to the Japanese ambassadors' proposals, and Stimson had called him earlier in the morning to inquire what his plans were. Mr. Hull sounded depressed and uncertain of his course. He had come to the conclusion, he said, that probably the best thing would be simply to tell "the Japs" that he had nothing more to propose.

When Bratton's reports were brought to his desk, Stimson called the President and asked whether he had heard anything about Japanese concentrations south of Formosa. Mr. Roosevelt had not. "He was shocked," Stimson later recalled, "and at once took it as further evidence of bad faith on the part of the Japanese." That seemed to settle the matter.

Bratton was baffled. Here they were, he thought, with knowledge of Japanese "intentions to attack the United States," and yet everybody was merely raising eyebrows and shrugging shoulders. But there was a reason for this attitude in Mr. Roosevelt's circle. The mood was set by the President himself. Now that the prospect of peace with Japan was slipping away fast and the issue of war was becoming paramount, the President felt his hands were still tied, not so much by his "constitutional difficulties," of which he had complained to Churchill at Placentia Bay, as by a set of firm pledges he had given in the heat of his 1940 campaign for a third term. Most binding (and, for that matter, the most embarrassing) was a solemn promise he had made in Boston to "the mothers and fathers of America."

"I have said this before," he told them on October 31, 1940, "but I shall say it again and again and again: your boys are not going into any foreign wars." Roosevelt was in part paraphrasing the pledge in the platform of the Democratic Party, but when he was reminded that the platform also contained the qualifying phrase "unless attacked," he chose to omit it to make his own pledge sound stronger.

A mere campaign promise, one might say—but it kept coming back again and again, to brake the march of events and well-nigh paralyze the American government at this critical period. It had even intruded upon a crucial session of the Cabinet the day before, on November 25. The President opened the meeting with a review of the Japanese problem, and Mr. Hull said: "They are poised for attack—they might attack at any time."

Mr. Roosevelt said yes, the Japanese were notorious for attacking without warning, and we might be attacked, he mused, "perhaps as soon as next Monday." What should we do? "The question was," Secretary Stimson wrote in his diary that night, "how could we maneuver them into the position of firing the first shot without allowing too much danger to ourselves."

It was a difficult proposition, he complained.

Shortly after Bratton reached his office on Thanksgiving morning, November 27, his conviction that war with Japan was now only seventy-two hours away became absolute. Awaiting him was the envelope from SIS with the latest intercepts, and among them he found a telegram from Nomura to Togo, reporting the receipt of the American note in the afternoon of the day before. The dispatch reflected the ambassador's despair. "Our failure and humiliation is now complete," he wrote abjectly.

Even more important as straws in the wind were two intercepted telegrams, from Major General Saburo Isoda, an old friend of Bratton's who was now serving as military attaché in Washington, and from Captain Ichiro Yokoyama, the naval attaché. They advised their Chiefs in the Army and Navy General Staffs that the negotiations had finally collapsed, and implied that war with the United States could not be delayed any longer.

General Marshall was still on maneuvers, and so Colonel Bratton once again passed the intercepts to Mr. Stimson, together with the latest report about the movement of still another enormous Japanese expeditionary force. This particular report was evaluated in G-2 as indicating "a possibility that [the Japanese] might be proceeding to the Philippines or to Burma to cut off the Burma Road, or to the Dutch East Indies," or might be moving "into Thailand from which they could be in a position to attack Singapore at the proper moment." An attack on Hawaii was not anticipated. But Bratton regarded attacks on American territories such as Dutch Harbor in Alaska and even the West Coast as distinct possibilities.

Mr. Stimson called Mr. Hull at once "to find out," as he phrased it, "what his final word had been with the Japanese"—in fact, to ascertain whether or not the note had been delivered. Hull now told him, almost casually, that he had "handed the note to the Japs," and for all practical purposes, had terminated the negotiations. His actual words were, as Mr. Stimson recorded them: "I wash my hands of the whole matter and it is now in the hands of you—the Army and the Navy." It was momentous information, but it had not been volunteered by Mr. Hull. It had to be solicited by Stimson.

The Secretary was shocked, and called the President in some agitation. But Mr. Roosevelt sounded cheerful about the whole affair. True, he said, the talks had been called off. But they had ended with "a magnificent statement prepared by Hull."

Although Mr. Hull had no more illusions and recognized that his own role in the crisis was at an end, he went along with his advisers, who continued to insist that the Japanese were bluffing and would back down at the last minute, giving the United States the time it needed to improve its defenses. Dr. Hornbeck in particular was pleased with the note, which he had been instrumental in drafting. Convinced that it would call the bluff of the Japanese, he spent the morning composing a long memorandum. A Delphic document entitled "Problem of Far Eastern Relations —Estimate of Situation and Certain Probabilities," it was designed to project the Japanese reaction to the stiff American note.

"In the opinion of the undersigned," he wrote, "the Japanese government does not desire or intend or expect to have forthwith armed conflict with the United States. . . . So far as relations directly between the United States and Japan are concerned there is less reason today than there was a week ago for the United States to be apprehensive lest Japan make 'war' on this country.

"Were it a matter of placing bets," he went on, "the undersigned would give odds of five to one that the United States and Japan will not be at 'war' on or before December 15 (the date by which General Gerow has affirmed that we would be 'in the clear' so far as consummation of certain disposals of our forces is concerned); would wager three to one that the United States and Japan will not be at 'war' on or before the 15th of January (i.e., seven weeks from now); would wager even money that the United States and Japan will not be at 'war' on or before March 1 (a date more than 90 days from now, and after the period during which it has been estimated by our strategists that it would be to our advantage for us to have 'time' for further preparation and disposals). . . .

"Stated briefly, the undersigned does not believe that this country is now on the immediate verge of 'war' in the Pacific."

Stimson was neither disposed to share the President's enthusiasm over Mr. Hull's note nor to take up Dr. Hornbeck on his wagers. Rather, he was inclined to accept Bratton's estimate that war with Japan would break out on Sunday, November 30. He now felt that something radical had to be done immediately. There was still time to anticipate the Japanese attack. His big office in the Munitions Building was turned into a command post. In the absence of the Chief of Staff, Stimson began issuing orders which only General Marshall had the authority to give.

Shortly after nine o'clock he authorized General Henry H. Arnold, chief of the Army Air Corps, to send two B-24's from San Francisco to Manila via the Japanese mandated islands—to fly high over the island fortresses of Truk and Jaluit and photograph them, "with the idea of trying to detect any naval concentrations that might be going on there." At nine-thirty he summoned Major General William Bryden, the Deputy Chief of Staff standing in for Marshall, and Brigadier General Gerow, chief of the War Plans Division.

In their presence, then, Stimson called Mr. Roosevelt and requested the President to authorize him to send unequivocal warnings to the danger zones—to the commanding generals at the Panama Canal, in the Presidio in San Francisco, at the Hawaiian Department, and especially to General MacArthur in the Philippines. The messages were to explain the situation and order them "to be on the *qui vive* for any attack."

For the President this was a historic decision, the definite shift of the crisis from the diplomatic to the military sphere. He weighed Stimson's request thoughtfully. Then he not only authorized but actually ordered his Secretary of War to send out what Roosevelt called "the final alert."

From then on Secretary Stimson was on firm grounds. He was

no longer acting as the civilian head of the War Department, usurping the prerogatives and functions of the Army's Chief of Staff, but as the President's deputy executing an order of the Commander-in-Chief.

He invited Secretary Knox and Admiral Stark over from the Navy Department, and reviewed the situation with them. Stark and Gerow continued to plead for time, but the Secretary cut them short. "I'd also be glad," he said, "to have time but I don't want it at the cost of humiliation of the United States or of backing down on any of our principles which would show weakness on our part."

At this point Gerow produced a paper. It was the draft of a message General Marshall had prepared before his departure from Washington, and left with his aide to send out should the negotiations break down. They had collapsed, but Gerow had not yet sent it out. It was a warning, to be sure, but its recipients in Hawaii and the Philippines would only have construed it merely as an alert for Condition 1: defense against sabotage and uprising within the Islands "with no particular threat from without."

The draft, as it was to go to General Walter C. Short at Fort Shafter, began by saying: "Negotiations with Japanese appear to be terminated to all practical purposes with only the barest possibilities that the Japanese Government might come back and offer to continue. Japanese future action unpredictable period."

Now Stimson intervened. He took the draft from Gerow, crossed out the "period" after "Japanese future action unpredictable," and added in his own hand the words "but hostile action possible at any moment." The whole sentence now read:

> Japanese future action unpredictable but hos-
> tile action possible at any moment period

Stimson's editing raised the warning to Alert No. 3, the "all-out alert requiring occupation of field positions." It went out as a priority dispatch in Stimson's version but over Marshall's name, eight minutes after eleven in the morning of November 27, 1941.*

* Upon their return to the Navy Department, Secretary Knox and Admiral Stark sent out an even stronger warning to Admiral Husband E. Kimmel, the Pacific Fleet's commander-in-chief at Pearl Harbor. "This dispatch," it read in part, "is to be considered a war warning. Negotiations with Japan looking toward stabilization of conditions in the Pacific have ceased and an aggressive

When the message was out of the way, and Knox and Stark were gone, General Gerow mentioned in passing that General Marshall and Admiral Stark had prepared an "estimate of the Far Eastern situation" that was scheduled to go to the White House later in the day. Stimson demanded to see it and Gerow produced a copy of the draft. It was a repetition of the familiar recommendation to "wait and see." Stimson did not like it. He told Gerow to rephrase it in more definite terms.

"I want to be sure," he said, "that the memorandum will not be considered as a recommendation to the President that he request Japan to reopen the conversations."

Early the next morning Colonel Bratton returned to the "front office" with information of "such formidable character," as Stimson called it, "with regard to the movements of Japanese forces along the Asiatic coast" that the Secretary decided to take it to the White House personally and right away. Though it was past nine o'clock the President was still in bed, feeling low from a sinus infection and even lower from its somewhat too vigorous treatment (or "overtreatment," as some said) by Admiral Ross T. McIntire, his physician.

Mr. Roosevelt read Bratton's reports and then said to Stimson: "We have three alternatives—either to do nothing or to give them something in the nature of an ultimatum stating a point beyond which we would fight or fight at once."

"Doing nothing is out of the question, Mr. President," Stimson replied. "As for the other alternative, the desirable thing to do from the point of view of our own safety would be to take the initiative and attack without further warning. It's axiomatic that offense is the best defense. It's always dangerous to wait and let the enemy make the first move."

Stimson was of the opinion that the warning the United States had given Japan in August after the occupation of Indochina was an "ultimatum" that would "justify" an attack without any fur-

---

move by Japan is expected within the next few days. . . . Execute an appropriate defensive deployment preparatory to carrying out the task assigned in WPL 46X." WPL 46 was the "Orange" part of the series of "Rainbow War Plans," providing that the Pacific Fleet move immediately against the Japanese-held Marshall Islands on the outbreak of war in the Far East.

ther ado. On the other hand, he agreed with the President that "the situation could be made more clean-cut [sic] from the point of view of public opinion if a further warning were given."

At noon the President held a meeting of his so-called War Council to review the situation on the basis of Bratton's latest intelligence. Stimson was there (accompanied by Marshall, who had returned from the Carolinas) and so were Hull, Knox and Admiral Stark, armed with reports of their own. The President had Bratton's dossier before him, read out aloud the most alarming passages of the reports, then invited a discussion about their implications. The opinions at the conference table ranged from the probability of Japanese landings at Thailand, Singapore and the East Indies to an attack on the Philippines or a thrust from Indochina to cut off the Burma Road. The possibility of an attack on Pearl Harbor or any American territory was not mentioned. All agreed that "if this expedition [described in Bratton's reports] was allowed to round the southern point of Indochina, this whole chain of disastrous events would be set on foot."

Stimson argued for an attack *without* warning. The others favored another "warning." The President brought up his pet idea of sending a personal message to the Emperor in which he would invite him to halt this mad drift into war, coupled with a special message to Congress reporting on the danger and explaining what the United States would face if it came to pass. In the end, however, nothing was decided.

It was indeed a strange meeting, held in an atmosphere of urgency and inanimation. Mr. Roosevelt was not in his best form. His sinuses were bothering him, and besides he had his mind on a promise he had given the polio patients at Warm Springs, Georgia, that he would spend Thanksgiving dinner with them. He had not been able to keep the date the night before, but now, yearning to take his sinuses out of Washington and himself out of the crisis, he was determined to go. He adjourned the meeting abruptly and left for Warm Springs immediately afterward.

If Bratton needed any more evidence to bolster his conviction that Japan would go to war the following Sunday, he received it on Friday, November 28, from two more intercepts. The first was the translation of another Togo telegram to Nomura, advising the ambassador that war had become a foregone conclusion as a result of the American government's uncompromising stand. "The United States had gone ahead," Togo wrote, "and presented this humiliating note. With a telegram that will be sent to you in two or three days containing the Imperial Government's views, talks will be *de facto* ruptured. This is inevitable. However, do not give the impression that the negotiations are broken off."

What intrigued Bratton most in Togo's dispatch was the announcement that a communication would be sent to the American government "in two or three days." Sunday was now less than three days away. The note of which Togo spoke could very well be Japan's declaration of war.

The other bit of "evidence" became famous as the "winds" message during the subsequent Pearl Harbor investigations. On November 19 the Cable Section of the Foreign Ministry sent a circular telegram to a number of Japanese diplomatic missions, with instructions that seemed typical of arrangements usually made on the eve of war. The *denshin-ka* advised its outposts that certain signals would be given in the weather reports of Radio Tokyo's daily Japanese-language short-wave broadcasts. References to the direction of the wind would be a code to inform them whether relations were about to be broken with the United States, Great Britain or Russia.

The telegram sent to Consul General Kita in Honolulu read in full:

In view of the serious international situation that may reach the most critical crisis at any moment, telegraphic communications between Japan and the countries of her adversaries are likely to be suspended. Consequently we will include in the middle and at the end of the weather reports broadcast in our Japanese-language news programs beamed to all points one or another or all of the following code phrases:

(1) HIGASHI NO KAZE AME [east wind rain] to mean that relations with America are not according to expectations.

(2) KITANOKAZE KUMORI [north wind cloudy] to mean the same concerning Japanese-Russian relations.

(3) NISHI NO KAZE HARE [west wind clear] to mean the same concerning relations with England (including the invasion of Thailand, Singapore, Malaya, the Netherlands East Indies and Eastern India).

When you hear any or all of these phrases repeated twice in the newscasts destroy your codes and confidential papers. It is desired that you treat this message with the utmost secrecy. Pass on this information to the addressees on your own circular list.

Since the "winds" code (as it came to be called in Washington) was given a very wide distribution and was being forwarded also to outposts which did not have any of the *denshin-ka*'s cipher machines, it had to be sent in one of the lower-grade diplomatic ciphers. In fact, it went out in the TSU system, the nineteenth variant of which SIS and Op-20-G had only recently recovered.

It was intercepted promptly, of course, but it took some time before the message could be decrypted. It became available to Bratton only in the morning of November 28. By then several slightly differing versions of the same circular had arrived in Washington from the British in Singapore and the Dutch intelligence service in Batavia.*

The "winds" code created a sensation in Washington. Colonel Sadtler and Commander Safford in particular were inclined to attribute extraordinary significance to it. As Safford later put it: "It meant war—and we knew that it meant war." Elaborate arrangements were made by both the Army and the Navy to monitor the Japanese newscasts for the code phrases. From November 28 on, twelve of the interception stations covered Radio Tokyo's newscast schedules with special monitoring staffs standing watch around the clock.

Although at first Bratton was skeptical about the significance of the "winds" code and regarded it merely as a precautionary meas-

* Thanks to the efforts of a Dutch cryptanalyst named W. A. van der Beck, the Dutch in the East Indies were also able to read the Japanese telegrams, but only those sent in TSU, OITE and L. Early in December 1941 they intercepted and decoded several of the "winds code" dispatches, including a circular from the Japanese ambassador in Bangkok, Thailand, to the Japanese consul general in Batavia, and one of Tokyo's round-robin telegrams. The Netherlands authorities in Bandoeng passed the information to the American military and naval attachés (Lieutenant Colonel Thorpe and Lieutenant Commander Slawson), who in turn notified Walter Foote, the American consul general in Batavia. Foote forwarded the information to the State Department on December 4, and Thorpe reported it to his Washington home office in a separate dispatch on the same day. However, these telegrams added nothing to what was already known through "Magic." Moreover, as Safford later noted, "the Dutch did not think that Japan was going to attack the United States, and Pearl Harbor came as a complete surprise to them."

ure normal in a crisis, he too became infected by Sadtler's and Safford's contagious excitement in the end. He requested the Foreign Broadcast Monitoring Service of the Federal Communications Commission to keep a day-and-night watch on the Tokyo broadcasts for what Safford had come to call the "execute" of the "winds" code.*

With the evidence seemingly overwhelming to support his contention, Bratton was now prepared to stake his whole reputation and whatever prestige G-2 had on the prognostication that war with Japan would break out within less than seventy-two hours. Those who knew him from calmer days and were used to his quiet ways could not make up their minds whether to be fascinated or bewildered by his abrupt metamorphosis. Disregarding chains of command and channels, he asserted himself with a vigor and eloquence few of his friends and colleagues had suspected in him. During these days Bratton was undoubtedly the busiest man in the whole Munitions Building. He carried the bad tidings up and down the long corridors. He prodded his placid chief, General Miles, to abandon his equanimity and timidity. He crashed the sacrosanct gates of Gerow's War Plans Division with warnings and pleas for action, and made a nuisance of himself everywhere he went.

Although his insistent demand that additional warnings be sent to the American commanders in the four major danger zones were turned down on the assumption that Stimson's message of November 27 would be sufficient to alert them, the high command awaited Bratton's sinister Sunday with something akin to bated breath.

But nothing happened. As General Marshall later put it, with reference to Foreign Minister Togo's deadline on which Bratton had based his prediction of things to come: "November 29 arrived and passed, and we entered into December without anything happening other than the continuation of these movements, which we could follow fairly well, down the China coast and

---

* Several times during the next nine days FCC monitors picked up what sounded like the ominous code, but the intercepts invariably turned out to be *bona fide* references to genuine atmospheric conditions. As we shall see, Safford later claimed that the "execute" had been broadcast and picked up, but Bratton steadfastly denied it.

headed quite plainly towards Thailand and the Gulf of Siam."

Bratton forfeited his stake. He was thoroughly discredited in the War Plans Division, whose calm apparently nothing could shake during these days. The Military Intelligence Division, whose prestige was at a low ebb anyway, suffered a serious loss of face.

It seemed that Colonel Bratton had cried wolf once too often.

23 Japan Deploys for War

DECEMBER 1, 1941 * . . . The resolution to make war with the United States was passed shortly after four o'clock in Room 1 in the east wing of the imperial palace. This afternoon session, called to sanction the decision the Cabinet had reached in the morning, was a formal and subdued affair, not because of the monumental nature of its agenda, but because of the presence of the Emperor. A self-effacing, nervous little man sitting stiffly on a slightly elevated platform in front of an ancient silk brocade screen, he peered with remonstrative eyes from behind rimless glasses at the conferees. Though his diffident glance was almost apologetic, it left them uncomfortable and contrite.

Aside from His Imperial Majesty, there were nineteen solemn men present. "I was there as Premier," General Hideki Tojo recalled later, "also Baron Hara, president of the Privy Council, and all or nearly all of the Cabinet ministers. The two Chiefs of Staff were also present." There were three other persons in attendance, in a more or less clerical capacity—Naoki Hoshino, secretary of the Cabinet; General Muto, chief of the War Ministry's Military Affairs Bureau; and Rear Admiral Takasumi Oka, the latter's opposite number in the Navy Ministry.

* All dates and times in this chapter are given in the local time of the place where the action occurs. Tokyo time, on which the Pearl Harbor striking force operated throughout its mission, was 19½ hours ahead of Hawaiian time and 25 hours ahead of Washington time. For instance, 0000 hours on December 1 in Tokyo was 4:30 A.M. on November 30 in Hawaii, 10 A.M. on November 30 in Washington.

They were seated at two long tables covered with heavy silken cloths, their bodies obsequiously half turned toward the Emperor, who did not utter a single word during the entire conference. Nevertheless, his silence conveyed a certain eloquence. The men around him knew only too well that His Majesty had grave doubts, if not actual misgivings, about the "final solution" they had assembled to ratify.

Since the decision to embark on war was about to be made because of the failure of the diplomats to preserve the peace, much of the time was given over to Foreign Minister Shigenori Togo. Grim and frigid, Togo read an "explanation" of the Japanese-American negotiations from a fourteen-page memorandum prepared by the permanent staff of his Foreign Ministry, and concluded with the very words the conference had been summoned to hear: "All things considered," he said in a voice so low that it was barely audible, "it is almost impossible to realize fully our claims by continuing the negotiations." But these men no longer cared for "explanations."

The decision was a mere formality. It was adopted unanimously in a two-sentence resolution: "Our negotiations with the United States regarding the execution of our national policy, adopted November 5, have finally failed. Japan will declare war on the United States, Britain and The Netherlands."

Wars are decided upon in all sorts of moods—in calm, calculated reflections or in frenzies of fervor—but, supposedly, always in a firm belief in the justness of one's cause and the certainty of ultimate victory. Yet in this conference room of the old palace, whose quaint medieval splendor lent an anachronistic touch to the proceedings, a pall of doubt and apprehension hung over the heads of the war makers.

When the resolution had been passed, Cabinet Secretary Hoshino felt a sudden chill in his spine. Sensing the historic salience of the moment, he glanced at his wrist watch to fix in his memory the exact time when Japan "turned off the lights of peace in Asia."

It was twelve minutes past four.

The phrase "will *declare* war" was a concession to the Emperor, who had insisted that hostilities be opened with a formal notice. So the remaining few minutes of the conference were devoted to the discussion of how to formulate the declaration of war and when to deliver it without jeopardizing Japan's plans by alerting the enemy.

The men at the conference were growing tired and restive, and still the problem remained unresolved. It was left to an *ad hoc* committee, composed of the Chiefs of the Army and Navy General Staffs, and Foreign Minister Togo, to produce a solution that would satisfy both the Emperor and the military's need for surprise.

At four-thirty the conference adjourned, and Japan, for all practical purposes, was at war.

Earlier in the day a Mitsubishi transport plane of the China expeditionary force was flying over the South China Sea, carrying Major Tomoyuki Sugisaka, a courier of the Imperial General Staff, bound for Chienchung, headquarters of the 23rd Army. General Tsutomu Sakai, its commander, had been alerted; he expected Sugisaka to reach his headquarters before noon. Now it was past three o'clock and the plane had not arrived.

General Sakai sent a reconnaissance plane to search for the overdue aircraft. The pilot spotted the wreckage of a big army transport near Waiyeung, some fifty miles northeast of Canton, a mountain stronghold the Japanese had tried repeatedly to wrest from the Chinese. The pilot observed that "the scene of the crash was already surrounded by the Chinese who were swarming like ants."

Sakai immediately ordered a rescue party to try to break through, but the rugged terrain and the strong Chinese forces in the area made access impossible. Late in the afternoon General Sakai reported the accident to the General Staff in Tokyo, for he was certain that it was Major Sugisaka's courier plane that had crashed.

Since tactical surprise was essential to success during the initial phase of the impending campaigns, the Japanese high command did all it could to conceal the deployment of its forces. Until now Colonel Hattori had been satisfied that the concealment was succeeding. But with the crash of Sugisaka's plane the situation had changed radically. The document the major was carrying was the final "General Order" to Sakai with all the minute details of the Hong Kong attack, and he probably had not had time to destroy it prior to the accident. Though it seemed possible that it had burned in the crash, Hattori felt obliged to assume that it had been thrown clear and had been found by the Chinese.

"If the order were found," Hattori later wrote, "Chungking would be informed immediately, and Chiang Kai-shek would alert Washington and London. If the United States and British forces were informed of Japan's intentions of opening hostilities, they might carry out an attack on us, in great force, prior to Japan's commencement of hostilities."

He alerted General Shinichi Tanaka, his chief in the Operations Bureau, and Tanaka recalled General Sugiyama, the Chief of Staff, from an inspection trip. By the time Sugiyama reached his office in Tokyo it was past ten o'clock in the evening, but he called Admiral Nagano, Chief of the Naval General Staff, and asked him to come over as quickly as possible to discuss a sudden emergency.

Sugiyama and Nagano now agreed that in the light of what had happened in China, they could not wait any longer to set the "final and definite" date for the commencement of the hostilities. They decided to begin operations on December 8, and to petition the Emperor to approve the date. By then it was almost midnight, too late for an audience in the palace. Arrangements were made to see the Emperor in the morning.

DECEMBER 2 . . . At ten-thirty in the morning, standing side by side before Hirohito, the two Chiefs of Staff described the emergency and asked the Emperor's permission to start the war on X-Day. The Emperor nodded his head. This was sufficient for Sugiyama and Nagano to rush back to their offices and issue the final orders.

Sugiyama sent his at two o'clock to Supreme Commander General Count Juichi Terauchi and to all the other army commanders, in the prearranged WASHI code. The signal consisted of only two words—HINODE YAMAGATA—hinode standing for "the date for the commencement of operations," and yamagata for "the 8th of December."

By four-forty General Terauchi's confirmation was in Sugiyama's hands. "I respectfully received the Imperial Headquarters'

WASHI that HINODE will be YAMAGATA," it read. "The whole Southern Army, whose morale is being elevated further, swears to relieve His Majesty's concern by accomplishing its duties under the August Virtue of His Majesty."

At five-thirty Admiral Yamamoto had his signal flashed to the fleets. It went out in two parts, in the new invulnerable ADMIRALS code, put on the air one after another in rapid succession. First he radioed: "NIITAKA-YAMA NOBORE [Ascend Mount Niitaka]" which was his code for "Launch the attack on the enemy as previously arranged." Then followed the second part of the signal, the number "1208." It meant: "The date for the commencement of hostilities has been set for December 8."

The Pearl Harbor striking force was at sea. Its thirty-two ships were steaming in two parallel columns at 17 to 24 knots, covering about 320 miles each day on the northern course which Commanders Suzuki and Maejima had charted on their voyage on the *Taiyo Maru*. The Japanese knew that American aircraft were patrolling the vast "danger zone," flying eight hundred miles south of Dutch Harbor and eight hundred miles north of Midway. The course of the striking force was, therefore, directly between the two patrolled areas. There was dense fog, but the storm Admiral Nagumo feared would blow up did not materialize. Not a single ship or plane had been encountered—so far.*

Nagumo's "magnificent air fleet" was about a thousand miles north of Midway when Commander Kazuyoshi Kochi, the task force communications officer, handed Yamamoto's signal to the commanding admiral. Nagumo read it somberly, then called for "*Banzai*"—"May the Empire endure for ten thousand years!"

In Japan a separate operation was on to cover the departure of the "Z" forces. At the various naval bases a normal volume of fleet traffic was being put on the air, most of it dummy transmissions. The regular radio operators of the carriers with the striking force had been kept at home to lend the outgoing signals the "swing" presumably known to the American monitors, for a radioman's touch on the key is as distinctive as his fingerprints. The usual number of sailors showed up in Tokyo on the Ginza, at the haunts

---

* The task force met only one vessel on its outward passage, and that was a Japanese freighter.

of the gobs at liberty from the Yokosuka naval base, but they were soldiers in sailors' uniforms, dressed for the occasion to mislead the American and British attachés. In Yokohama harbor the *Tatsuta Maru*, flagship of the NYK line, was under steam to sail later in the day for San Francisco. Under the circumstances it would have been impossible to cancel her sailing without attracting attention. In the afternoon Commander Toshikazu Ohmae boarded the liner and handed her master a sealed box with instructions to "open it at oooo, December 8." The box contained a loaded pistol and the order to return to Yokohama, observing radio silence on the way back.*

In the afternoon Director Kumaichi Yamamoto of the Foreign Ministry's Bureau of American Affairs, called a meeting of his aides in his office in the main building on the *gaimu-sho* compound, a white, castlelike structure that was once the mansion of the feudal lord of Kuroda. He, too, had a duty to perform. The imperial conference had left the Foreign Ministry with one last important diplomatic function. There would be a hiatus of six days until X-Day, and the *gaimu-sho* had been given the job of putting up the smoke screen behind which the Emperor's forces could complete their deployment.

The assignment was much to Yamamoto's liking. In the hierarchy of the Foreign Ministry he represented the aggressive, expansionist faction. Although a veteran career diplomat, Yamamoto was committed to the policies of the militarists, at whose councils he represented the *gaimu-sho* and whose spokesman he was within the Foreign Ministry.

As soon as the imperial conference adjourned, Yamamoto began to work on what he called the "outline of future diplomatic measures regarding the United States." It was the operations order for the maneuver to lull the Americans. "Although," his memorandum read, "it will be necessary to break off the negotiations at the proper time, we must make it our main objective for the present to guard our future course, lest our real intentions are

---

* Commander Ohmae was the officer whose romantic escapade in Davenport, Iowa, a few years before had contributed to the unraveling of the secrets of the TYPE NO. 91 cipher unit. The *Tatsuta Maru* sailed on schedule but turned around five days out and reached Yokohama without incident.

found out. We must therefore give the appearance of our willingness to continue the negotiations, so as to facilitate the execution of our future plans."

He then sent a telegram to Ambassador Nomura: "The date set in dispatch No. 812 has come and gone, and the situation continues to be critical. However, to prevent the United States from becoming suspicious we have been advising the press and others that though there are some wide differences between Japan and the United States, the negotiations are continuing."

By his direction the Ambassador and Mr. Kurusu were to assure Mr. Hull that they were merely waiting for new instructions from Tokyo before resuming the talks. Yamamoto told them in so many words to keep talking to the bitter end "with a show of sincerity."

Thus began the last phase of what had essentially been a "battle of the telegrams." The air was now filled with spurious diplomatic dispatches to create the impression that this tottering peace could be preserved after all.

Although he was not admitted to the secret, Consul General Nagao Kita in Honolulu had no doubt that the war was only a few days away. He was at his desk almost around the clock, managing with brisk efficiency the final maneuvers before zero hour.

Only Ensign Yoshikawa was unruffled. He was still carrying out his secret mission without changing his daily routine at play. He continued to go swimming off the beaches, hiking on the highways around Pearl Harbor and sailing in a twin-hulled catamaran, close to the areas in which he had a special interest. His sightseeing enabled him to let Ogawa know that on this day two American battleships were anchored in Area A-KT, four more in Area A-FV, and that the heavy cruiser *Portland* was in the repair dock at the Navy Yard.

Then, however, four telegrams came in to put an end to this perfunctory espionage operation. A telegram from Cable Chief Kameyama brought a new code with "hidden words" and instructions to the code clerk to use it "until the final moment" in his "misleading-language dispatches." Another cable ordered the consul general to burn all his codes except a single copy of his OITE system. Kita immediately complied with the order, leaving this key outpost with nothing but a low-security system even while the messages it was sending to Tokyo increased in secrecy.

The third telegram concerned Yoshikawa. It was from Captain Ogawa, his last message in the TSU system, with a special notation to treat it most secretly. "In view of the present situation," Ogawa wrote, "the presence in port of battleships, aircraft carriers and cruisers is of the greatest importance. Hereafter report to me daily to the utmost of your ability.

"Advise me whether or not there are any observation balloons over Pearl Harbor or if there are any indications that they are likely to be used. Also let me know whether or not the battleships are protected by anti-torpedo nets."

The fourth telegram instructed Kita to forward at once the signal system Otto Kühn was devising. Kita immediately made arrangements to contact Kühn. He addressed a post card to Box 1476 at the main post office in Honolulu, inviting his "friend" to meet him "at the usual place" the next morning. He signed it "Jimmy" and gave it to Ichitaro Ozaki, the consulate's driver, to mail at the post office itself.

DECEMBER 3 . . . "Dr." Kühn, as Otto was now titling himself, found the post card in his box and went immediately to "the usual place"—a beauty parlor in downtown Honolulu. Waiting for him there was the young man he knew as Vice-Consul Morimura.

Kühn came fully prepared, even bringing along a "ships-in-port" report of his own. He told "Morimura" (who was, of course, Ensign Yoshikawa) that at his last count there were "seven battleships, two aircraft carriers, forty destroyers and twenty-seven submarines in Hawaiian waters"—almost the entire Pacific Fleet, as it were. This started an argument. Yoshikawa, who thought he knew better, voiced the opinion that Kühn was "way off" in his count, and the German shot back that he never made a mistake.

But then he calmed down and gave the ensign the "simplified system of signaling" which Captain Ogawa had commissioned him to draw up. It was neatly written down on several sheets of paper, in English but in Gothic script, and looked most professional, since Kühn had prepared the code part of it in the familiar arrangement of signal codes.

It turned out to be a numbers code running from 1 to 8, each number signifying a different movement of diverse types of ships: Nos. 1, 3 and 6 to indicate the battleships at division strength, Nos. 2, 4, 5 and 8 the aircraft carriers. The system provided for four methods of signals with separate arrangements for day and night. To indicate the various code numbers, Kühn proposed (1) to show lights in the dormer windows of his houses at Kalama and Lanikai; * (2) to display a star and/or the Roman numeral III at the top of the sail of a boat off Lanikai Beach (despite the fact that he did not own such a boat); (3) to place a series of want ads on the radio, such as "Chinese rug for sale" (to stand for signals 3 or 6), "Chicken farm for sale" (meaning Nos. 4 or 7), and "Beauty-parlor operator wanted" (for Nos. 5 or 8).

A fourth method was devised for the eventuality that none of the other signals could be sent. Kühn proposed to give fire or smoke signals by burning garbage at a certain location high up on Maui Island at specific times, each hourly period between seven and ten o'clock in the evening, indicating a different signal. It looked like an ingenious system as a whole. Since, for instance, lights in several windows might have attracted attention, Kühn suggested that he light no more than one or two windows in the attics, and the time period during which they were lit would signify the number of the code.

The system also had a number of interesting features that, in hindsight, stand out as significant clues. Apparently on further instructions from Ogawa (of which no record survives) Kühn had drawn up his system only for the six-day period ending on December 6. Moreover, since this was basically a visual system (except for the want ads), it presupposed the presence of Japanese vessels in Hawaiian waters, specifically in the Kaiwi Channel east of Oahu and west of Maui, through which the American fleet was regularly passing on its way to or from Pearl Harbor. The idea was for Japanese submarines to monitor the signals and relay the last-minute intelligence they furnished to Admiral Nagumo's striking force.

During the night Yoshikawa went boating off Kalama to try out the system. When he found that it worked, he incorporated the

---

* He persisted in including his beach house at Lanikai in the system even though it was occupied by the two Army couples to whom he had rented it and whose presence would have made signaling from there impossible.

whole scheme in a long telegram (the longest he ever filed) and
sent it to Tokyo for Ogawa's approval.

Behind its staid façade the consulate was now a beehive. The
hustle and bustle baffled Tada, the consul general's personal cook.
He sneaked upstairs for a closer look, then rushed back to the
kitchen and called a friend of his on the telephone.

"Listen, Otozo," he whispered in an excited voice. "There will
be war. Kita-*san* is burning his papers."

In the Foreign Ministry back in Tokyo, Kameyama's Cable
Section was working overtime. Telegrams to Japanese envoys in
Washington, London, Berlin, Rome, and around the world, were
flowing from Director Yamamoto's bureau to the *denshin-ka*
downstairs.

Kameyama was taking a certain risk by sending a series of
telegrams of his own to the missions abroad with orders to destroy
their codes in a low-grade cipher he himself was not positive was
safe. He even appended a telltale little note to telegrams going to
many of the consuls, including Kita in Honolulu. "The above," it
read, "is preparatory to an emergency situation and is for your
information only. Remain steadfast and calm!"

A pattern began to develop in the telegrams. The Japanese
ambassador in Rome reported that he had asked the Duce:
"Should Japan declare war on the United States and Great Britain
would Italy do likewise?" and quoted Mussolini as replying: "But
of course!" A cable from Bangkok spoke darkly of certain "cur-
rency arrangements for Thailand" to be ready "for an emergency
situation." A long telegram from Peking, signed by the commanding general of the army in North China and his staff, began with
the sentence: "This will be a war which will decide the rise or fall
of the Japanese Empire."

Yamamoto sent word to Terasaki, chief of the intelligence
service in Washington, to leave the United States at once, together with members of his staff. A new code was issued with
"hidden words" and sent to the missions in the danger zones "to
expedite the dispatch of the messages by forgoing the time-consuming process of encrypting."

DECEMBER 4 . . . In Saigon General Yamashita issued his orders to the 25th Army, bound for Malaya and Thailand. General

Sakai's troops began their march to their battle stations in the hinterland of Hong Kong. Low-flying little planes, their insignia painted out, appeared over southern Thailand.

Nagumo's task force spent the day refueling.

In Batavia the Japanese consul general was trying to fathom the broader implications of a series of cryptic telegrams pouring in from the Foreign Ministry. The latest, received early in the morning, made him fear the worst. It contained the "winds" code, to be broadcast in the regular weather reports "when the crisis reaches its most critical stage."

The consul turned on his radio, tuned it to the short-wave transmitter of Radio Tokyo and waited for the weather report. There came no mention of any east, west or north winds. None of the code phrases Kameyama had prepared for the ultimate emergency were included in the broadcast. But the consul was taking no chances. He decided to burn his papers anyway.

He had his servants carry the secret files of the consulate general into the back yard. He himself took out the code books and the ciphers. His houseboy arranged the files in a loose pile and ignited it, and the consul threw the code books into the flames. He stepped back to watch the fire, then looked over the fence at his neighbor's back yard, where a spiral of grayish smoke was curling skyward. It was the back yard of Walter Foote, the American consul general in Java. He, too, was burning his codes and papers.

There was only one issue still unsettled in Tokyo, and it turned out to be a thorny one. It was the question of how to meet the Emperor's demand that war be declared formally before the commencement of hostilities, as was mandatory under Article 1 of the Third Hague Convention, of which Japan was one of the signatories. "See to it," Hirohito had told General Tojo after the imperial conference, "that hostilities will not be started before the note is delivered."

Toshikazu Kase, section chief in Yamamoto's bureau, had worked for days on solving this problem. He finally hit upon the idea of a diplomatic note to be handed the Americans "prior to the launching of military operations" that could be construed as a kind of declaration of war without immediately alerting the United States. What his labors produced was a three-thousand-word document which the Foreign Ministry called *saigo no tsu-koku*, or "final notification," as distinguished from *saigo no tsucho*, or "ultimatum," the presentation of which had been considered but was ruled out.

Foreign Minister Togo presented Kase's paper to the *ad hoc* committee, with pointed references to the pertinent article of the Hague Convention. Nowhere in Kase's draft was the attack on Pearl Harbor as much as hinted at, of course. Neither did his note indicate that Japan would be launching military operations in the immediate wake of the delivery of the document.

Admiral Yamamoto, who needed total surprise for the success of his "Plan Z," protested vigorously the very idea of such a note. He threatened to call off the Pearl Harbor operation if the Emperor and the Foreign Minister insisted on going through with the delivery of even the vaguest notification to the United States before the raid. Debate over the note raged throughout the day and the *ad hoc* committee adjourned without reaching a decision.

Otherwise calm settled over the secret scene. Even the telegrams flared up only once, and briefly, in an exchange between Kameyama and Counselor Sadao Iguchi at the embassy in Washington. Iguchi had received orders to destroy all the embassy's coding paraphernalia, including both of the B units, by using certain chemicals the naval attaché had for this eventuality. But Counselor Iguchi considered the order impractical. How could he destroy the last of the cipher machines while negotiations were continuing, and still enable the ambassador to communicate with Tokyo safely? Iguchi asked the cable chief's permission to "delay for a while yet the destruction of the one cipher machine." Kameyama responded promptly, granting the permission.

DECEMBER 5 . . . The expeditionary force going to Thailand and Malaya left Samah at dawn. "The moon," wrote Colonel Tsuji while sailing with the convoy on the *Ryujo Maru*, the command ship, "like a tray, was sinking in the western sea, and the deep-red sun showed its face to the east. Samah Harbor, shimmering with gold and silver waves, was as beautiful as a picture.

"The men on the convoy of twenty ships, confident of victory, looked toward the bows of their ships, with the radiant sun behind them and the light of the sinking moon ahead, as the navy formed in two lines to right and left of the convoy as it ploughed through the waves heading away from the harbor.

"This was surely the starting point which would determine the destiny of the nation for the next century. The die was cast."

Although it was raining in the morning, Ensign Yoshikawa was driven to John Rodgers Airport, where he rented a Piper Cub for a flight over the harbor. A cable had come in earlier in the morning with another urgent query from Ogawa. "Please report comprehensively," it read, "on the American fleet."

After his flight he walked through Pearl City to the end of the peninsula, where he could survey the airfield on Ford Island and the cruisers moored in Pearl Harbor. Beyond them he saw the upper structure of the battleships.

It was Friday afternoon. The fleet was in.

From all over, telegrams were pouring into the Cable Section with a single word: "HARUNA." It was Kameyama's secret word, for "Codes destroyed by burning in accordance with your instructions."

In the afternoon Vice-Admiral Jinsaburo Ito arrived unexpectedly at the *gaimu-sho* to see Foreign Minister Togo. He was accompanied by General Tanaka, chief of the Army General Staff's Operations Bureau. Ito told Togo that he had come as the representative of the Chief of the Naval General Staff to discuss the timing of the delivery of Kase's note. Togo had proposed that it be delivered in Washington and London six hours before the commencement of hostilities. General Sugiyama had suggested that the interval be cut to two hours, but Admiral Nagano was unwilling to take even that much of a risk. At his insistence the margin was reduced to one and a half hours, in a compromise that recognized the letter of the Hague Convention but was not likely to give the Americans enough time to take any precautionary measures.

The attack against Pearl Harbor was only sixty hours away. But Admiral Ito had not come to reveal the momentous project even to the Foreign Minister. He came to say that Admiral Nagano had made a mistake. He now demanded that the time of delivery be changed again—cut to no more than a half-hour before the attack.

"How much time do you need," Togo asked, "between the notification and the attack?"

"That is an operational secret," Ito replied, "and cannot be divulged."

"Will there be sufficient margin of time before the commencement of hostilities," the Foreign Minister persisted, "if the note is delivered at one o'clock Washington time Sunday afternoon?"

"The margin of time will be *sufficient*," Admiral Ito said with emphasis.

The striking force was still forty-three hours from its target when another Japanese fleet reached its destination after nightfall, only eight and a half miles from the mouth of Pearl Harbor. It was the advance expeditionary force of twenty-seven submarines, most of them of the long-range I-type, sent by Yamamoto on a triple mission: to conduct reconnaissance, transmit intelligence to the striking force, and eventually to join the issue by hunting down and torpedoing ships that escaped the air attack.

They had had a grueling seventeen-day journey in heavy seas across a fogbound ocean, and now they dispersed to take up their preassigned scouting and patrolling stations. Five of the largest subs moved to the harbor's mouth to launch yet another flotilla, the special attack unit of midget submarines. In one of them Ensign Kazuo Sakamaki, just turned twenty-three, was preparing for his "sacrifice mission" with the ritual of a *ronin* sentenced to commit *hara-kiri*. He had brought along a small bottle of perfume, "in the best tradition of the old Japanese warriors," to scent himself before going to battle. "Then I could die gloriously," Sakamaki explained, "like cherry blossoms falling to the ground."

In the midst of his gloom he caught himself, joined his comrades in the mother sub, and invited them to intone the *Kuroda Bushi*, a stirring old song of the *samurai*, with a rather somber melody.*

---

* "Drink *sake*, drink *sake*, for if you can drink so much as to swallow this spear, the mightiest in all Japan, you'll be a true *samurai* of Kuroda." Ensign Sakamaki was the sole survivor of the midget submarine attack on December

DECEMBER 6 . . . At eight o'clock in the morning Commander Kanjiro Ono, Admiral Nagumo's intelligence officer, handed his chief one of the last signals from Tokyo. It gave the number and position of the American ships at Pearl on the basis of Ensign Yoshikawa's report of the 5th. The absence of the carriers darkened Nagumo's mood. He knew that the *Saratoga* was on the West Coast. But that still left the *Enterprise* and the *Lexington* in Hawaiian waters—perhaps looking for him.

Yamamoto had ordered him to abandon his mission and return to Japan if discovered prior to December 6.* But Ono reassured his admiral. He had been keeping vigil over the American radio traffic, and nothing he had picked up indicated even remotely that they were on to the game. Throughout the force, radios were tuned to the Honolulu stations, coming in "bright and lively." At 12:45 there was a Japanese program on KGMB, conducted by George Fujita, but the pilots preferred "Plantation Melodies" at 3:05 P.M. and "Swing Nocturne" from 11:15 to midnight.

Colonel Hattori was reassured at last. "Since the night of December 1, the Imperial General Headquarters had been deeply worried about the possible reaction from the plane accident of Major Sugisaka," he wrote in his war diary. "But there was no sign up to the 6th. After all, the classified documents seemed not to have fallen into enemy hands."

He could now confidently prepare the day's Intelligence Summary for the Chief of Staff, the last he would write before the outbreak of the war.

"The United States and Great Britain," he accurately wrote, "are believed to be gradually obtaining information concerning the progress of Japan's operational preparations, but it is considered that they have not yet grasped the situation. In other words, it may be known to them that Japan will direct her military opera-

---

7. He lived to tell this story of his night off Pearl Harbor, and to criticize Consul General Kita and his aides for sending "wrong information" about the "locations of the ships of the Pacific Fleet" in Pearl Harbor at the time of the attack.

* Nagumo's orders included the stipulation that he hold himself in readiness to return "should the negotiations with the United States prove successful." However, it was left to his discretion to decide what to do "if discovered 7 December (East Longitude date)."

tions toward the south, but their estimate as to the specific area of operations will be a wild guess.

"It appears that they have placed greater probability on Japan's advancing into Thailand to cut off the Burma Route, than attacking American and British territories or the Dutch East Indies. Meanwhile the Chungkirig authorities are believed to be seriously concerned over a possible Yunnan operation by the Japanese army, and are frantically devising countermeasures.

"Some quarters of the United States and Great Britain think that Japan plans to attack Singapore, but they do not seem to expect any attack on other areas. Furthermore, it is observed that some think that Japan's military movement in the southern area might be a maneuver to accelerate her negotiations with the United States." *

Shortly before five o'clock in the evening, Director Yamamoto called Cable Chief Kameyama on the phone and told him to place his Section on a war footing. Simultaneously Kase arrived at the *denshin-ka* with copies of two telegrams consigned for Washington, and asked Kameyama to send them out immediately, encrypted on the BEI-GWA, the B machine.

One was a personal note from Yamamoto to his friends Counselor Sadao Iguchi and First Secretary Shiroji Yuki, who had recently arrived in the United States to aid in the negotiations. It turned out to be a highly emotional farewell message, expressing the Ministry's thanks for their "great efforts in behalf of our country in the face of all the difficulties in coping with the unprecedented crisis." It went out at seven-thirty.

At four minutes to eight Senior Code Clerk Tokuji Oda, chief operator of the B unit, completed the encoding of the second telegram. Signed "Togo," it was a three-paragraph message from the Foreign Minister to Ambassador Nomura. Clerk Oda marked the finished crypt "state secret," to indicate its supremely confidential nature, and passed it by teletype to the Central Telegraph

---

* Hattori's last-minute summary demonstrated the extraordinary astuteness of the man, but also the high quality of Japanese intelligence coverage of Washington and London. Parts of the summary read as if they had been lifted verbatim from American and British documents, indicating that the Japanese were putting their own Code Research Groups to good use.

Office, with a note that it must be sent out at once. According to the log of the *denshin-ka*, the message left Tokyo via MKY (Mackay Radio) at ten minutes after nine, which was ten minutes past seven in the morning of December 6 in Washington. This telegram was to gain fame as the so-called pilot message. However, it did not seem to contain anything that might hint at the further deterioration in the situation, bad as it already was. It merely alerted the ambassador to a forthcoming cable containing the text of a "very long memorandum." This was to be sent in fourteen parts and was presumably Tokyo's answer to the American note of November 26. The pilot message instructed Nomura to make all necessary arrangements so that the memorandum could be presented to the American government promptly, the exact time to be specified in a separate telegram that would be sent shortly.

The embassy received the cable at high noon in Washington. It was decoded in just fifteen minutes by Chief Cipher Clerk Takeshi Kajiwara, and was taken to Admiral Nomura by First Secretary Yuki. Then came another cable, instructing the ambassador to use none of the embassy's regular typists in the transcription of the mysterious memorandum, but to have it transcribed by a member of the diplomatic staff.

Admiral Nomura alerted the Code Room. Its full complement of five cipher clerks under Telegraph Official Masara Horiuchi was told to stand by. And since no ordinary typist was allowed to handle the memorandum, Nomura delegated one of his senior diplomatic aides, First Secretary Katsuzo Okumura, to do the typing. The task fell to Okumura simply because he was the only member of the diplomatic staff who could type, albeit by the two-finger method. Chancellor Yoriyasu Nakajima and Secretary Yuki were then detailed to proofread the final version of the text, an important assignment, as it turned out, in view of Okumura's deficiency at the typewriter.

Back in Tokyo, the code clerks were busy putting the memorandum itself through the B unit. "I recall," Kameyama later wrote, "that I received the original copy of the memorandum in the afternoon of December 6, from Toshikazu Kase, chief of the First Section of the American Bureau, and had it encoded immediately, part by part." The Japanese text, which had been approved by the entire Cabinet two days before, had been translated into English by Kase, partly to expedite its handling at the Washington end, and partly to prevent any errors or possible misinterpretations from slipping into the text.

It took Chief Clerk Oda thirty minutes to encode Part 8 of the memorandum, the first to be ready to be sent to the Central Telegraph Office. Thirteen parts of the message were to be sent out for the time being. When Kameyama inquired about the fourteenth part, Kase told him to await instructions.

Working from twenty to thirty minutes on each part, depending on its length, the code clerks finished the job shortly after eight o'clock. Half an hour later the memorandum started moving out of the Cable Section. The final copy of the first thirteen parts was at the Central Telegraph Office at twenty minutes past midnight on December 7 (Tokyo time). The message had been put on the air at ten minutes past ten the previous evening and was again sent at one-fifty in the morning on the 7th, on two separate channels to ensure safe and accurate transmission and reception. The first cable moved via Mackay Radio. Then followed the identical text via RCA.

Early in the morning in Hawaii, Code Clerk Tsukikawa handed Yoshikawa an "urgent" telegram from Ogawa that had just arrived: "Please report immediately re the latter part of my No. 123 the movements of the fleet subsequent to the 4th."

It referred to the telegram of December 2 in which the Third Bureau had queried the ensign about the observation balloons over Pearl Harbor and the anti-torpedo nets. Yoshikawa had so far neglected to reply, but now he called Mikami, who was supposed to check up on the defenses of the harbor, and the cab driver assured him that there was no reason for apprehension on this score.

"I have never seen any torpedo nets used on my trips to the harbor," Mikami said. "And I am positive that the Americans have no anti-airplane balloons. They would be impractical for use around Pearl Harbor because they would give away the exact location of the objective."

Yoshikawa drafted a telegram for Ogawa—the most crucial and potentially most indiscreet communication he would ever send. It was his next to last report and it read:

(1) In my opinion the battleships do not have torpedo nets. The details are not known. I will report the results of my investigation.

(2) . . . . At the present time there are no signs of barrage balloon equipment. In addition, it is difficult to imagine that they actually have any. Even though some preparations had been made, for they must control the air over the harbor and the runways of the airports in Pearl Harbor, at Hickam, Ford and Ewa, there are limitations imposed upon the balloon defense of Pearl Harbor.

Then, sensing that his "work was almost done" and carried away by the excitement of the moment, he added a thought he was not supposed to have even in the back of his mind, much less express. "I imagine," he wrote as an afterthought, "that in all probability there is considerable opportunity left to take advantage for a surprise attack against these places."

There was only one other task left for him on this day. Kotoshirodo, Seki and Yoshikawa himself had been out on their routes the whole day, checking the fleet in the harbor until sunset. The carriers were gone, and so were, Yoshikawa believed, all the heavy cruisers. But the rest of the fleet was in. The ships were at their moorings, and nothing indicated that any of them was planning to depart before Monday.

At nine o'clock Yoshikawa wrote up his final ship-movement report:

The following ships were observed at anchor on the 6th: 9 battleships, 3 light cruisers, 3 submarine tenders, 17 destroyers. In addition there were 4 light cruisers and 2 destroyers lying at docks.

It appears that no air reconnaissance is being conducted by the fleet air arm.*

"So it was," Yoshikawa wrote after the war, "that as I sat at my desk in the darkened consulate building in Honolulu late in the

---

* His count of the ships was not exact. In actual fact, eight of the battleships were at their moorings, one was in dock. The heavy cruisers, which he believed had left, were in port, and there were six light cruisers riding at anchor. Instead of the nineteen destroyers he reported, there were twenty-nine. In addition, four minesweepers and eight mine layers were moored in Area D. But the discrepancies did not matter. Yoshikawa correctly reported the crucial intelligence that the fleet was in and that air reconnaissance was conspicuous by its absence.

evening on 6 December, I knew that the message I was working on might well be the last which the Japanese attack-force commander would receive before the attack. And so it proved to be.

"After giving the message . . . to the waiting code clerk for encryption into the diplomatic code and transmission to Tokyo, I strolled about the consulate grounds before turning in, as was my custom. The bright haze in the distance indicated that the lights were on at the Pearl Harbor naval base, and I could hear no patrolling aircraft aloft. It was a quiet Saturday night and all seemed normal, so I finally turned in and slept restlessly until morning."

At about the same time, the striking force reached the meridian of Oahu at a point about five hundred miles north of the island. Admiral Yamamoto's final message had just been received in the *Akagi*. It repeated the "Mount Niitaka" code and went on to say: "The moment has arrived! The rise or fall of our Empire is at stake!"

The attack pilots assembled in the carriers to receive their last briefings from their group leaders. And then the actual "Z" flag which admiral Togo had flown in the Battle of Tsushima Strait thirty-six years before was hoisted to the masthead of the flagship.

It was not until four o'clock in the afternoon of December 7 in Tokyo that Section Chief Kase told Kameyama to move the fourteenth part of the *saigo no tsukoku*, the "final notification." Again the telegram was sent out on two circuits, at five o'clock via MKY and at six via RCA. Then at six twenty-eight, and again at six-thirty, another dispatch was sent. It instructed Ambassador Nomura and Special Envoy Kurusu to deliver the note—"into the hands of Secretary Hull if possible"—at exactly one o'clock on December 7, Washington time.

Then a minor mishap was discovered. A line had been left out of a paragraph in the note. This, and the ungarbling of the word "assertions" in the third part to read "proposals," necessitated brief follow-up cables on both channels to correct the errors.

By then it was twenty minutes past five in the morning on December 7 in Washington.

The capital was sound asleep on the Sunday that was to go down in history as the Day of Infamy.

24

A Week of Indecision

As the crisis moved into December, American communications intelligence continued in a turmoil. On December 1, just as Commander Holmes in Hawaii had succeeded in lining up the calls the Japanese had introduced a month before, the service signs of the forces afloat were changed again. Holmes commented on the surprising development: "The fact that [they] lasted only one month indicates an additional progressive step in preparing for active operations on a large scale. It appears that the Japanese navy is adopting more and more security provisions."

The Japanese confused the picture still further with additional measures of concealment. On the eve of the change they transmitted a considerable number of old messages to pad the volume of the traffic. Then, after the change, they returned traffic to normal. This gave the impression that except for their Second Fleet, which moved with almost deliberate conspicuousness toward Indochina, none of their other fleets was operating outside of Japanese waters.

Holmes was understandably baffled by these tricks. There was nothing he could report on the First, Third, Fourth or Fifth fleets, no apparent change in the dispositions of the Combined Air Force. As far as the submarines were concerned, he assumed they were "somewhere" east of the Yokosuka-Chichijima area, but presumably not far from their home waters. He could find no sign of the carriers.

When his daily summaries continued to state the stereotype

that he had "no information on submarines or carriers," Admiral Kimmel first sent Lieutenant Commander Edwin T. Layton, his fleet intelligence officer, to Rochefort and Holmes, then went himself to impress upon them the importance of "finding" the carriers. But Rochefort could tell the admiral only: "There is an almost complete blank of information on them, sir, but," he added, "since over two hundred service calls have been partially identified since the change on the first of December and not a single carrier call has been received, it is evident that carrier traffic is at a low ebb."

"Do you mean to say they could be rounding Diamond Head and you wouldn't know it?" Kimmel asked Layton, who could reply only that he hoped "they would be sighted before that."

In the midst of this setback, an interdepartmental squabble occurred in which the security bureaucrats in Hawaii gave up the Navy's next-to-last means of surveillance, the DIO's taps on the telephones at the Japanese consulate.

In November the FBI had placed a tap on the phone of Kenzi Kimura, general manager of the NYK line, in the basement of the Dillingham Building, where he had his offices. But the tap—a jumper placed across the connections in a junction box—was uncovered by a workman, and a representative of the telephone company told the DIO about the discovery. Robert L. Shivers, the FBI agent in charge, thereupon upbraided the manager of the phone company for revealing, as he put it, FBI secrets to the Office of Naval Intelligence. When Shivers' indiscreet protest was related to Captain Mayfield, the district intelligence officer, he peremptorily ordered that all taps be removed from the consulate's phones. His reason for this was his "concern at the violation of security," and that some "incident of international import might result from such violations." The DIO's tapping of telephones in Hawaii was a secret second only to that of "Magic." Even Admiral C. C. Bloch, commandant of the 14th Naval District, was not told of this activity "in order that he might be spared any possible embarrassment." *

---

* The FBI continued its surveillance of the consulate over its single tap on the telephone of Kita's cook and overheard his excited conversation on December 3 about the consul's burning of his papers. This was an important straw in the wind, and despite the recent quarrel Shivers immediately for-

On this same December 2 the United States Navy decided against the opening up of a friendly channel that could have aided its surveillance of the Japanese navy. On October 8 the Admiralty had proposed that the two navies co-ordinate their communications procedures in the emergency and introduce an Anglo-American code to facilitate and expedite "the exchange of information." The suggestion was ignored for forty-five days. Now at last Admiral Stark answered it, in the negative. "Existing communication channels and procedures," he cabled the Admiralty via the American ambassador in London, "are considered wholly adequate for the transmission of urgent and important information and for insuring that information of this character receives the prompt attention of the appropriate high authorities in Washington. . . . In view of the foregoing it is not believed that any new arrangements need to be made."

On November 30, 1941, despite Hull's and Stimson's warnings that relations with Japan had left the bounds of diplomacy, F.D.R. still persisted in the belief that he was gaining the time the Army and the Navy were pleading for. And he was confident that the State Department's note of November 26—conspicuously marked "tentative" to indicate that it was still leaving the door ajar—would bring an answering note through normal diplomatic channels, and not war.*

It was, therefore, with a light heart and in a buoyant spirit that the President sat down with the patients in Warm Springs for a belated Thanksgiving dinner. But in the midst of it Lieutenant Commander George Fox, his physical therapist, had to wheel him out to answer a call from Washington. Mr. Hull was calling to tell the President that Premier Tojo had proclaimed in a "bellicose speech" that Japan was "morally bound for the honor and pride of

---

warded the information to Captain Mayfield as well as to Colonel Bicknell in the Army's Contact Office. Mayfield did nothing with the information, but Bicknell personally gave it to General Short at a staff meeting on December 6.

* Ambassador Nomura, however, omitted to transmit to Tokyo the conspicuous reference to the "tentative" character of the American proposals and thus created the impression that they represented the definitive and final terms of the United States.

mankind" to "purge" Great Britain and the United States "from all of East Asia with a vengeance." Hull construed the statement as "a last straw" and decided to call the President about it. He now advised Mr. Roosevelt to return to Washington immediately because a Japanese attack seemed imminent.

The President left at once and arrived back in Washington in the morning of December 1, only to find that what had threatened to develop into an explosive incident had blown out meekly. Alarmed over Tojo's intemperate remarks, and more anxious than ever to lull the Americans a little longer, the Japanese went to some lengths to disavow their Premier.

On December 1 Ambassador Grew cabled from Tokyo that he had received what amounted to an apology for Tojo's statements and that "several prominent Japanese" with whom he had discussed the incident "all appear to desire continuance of the Washington conversations."

There would have been ample reason for the President to remain uneasy despite Mr. Grew's reassuring cable. The "magics" (which he was now seeing in the full text of the intercepts) continued to carry their disturbing message. Three which awaited him on his return in particular seemed to bear out Hull's apprehension over Tojo's speech rather than Grew's optimistic interpretation.

One intercept showed that the Japanese were transferring First Secretary Terasaki from their embassy in the United States to Argentina. Since he was, according to Kramer, "head of Japanese espionage in Western Hemisphere," this seemed to indicate, as Kramer indeed pointed out in a footnote, that Tokyo was dismantling its intelligence service in the United States and establishing it in a neutral American country, presumably because rupture of relations or war would make it impossible for Terasaki to continue to function in Washington.

The second was the set of telegrams from Kameyama to the various Japanese missions abroad arranging for the gradual destruction of their code material and confidential papers.

The third was a dispatch from Foreign Minister Togo instructing Ambassador Oshima in Berlin to see Hitler and Ribbentrop and tell them "very secretly . . . that there is extreme danger that war may suddenly break out between the Anglo-Saxon nations and

Japan through some clash of arms," and that "the time of the breaking out of this war may come quicker than anyone dreams." When Captain Beardall showed the Togo telegram to Mr. Roosevelt, the President spent some time studying it. The next day he asked the naval aide to bring it back from the files, for he wanted to read it again. It made an enormous impression on him. Even much later it stuck in his mind as the one intercept he had seen that convinced him of the seriousness of the Japanese threat. On this December 2 the President seemed to be sure that some warlike action was imminent and that the United States might not be as immune as he had thought. He sent for Stimson, Knox and Sumner Welles (the latter substituting for Secretary Hull, who went to bed for a day to recoup his strength that was beginning to crumble under the strain of the crisis). This was virtually the only time during this period that the President showed vigor, determination and initiative to counter the Japanese moves with a number of American arrangements.

A flurry of action ensued in the Navy Department, as reflected in a number of OPNAV signals sent during the day to Admiral Hart of the Asiatic Fleet, Admiral Kimmel in Pearl Harbor, and the commandants of the 14th and 16th Naval districts. They were told that the Japanese missions at Hong Kong, Singapore, Batavia, Manila, Washington and London had been ordered to "destroy most of their codes and ciphers, and to burn all other important confidential and secret documents." An "action dispatch" to Hart and the commandant of the 16th Naval District went so far as to actually mention a "magic"—the one in which Kameyama had ordered Washington to destroy the B machine and had instructed the consul general in Batavia "to return [his] machine to Tokyo at once."

More important, Admiral Hart in Manila was ordered to "charter three small vessels [within two days after receipt this dispatch] to form 'defensive information patrol.'" To be stationed off the Indochina coast between Hainan Island and Hué, between Camranh Bay and Cape St. Jacques, and off Point Camau, they were to "observe and report by radio Japanese movements in West China Sea and Gulf of Siam." At the same time, Hart was ordered to inform Admiral Stark "what reconnaissance measures are being regularly performed at sea by both army and navy and whether by air, surface vessels or submarines." He was invited to give his opinion "as to the effectiveness of these latter measures."

It seems, however, that these dispatches exhausted the energies which had inspired them. Hart was left no time to organize a "defensive information patrol" or even to improve his existing "reconnaissance measures." There was no follow-up from Washington.

The woes of the Navy's communications intelligence apparatus were not yet over. The final blow came on December 4, when the Japanese also changed their FLEET code, the only remaining naval system from which the United States Navy could still cull a modicum of information. This change was not entirely unexpected. The Japanese regularly revised this code every six months. The change was in fact overdue since December 1, and the American analysts were surprised when it failed to materialize. When it was finally made, four days behind schedule, Commander Safford set his best code crackers to work on the new code. But their progress was slow. And with the change of JN-25—the twenty-fifth variant of the old JN series—the United States Navy apparently lost the last remaining channel through which intelligence could be obtained about Japanese designs, especially those on Pearl Harbor.

There appeared, however fleetingly at this point, a bright spot in the dismal picture, a development of potentially enormous significance. A channel had suddenly opened up in Hawaii itself that promised to aid materially in compensating for the loss of the other sources.

An arrangement was worked out on December 2 whereby George Street, the district manager of RCA in Hawaii, would co-operate at last with Captain Mayfield by preparing copies of the Japanese telegrams on blank sheets of paper, giving the full text of the messages but including as little data as possible about their origins and addressees. No written records, such as lists of transmittal or receipts, would be used. The copies, placed in unmarked envelopes, would be picked up by Captain Mayfield in person each morning at Street's office on S. King Street.

At eleven o'clock in the morning on December 3, Mayfield went to the RCA office and was given the first envelope containing every single telegram the Japanese consulate had filed with RCA during the first three days of the month. Most of them were in plain text, but five were crypts. The next morning Street gave Mayfield another envelope with a number of telegrams, four of which were in crypt.

What had seemed to be a gold mine of an intelligence source proved disappointing. The plain-text telegrams revealed nothing new. And the dispatches in code could not be puzzled out. The DIO had an excellent linguist on his staff in the person of Commander Carr, but no cryptanalysts. Moreover, neither the 14th Naval District nor the Pacific Fleet Communications Office had cryptanalytical branches.

Mayfield knew, however, of a mysterious outfit tucked away in the Naval Radio Station at Aiea that was rumored to be engaged in such work. It was nominally attached to the Naval District but was actually operating as an autonomous organization beyond the commandant's jurisdiction, reporting directly to Naval Communications in Washington. It was, of course, Commander Rochefort's organization. A field unit of Safford's Op-20-G, it was an integral part of the Navy's own top-secret cryptological effort that had nothing to do either with the Naval District or, indeed, with "Magic." Though its proper name was "Communications Intelligence Unit," it was here called "Combat Intelligence Unit" to camouflage its functions while retaining the initials C and I and, as Rochefort put it, place it "on a military footing."

Mayfield now faced the alternative of either routing the encrypted telegrams to Washington through slow channels, with the prospect of never seeing anything of them again, or penetrating behind the high wall Rochefort had erected around his C/I Unit. On December 5, two days after he had started receiving the copies from Street, he took the batch to Rochefort and asked him to decrypt them for him. The Unit was far too busy to devote its attention to any extra work, and was not equipped to tackle any diplomatic systems. It was working on the tough new FLAG OFFICERS cipher and several other Japanese systems, all of them *naval*, such as the Imperial Navy's 267 (personnel) code, administrative code and a code used in the mandated islands.

Lieutenant Commander Dyer, the chief cryptanalyst, designated one of his minor assistants, a petty officer named Farnsley

C. Woodward, to see what he could do about the consular tele-grams. Woodward had come to the Unit only recently from Shanghai, where he had worked from 1938 to August 13, 1941, at the station Zacharias had established in 1927. In the Rochefort organization he had several duties to perform, one of which was cryptanalysis.

A lone yeoman was thus assigned to attack what potentially was one of the most important sources of intelligence about the Japa-nese, at a time when all other channels were effectively blocked off. Working sixteen hours each day on December 5 and 6, Wood-ward had no difficulty with crypts in the consulate's low-grade LA system, a simple abbreviating code with which the Unit was familiar. But it was a different matter with messages encoded in OITE—what we called PA-K2—which used a code base with a trans-position system. Since the Unit was not supposed to work on anything connected with "Magic" and had no experience with the diplomatic systems, Woodward had to attack the code from scratch. Rochefort had several RIPs—Radio Intelligence Publica-tions issued by Op-20-G, which included research material about all Japanese systems currently read—but Woodward found noth-ing in any of them to aid his "take-out" of the OITE code.

The result was that Mayfield's coup in obtaining Yoshikawa's last-minute messages at their source, on the day of their filing, in perfect copies of their ungarbled originals, went completely to waste. There were two key telegrams in this batch: the dispatch of December 3 in which Kühn's signal system was forwarded to Tokyo, and Yoshikawa's next-to-last report of December 6 with information about the anti-torpedo nets, barrage balloons and his comment that this would be a good time to mount a surprise attack. But since Woodward could not as much as break into the code before December 9, and, therefore, could not even guess at the contents of the messages, these vital telegrams in our hands proved as useless as if Mayfield had never succeeded in getting them.

At this time Mr. Roosevelt ran into an embarrassing controversy with President Manuel Quezon of the Philippines, who, in the face of the Japanese challenge, could neither understand nor tolerate F.D.R.'s apparent inertia any longer. On November 28 Quezon had erupted in a National Heroes Day speech at the University of the Philippines in which he denounced Roosevelt in bitter words. If war were to come, he said, the civilian population of the Philippines would be unprotected. The inadequacy of preparations was due, he charged, to his being blocked in his efforts to provide for civilian defense by the President of the United States. He attributed Mr. Roosevelt's inaction to "ignorance and bad faith."

Stung by Quezon's accusations and feeling that something really needed to be done if he was to deny the Japanese all the initiative, Roosevelt pondered just what action he could take without running the risk of committing the first overt act in a shooting war. He thought of sending a personal letter to the Emperor to invite him to join in an effort to halt this mad rush to war. But Hull and his associates strenuously objected to the idea, arguing that such a message would be of "doubtful efficacy" and "might even cause . . . complications."

Churchill was urging Roosevelt to issue a warning to the Japanese in no uncertain terms, that any further act of aggression on their part would have "the gravest consequences." The President agreed that such a "plain declaration" was the "one important method unused in averting war," and he wanted to make it in the form of a special message to Congress in which he would "spill the beans," as he told Hull and Stimson. But the sudden quiet on the crisis front persuaded him to defer both the letter to the Emperor and the message to Congress. He let Congress adjourn for a long weekend on Thursday, December 4. There would be ample time to do "something" next week.

Since the Japanese were now eager to keep things on an even keel until their X-Day, they tried to avoid doing anything on their part that might disturb the precarious balance and the curious calm of these days. Their telegrams became more discreet, more taciturn, and fewer in number. Director Yamamoto of the Foreign Ministry even asked Nomura and Kurusu to do without cables as far as possible and use the transpacific telephone instead. In order to ensure the secrecy of these conversations, he sent them a list with a set of code words in which the President was "Miss Kimiko" and Mr. Hull "Miss Umeko"; the negotiations were referred to as "matchmaking"; and the pending war was a "child" about to be born.

Unhappily for the Japanese, "Magic" also eavesdropped on their conversations. And since the "hidden word" code had been sent ahead in a telegram that was promptly intercepted and decrypted by the Navy, the real meaning of this bizarre "matchmaking" could not be concealed from the Americans.

During this final week before Pearl Harbor, American diplomacy degenerated into nothing but interoffice dialogues and bureaucratic paper work. The spoken and written words wasted on the crisis during these last few days ran into hundreds of thousands of ephemeral words. The State Department thus spent innumerable man-hours drafting and redrafting the President's proposed letter to Hirohito it did not really want to be sent. The experts locked themselves up in endless conferences debating issues which were patently beyond any more discussion. They used relays of stenographers in mass-producing memoranda that conjugated the themes of the crisis in all their moods, tenses and inflections, without adding anything new to what had already been thrashed out.

When these officials were not busy writing their own memoranda, they were engaged in reading the memos of their colleagues. These memos were crisscrossing one another and were sent around full circle within the Department "for information and comment." While they generated very little information, the comments they elicited merely added to the confusion. A memorandum circulating a British suggestion that some sort of arrangement ought to be made with the Japanese for the exchange of diplomatic personnel in the event of war, drew the comment, "Do not clearly perceive a need," from Dr. Hornbeck, and the remark, "It would appear highly desirable to take such a step immediately," from Joseph Green, chief of the Department's Special Division.

While the contours of the Japanese conspiracy could be traced by "Magic" from more than ten thousand miles away, an insidious plot brewing in Washington itself remained totally undetected. Early in December a group of dissident officers motivated by anti-Roosevelt, anti-British sentiments removed a number of top-secret documents from the files of the War Department with a view to exposing this country's war plans. It was a blatant effort to frustrate American aid to Britain and what was called Roosevelt's conspiracy to sneak the United States into the war. The documents included the Joint Strategic Estimate of September 11, 1941, signed by General Marshall and Admiral Stark. It summarized such strategic studies and plans as the CNO ("Plan Dog") Memorandum of November 12, 1940; the ABC-1 staff agreements with the British of March 1941; and the Joint Army-Navy War Plan, the so-called "Rainbow No. 5." The Joint Estimate described the strengths of the forces and arms production the United States needed "to assure the defeat of Germany and Italy, and also, if necessary, Japan."

It was now smuggled to the isolationist group of newspapers controlled by the McCormick-Patterson clan, the Chicago *Tribune*, the Washington *Times-Herald*, and the New York *Daily News*. The papers prepared the publication in the utmost secrecy and issued it simultaneously as the "Roosevelt War Plan" in the morning of December 4, under a Washington date line.

This revelation of America's most vital military secrets created a national emergency that overshadowed the international crisis. An investigation was ordered by the President of the source from which the Chicago *Tribune* and its sister publications had obtained the documents. Their authenticity was publicly acknowledged by Secretaries Stimson and Knox. Mr. Knox described them as "the most secret documents in the possession of the United States Government," and Mr. Stimson explained that they were "unfinished studies of our production requirements for national defense."

The isolationists hailed their publication as a mortal blow to Roosevelt's "undeclared war." On December 5 the *Times-Herald* headlined: "War Plan Exposé Rocks Capital, Perils Army Appropriation Bill—Administration Fears Nation's Wrath Over Secret Project—Congress in Uproar." Secretary Stimson released an indignant statement:

"While this publication will doubtless be a gratification to our potential enemies and a possible source of impairment and embarrassment to our national defense, the chief evil of their publication is the revelation that there should be among us any group of persons so lacking in appreciation of the danger that confronts the country, and so wanting in loyalty and patriotism to their government that they would be willing to take and publish such papers."

The Japanese high command privately greeted the appearance of the Joint Strategic Estimate as proof positive that the United States was not ready for a major war even in one ocean, much less in two, and welcomed its publication for the embarrassment it was causing Roosevelt.

The impact of the publication of the documents on the home front was considerable. The debate the Chicago *Tribune's* startling scoop had engendered, momentarily diverted attention from the Japanese threat, both in public and at the White House.*

On the day Captain Mayfield managed to gain access to the Japanese consulate's confidential dispatches at their source, an unusual amount of first-hand data became available about Japanese moves toward war and, in fact, about their plan to attack Pearl Harbor.

In Honolulu the telegram containing Kühn's scheme of signaling was filed with and transmitted by RCA, and was intercepted by no fewer than three separate operations: by Captain Mayfield, who was given a copy of the original by Manager Street of RCA; by the Army's MS-7 at Fort Hunt, Virginia; and by the Navy's Station M in Cheltenham, Maryland. MS-5, the mystery station at Fort Shafter, picked up Captain Ogawa's telegram to Kita with the order that the consulate report daily henceforth the movements of ships (instead of twice a week as heretofore) and asking details of the anti-torpedo nets and barrage balloons at Pearl Harbor.

Neither intercept was processed when picked up. But in Washington a "strictly secret" telegram of December 2 from Tokyo—ordering the embassy to "destroy all codes except one, one of the cipher machines, and all confidential documents"—became available in translation. The message was the classic order usually issued on the eve of war, and Colonel Bratton immediately recognized it

---

* The first reports of the investigation President Roosevelt had ordered to discover the sources of the "leak" reached the White House on December 9, when the nation was already at war. The President thought it better not to press the probe further. Hence no legal proceedings nor disciplinary action was ever initiated to punish those responsible for disclosing our defense secrets. The identity of the people from whom the documents were procured has never been revealed.

as such. But he now found himself in an awkward position. He had lost face badly with his prediction that war with Japan would break out on November 30, and was ridiculed as a "worry-bird" in the War Plans Division. He felt deeply the humiliation of his debacle and hardly dared to show himself at the "front offices" in the Munitions Building.

But now the code-destruction telegram propelled him back into action. He sent Lieutenant Schindel from his Section up Massachusetts Avenue to ascertain whether the embassy was complying with the order. Judging from the grayish-white smoke escaping through one of the chimneys of the quaint embassy building, Schindel concluded that they were and so reported back to Bratton, who took the intercept and the lieutenant's report to General Miles. At Miles's suggestion he then went to War Plans, gave his opinion that this was "the culmination of the complete revelation of Japanese intentions" and said that it was construed by G-2 as meaning "immediate war." He suggested that War Plans send another warning to the overseas commands, but Gerow turned him down. "I think they have had plenty of notification," he said and told Bratton rather curtly that he did not wish to discuss the matter any further.

As was his practice when he could not make any headway with his fellow officers in the War Department, Bratton went over to the Navy Department to review the situation with Commander McCollum, his opposite number in ONI. The problem of further warnings, especially to Hawaii, was explored in an impromptu conference attended by Admiral Noyes of Naval Communications, Captain Wilkinson, the Director of Naval Intelligence, McCollum and Bratton. The evidence was impressive. Aside from the latest code-destruction message, the "winds" code was haunting the scene. Wilkinson was, therefore, all in favor of another warning signal to Kimmel. Noyes, however, objected on the ground that it would be "an insult to the intelligence of the admiral."

"I do not agree with you," Wilkinson said. "Admiral Kimmel is a very busy man." But Noyes persisted in his objection and refused to transmit any further warnings.

Bratton returned to Miles with an idea to circumvent Noyes's objections. McCollum had revealed to Bratton the existence of

Rochefort's organization and that Rochefort himself was aware of the "winds" message inasmuch as his interception stations had orders to monitor for "the implementing message." McCollum had suggested that as a way out of their difficulty Miles send a message to Colonel Kendall J. Fielder, General Short's G-2 at Fort Shafter, "to see Rochefort at once." It was assumed that Rochefort would then warn Fielder and somehow the warning would reach Kimmel in the end.

Miles agreed to send a message and Bratton then composed one that read: "Commander Rochefort, who can be located through the 14th Naval District, has some information on Japanese broadcasts in which weather reports are mentioned that you must obtain. Contact him at once."

The message went out as "Secret Cablegram No. 519" a few minutes before noon on December 5, but it evaporated as soon as it reached Fort Shafter. Fielder chose to ignore it when he found that Commander Rochefort was the officer in charge of a *combat* intelligence unit. On the principle that "there is no combat intelligence unless there is combat," he decided not to contact Rochefort or, for that matter, probe the obscure meaning of the message. The next-to-last chance to alert Short and Kimmel to the acuteness of the danger, even if only in an indirect way, was thus missed.

On the same day, December 5, excitement flared up in a limited circle when, by a set of circumstances which have never been fully explained, it was briefly believed that Op-20-G had picked up the "winds code" phrase "War with the United States, war with Great Britain, peace with Russia" * on one of the Japanese weather broadcasts of the day. Supposedly it was Lieutenant Francis M. Brotherhood, one of Safford's young watch officers in his decrypting section, who had stumbled upon the code phrase and sent word to Admiral Noyes that "the execute was in."

This seems highly irregular in itself, if only because an intercept

---

* This is Commander Safford's rather arbitrary version of the code's translation, unjustified by any of the Japanese texts. None of the "winds code" phrases referred to "war" but merely to a deterioration or a rupture of diplomatic relations. Safford is the foremost proponent of the theory—for it is hardly more than a theory—that the "execute" of the "winds" code was actually broadcast and picked up in any such explicit terms.

of such importance would have been handled by Safford or by Commander L. W. Parke, chief of the decrypting section, and not by a junior officer of the watch. To add puzzlement to the mystery, Noyes then called not someone within the Navy or connected with "Magic," but Colonel Otis K. Sadtler in the Signal Corps to tell him: "The message is in!"

The colonel had no business to be in these proceedings. According to the Signal Corps organization chart, he supervised signal intelligence but had no proper part in it and no authority whatever to influence any of its activities. However, Sadtler now plunged into the emergency, violating every rule and channel along the line. He rushed to General Miles in the Intelligence Division with the news, as far as it went, but was asked by Miles to contact Noyes in person to obtain more information about the crucial intercept and ascertain its precise wording. By then, however, Noyes's own excitement and interest in the matter had subsided. He told Sadtler he had more important things to do.

Without having verified the exact wording of the intercept, Sadtler took it upon himself to go to the War Plans Division with the suggestion that a warning be sent to Hawaii. Gerow told him what he had said to Bratton—that they had ample warning and no further message would be necessary. Sadtler then took his plea to Colonel Walter Bedell Smith, secretary of the General Staff. Smith was completely baffled by the call. For one thing, Sadtler was outside the "Magic" circle, had no connection with Intelligence and was not a member of the General Staff. As a matter of fact, Smith himself was not one of the Ultras and was, therefore, actually forbidden to undertake anything connected with "Magic."

"Why don't you take it up with War Plans or G-2?" Smith asked, and when Sadtler said that he had but both had declined to do anything about it, the ulcer-ridden Smith had enough. He gruffly asked Sadtler to mind his own business and leave him alone.

As a last resort Sadtler returned to Miles and related his experience, hoping that the G-2 chief would undertake what Gerow and Smith had refused to do. But now Miles also washed his hands of the matter. "I feel," he said, "I cannot go over General Gerow's decision."

There the matter ended. No action whatever was taken. The mysterious execute of the fabled "winds" code passed into history as one of the unresolved puzzles in the prelude to Pearl Harbor.*

* Captain Safford still insists that the "execute" was picked up and seen by those in the War and Navy departments who had the authority to do something about it. Colonel Bratton and most of the others involved in the "Magic" operation disclaimed any knowledge of it and, indeed, declared categorically that no "execute" was ever picked up. During this author's independent researches, however, an "execute" was found among the papers of the Japanese consulate general in Honolulu. It was a telegram in the OITE (PA-K2) system, No. 864 in the Tokyo–Honolulu series, sent at nine in the evening on December 6 via RCA and received in Honolulu at three-twenty in the morning on the 7th. It read: "Relations strained between Japan and the United States and Britain," a text close to the translation of two of the three code phrases to which the consulate had been alerted on November 19.

The historic telegram was seized in the morning of December 7 with the other papers which Consul General Kita had not had time to destroy. It is now in the Pearl Harbor files of the FBI. There is therefore this hard evidence on hand to corroborate Safford's contention that an "execute" was sent out by the Japanese, but nothing to substantiate his claim that it was broadcast in a weather report on December 5 and that it had been picked up by one of the American interception stations.

25

"Magic" on the Eve

Whatever excitement there was in the "Magic" circle the day before seems to have diminished considerably by the morning of December 6 when the staffs of SIS and Op-20-G assembled at their desks. It was Saturday. Work at both places would cease around noon except for Commander Safford's watch in his decrypting section, operating the PURPLE machine day and night.

Safford himself was relaxed. He was planning to go home early and take the rest of the weekend off. Kramer was making his rounds as usual, delivering a few intercepts (none of which seemed urgent or important) at the White House and calling at his stations in the Navy Department.

In Kramer's absence his confidential yeoman, Chief Ships Clerk H. L. Bryant, presided over the Cryptographic Section's six translators, who for the first time in weeks had no top priority messages before them requiring their immediate attention. After the hectic traffic of the previous days, PURPLE calmed down. There were hardly any telegrams going out from Nomura or coming in from Togo—apparently they had told each other everything that needed to be said.

One of the translators was a novice. She had been with the Section for a little over two weeks, still tense and exhilarated as outsiders usually are when suddenly they find themselves inside an intelligence organization. She was a plain woman of thirty-eight, Dorothy Edgers by name, married, a schoolteacher by profession. She had lived in Japan for more than thirty years and held a diploma to teach Japanese to Japanese pupils up to the high school level. Her command of the language was perfect, and her eagerness to work hard and do her best at this mystery-shrouded, scintillating job was usually not in evidence among Kramer's regular crew of translators.

Neither Commander Kramer nor Chief Bryant had assigned any special work to her, although she had a number of decrypted intercepts before her in the incoming basket awaiting translation. However, they were all in the "deferred" category, and "magics" of this kind would be left in the baskets for weeks at times before having their processing completed with the translation.

Both eager and bored, and loath just to sit there doing nothing, Mrs. Edgers pulled up the basket and began to scan the intercepts. The more she read them, the more engrossed and intrigued she became. To her mind these were important messages, and it seemed most urgent not to leave them gathering dust in the crisis. One of the "magics" she glanced at was dated December 2 and intercepted on the same day by the Army monitoring station in Hawaii. It was Ogawa's telegram to Kita instructing the consulate to file its ship-movement reports daily henceforth and inquiring about the torpedo nets and balloons at Pearl Harbor.

Another telegram was considerably older—dated November 24, when it was also intercepted by the Army station at the Presidio. A long dispatch sent in two parts, it seemed to be a most detailed report on "the manner in which the American fleet moves"—the battleships, aircraft carriers and cruisers, down to the lowliest mine sweepers. She found a third, dating back to November 28, that had been intercepted by the Army station at Fort Hunt just outside of Washington. It spoke of eight B-17 planes stationed at Midway and of the range of the anti-aircraft guns the Americans had on the island. It was labeled "Military Report," though it seemed to have originated at the consulate in Hawaii.

Mrs. Edgers then pulled out what appeared to be the longest intercept in the basket, its Japanese-language transcript covering sheet after sheet. It was one of the more recent "magics," only three days old, and had been routed to her that very morning. Its markings showed that it had been picked up by both Fort Hunt and the Navy's own Station M at Cheltenham.

As Mrs. Edgers began reading it—actually devouring it word for word instead of just glancing at it as she did with the other intercepts—she felt galvanized by what she read. As she remembered the dispatch even four years later, it was "a message saying how they were going to communicate from Honolulu to the parties interested information on our fleet movements from Honolulu, and apparently it was something which they had had previous arrangements but they had changed some of the minor details of how to go about it."

She went on to say: "I think there was something to do with lights, a window of a certain house, and there was also something about newspaper advertising."

It was Consul General Kita's telegram of December 3 to Tokyo, transmitting Otto Kühn's scheme of signals to Japanese ships lurking off shore. Mrs. Edgers was completely unfamiliar with any such things as strategy or espionage or the ruses of war. But she now sensed intuitively that the intercept she was holding in her hand had some bearing on every one of them. And she concluded that this special arrangement prepared for Pearl Harbor indicated rather unmistakably that the Japanese had something in store for the base and that the fleet at Pearl appeared to be in jeopardy.

She showed the intercept to one of her colleagues, senior translator Fred C. Woodrough, Jr., who felt that she was absolutely justified in her apprehension. Then she called it to the attention of Chief Bryant, suggesting that he call back Commander Kramer and start the processing of the intercept at once. Bryant agreed that the intercept was "interesting" but he did not think that it warranted any special attention on a weekend. It was too long, he said. Dorothy could never finish the translation by noon. It would "keep" till Monday!

But she refused to put it aside. She returned to her desk and on her own initiative began translating the intercept for Kramer, who, she was positive, would recognize, even as she did, its grave significance and urgency. At twelve o'clock the other translators went home. Mrs. Edgers remained behind with Chief Bryant in the nearly deserted office, she working on the translation, the chief just waiting to be relieved by his superior officer so that he, too, could go home for the weekend.

Kramer showed up at three o'clock, just when Mrs. Edgers was completing the final paragraph of her translation: "If the above signals and wireless messages cannot be made from Oahu, then on Maui Island, 6 miles to the northward of Kula Sanatorium . . . at a point halfway between Lower Kula Road and Haleakala Road (latitude 20° 40′N., longitude 156° 19′W., visible from seaward to the southeast and southwest of Maui Island) the following signal bonfires will be made daily until your EXEX signal is received: from 7 to 8, Signal 3 or 6, from 8 to 9, Signal 4 or 7, from 9 to 10, Signal 5 or 8."

She rushed to Kramer with her copy and he read it through still standing up. But instead of becoming electrified by the message, as Mrs. Edgers was, he showed some irritation with her for staying after office hours to work on a "deferred" intercept. In his annoyance he started to criticize her translation and sat down to edit the copy, changing a word here or a phrase there, to make it sound more "professional." He worked at it for a few minutes, then said: "This needs a lot of work, Mrs. Edgers. Why don't you run along now? We'll finish the editing sometime next week."

Mrs. Edgers tried to protest. "But, Commander," she said, "don't you think that this intercept ought to be distributed right away?"

"You just go home, Mrs. Edgers," Kramer said. "We'll get back to this piece on Monday."

When Colonel Bratton found out about this incident after the war and had his first opportunity to read the old intercept, he summed up what must be history's own verdict in this strange case: "If we had gotten that message on [December 6] . . . the whole picture would have been different." *

---

* Testifying before the Joint Congressional Committee on February 11, 1946, Kramer described Mrs. Edgers as "still unfamiliar with the practices and procedures in my office" and was, therefore, not especially qualified to adjudge what was important and what was not among the intercepts. He dismissed the intercept itself as "containing information that was not materially different than information we already had." He persisted in criticizing Mrs. Edgers' translation, claiming that he had to spend "several days [December 8, 9 and 10, after the attack] cleaning garbles and working with this message before it was completed in the form you now see it." He went on to claim that he had had "no clue to the subject or importance of this message," and protested that anyway it was December 6, an even day, "a date of Army responsibility." Beyond that he had no clear recollection of the incident. Mrs. Edgers had been heard briefly by the Hewitt Inquiry on June 22, 1945, but was never called to testify in any of the other investigations.

This was one of forty-nine espionage messages from the Tokyo–Honolulu circuit, eighteen of which had been intercepted and were available to Commander McCollum and Lieutenant Commander Watts in the Office of Naval Intelligence during a period of twenty-one days between November 15 and the end of December 6, 1941.* Seven of them were routine, but eleven were of crucial importance. They indicated at the least that the Japanese had an interest in Pearl Harbor at a time when it was abundantly clear that they were moving into war. At the most they supplied conclusive clues that they were preparing to attack the fleet at Pearl Harbor.

Here, however, the fateful error of the arrangement that had placed this traffic in the "deferred" category of "magics" came home to roost. Since no priority had been assigned to this particular traffic, only three of the eleven key messages were processed before the attack. They were Captain Ogawa's telegram of November 15, instructing Ensign Yoshikawa to report the movement of the ships "twice a week"; his telegram of November 20, ordering Yoshikawa to subject the fleet air bases on Oahu to special scrutiny; and his dispatch of November 18, requesting information about Mamala Bay and other strategic points around Honolulu. Even they were left in garbled translations. "Mamala Bay" came out as "Manila Bay," and the word "air" was omitted from Ogawa's query about the fleet air bases.

The others were intercepted promptly, but their processing required from two to twenty-eight days and was completed only when these messages suddenly gained the attention they should have warranted before the attack. Let us see, then, how and when these intercepts were processed.

• Yoshikawa's report on the exercises of the Pacific Fleet was sent on November 24, was intercepted on the same day by the Army, but was not decrypted and translated by SIS until December 16, twenty-two days after it had been picked up and nine days after the attack.

• Captain Ogawa's order to report the movements of the capital

---

* They were serial numbers 111 to 128 from Captain Ogawa to Consul General Kita, and Nos. 222 to 254 from Kita to the "Chief, Intelligence Bureau, Naval General Staff."

ships, dated November 28, was also handled by the Army. It was intercepted on November 28 but processed only on December 8, after a delay of ten days—the day after the attack.

• Yoshikawa's long, two-part report about the fleet's schedule, sent on December 1 and intercepted on the same day by the Army, was processed by the Navy on December 10.

• Ogawa's instructions of December 2, asking for daily ship-movement reports henceforth and for information about Oahu's ground and air defenses, required twenty-eight days to be processed. It became available in two different intercepts: one obtained by Captain Mayfield from RCA, the other picked up by MS-5, the Army's mystery station at Fort Shafter. The Mayfield copy was neither processed by the C/I Unit in Hawaii nor forwarded to Washington for decrypting. The MS-5 intercept had the worst career in the experience of the whole "Magic" operation. It was not decrypted until December 23, twenty-one days after MS-5 had picked it up. Even then it took another full week before it was finally translated—on December 30. "Reason for the long delay not known," Commander Safford noted in his *Index of Translations*, "but apparently someone fumbled the ball."

• The telegram of December 3 that contained Otto Kühn's system of signals was translated in full by Mrs. Edgers by two-thirty on December 6, but was then put aside by Commander Kramer. Its processing was completed only on December 11, four days after the attack and eight days after it had been intercepted.

• Captain Ogawa's telegram of December 5 (Tokyo time), in which he asked Yoshikawa to "wire immediately the movements of the Pacific Fleet subsequent to the 4th" and showed his special interest in the battleships at Pearl Harbor, was intercepted by the Army and translated in SIS on December 12, five days after the attack.

• Yoshikawa's telegram of December 6, in which he reported on the absence of anti-torpedo nets and barrage balloons, and ventured the opinion that this would be an opportune moment for an attack on the fleet assembled in Pearl Harbor, was intercepted and forwarded promptly by Master Sergeant Martin from the Presidio. But Mayfield did not get it until early on December 8, since he had not picked up the envelope from Mr. Street at RCA on Sunday.

SIS processed the intercept on December 8, too late to do any good, but at least its translation was accurate. The message had a different fate at the C/I Unit in Hawaii. Woodward succeeded in breaking into the OITE system at dawn on December 9 and had it fairly well solved by the 10th, beginning immediately to "take out" the messages. This telegram was among the first he decrypted. It was then forwarded to Captain Joseph Finnegan, USN, a former language student in Japan who had been attached to Rochefort's unit only on December 9 when additional translators were needed to cope with the increased volume of intercepts. Apparently Finnegan's knowledge of the Japanese language left much to be desired. Inexplicably and inexcusably even at this late stage, Finnegan translated Yoshikawa's key sentence, "I imagine that in all probability there is considerable opportunity left to take advantage for a surprise attack against these places," to read, "The whole matter seems to have been dropped."

• Yoshikawa's final message, in which he gave the vital information that no air reconnaissance was being conducted by any Navy patrol planes, was processed on December 8 in SIS—for the record rather than for any useful purpose. At last the enormous significance of these espionage messages was fully recognized. And while previously they had been kept at the bottom of the "deferred" pile, now, when it was too late, they were given top priority, but merely in the belief that they might supply valuable clues for counterespionage.

The inferior treatment accorded to the traffic of the Japanese consulate in Hawaii was no mere oversight or bureaucratic expediency. It was a deliberate arrangement, the product of inefficiency, bad judgment and arrogance. Since Mayfield and his colleagues had failed to discover that in Yoshikawa's mission a major espionage operation was in progress at the consulate, our counterespionage effort in Hawaii proved woefully deficient. The assumption that the "Japanese diplomatic service," honeycombed as it was with espionage operatives and working hand in glove with the Third Bureau, was incapable of good intelligence work was the result of professional conceit on the part of the officers in ONI.

The arrangement had remained unchanged even after Ogawa's telegram of September 24 setting up a grid system for Pearl

Harbor, although the increasing density of Yoshikawa's reports should have recommended the utmost attention for these "magics." As Major General Myron C. Cramer, the Judge Advocate General later put it in his report to the Secretary of War, "a keener and more incisive analysis by the Intelligence sections of either service of the over-all picture presented by these intercepts . . . might have led to an anticipation of the possibility, at least, of an attack on Pearl Harbor at or about the time it actually occurred."

The unwise handling of the espionage messages, however, was the exception to the rule. By and large "Magic" operated smoothly, especially insofar as its PURPLE part was concerned.* It was, in fact, never better than during the month immediately before the outbreak of the Pacific war. Between November 1 and December 5, a total of 1828 intercepts were received in SIS and Op-20-G, of which about 1750 were actually processed, at least up to a point. From November 15 on, the people of "Magic" worked superbly under enormous pressure—on overtime, for which no compensation was paid. During the twenty-day period between November 17 and December 7, SIS and Op-20-G handled an average of fifty "magics" each day, many of them high-priority PURPLES whose processing demanded extra care.

But in the morning of December 6 this admirable fluency and precision of "Magic" suddenly broke and the activity became perfunctory if not actually slipshod. Perhaps this abrupt relaxation was a natural reaction to the immense tension of the previous weeks. Or perhaps it was just the effect of a balmy weekend. Whatever it was, the reins were loosened in both SIS and Op-20-G and the staffs were taking it easy. Traffic was light anyway, and there were no PURPLES in the backlog. In the Navy, even the PURPLE watch was extemporized. One of its four officers, Lieutenant Felix Brown, had gone off on his Christmas vacation, and his stand-in did not know any too well how to operate the machine or set the keys. The rest of the staff was idling.

---

* This is easy to understand if we bear in mind that PURPLE was a machine cipher yielding solutions almost automatically. "Magic" was not as good and prompt when it came to the recovery of the conventional codes and ciphers, and the "reading" of messages the Japanese were sending in them.

In SIS everybody, from Lieutenant Colonel Rex W. Minckler, the officer in charge, down to Miss Ray Cave, a typist, went home between noon and one o'clock. The PURPLE machine was left unattended in its cage. Nothing in either agency showed that the United States was in the midst of a supreme crisis or that this was the nerve center of its major intelligence activity.

But even as they relaxed and then closed down, a new emergency was already on. The Japanese had begun to move the final series of telegrams (known as the 900-Serial) with which the Foreign Ministry was ushering in the war. The sequence of these dispatches began with telegram No. 901 from Togo to Nomura, advising the ambassador that a very long message was about to be sent in fourteen parts for delivery to the American government. Within a little over six hours, this series produced twelve dispatches—Nos. 901 to 912—arriving in twenty-five separate telegrams.

Since seven-fifteen * (when the so-called pilot message was picked up at Puget Sound) the monitors were busy. But though this sudden upsurge of the traffic was most unusual, especially for a Saturday, nobody at Station S thought it necessary to alert Washington. So while the interceptors had their hands full taking down one telegram after another, the operation was allowed to subside, then cease at the Washington end. As a result, six precious hours were lost. The sudden inefficiency of the PURPLE operation added another four or five hours to the time that went to waste while the people of "Magic" "fumbled the ball."

There is no record extant or accessible to show when Station S teletyped the pilot message to Washington. The telegram made its first official appearance at five minutes past noon when it arrived in SIS, brought over from Op-20-G by a messenger, since this was the Army's turn to decrypt and translate. Again the logs keep silent about the timetable on which the message was processed. But by the time the inexperienced watch officer in Op-20-GY got around to relaying the pilot message to the Army, everybody except Captain Robert E. Schukraft, the officer in charge of interception, had gone home. However, Schukraft somehow sensed that this was an important intercept and called Major Harold

* All time designations in this chapter are E.S.T. At 7:15 A.M. in Washington it was 4:15 A.M. on Bainbridge Island.

Doud, head of the decrypting section, and Doud rushed back to his office to start processing it.

By then it was one o'clock. Impressed by the ominous tone of the pilot message, Doud telephoned Colonel Minckler at home, told him that it seemed the Japanese had opened up with a barrage of telegrams and that a lot of activity could be expected during the next few hours. Minckler authorized him to call back the staff. They began to arrive in the Munitions Building at two o'clock for an extra tour of duty that was to stretch through the next twenty-four hours for most of them.

Finally, at three o'clock (almost eight hours after it had been intercepted), copies of the pilot message were delivered to Colonel Bratton, who was keeping vigil at his desk in G-2. Through a slip-up no copies were delivered to the Navy (in fact, Kramer did not get his set until Sunday morning).

While waiting for the decrypted note (it was in English and needed no translation), Bratton went to see McCollum. At this point he did not know any more about the Japanese deployment than what he had known the day or indeed almost a week before. At ten-forty, however, the State Department had received the summary of a set of alarming British intelligence reports sent by Ambassador John G. Winant from London, showing that the Japanese convoys in the China Sea were nearing their presumed destinations. The dispatch was not forwarded to either Bratton or McCollum. "It took," Bratton later said, "what I thought was an unreasonably long time for us to get any type of intelligence out of the State Department during this time." However, he added, he did not need any more messages to know that war with Japan was highly probable at this time, and McCollum agreed. But where would it come? Where were the Japs most likely to attack? All reports indicated that they were moving toward the Kra Peninsula, so Thailand seemed to be their most likely destination. How about the Dutch East Indies? What of the Philippines? They agreed that both areas were in danger.

Then Bratton raised the question: "Do you think they might attack American territory—Dutch Harbor, for instance, or the West Coast? And how about Pearl Harbor?"

Out of the question, McCollum said. For one thing, he said, reiterating his usual theme, the Japs wouldn't dare to make a frontal attack on any American installations. For another, *the American fleet was not in Pearl Harbor.* As Bratton later recalled the conversation, McCollum made the point without qualification. He had a huge map on the wall that showed the position of all navy vessels on the seven seas, including American ships. McCollum stepped up to it for emphasis as he pointed to where Pearl Harbor was, and with a finger on the spot he repeated that "no major units of Admiral Kimmel's fleet were at Pearl."

"Are you sure these people are properly alerted?" Bratton asked. "Are they on the job? Have they been properly warned?"

"Oh, yes," McCollum said. "The fleet is either gone or is about to go to sea." As it happened, the Japanese knew better the whereabouts of the Pacific Fleet than the chief of the Far Eastern Section of the American Naval Intelligence Service.

The Cable Section in Tokyo had started moving the long telegram at eight o'clock in the morning on December 6 and Station S began picking it up three minutes later, but no part of it was forwarded to Washington until shortly before noon. However, the telegram was also intercepted at Station M at nearby Cheltenham and had already been teletyped to Op-20-G between nine and ten o'clock. The young officer standing watch for Lieutenant Brown started processing it and had the second part of the message through the PURPLE when he remembered that this was the Army's day and abandoned it for the time being.

Then another snafu developed. When at last Station S also began to move the long intercept, at eleven forty-five, the whole schedule was sent over to the Army for processing. But it was then returned to the Navy because everybody had gone home by then, and no operator was left in SIS to handle the army's PURPLE.

It therefore fell to the inexperienced young officer in Op-20-GY to put the intercept through the machine. But he had trouble setting the key, then so completely upset the machine that no part of the message could be decrypted on it. Safford was around, breathing down the poor boy's neck, yet he did not know either how to set the key or fix the machine. He phoned Lieutenant George Lynn, the senior watch officer, who was off, and asked him to come in and straighten things out. Lynn arrived at four o'clock, to stand the whole watch till midnight, and found the machine badly disarrayed. He set to adjusting it as Safford waited around. After a while Safford looked at his watch. It was four-thirty. He went for his hat and coat. "There is nothing I can do but get in your way and make you nervous, George," he said. "I'm going home." It was the first weekend he was to have to himself in more than a month.

Lynn had the machine working by five o'clock, set the key and started decrypting the message. He completed the work shortly after seven and called SIS to lend him a typist because Safford, unlike Minckler, had not considered it necessary to recall the civilian members of his staff. Miss Cave was sent over from the Munitions Building to type up the three-thousand-word message up to and including its thirteenth part, all that had been intercepted.

At nine o'clock Bratton received his six copies of the transcript, typed up on the Navy's confidential message form, and called General Miles at home to clear the procedure with him. Miles was at Captain Wilkinson's dinner party, but the person who answered the phone did not know where he was. Bratton left word for the general to phone him at his home when he returned, no matter how late it would be. Then he called Major Doud at SIS and asked him: "What happened to the fourteenth part of this message?"

"I don't know, sir," Doud said, somewhat concerned. "Either the Navy missed it or the Japs haven't sent it yet."

Bratton then called Lieutenant Colonel Carlisle C. Dusenbury, his principal assistant, to his desk and told him: "I'm pooped, you better take over. Wait here for the fourteenth part of this message and call me at my house as soon as you get it."

On his way home he stopped at the State Department and left the locked pouch with the thirteen parts in the care of the night duty officer, to be handed to Secretary Hull in the morning. Then he went home, turned in at once, and was awakened shortly after eleven o'clock by Miles returning his call. The general had already seen the transcript in Captain Wilkinson's house and now told Bratton to forget about it as long as it was unfinished. Bratton asked whether it should not be taken to General Marshall as it was, but Miles said no. There was no point in disturbing the Chief of Staff so late at night with an incomplete "magic." Then both men retired for the night. When the fourteenth part failed to come in by midnight, Colonel Dusenbury also went home.

Commander Kramer waited patiently at his desk in ONI for his six copies of the message, and when they arrived he waited a little longer, this time for his wife, who was going to pick him up at nine o'clock with their Chevrolet to drive him around on his route. He did not need to consult anyone about his plans. He had made up his mind to deliver the message to every single addressee on his distribution list before the night was out—to Secretary Knox, Admirals Stark and Turner, Captains Ingersoll and Wilkinson, and yes, to the White House.

His wife arrived with the car a few minutes past nine, and Kramer went down to the deserted Constitution Avenue to start out on his nocturnal rounds. When he was seated in the car he told Mrs. Kramer to drive him to the White House.

He wanted the President to be the first to see this intercept.

26

F.D.R.—December 6, 1941

President Franklin D. Roosevelt woke up in pain from his sinus infection, dreading the treatment Admiral McIntire would insist on giving him in the morning. But as for his other woe—his trouble with Japan—his anxiety had subsided.

The Japanese had the initiative and there was little the President could do to seize it from them before they showed their hand. He had made up his mind to "keep the record clean" and to let them "commit the first overt act." In the meantime he would indulge in what Dumas *père* called the epitome of human wisdom —wait and hope.

This promised to be a quiet Saturday. Mr. Roosevelt had only two firm engagements on his official calendar, and they had nothing to do with the crisis. Harold Smith, the Director of the Budget, was expected at eleven to present some items of the new budget. And Attorney General Francis Biddle had asked to see him to go over a speech he, Biddle, was to deliver in Detroit on December 7.

After Dr. McIntire had treated his sinuses the President, dressed in a gray jacket and a pair of slacks, went to his desk in the oval study at nine forty-five. At ten Associate Justice William O. Douglas dropped in unexpectedly ("It's always good to see you, Bill") to talk about diverse subjects occupying his versatile mind. The President was with Douglas when "Hackie" (Louise Hachmeister, chief switchboard operator at the White House) put through a call on the scrambler phone. Mr. Hull was calling on the special line (which the Signal Corps had recently put in) to say that an urgent cable had just come in from Ambassador Winant in London, forwarding "the Admiralty's latest dope about the Japs." The President had no time to ponder the call. Usher Charles K. Claunch announced Smith, and the budget session was on. For the next eighty minutes the President was engrossed in figures, except for two interruptions. First Mr. Hull called back to give Mr. Roosevelt a summary of Winant's cable. According to the Admiralty, he said, a Japanese fleet of transports, cruisers and destroyers had been sighted moving from Indochina toward the Kra Isthmus, a narrow neck of land between the Bay of Bengal and the Gulf of Siam connecting the Malay Peninsula with Thailand. Then Admiral Stark phoned; he had received a signal from Admiral Thomas C. Hart, commander-in-chief of the Asiatic Fleet, relaying a report of British Intelligence from Singapore about "two large Japanese convoys proceeding on a western course, destination uncertain, perhaps Bangkok, perhaps Kra." Hart also reported that his own scouting forces had sighted thirty Japanese transports in Camranh Bay, escorted by a heavy cruiser.

Commenting on the increased defense appropriations in the light of these reports, the President remarked to Smith that "we might be at war with Japan although no one knew." Smith was so intrigued by the offhand statement that he jotted it down on a piece of paper as soon as he left the President's study, and entered it in his diary that same afternoon. What did the President mean by "nobody knew"? Didn't he know?

On this December 6 the President was exceptionally well informed on some aspects of the crisis and yet, at the same time, he was woefully in the dark about the nature and direction of the immediate threat. He concluded from the "magics" that the Japanese were now ready to do what Ambassador Grew had told the State Department already on November 3—"rush headlong into a suicidal struggle." But he did not see as clearly as Grew that "armed conflict with the United States may come with dangerous and dramatic suddenness."

Mr. Roosevelt knew of Tokyo's instructions to the Japanese diplomatic missions to destroy their codes and ciphers and use emergency "hidden words" instead. He knew that their move to war was gaining momentum by the hour. But he did not know where they would strike and what plans they had for the United States.

His ignorance of what turned out to be the crucial aspects of the crisis, namely the Japanese design on the United States, was due to tangible and intangible factors, to the state of signal technology and communication efficiency,* to human, material and natural elements.

Though much was made later of some last-minute intelligence reports—most of them from British sources—that should have alerted the President to the imminence of the attack, in reality the hard information they contained was scant, spotty and inconclusive. In the Canton area, for instance, British Intelligence had ruled out an attack on Hong Kong because, as it was estimated, "the Japanese forces in South China [were considered] insufficient for a major attack upon the Colony."

British seaward reconnaissance out of Malaya covered an area stretching from Kota Bahru to Point Camau, thence southeast to the Anambas Islands and westward back to Kuantan on the Malay Peninsula. But the Gulf of Siam was beyond the range of the one or two twin-engine Hudsons conducting the reconnaissance and was, therefore, completely uncovered. Moreover, the weather was extremely bad over the South China Sea. Rainstorms and the low clouds of the northeast monsoon seriously reduced visibility. As a result there were only six sightings, all of them on December 5, three by the same reconnaissance plane.

On December 6 the Japanese moved out of the British reconnaissance area and remained totally undetected henceforth. In the morning a Catalina flying boat was sent from Kota Bahru to look for them, but the plane was never seen again and nothing was ever heard from it. As we now know, it was shot down by the Japanese at one-thirty in the afternoon, with what was the first shot fired in the Pacific war. However, Singapore attributed the failure of the plane to return to some mishap in the bad weather and not to enemy action.**

* Communication inefficiency persisted as a serious detrimental factor in presidential decisions and was partly responsible twenty-one years later for the fiasco in the Bay of Pigs.
** The Japanese going to Thailand and Malaya were not seen again before dawn on December 7, when the defenders of Kota Bahru woke up and saw

Nothing was known about the 21st and 23rd air flotillas of Vice-Admiral Tsukahara's Eleventh Air Fleet, waiting at Formosa and at Palau in the Carolines to strike at the Philippines, scheduled to take place three hours after the raid on Pearl Harbor. There was no information whatever about the big striking force of six carriers and two battleships heading for Pearl Harbor. Communications intelligence had failed to locate the "missing" carriers and submarines. All it was picking up was very heavy traffic, but most of it consisted of old messages that were being retransmitted.

Admiral Nagumo's luck in escaping detection on his long voyage had been due partly to the limitations and laxness of the American reconnaissance effort, but mostly to the weather—gales, high seas and thick fog. On December 6, too, the sea was running, a brisk northeast trade wind was blowing and fog was enveloping the ocean.

As far as Hawaii was concerned, the President was never told that Pearl Harbor was in jeopardy. Although every American war plan made a provision for an attack on the Pacific Fleet's major base, such an attack was now neither expected nor anticipated. In a basic summary the Intelligence Branch of G-2 had prepared on November 27 for presentation to the President there was no mention of Pearl Harbor. When he was specifically queried by the President, Admiral Stark assured him that the base was in no danger and that the fleet was at sea.

The President was never shown any of the intercepted espionage messages and was never apprised that such reports to Tokyo existed at all. In fact, he was left completely in the dark about any such Japanese activity in Hawaii, and was told only that some sabotage by local Japanese elements could be expected in the event of a Japanese-American war.

Even in the diplomatic sphere of "Magic," Mr. Roosevelt was inadequately serviced. The crucial last-minute messages of the 900-Serial were taken to the White House only around ten in the morning on December 7, although several of them had been on hand since the 6th. Captain Beardall then chose only the last part of the long note for presentation to the President. Seven other

_____
Japanese transports anchored off the beach, getting ready to disembark their troops under the heavy covering fire of their naval escorts.

intercepts which Commander Kramer had in the "book"—including the pilot message and the vital telegram instructing Ambassador Nomura to deliver the note at one o'clock—were never submitted to the President.

While the President was busy with other matters of state, elsewhere in Washington the crisis continued as usual. Most of it was conducted on the special "safe line" that ran through the White House switchboard. Secretary Knox had been at his desk in the Navy Department since nine o'clock, calling everybody he could raise—Sumner Welles in the State Department; Jesse Jones; the Postmaster General; and, several times, Secretary Stimson, who had arrived in his office at ten-thirty.

Mr. Hull came in at ten o'clock to find Winant's cable. When he conveyed it to the President he was told to let Admiral Stark know. This started a round robin of other calls, as Admiral Stark phoned General Marshall about it, then talked with Mr. Hull to elaborate on the Winant message and add his own information.

The last call on this secret line was made at nine minutes after one, when Stark talked to Hull for the third time. Then the phone was silent. No more calls were made on it throughout the afternoon—not, in fact, until eight-thirty, when Knox resumed his telephoning about the crisis.

At the time Admiral Stark was discussing the probable meaning of the intelligence reports with the Secretary of State, the President was having his modest lunch from a tray at his desk, with Harry Hopkins and Miss Grace Tully, his secretary, keeping him company. Little if anything in their conversation bore on the crisis. Miss Tully told the President that she had been invited to a cocktail party which the columnist Richard Harkness was giving in the Mayflower Hotel, and asked whether she could have the afternoon off. Mr. Roosevelt said by all means, he had nothing important on the agenda that would require her presence at the White House.

This was the last "decision" the President made on this afternoon that survives on the record. The next time we see him is around five-thirty mixing martinis for himself and his friend Vincent Astor, who had dropped in for a chat, and waiting for Miss

Tully to return posthaste from the party after having been summoned back to duty for some urgent dictation. There is nothing in the President's voluminous records to document firmly what happened in the intervening time, but these must have been his busiest hours on this Saturday. There had been a sudden upsurge of activity at the White House as huge official limousines drove up at the north portico shortly after lunch, somber gentlemen alighted from them and disappeared behind the glass door that opened briefly to admit and closed quickly to conceal them.

One of these men was Secretary Hull. Another was Lord Halifax, the British ambassador. A third was the key figure in this clandestine rendezvous, Robert G. Casey, the Australian minister in Washington. About two hours later, around four o'clock, the glass door opened again, the gentlemen emerged from the Executive Mansion, the limousines drove up and drove away, then Saturday's customary calm returned to the White House. As far as the President's log is concerned, these men were not at the White House that afternoon. When no American documents were found to shed light on these obscure hours, the congressional investigators of the Pearl Harbor attack sought documentation from the British and Australian governments, but their persistent efforts were poorly rewarded.

An attempt was made to dig up some pertinent material with the help of Miss Tully, who was, after all, the keeper of the President's confidences and the custodian of his secret papers. But no matter how thoroughly she searched the files, Miss Tully said, nothing could be unearthed. On April 17, 1946, she acknowledged that a "certain subject" had been discussed by the President with Mr. Casey and Lord Halifax "but, of course," she wrote, "no record was ever made of such conversations."

What were "such conversations"?

In order to answer this question (with evidence that is but circumstantial, to be sure, but most persuasive nevertheless) one has to go back a few days, to Thursday, December 4, in Melbourne, Australia, at five o'clock in the afternoon, to a conference called by Air Chief Marshal Sir Charles Burnett, posted by the RAF to command the Royal Australian Air Force. It was attended by Commander Saom (or Soam) of the Dutch navy, serving as liaison officer in Australia; Colonel Merle Smith, the American military attaché; and Lieutenant Robert L. O'Dell, his young aide. Colonel Smith had been summoned by the Air Chief Marshal to listen to some momentous intelligence Sir Charles had just received from Vice-Admiral C. E. L. Helfrich, commander-in-chief of the Netherlands navy in the East Indies. It reported movement of Japanese convoys well beyond the geographical line which the United States regarded as the boundary of normal peaceful penetration by Japanese military or naval forces.

Commander Saom then told Colonel Smith, explicitly for the information of the United States government, that the Netherlands authorities in the East Indies, with the approval of the government in The Hague, had "ordered the execution of the Rainbow Plan A-2 . . . which was part of the joint Abducan Plan." * "That was significant," Lieutenant O'Dell later said, "because the plan called for joint operations for the Australians and the Dutch, and to the best of my knowledge, our Navy, if nothing else. That was to go into effect only in case of war and here the Dutch had ordered it. That was the definite information —that it had gone into effect."

As the Dutch had it "doped out," the convoys their scouting forces and reconnaissance planes had spotted in the South China Sea "could get to somewhere, either the Philippines or the Indies within . . . sixty hours."

Back in his office Colonel Smith reviewed the situation with Captain Charles A. Coursey, the American naval attaché. Coursey recommended that they do nothing—this was "too hot" a matter for them to burn their fingers with. Smith decided to act on his own. He ordered Lieutenant O'Dell to draft a cable with the information Air Chief Marshal Burnett and Commander Saom had just imparted to him, and send it out in two copies. One was for General MacArthur in Manila, the other for the commanding general of the Hawaiian Department, with the request to repeat it to the Military Intelligence Division in Washington for the information of the Chief of Staff.

O'Dell had just finished encrypting the message in two different codes when Burnett called Smith and asked him to delay sending the cable, pending a meeting of the Australian Cabinet later

* The American-British-Dutch-Canadian plan of the Quebec Conference.

during the night. The cable was held for twelve hours, until the morning of the 5th in Australia, after the War Cabinet of Prime Minister John Curtin had met and made its own arrangements.

It was as a direct sequel to this Cabinet meeting in Melbourne that Mr. Casey went to the White House on this Saturday afternoon. His mission was in part to place the momentous intelligence before the President. Casey acted upon instructions from the Australian government to find out whether the President would be willing to invoke the provisions which the "Abducan Plan" contained for such an eventuality. But he also went to the White House on behalf of Mr. Churchill to invite Mr. Roosevelt to join the British and Dominion governments in a final warning to Japan, which would say in part: "They feel bound . . . to warn the Japanese government in the most solemn manner that if Japan attempts to establish her influence in Thailand by force or threat of force, she will do so at her own peril. . . . Should hostilities unfortunately result, the responsibility will rest with Japan."

There is reason to believe that the President still refused to commit the United States either to participation in the execution of the "Abducan Plan" or in sending the warning to Tokyo. However, his refusal must have been presented in rather ambiguous terms, for Lord Halifax construed it as an actual acceptance of their invitation on both scores, and so reported to London.

Whatever the conversations were, their impact can be reconstructed on the basis of a series of rapid-fire developments that occurred in the immediate wake of this White House conference. Within hours Air Chief Marshal Sir Robert Brooke-Popham, commander-in-chief of the British forces in the Far East, received word from London that the United States had agreed to full American participation in the "Abducan Plan," and would join the British and Dutch forces in the event of a Japanese attack even if American territories were not involved.

Immediately after Brooke-Popham's receipt of the signal from London, Captain John M. Creighton, the American naval representative at his headquarters in Singapore, relayed the information to Admiral Hart in Manila. His coded signal read:

"On Saturday Brooke-Popham received from War Department London:

" 'We have now received assurance of American armed support in case as follows: *Affirm* /if/ we are obliged execute our plans to forestall Japs landing Isthmus of Kra or take action in reply to Nips invasion any other part of Siam; *Baker* if Dutch Indies are attacked and we go to their defense; *Cast* if Japs attack us.'

"Therefore without reference to London put plan in action if first you have good info Jap expedition advancing with the apparent intention of landing in Kra, second if Nips violate any part of Thailand.

"Para: if NEI are attacked put into operation plans agreed upon between Britsh and Dutch."

Hart was with Vice-Admiral Sir Tom Phillips of the Royal Navy, who had just been named naval commander in Singapore and was paying a courtesy visit to him, when Creighton's telegram was brought in, together with a report that "a large Japanese convoy known to have been in Camranh Bay, Indochina, had put out to sea and was heading for the Gulf of Siam." Hart excused himself, then returned to bid farewell to Phillips, who had decided to rush back to Singapore.

"I have just ordered my destroyers at Balikpapan [on Borneo] to proceed to Batavia on pretext of rest and leave," Hart told Phillips in parting. "Actually they will join your forces."

While Mr. Hull was at the White House a second cable came in from Winant, at five minutes after three, with more intelligence from the Admiralty. A twin-engine Hudson of the First G.R. Squadron, on a reconnaissance mission operating from Kota Bahru, had at the extreme limit of its range sighted several Japanese convoys with naval escort some eighty miles southeast of Point Camau. It had sent back three reports: the first, of three transports with a cruiser as escort steering approximately northwest; * the second, of twenty-two transports seen considerably farther east with a heavy escort of cruisers and destroyers steering west; and a third, similar to the second, but the position given was slightly to the south.**

* This convoy was carrying the Japanese 143rd Infantry Regiment bound for Thailand and Malaya.
** The second and third sightings were in fact of the same convoy, carrying the advance contingents of the 5th Division of Lieutenant General Matsui to Malaya.

According to the Admiralty, the convoys were about fourteen hours' sailing time (when sighted at twelve minutes past noon, local time) from Kra, which was now firmly believed to be their destination. The convoys the Dutch had sighted on the 3rd and 4th, presumably heading for the East Indies and the Philippines, were now approaching the points where the invaders were scheduled to jump off. War, it seemed, was only a few hours in coming.

One of the emergency decisions definitely agreed upon at Roosevelt's conference with Halifax and Casey was to send F.D.R.'s long-planned but long-delayed personal letter to the Emperor. Mr. Roosevelt presented it as his last resort, his final attempt to avert the clash of arms.*

Miss Tully was back at the White House, taking down the letter the President dictated from various drafts the State Department had reluctantly prepared.

"Almost a century ago," it began in the President's revised final version, "the President of the United States addressed to the Emperor of Japan a message extending an offer of friendship of the people of the United States to the people of Japan. . . . Only in situations of extraordinary importance to our two countries need I address to Your Majesty messages on matters of state. I feel I should now so address you because of the deep and far-reaching emergency which appears to be in formation." It ended with the plea: "I address myself to Your Majesty at this moment in the fervent hope that Your Majesty may, as I am doing, give thought in this definite emergency to ways of dispelling the dark clouds. I am confident that both of us, for the sake of the peoples not only of our own great countries but for the sake of humanity in neighboring territories, have a sacred duty to restore traditional amity and prevent further death and destruction in the world."

Shortly before seven o'clock the President proofread Miss Tully's finished copy, then scribbled on it a note to Secretary

---

* According to a telegram from Australia to London, reporting details of Minister Casey's conversation at the White House: "1) President has decided to send message to Emperor. 2) President's subsequent procedure is that if no answer is received by him from the Emperor by Monday evening, a) he will issue his warning on Tuesday afternoon or evening, b) warning or equivalent by British or others will not follow until Wednesday morning, i.e., after his own warning has been delivered repeatedly to Tokyo and Washington."

Hull: "Dear Cordell: Shoot this to Grew—I think can go in gray code—saves time—I don't mind if it gets picked up. FDR." He then went upstairs, changed, and joined Mrs. Roosevelt at a dinner party she was giving for Sir Wilfred French, a British vice-admiral, his wife, and a party of friends and house guests. But he left the dinner abruptly without waiting for the dessert. He returned to his oval study to keep watch like the lookout in the crow's nest of a fogbound ship.

If the President had seemed restive at Mrs. Roosevelt's dinner table, nothing in his manner in the oval study indicated that he was uneasy and apprehensive. If anything, he appeared to be more composed and relaxed than usual, settling comfortably into the sinecure of the evening.

The room was dimly lit by the green-shaded lamp on the President's desk, casting shadows on the pastel walls, on the thick beige carpet, and on the sofa where Harry L. Hopkins sat, trying to stay awake. He had come out of the hospital only a few days before and was not feeling too well. But he was, as ever, the available man, sharing this lonely vigil with the President.

Mr. Roosevelt was toying with his stamp collection and chatting with Hopkins. He talked easily, in a low key, skipping from one topic to another as they came to his mind. He discussed a few more serious matters, like the indiscretion of the Chicago *Tribune,* and his new budget, which he had worked on that morning with Harold Smith, musing about the mayhem Congress was likely to do to it.

But mostly the conversation was in a lighter and even somewhat frivolous vein. He joked about Vincent Astor, his friend and Dutchess County neighbor who had visited him that afternoon, trying to "unload," as the President put it, his costly yacht on the United States Navy. And he brought up a favorite topic of his that recurred often in his nostalgic chats with his closest confidant—retirement to a cozy secluded spot in Florida. Even in the midst of the uncertainties and dangers of these days, Roosevelt remained preoccupied with his plans for a fishing retreat at Key West for Harry Hopkins and himself.

At nine-thirty the door opened quietly, and an usher announced a visitor: "Lieutenant Schulz, Mr. President." Behind the usher was a handsome lad in his twenties, flushed with the excitement of this nocturnal mission to his Commander-in-Chief. He was Lieutenant Robert Lester Schulz from Iowa, Annapolis class of 1934. A week before, he had been sent on temporary duty to the White House to act as assistant to the naval aide.

Captain Beardall had gone home at five-thirty, then on to the dinner party at Captain Wilkinson's house, leaving it to young Schulz to handle whatever urgent messages might still come over from the Office of Naval Intelligence. Thus Schulz had to take to the President a pouchful of dispatches that had just been brought in by Commander Kramer.

Schulz stood at attention at the President's desk, on which he had placed the locked pouch. Then he unlocked it quickly with a key Captain Beardall had entrusted to him, and laid the "book" before the President. There were six documents in it.

On top was a dispatch reporting on the Rostov front in Russia where the Red Army was going over to a promising counteroffensive. Next was a telegram with a description of gains Field Marshal Erwin Rommel's Afrika Korps had scored at Tobruk. Another dispatch was the report of a conversation Admiral Nomura and Saburo Kurusu had had with Secretary Hull the day before.

Three brief telegrams involved a controversial First Secretary of the Japanese embassy and a cipher apparatus referred to as "the B-machine."

The President scanned the dispatches briefly, then picked up the telegram at the bottom of the pile. It consisted of some fifteen pages, fastened together in a sheaf with a paper clip, its text typed on the Navy Department's secret-message forms. Mr. Roosevelt read it avidly but quickly, at a rate of about three hundred words per minute, somewhat too fast to allow careful study of the long dispatch.

When he had finished he scooped up the sheets and handed them to Hopkins, who was now on his feet, pacing up and down. Mr. Roosevelt waited for about ten minutes while Hopkins read the document. Then, recovering it for another glance, he said: "This means war."

He said it quietly, without any bathos, in a voice that betrayed no emotions but stated simply a seemingly inescapable fact. The President and Hopkins went on to discuss the document for another five minutes, in the presence of Lieutenant Schulz.

"Hopkins agreed," the lieutenant later said in recalling their conversation. "The substance of it was—I believe Mr. Hopkins mentioned it first—that since war was imminent, the Japanese intended to strike first, when they were ready, at a moment when all was opportune for them, when their forces were most properly deployed for their advantage. Indochina in particular was mentioned because the Japanese forces had landed there and there were indications of where they would move next. The President mentioned a message he had sent to the Japanese Emperor concerning the presence of Japanese troops in Indochina, in effect requesting their withdrawal.

"Mr. Hopkins then expressed the view," Schulz added, "that since war was undoubtedly going to come at the convenience of the Japanese, it was too bad that we could not strike the first blow and prevent any sort of surprise. The President nodded and said, 'No, we can't do that. We're a democracy and a peaceful people.' Then he raised his voice, and this much I remember definitely. He said, 'But we have a good record.' "

Lieutenant Schulz then picked up the papers and returned them to the pouch for delivery back to the Navy. Commander Kramer was waiting downstairs, drumming with nervous fingers on a long table at which he was sitting in the deserted mail room in the White House basement.

"One thing is abundantly clear," Robert E. Sherwood later wrote. "Roosevelt at that moment faced the most grievous dilemma of his entire career."

27

The Creeping Hours

On December 7, 1941, General George C. Marshall woke up at six-thirty and was dressed in his riding togs by seven. It was the exact time he usually got up when he was at home in Quarters Number 1, the Chief of Staff's red brick house at Fort Myer. The day promised to be fine for this time of the year. Clouds, their linings faintly lit by the hesitant rays of the rising sun, rolled in the sky, certain to burn away before long in the morning. The temperature was just a notch below fifty.

Breakfast was served at a quarter to eight by Sergeant Seapman, the general's colored orderly, in Mrs. Marshall's bedroom. This was the only departure from their routine. On weekdays the Marshalls breakfasted quickly at seven sharp, then the general would leave for the ten-minute drive to the Munitions Building and be in his office at seven-thirty.

But on Sundays he lingered awhile longer, and on this particular Sunday even somewhat longer than usual. Mrs. Marshall had slipped on a rug a few weeks before and broken four ribs, and she still had some difficulty getting around, even to the sun porch, where they usually had their meals and spent most of their time at home. She had been in Florida convalescing at the home of her sister and returned only the day before. This was their first breakfast together in a week.

The only time the general had to himself was on Sundays and

Mrs. Marshall insisted that he spend it at leisure. Accordingly, Marshall would go horseback riding in the morning, then lounge for the rest of the day on the sun porch, reading the books Colonel Joseph E. Greene, editor of the *Infantry Journal*, had picked for the Chief.

The general was totally unaware of the developments of the night. His staff knew that he retired regularly at nine o'clock and did not like to be disturbed with loose ends. The President, who talked over the incoming Japanese note with Admiral Stark, did not deem it necessary to call him about it. Marshall was an aloof, distant man who lived in Olympian seclusion. He had been Chief of Staff nearly a year before he "received the Army." As Mrs. Marshall later put it: "Few of the officers had ever been in the Chief of Staff's house, many did not know him even by sight."

Communication with him was mostly through Colonel Bedell Smith or the other secretaries of the General Staff. "I think," Marshall said repeatedly, "I prize my privacy more than anything else," and his associates were made aware that he disliked intrusions upon it. This was one of the reasons why he, alone among all the senior officers of the Army, never had a personal aide. Perhaps if he had had one, history would have taken a different turn on this Sunday.

Sergeant Powder, who doubled as his driver and groom, had orders to be at the house at nine o'clock with King Story, the General's bay gelding. Powder was there at nine sharp waiting with the horse when Marshall came out with Fleet, his Dalmatian, at his heels. He left promptly, a trim, erect, lonely figure mounted on the fine tall horse, accompanied only by his coach dog. He was expected back around ten o'clock.

As the day broke, the Japanese were launching the 183 planes of Admiral Nagumo's striking force for the flight to Pearl Harbor, still some 230 miles away. Their objective was explicit—the American fleet. If the ships remained at their moorings, the operation was certain to succeed. But at this hour the big ships of the Pacific Fleet could still quit port, disperse and escape the bombs and torpedoes. How was this precious time used by the Americans?

In his subsequent account of this morning, Admiral Ross T.

McIntire, the President's physician, spoke of a vague tenseness in the air as the men closest to the crisis, exhausted and nearly numb, tried to catch a little rest and steady their nerves. Viewed in retrospect, the Washington scene resembled the climax of one of those contrived melodramas in which the ominous meaning of every passing minute used to be accentuated by the ponderous ticking of a big clock on the wall.

The newspapers on this indolent Sunday morning reflected the uncertainties of the crisis. The *New York Times* and the Washington *Post* reported as accurately as the intelligence dispatches the movements of the Japanese convoys. But their stories around the news tended to take the sting out of the alarming reports. "Over in Japan," wrote Edwin L. James of the *New York Times* in his editorial, "the sword rattling goes on with all sorts of threats and dire predictions of what will happen if the United States tries to tell Tokyo what to do; yet the echo in Washington does not hurt the eardrums." He asserted that the Japanese spokesmen in the capital wished to continue the negotiations. "Obviously," he wrote, "one may argue that Tokyo is seeking to gain time in which to get into better shape for the threatened war. One may also argue, however, that Japan does not wish war."

This was also the trend of thought on Capitol Hill. Senator Walter F. George of Georgia perceived "a hopeful sign" in the rumors that Japan would soon answer Mr. Hull's note of November 26. "I have had the view all along," he told a reporter, "that the Japanese did not want to force the issue." Senator George W. Norris of Nebraska thought that the Japanese were just about ready "to back down."

This, then, was what the handful of men involved in the emergency read in bed or at breakfast. In the War Department, only the wheels of the Signal Intelligence Service were turning at full speed. Otherwise the Department operated on its peacetime Sunday schedule. General Miles of G-2 was not even planning to go to his office. Neither was General Gerow of War Plans. Nobody had bothered to tell him about the arrival of the Japanese note.

Next door in the Navy Building this was Op-20-G's day to process the intercepts. Although the Tokyo–Washington circuit had been unusually busy the day before with the telegrams of the

900-Serial, there was a long lull from eight minutes before noon on December 6, when the thirteenth part of the note had been picked up by Station S. Since only one more telegram of any real importance was expected to come through in the same series—the concluding passage of the note—Op-20-G was holding to its weekend schedule with only a skeleton staff standing watch.

Commander Safford was at home, sleeping off a long night on the town. Lieutenant Francis M. Brotherhood had the shrimp shift at the PURPLE, and was waiting to be relieved at eight in the morning by Lieutenant Alfred V. Pering, another watch officer. Commander Kramer alone was eager to get back into harness to see what the rest of the Japanese note would say. Though he had been up until two o'clock making his rounds, he was back at the Navy Department at seven-thirty, the first officer to show up in the Office of Naval Intelligence. Commander McCollum arrived at eight to relieve Commander Watts, who had stood watch during the night. Captain Wilkinson came in next, at eight-thirty.

The lull in "Magic" lasted until shortly before dawn at Puget Sound. Then the Tokyo–Washington circuit became busier than ever. A slew of telegrams of the same serial—all brief and addressed to Ambassador Nomura in his special CA code—was intercepted in rapid succession, keeping Station S working steadily for over three hours. Reception conditions were excellent at Bainbridge Island. The station sent word to Lieutenant Brotherhood that it was intercepting everything "solid."

By three-ten three telegrams of the series—Nos. 902 to 904—had been picked up and recorded. By four thirty-seven the "schedule" was up to No. 907 and the telegrams were still coming. At seven minutes after five the station intercepted No. 910, then Nos. 911 and 912. After that the circuit went dead again. Station S had not missed a single dispatch. By seven o'clock it had the entire "schedule of transmissions" on the teletype to Washington.

No. 902 arrived shortly before seven and Lieutenant Brotherhood decrypted it before going home. The text came out clear in English and Brotherhood passed it on to Kramer as soon as he arrived. This was what he had come in for so early. It was the missing last part of the Japanese note.

Kramer showed it to Wilkinson and McCollum, then made up the "book," putting the intercept in the loose-leaf binder for presentation to his "clients." He picked a few other "magics" from the previous day to go with No. 902 (which he included in full)— the telegram instructing Nomura to use one of his career officers in typing up the note, a query from Tokyo about the President's message to the Emperor, but not the pilot message. It still had not come over from SIS.

Kramer was just about to leave on his rounds when Lieutenant Pering came in with two more PURPLE intercepts he had just decrypted. They were Nos. 907 and 910. Unlike the long note, which was in English throughout, they were in Japanese and required further processing. But even a quick glance at them gave Kramer a jolt. When the Japanese had first announced the sending of the note they instructed Nomura to hold it until further notice. Rightly or wrongly this gave Kramer and Bratton a sense of relief, a feeling that things would not come to a head from one moment to another.

But now one of the telegrams Pering brought over was ordering Nomura to "please submit to the United States Government (if possible to the Secretary of State) our reply to the United States at 1:00 P.M. on the 7th your time." The second intercept made the first seem even more ominous. "After deciphering Part 14 of my No. 902 and also Nos. 907, 908, and 909," it read, "please destroy at once the remaining cipher machine and all machine codes. Also dispose in like manner secret documents."

The obvious urgency of these telegrams was not lost on Kramer. But he was anxious to get on with the job of delivering the concluding passage of the note to the White House and to Secretary Knox, who would be waiting for it at the State Department, where he had a conference scheduled for ten o'clock with Secretaries Hull and Stimson. He stopped just long enough to figure out on a navigator's plotting circle what the time would be at the various danger spots in East Asia and the Pacific when Nomura appeared at the State Department with the note.

Well, he told Chief Bryant, one o'clock in Washington would be two o'clock in the morning in Manila and seven-thirty in the morning in Hawaii. The deadline of the delivery, he said, "tied

with the sun and [the Japanese] movements in progress elsewhere"
—it could very well be the zero hour they had set to begin "some
amphibian landing operations." *

He then asked Bryant to take the telegrams over to SIS for
translation and to tell Major Doud to send them back to him as
soon as it was completed. This was the Navy's day to process them
but Kramer's translators had the Sunday off, and he himself could
not spare the time to do any work on them. Shortly after nine-
thirty, he left the Navy Building for the White House and the
State Department, carrying the "book" that now held the entire
Japanese note and a couple of additional intercepts left from the
crop of the day before.

As Kramer began his rounds it was still night in Hawaii—almost
three hours to sunrise and four hours to the fatal moment of the
attack. It was an exceptionally tranquil night, breezy and balmy.
Nightcaps of the trade-wind clouds that broke loose from the
mountains floated indolently over the dark-green cane fields on the
slopes of Aiea and the deep blue of the Pearl Harbor lochs.

In the harbor, only the contours of the buildings were visible
and the silhouettes of the ships edged off the darkness. There were
ninety-four of them strung out around Ford Island, some moored
singly, others in the docks, but most of them anchored in pairs
side by side. The ships were in Condition 3 of readiness, which
was automatically set whenever the fleet was in the harbor. Despite the "war warning" of November 27—indeed, in the face of
what he had read in the Honolulu newspapers on Saturday—Admiral Kimmel neglected to make any arrangements for further
security of his men and ships. Why should he? Only four days

* In his testimony before the Navy Court of Inquiry held two and a half
years later (in the summer of 1944), Safford stated under oath that Kramer
had told him that he warned everybody he saw in the morning of December 7
that Nomura's instructions to deliver the note at one o'clock "means a sunrise
attack on Pearl Harbor today and possibly a midnight attack on Manila." But
Kramer swore that he had "never intended in the least to imply that those
remarks I made indicated an attack on Pearl Harbor or, in fact, any overt
intention on the part of the Japanese directed toward the United States."
However, the fact that he computed the time specifically for Manila and Pearl
Harbor showed clearly that he was at least apprehensive about those two
points toward which, in actual fact, the Japanese were moving.

before, Captain Charles H. McMorris, his war plans officer, had assured him categorically that there would "never" be an attack on Pearl Harbor from the air.

Downtown Honolulu was lively but no more so than other Saturday nights when the fleet was in. A "battle of the bands" was held at the Naval Receiving Station, the musicians from the battleship *Pennsylvania* blaring their way into the lead. Fort Street, ablaze with Christmas ornaments, was crowded until well past midnight, and a number of dances celebrating football victories continued until the small hours. But now the brief pleasures of shore liberty were over, and though many of the officers stayed off their ships on weekend passes, the men were back and asleep in their bunks.*

It was four o'clock, the end of the middle watch. The morning watches, to stand till eight o'clock, had just come on but the men idled the time away. None of the batteries was manned. Ammunition was kept in locked boxes. The plotting rooms were deserted. Only three small vessels of the fleet were under way—the destroyer *Ward* on inshore patrol all by herself, and two small converted mine craft, the *Condor* and the *Crossbill*, sweeping the entrance channel to Pearl Harbor for magnetic mines. Otherwise the fleet was asleep. The ships had their anchor lights on, but there was not even a trace of smoke from any of them in the harbor.

Watch throughout the Navy Yard was perfunctory. The gate of the anti-torpedo net in the channel was supposed to be kept closed from sunset to sunrise except to allow an occasional ship to stand in; but the men on the gate ship kept opening and closing and opening it rather erratically.

In the Communications Office of the 14th Naval District two young officers of the Naval Reserve stood the 8 P.M. to 8 A.M. watch—Ensign Oliver H. Underkofler at the open loudspeaker and Ensign Gordon F. Kennedy in the coding vault. In a real sense, this office was the sentinel of the big base—monitoring the inshore frequency to pick up the signals of the ships patrolling around the mouth of the channel. The officer on this loudspeaker watch was expected to relay whatever messages he heard to those

---

* Rumors and charges that "hundreds of officers and men of the fleet were absent from duty because suffering from hangovers on Sunday morning" were later proved "unqualifiedly false."

they were actually meant for, or listen in on voice transmissions for telltale evidence of any untoward incidents.

But this was a quiet night when nothing seemed to be happening, and Ensign Underkofler turned in at two-thirty. Since Kennedy in his isolated vault could not hear the loudspeaker, there was now nobody left to listen. "I do not recall a single man," Underkofler said afterward, "that was on watch that morning."

While he was asleep, however, his unattended loudspeaker gave forth with a spirited conversation between DZ5Y and DN3L, call signs of the *Ward* and the *Condor*. Sweeping at the lower end of the channel, at three forty-two, the *Condor* sighted what Lieutenant Monroe H. Hubbell, her commanding officer, thought was a periscope moving in the dark water. There was nothing he himself could do, but he spotted the *Ward* near by and signaled her by flashing his blinker: "Submarine is standing 1000 yards to the westward."

The *Ward* immediately went to General Quarters, slowed to 10 knots and began a sonar search, but found nothing. Half an hour later Commander William W. Outerbridge, her commanding officer, called Hubbell on his radio to ask: "What was the approximate distance and course of the submarine that you sighted?"

"The course was about what we were steering at the time," Hubbell replied, "020 magnetic and about 1000 yards from the entrance, apparently heading for the entrance."

Outerbridge realized that he had been searching in the wrong direction. He went westward, found nothing there either, called off the search, and turned in.

Ensign Underkofler slept through this conversation.

At about this same time the *Crossbill* was ready to stand in. The gate was opened for her, and since sunrise was approaching, it was left open from then on. It was eight minutes past five in Pearl—thirty-eight minutes past ten in Washington.

Colonel Bratton arrived on Independence Avenue at nine o'clock, entering the Munitions Building with Lieutenant Colonel John R. Deane, one of the assistant secretaries of the General Staff who was to be the duty officer in General Marshall's outer office on this Sunday. Bratton found the fourteenth part of the Japanese note waiting for him—Colonel Dusenbury had come in earlier,

taken a copy of the intercept to Marshall's office, left another copy
in War Plans and carried the third copy to the State Department
to complete the delivery to Mr. Hull.

Until this moment Bratton had not been inclined to make
much of the fourteen-part note. In his opinion it was the long-
awaited Japanese reply to the American note of November 26.
"We just don't barge off to war whenever the spirit moves us" was
his way of putting it later. "We have to go through certain
formalities." This, then, seemed to be one of the formalities. "This
was primarily of . . . immediate interest to the Secretary of
State," he said, "not to the Secretary of War or the Chief of the
General Staff, for it was not an ultimatum, it was not a declaration
of war, nor was it a severance of diplomatic relations."

If anything, it had a reassuring undertone. As he viewed the
note with its pilot message, it indicated that "we probably had a
little bit more time before the shooting war started." "There was
nothing [to it] even after the arrival of the fourteenth part,"
Bratton said. "There was no military significance to its presence in
Washington as long as the Japanese ambassador kept the note
locked up in his safe."

As he was reading the fourteenth part, however, Major Doud
came in with the intercept of the one o'clock-delivery message.
Now the whole crisis gained a different complexion. Immediately
upon its receipt, Bratton later claimed, he "became convinced the
Japanese were going to attack some American installation in the
Pacific area." It stunned him, he said, into frenzied activity. He
picked it up and literally ran with it next door looking for General
Miles, then down the corridor to War Plans, finally to Deane in the
front office asking for General Marshall. None of these officers was
in, so Bratton dashed back to his own office, and on his own
initiative and without going through channels, put in a call to
General Marshall at his quarters in Fort Myer.

Sergeant Aguirre, one of Marshall's orderlies, answered the
phone and told Bratton that the general had left the house about
ten minutes before, to go horseback riding.

"Well," Bratton said, "you know generally where he goes. Do
you think you could get ahold of him?"

"Yes, sir," Aguirre said, "I think I can find him."

"Please go out at once," Bratton said, "get assistance if necessary, and find General Marshall—tell him who I am and ask him to go to the nearest telephone, that it is vitally important that I communicate with him at the earliest practicable moment."

Sergeant Aguirre said he would do so.

Bratton then called General Miles at his home and told him what he had done. "You better come down at once," he said to Miles. "General Marshall may want to see you and talk with you." Then he called Gerow and advised him to come to his office as fast as he could make it.

With the intercept in hand Bratton returned to the front office to see if Deane had any word from the general. There was no word. He then went back to his own office again, to wait for the call from Marshall.

Walking up 16th Street toward Pennsylvania Avenue, Commander Kramer pondered the portent of the one o'clock-delivery note. He was quite wrought up by the time he reached the White House, where Captain Beardall had just arrived to find that he was the only presidential aide to put in an appearance. He had come on his own initiative, perhaps because he was a bit uneasy about the night before, when he had left the presentation of the thirteen parts of the important Japanese note to a junior grade lieutenant. Now he wanted to be on hand to deliver the fourteenth part as soon as it came in.

Kramer found Beardall in General Watson's office and gave him the "book." He told him also that Nomura had orders to deliver the note to Mr. Hull at one o'clock, which could be the time set for the launching of some operations. Beardall then went upstairs to Mr. Roosevelt's quarters. The President was still in bed, reading the papers; he took the intercept from the naval aide and went through it quickly. "The Japanese government regrets," it read, "to have to notify hereby the American government that in view of the attitude of the American government that [sic] it cannot but consider that it is impossible to reach an agreement through further negotiations."

It was exactly what he had expected: notice that the talks would be terminated but not an announcement of a break in diplomatic relations, certainly not a declaration of war. The President remarked to Beardall: "It looks like the Japs are going to break off the negotiations."

During the meeting, which lasted only a few minutes, Beardall said little if anything. As far as he could later recall it, he did not tell the President that Nomura had received instructions to deliver the note at one o'clock or mention Kramer's remark that the timing could mean the beginning of military operations somewhere. Mr. Roosevelt did not seem perturbed. He thanked his naval aide, then returned the intercept. It did not strike him as something that needed further attention.

Beardall then left for the Navy Building while Kramer crossed to the State Department, where Mr. Knox was waiting for his copy of the intercept. Kramer handed the "book" to John F. Stone, Mr. Hull's personal assistant, with an oral message for Secretary Knox repeating what he had told Bryant and Beardall about the coincidence in the timing of the delivery note. In Mr. Hull's anteroom Kramer met Dr. Hornbeck, Hamilton and Ballantine, and informed them, too, of the peculiar significance of the one o'clock delivery. As Hamilton remembered the conversation, Kramer "remarked on that occasion, in reference to the matter of an appointment for the Japanese ambassador to see the Secretary of State at 1:00 P.M. on December 7 that the naming of the hour might mean that it was the hour for some Japanese movement." But no mention was made of Pearl Harbor or Hawaii.

From the State Department, Kramer returned to his office, picked up the processed intercepts that had come over from SIS during his absence and set out on his delivery route within the Department. None of his clients was at his desk. They all were at a conference with the Chief of Naval Operations.

It was now past ten o'clock—around four-thirty in the morning at Pearl—and Marshall was still out, but his opposite number in stragetic command and responsibility in the Navy, Admiral Harold R. Stark, was at his desk, an arm's length from the telephone over which this whole awesome problem could have been resolved with a three-minute call.

"Betty" Stark impressed the President as a keen strategic thinker and pleased him with his enthusiastic support of the British in the Atlantic in the "undeclared war." In fact, the CNO was a scholarly, wise and progressive-minded officer, free of the prejudices of a navy that, according to Secretary Stimson, "frequently seemed to retire from the realm of logic into a dim religious world in which Neptune was God, Mahan his prophet, and the United States Navy the only true Church."

His erudition, articulateness and modesty, however, concealed his shortcomings. He lacked the ability to make quick decisions and the ruthlessness to organize and run the Navy Department tightly and efficiently. His laissez-faire created rampant inadequacies that left the Navy floundering, both mentally and physically unprepared for war. If the General Staff was paralyzed by the fact that Marshall was incommunicado, the Navy could have acted, for Stark was there. Moreover, it was his fleets in Pearl and Manila that stood out in front of the crisis and could be expected to bear the brunt of the onslaught.

Stark knew that the thirteen parts of the note had come in. He was the only high commander with whom the President had discussed it the night before, around eleven-thirty, when the CNO returned to his house on the Naval Observatory grounds from the theater. The fourteenth part of the note had been brought to him shortly after nine o'clock this morning, as soon as he arrived at his desk, by Captain Wilkinson and Commander McCollum. They stayed with Stark to discuss its possible meaning. Shortly afterward the intercepts of the telegrams with the one o'clock deadline and the order to destroy the last remaining cipher machine were brought in by Commander Kramer.

By then Stark's office had crowded up. All his top associates (except Admiral Turner) were at his side. Noyes was there from Naval Communications, and Captain Schuirmann, the Navy's liaison officer to the State Department, as was Admiral Ingersoll, the "brain" of Operations. They were joined by Captain Beardall, who had come over from the White House, sensing the urgency of the hour and eager to be closer to the rapidly developing events.

None of these men expected that the Japanese would "dare" to strike at Pearl Harbor. McCollum persisted in his assumption that the fleet was at sea. Wilkinson and the others had their apprehension focused on the Gulf of Siam, Singapore and the East Indies. But they knew of Japanese concentrations in the Marshalls and regarded them, intuitively rather than rationally, as a probable threat to Oahu. They suggested to the CNO, in the deferential manner of their relationship, that he do something. "Why don't you pick up the telephone," Wilkinson asked, "and call Admiral Kimmel?" *

Stark reached for the phone to put in the call. But then he thought it over. It was ten thirty-five in Washington but only five minutes past five in Hawaii, an ungodly hour to disturb Admiral Kimmel in his sleep. For another thing, Stark was addicted to the Navy protocol by whose rules it was definitely *not* the function or duty of the high command in Washington to "direct and supervise the detailed administration of commanders in the field." It was, in fact, the fundamental policy in both the Navy and Army high commands "not to interfere unduly with commanders in the field whose records justified the assumption of great responsibilities." The idea of telling Kimmel what to do or not to do was "repugnant" to the Washington staffs. Last but not least, Stark did not think that Pearl Harbor was in danger. He held to the thought he had expressed in a letter to Kimmel as recently as October 17: "Personally I do not believe the Japs are going to sail into us."

As he was holding the telephone he shook his head and said no, he would rather call the President. He reached the White House switchboard promptly, only to be told that the President's line was busy. Stark replaced the receiver and left it at that. He called for Admiral Turner, who came over quickly, but Stark did not deem it necessary to tell him about the Japanese deadline or the order to destroy the B machine. Rather, he began to discuss with him a recent letter from Admiral Hart requesting clarification of the duties of the Asiatic Fleet in a war that would *not* involve the United States.

The conference in the CNO's office disbanded. The men Stark

---

* The intriguing question as to why the telephone was never used in the emergency was raised by the various Pearl Harbor investigations and was answered by General Marshall, who said: "The telephone was not considered as means of transmission because, in the nature of things, it would have been too time-consuming." The Chief of Staff testified further: "From our own experience, my own experience, even now [in 1944] our telephone is a long-time procedure. . . . we now find we do a little bit better by teletype than we do on the telephone." No teletype link with the Hawaiian Department existed prior to the Pearl Harbor attack.

had dismissed when Turner came in went over to Room 2601, the office of the watch, banding together like a flock of apprehensive birds before a storm. They talked and talked, but their conversation was neither of substance nor consequence. Stark's "so what" attitude, as McCollum described the CNO's reaction to the latest intercepts, had rendered them totally impotent.

Nothing more was done by anybody in the Navy to act upon the alarm sounded by the morning's intercepts. "The basic trouble was," Admiral Ernest J. King, Stark's successor as CNO, told Admiral Zacharias, "that the Navy failed to appreciate what the Japanese could and did do." * And in his post-mortem on the disaster he wrote: "Even two hours' advance warning would have been of great value alerting planes and in augmenting the condition of readiness existing on board ship," concluding that "lack of efficiency in Admiral Stark's organization" was one of the major contributing factors in the disaster.

On Sunday mornings General Marshall usually went out on King Story for an hour, but he rode for another twenty minutes this day. And while most of the time he followed the winding bridle paths of Rock Creek Park in the District of Columbia, he now decided to go to the Virginia side of Potomac Park. As a result, Sergeant Aguirre searched for him in vain. And it was not until his return to his quarters at Fort Myer that the orderly could

* The commander's conduct in a situation confronting Stark in Washington and Kimmel in Pearl Harbor is lucidly described in *Sound Military Decision*, by Admiral E. C. Kalbfus, who wrote: "In his estimate, however, the commander's interest is not confined to what the enemy will *probably do*; *probabilities are subject to change*, and do not, therefore, cover the whole field of capabilities. The commander is not exclusively interested in what the enemy *may intend to do*, or even in what the enemy may be known, at the time, to intend to do; such *intentions are also subject to change*. The commander is interested in *everything that the enemy can do* which may materially influence the commander's own course of action." And Secretary Stimson said in this connection: "The outpost commander is like a sentinel on duty in face of the enemy. . . . He must assume that the enemy will attack at the time and in the way in which it will be most difficult to defeat him. . . . It is [the commander's duty] to meet him at his post at any time and to make the best possible fight that can be made against him with the weapons with which he has been supplied." Whatever the extenuating circumstances of Kimmel's conduct may have been, he did not meet the challenge of December 7 according to Kalbfus' concept of the commander's interest or Stimson's postulate of his duties.

give him Colonel Bratton's message. By then it was twenty-five minutes past ten.

Marshall called Bratton and the colonel explained, in the guarded language of "Magic," that he had "a most important message" which made it imperative that he see the general at once. Assuming that Marshall was phoning him from a booth somewhere en route, he suggested that if the Chief of Staff stayed where he was calling from, he would get a car and bring the message to him right away.

"No," Marshall said, "don't bother to do that. I'm coming down to my office. You can give it to me there."

Bratton figured that it would take the general ten to fifteen minutes to get to his office, and waited for him in the hall, intercepts in hand. But Marshall was in no hurry. He showered and changed, then sent for his official limousine that was parked at the Munitions Building on the other side of the Potomac.

When Marshall failed to arrive, Bratton returned to his own office to wait there for his call. The minutes passed. They grew into half an hour—it was now eleven o'clock—and Marshall still did not show up.

Bratton returned to the landing at the top of the staircase off the main entrance to resume his vigil in front of the general's office, hoping to meet him on his way in. Then another fifteen minutes went by and Bratton, now finding the strain of the delay unbearable, went into Colonel Deane's office to await Marshall's arrival there and share his suspense with a colleague.

There were two doors opening into the Chief of Staff's office, one directly off the hall, the other from the adjacent office, where Deane was now sitting with Bratton. A few minutes after Bratton had left his post outside, Marshall arrived and went into his office straight through the door from the landing. Five more minutes then passed before Bratton found out that the general had come in and was at his desk. There was a sign on the door from the secretaries' room, put there by Marshall himself: "Once you open this door, WALK IN, no matter what is going on inside."

Bratton now opened it and entered, and found Marshall reading the fourteen-part note aloud, his first opportunity to familiarize himself with it. Holding out the intercept he had in his hand, Bratton tried to interrupt him, saying that he had this most important message which the general ought to see before going any further with the reading of the long note. But Marshall droned on. He did not get around to looking at the intercept of the one o'clock-delivery message until he had gone all the way through the fourteen parts of the Japanese note.

By then he was surrounded by other members of his staff who had drifted in—General Miles, General Gerow and Colonel Bundy—and Marshall polled them one by one on what they thought the significance of the delivery message could be and how they evaluated the situation in its light. They agreed that the Japanese intended to attack somewhere in the Pacific at or shortly after one o'clock that afternoon.

At this point General Marshall drew a scratch pad toward himself and wrote out a message in longhand, to be sent to the commanding generals in the Philippines, in the Canal Zone, in Hawaii, and in the Presidio. It read: "The Japanese are presenting at 1 P.M. Eastern Standard Time today what amounts to an ultimatum. Also they are under orders to destroy their code machine immediately. Just what significance the hour set may have we do not know, but be on alert accordingly."

When he reached the bottom of the page he picked up the phone and called Admiral Stark, explained to him what he had written and what he proposed to do, inviting Stark to join him in the warning. He listened to the CNO's answer, then turned to his staff and said: "Admiral Stark doesn't think that any additional warning is necessary."

A few minutes later the phone rang. It was Stark calling back, asking that Marshall add the words "Inform the Navy" to his message, after all. As Stark later explained his change of mind: "I put the phone up . . . and stopped, and in a matter of seconds or certainly in a few minutes and thought, well, it can't do any harm, there may be something unusual about it . . . I turned back and picked up the phone. He had not yet sent the message, and I said, perhaps you are right. I think you had better go ahead and I would like to have you make sure that it goes to the naval opposites where this message was going which was throughout the commands in the broad Pacific.

"I also asked General Marshall," Stark continued, "knowing that the time was rather short, whether or not he would get it out quickly. I told him our own system under pressure was very fast.

And he said, no, that he was sure he could get it out quickly also."

General Marshall added the three words "Inform the Navy" at the bottom of the penciled message, handed the sheet to Bratton and told him: "Take it to the Message Center and see to it that it gets dispatched at once by the fastest safe means." As Bratton was leaving, Gerow called after him: "If there's any question of priority," he said, "give it first to the Philippines." The Message Center was down the hall, close enough for Bratton to reach in less than a minute. He took Marshall's note directly to Colonel Edward F. French, chief of Traffic Operations. French looked at the yellow sheet from the scratch pad and recoiled. "You'd better help me, Rufe," he said, "getting this into legible copy. Neither I nor my clerk here can read General Marshall's handwriting."

So Bratton took the sheet and dictated the message to the typist in the outside office. When it was typed up he brought the copy back to French, looking at his watch to check out the exact time of the delivery. It was two minutes before noon. He then walked back to Marshall's office, only to be sent back to the Message Center. "Find out," Marshall told him, "how long it's going to take for this message to be delivered to its addresses." French then told Bratton: "It's already in the works. Will take maybe thirty to forty minutes to be delivered."

It went out at once to MacArthur in the Philippines, to the Canal Zone next, and then to the Presidio. But when French himself took the message to the Signal Center, he was told that the direct channel to Fort Shafter had been out since ten-thirty because of atmospheric conditions. No matter how they tried, they could not get through and raise the Signal Office on Oahu.

French now had three choices to dispatch the message. The channel was open between Washington and San Francisco, and also between San Francisco and Fort Shafter. So he could have moved the message in a relay from the Signal Center in the Munitions Building to the Presidio, have it taken down there and retransmitted to Hawaii—going by Army facilities all the way from the War Department to the Hawaiian Department.

Or he could have given it to the Navy, whose channel with the Naval Radio Station at Aiea was open and which, as Stark had told Marshall, could be very fast under pressure.

Or as a last resort, he could send it via Western Union.

French ruled against his own facilities. As he later insisted, the relay method through San Francisco would have been slow. He also decided against giving the message to the Navy for transmission—not on his life would he admit to Op-20 that his channel was dead while the Navy managed to keep its line open.

He filed the telegram with Western Union, even though he knew that it also had no direct link with Honolulu: the telegram would go by cable from Washington to San Francisco, it would be relayed to the RCA office there by pneumatic tube, then radioed to RCA in Honolulu, delivered by messenger to the Signal Officer at Fort Shafter, about five miles from RCA's downtown office, then sent to the Adjutant Generals Office for delivery to General Short.

This was the method Colonel French chose as "the fastest safe means" to get the Marshall message to Short and Kimmel. He spent a quarter of an hour making up his mind. The telegram was given to Western Union at seventeen minutes past noon.

Japan was now *de facto* at war.

While all this was going on, Japanese troops occupied the International Settlement in Shanghai, shelled the British beach defenses at Kota Bahru, and began landings in northern Malaya. Simultaneously they landed at Singora and Pattani in Thailand and started their advance toward the Malayan border.

Two scout planes had been catapulted from the heavy cruisers of Admiral Nagumo's striking force; and almost at the very moment when General Marshall arrived in his office in the Munitions Building, the six carriers began to launch their planes for the two-hour flight to Pearl.

And exactly when French sent Marshall's warning message to Western Union, Ensign Underkofler at the Communications Office of the 14th Naval District was jolted out of his sleep. His loudspeaker was blaring out DW2X, his call sign. A message was coming in from Commander Outerbridge in the *Ward*.

Shortly after six o'clock the commander had been called back to the bridge because the elusive submarine had been sighted again. He had had no doubt at all in his mind, as he later put it, what to do, went to General Quarters again, at six thirty-three attacked with his guns and dropped depth charges in front of the submarine as she was trying to sneak into Pearl Harbor in the wake of the *Antares*, a supply ship on her way toward the open gate. "We have attacked fired upon and dropped depth charges upon submarine operating in defensive sea area," Outerbridge signaled. He could have told more: he had sunk the sub.

In actual fact, this was his second message. He had radioed a shorter and less explicit one fifteen minutes earlier, then thought, "Well, now, maybe I'd better be more definite," and put on the air a second message with details of the encounter.

Underkofler was asleep and did not hear the first call coming in. Fifteen precious minutes were thus lost, and then more time was wasted in getting Outerbridge's signal to higher-ups. "A not very bright yeoman" took so long in decoding it that the Naval District duty officer did not receive it until twelve minutes past seven. He passed the word to Admiral Bloch, who immediately ordered the destroyer *Monaghan* to go to the aid of the *Ward*.

At seven twenty-five Bloch's office notified Admiral Kimmel's duty officer. Eight minutes later General Marshall's message arrived at the RCA office in downtown Honolulu. It had been handled with dispatch in transit, requiring only forty-six minutes from the moment Colonel French filed it to its arrival in Hawaii. But it still had a long way to go.

The fleet switchboard was badly congested and it was only after some more delay that the fleet duty officer managed to get through to Kimmel with word about the *Ward's* venture, which had occurred more than an hour before. "I'll be right down," the commander-in-chief said. He quickly canceled a golf date he had with General Short, and was on his way to headquarters in response to this call when the first bombs began to drop.

Somehow President Roosevelt had become the forgotten man of the crisis. He had no visitors and his telephone was quieter than usual, even for a Sunday. There was no sudden rush of calls to him when the fourteenth part of the note came in, not even after the arrival of the one o'clock-delivery message.

His sinuses had become worse and he decided to stay in bed as long as he could, feeling very low from the pain. Dr. McIntire came in after Captain Beardall had left, and stayed at his bedside for two hours, his sole companion of the morning. The admiral is thus the only witness to the President's final hours before the attack.

"I sat with him," McIntire wrote in his brief reference to these historic hours, "on that Sunday morning from ten to twelve o'clock, while Mr. Hull was waiting over in the State Department for the Japanese envoys to bring their government's reply to the American note, and the President made it clear that he counted only on the usual evasions."

There was in McIntire's entire narrative only one other paragraph with a bearing on the climax of the crisis. "We knew," he wrote, "that [Mr. Roosevelt] was deeply concerned over the unsatisfactory nature of Nomura's and Kurusu's conversations with Secretary Hull; yet it was his firm conviction that even the madness of Japan's military masters would not risk war with the United States. It might well be that they would take advantage of Great Britain's extremity and strike at Singapore or some other point in the Far East, but an attack on any American possession did not enter his thought."

At noon Dr. McIntire left to have lunch at home. The President got up, dressed in a pair of flannel slacks and put on an old gray sweater he had "inherited" from his son James. Then he had himself wheeled to the oval study, planning to have his lunch there from a tray and spend the afternoon alone with his stamp collection.

28

"This Is Pearl!"

The Japanese embassy in Washington was a beehive, crowded with the regular staff on duty to the last man, and with friends and trusted newspapermen who were attracted to the scene by the portentous hour. They filled every office in the low and dainty cream-colored building on Massachusetts Avenue and overflowed to the rumpus room in the basement, playing billiards or listening to the radio as they waited.

In Ambassador Nomura's bungling management, the last act of the drama became a comedy of errors which would have been hilarious in any other circumstances. As it was, the hustle and foolish fumblings of these last hours were more in keeping with the trickeries and deceptions the Japanese practiced, now even beyond the bitter end. In the final convulsions of Japanese-American relations, diplomacy not only lost the game, it also lost its dignity.

The thirteen telegrams containing the first three-thousand-odd words of the note arrived Saturday night and were given to Senior Telegraph Officer Horiuchi in the Code Room for decrypting. The whole cipher staff was present and working. But the clerks had managed to complete only eight parts of the note when they were called away to attend a farewell dinner that Counselor Iguchi was giving for Secretary Terasaki, who was about to leave for his new post in Buenos Aires.

At nine-thirty, straight from the dinner and filled with *sake*, Horiuchi and the five code clerks—Kajiwara, Hori, Kawabata, Kondo and Yoshida—returned to their strong room to continue the decrypting. They finished all thirteen parts of the note shortly before midnight. Secretary Yuki took the copy to Ambassador Nomura's private quarters, ordering Horiuchi to keep his staff at the embassy, to be on hand when the final part of the note came in. Horiuchi put them to work on destroying the remnants of the three other cipher machines with the acid he had obtained from the naval attaché two days before. They completed the task at three o'clock in the morning. But the last part of the note had still not arrived, so Counselor Iguchi let the clerks go home to turn in, keeping only Kondo behind to stand watch.

Nomura had delayed the typing of the incomplete note, and nothing was done on it or on anything else during the night. At seven o'clock, however, messengers from the RCA office began to deliver telegrams, and kept coming for the next hour. Every one of the telegrams was marked "urgent." Yet now, aside from Kondo, who was sound asleep on a cot in the Code Room, no clerk was at the embassy to decode them. Counselor Iguchi awakened Kondo and told him to call back his colleagues.

This started a minor palace revolution. The clerks balked at the order. Protesting that they had barely had time even to doze off, they refused to return to the embassy. It was not until ten o'clock, and then only upon strict orders from Iguchi, that they finally came back, grumbling, to the pile of telegrams awaiting them.

The first of the dispatches which Clerk Kajiwara put through the remaining cipher machine was No. 908 from Foreign Minister Togo, expressing his "deepest thanks" to Nomura and Kurusu for their "valiant effort." Next to be processed was No. 909, a message of commendation from Director Yamamoto of the Foreign Ministry's Bureau of American Affairs to Counselor Iguchi and Secretary Yuki.

Only when these ceremonial dispatches were out of the way did the code clerks reach the more important telegrams, at ten-forty. It took them twenty minutes to decrypt No. 902, which was Part Fourteen of the note. Then Clerk Hori completed the decrypting of telegram No. 907, which had been delivered at eight o'clock that morning. It was Togo's instruction to Nomura to deliver the note at one o'clock. Now the whole embassy became electrified.

Together with the transcript of the fourteenth part of the note in English, Secretary Yuki took the telegram upstairs to an outer office in Ambassador Nomura's quarters, where First Secretary Katsuzo Okumura was sweating over a typewriter, copying the other parts. When ordered to have the note typed up not by any of the regular typists but by a member of the diplomatic staff, Nomura had chosen Okumura for the job simply because he was the only career officer at the embassy who "could operate a typewriter at all decently."

He had been at it since eight o'clock in the morning but was making slow progress, pecking out the letters laboriously, banging down the keys and making mistakes in the text. By eleven o'clock he had completed the typing of the thirteen parts, but then he decided that his copy was not neat enough for such a historic document and was marred by far too many errors. He returned a fresh sheet to the typewriter and started from scratch to peck out a cleaner copy.

He continued to make mistakes almost on every line, spending time and more time erasing them, typing and retyping, finishing half a page only to discover that he had left out words, inserting fresh sheets of paper in the machine, starting the pages over, sweating profusely as Chancellor Tsutomu Nishiyama and Secretary Yuki were spurring him on to please hurry up.

When Okumura had only 136 words of the final passage still left to type up, Ambassador Nomura sent for Junior Interpreter Enseki and asked him to arrange an appointment for him with Secretary Hull for one o'clock. At the State Department, Enseki was connected with John F. Stone, the Secretary's personal assistant, who told him that Mr. Hull had a luncheon date and that therefore their Excellencies, Nomura and Kurusu, would have to see Sumner Welles instead. But a few minutes later Joseph Ballantine called back to say that Mr. Hull would be able to see the envoys after all, at one o'clock as requested, at his office in the Old State Building.

Okumura was still sweating over the last part of the note. It was already twelve-thirty when its finished typescript was taken to the adjoining room to be proofread by Nishiyama and Yuki. A few more errors were then discovered and the transcript was returned to Okumura for retyping. As it became clear that the corrections could not be made in time for Nomura and Kurusu to keep the one o'clock appointment, Enseki was asked to call again to change the appointment to one-thirty. John Stone checked with Mr. Hull, then told the young interpreter that "the Secretary will expect the ambassadors as soon as their preparations are completed."

At ten minutes of two Okumura finally had the entire note in type. Nomura and Kurusu, waiting downstairs in the main hall, received the note from Yuki, climbed into their limousine and drove up Massachusetts Avenue to Pennsylvania, to the Old State Building. They reached the diplomatic waiting room at five minutes past two.

Sometime between one twenty-five and one forty-five (the exact minute was not recorded) the phone rang in Admiral Noyes's office in Naval Communications. A radioman from the watch was calling to relay a message that the Mare Island Navy Station in San Francisco Bay had picked up a few minutes before. It was a terse signal which Rear Admiral Patrick N. L. Bellinger, commanding the air arm of the Pacific Fleet, had broadcast from his headquarters on Ford Island at two minutes before eight, three minutes after Rear Admiral W. R. Furlong, the Mine Force commander, had spotted low-flying planes over Pearl Harbor, with the insignia of the Imperial Navy, and heard the explosion of bombs.

Bellinger's historic signal read:

Air raid Pearl Harbor—this is no drill *

Noyes took down the words and rushed to Secretary Knox with them. He ran into the Secretary in the corridor on his way to lunch. Knox looked at the scrap of paper, then said to Captain John H. Dillon, his Marine aide, who was standing at his side: "My God, this can't be true! This must mean the Philippines!"

"No, sir," said Admiral Stark, who was just coming up to go to lunch with the Secretary. "This is Pearl!"

Knox returned to his office, went for his direct phone to the White House, got through to the President in seconds, and told him the news. Mr. Roosevelt then called Secretary Hull, even as the two Japanese envoys were waiting outside his office.

"Cordell," he said in a steady but clipped voice, "Knox has just

---

* Bellinger's broadcast was followed at eight o'clock by a signal from Kimmel: "This is not a drill!"

called with the report that the Japs have attacked Pearl Harbor."
"Has it been confirmed?" Mr. Hull asked, punctilious as always.
"No, not yet," the President said. "I have it only from Knox."
"I'd like you to have it confirmed," Hull said, "and call me back
before I receive Nomura and Kurusu. They're outside in the
waiting room."

With that Mr. Hull turned to Ballantine and his legal adviser,
Green H. Hackworth, who were with him in the room, and said:
"The President has an unconfirmed report that the Japanese have
attacked Pearl Harbor. The Japanese ambassadors are waiting to
see me. I know what they want. They are going to turn us down
on our note of November twenty-six. Perhaps they want to tell us
that war has been declared. I'm rather inclined not to see them."

But at exactly two-twenty, as Hackworth left, Mr. Hull asked
Ballantine to bring in the two ambassadors. They bowed their way
in, presented the note, Nomura explaining that he had instructions to deliver it at one o'clock sharp and apologizing that difficulties in decoding and transcribing had delayed them.

Mr. Hull "made a pretense" of glancing through the note. Its
contents were, of course, known to him but, as he later said, he
could give no indication that he knew what they were. When he
had finished skimming the pages, he turned to Nomura and "put
[his] eye on him."

"In all my fifty years of public service," he told the squirming
ambassadors in his slow Tennessee mountain drawl, "I have never
seen a document that was more crowded with infamous falsehoods
and distortions—infamous falsehoods and distortions on a scale so
huge that I never imagined until today that any government on
this planet was capable of uttering them."

The final Hull-Nomura meeting was in keeping with the pathetic ineptitude that had marked the handling of the discussions
from the outset. The slipshod bureaucracy that delayed the processing of the note for hours defeated the purpose its authors had
designed for it.

The Emperor did not get his wish. The Japanese had struck
without warning.

It was now almost three o'clock.
The first enemy forces had pounded the Pearl Harbor base and

the airfields on Oahu for a whole hour. At the White House, the President was getting first details of the attack in a hastily written memorandum prepared by Colonel Walter Bedell Smith, secretary of the General Staff, from messages General Short started sending in.

"Japanese enemy dive bombers," the memo read, "estimated number sixty, attacked Hickam Field, Wheeler Field and Pearl Harbor at 0800. Extensive damage to at least three hangers [sic] at Wheeler Field, three at Hickam Field, and two planes caught on ground. Unconfirmed that ships in Pearl Harbor badly damaged. Marine field Ewa also badly damaged."

Later a second report was sent over by Smith. "Enemy submarines off Oahu," this one read. "Two American battleships sunk. Big fires along hangers still burning at Hickam Field. No Japanese bombers identified. Estimated from 60 to 100 dive bombers participated in attack on Oahu."

Then came the first report on the casualties: "Known dead, 38 . . . wounded 355 of which 20 to 50 may die . . ."

In Honolulu, Consul General Kita and his entire staff huddled in the office building while Samon Tsukikawa, the code clerk, was busy destroying whatever was still left of confidential papers and code materials. The brazier in the Code Room was too small for so big a pile, so he tried desperately to burn it in the bathtub. But in the damp air of the stuffy little bathroom the papers would not catch fire.

The muffled sound of explosions could be heard in the distance and a thick pall of smoke boiled into the sky over Pearl Harbor.

A car drove up at the Nuuanu Avenue gate—it was Mikami's familiar cab. Johnny got out, walked into the building and told Kimie Doue, the consulate's pretty Nisei receptionist: "Harada-san is waiting in the car at the gate to take Kita-san to Ala Wai."

Kimie went into the consul general's office, then returned promptly and told Mikami: "Please tell Harada-san that Kita-san regrets he will not be able to play golf with him this morning."

The dispatch addressed to "Commanding General Hawaiian Department Fort Shafter, T. H."—and bearing no mark to indicate that it was special or urgent—had been in one of the pigeonholes of incoming telegrams at the RCA office in Honolulu since seven thirty-three. So strange was this battle at Pearl Harbor that the people of the city, only a few miles away and watching the angry planes and the anti-aircraft bursts, did not really know what was going on.

This was now war—but Manager Street was keeping an efficient office and did not let the attack interfere with proper procedures. He called his messengers—young Nisei without exception, who had reported for work at half past seven—and told them to start delivering the telegrams that Ed Klein, the traffic clerk, had sorted in the pigeonholes of a big board on the wall. A young man named Tadao Fuchikami went to the board, and from the slot marked "Kalihi" he took the telegrams consigned to the district in which Fort Shafter was located. He arranged them by delivery areas—the one for Fort Shafter had to await its turn, since it was the most distant destination on this route, about five miles away. Then he went for his motorbike and rode off, going first to Vineyard Street, where he had a telegram for a doctor.

It needed courage for a "Jap boy" like Tadao to go to Fort Shafter this morning. He could be anything—a bona fide messenger of RCA, but also a spy or perhaps a saboteur. But Fuchikami went on his way without thinking of the perils of his journey. He was no "Jap." He was an American.

It took him until a quarter of twelve—almost four hours—to make it to the Fort. Traffic was heavy and chaotic. He ran into two roadblocks—one manned by Territorial Guardsmen who eyed him suspiciously and allowed him to proceed only after they had checked his credentials, the other by soldiers from the Regular Army whose young lieutenant detained him, for his own protection.

But when he reached the Fort on his Indian Scout bike, the sentry at the main gate just waved him in. He rode to the Signal Office and left the telegram with the desk sergeant.

It was put into the hopper with other messages for the commanding general, and stayed unattended for the longest period on its way from Washington, three hours and thirteen minutes. At last it was delivered to the Adjutant Generals Office, at two minutes before three, but General Short did not receive it until after four o'clock, nine hours after it had arrived at RCA downtown. The dispatch General Marshall had ordered sent by "the fastest safe means" was in transit a total of ten hours and thirty-eight minutes, from the time it had been filed by Colonel Bratton at the War Department Message Center to its delivery into General Short's hands.

In Washington the wheels of "Magic" were still turning but the machine was running empty. No more messages came in on the Tokyo–Washington circuit for some time—until an intercept, forwarded by Station S from Puget Sound, appeared on the teletype at last.

As the steel fingers of the clicking machine rapped out the letters on the yellow paper, the message began to form. It was in plain text and in English.

"C . . . I . . . R . . . C . . . U . . . L . . . A . . . R . . . N . . . O . . . 2 . . . 5 . . . O . . . 7 . . .

It was "Circular No. 2507" from the Foreign Ministry in Tokyo to all Japanese diplomatic missions abroad.

"The Imperial Naval Air Force," it read, "has damaged three United States battleships and sunk three in the Battle of Hawaii. Those sunk were the *Arizona* . . . the *Oklahoma* . . . and the *West Virginia* . . ."

One phase of "Operation Magic" was over.

Acknowledgments

It may be unusual to begin a formal voucher of thanks on a negative note, by listing some of those who could have aided my researches but did not. I think, however, that it is not without interest to show how the writer of a book like this has to labor to obtain the stones of which his mosaic is built.

Some of the people who were connected with the "Magic" operation are taciturn or secretive by nature or consider themselves bound to discretion by their vows of silence. No help can be expected for such an effort from any government agency, although I hasten to add that neither did anyone try to impede my research. I was very much on my own in this endeavor and had to piece together much of the evidence presented in this book from widely scattered references that could be found in no previous books, and only with difficulty and diligence in the documents. As a matter of fact, I would not have undertaken the writing of this book had I not had a few significant advantages to begin with.

I spent four years during World War II in the Office of Naval Intelligence, in charge of research and planning in the Special Warfare Branch, and had ample opportunity of observing from close quarters the workings of the American intelligence apparatus. In ONI, I worked closely with Comdr. (later Rear Adm.) Cecil Henry Coggins who had been on special intelligence duty in Pearl Harbor just before and briefly after the outbreak of the war. I had the privilege of working as a consultant for the late Secretary of the Navy Frank Knox during the weeks immediately preceding the Pearl Harbor attack. I was associated with the late Rear Adm. Ellis M. Zacharias, my chief during World War II and friend after it; and had unrestricted access to his files and memories when I helped him write his autobiography, *Secret Missions: The Story of an Intelligence Officer,* and collaborated with him in the writing of *Behind Closed Doors: The Secret History of the Cold War.*

These, then, are my basic credentials. In the course of researching this book, I have spoken to or corresponded with a great many people who were generous in giving me the benefit of their knowledge and recollections. Major aid (and, occasionally, comfort) was given me by Boris Hagelin, Jr., Lt. Comdr. Charles

C. Hiles, Brig. Gen. Frank McCarthy, and (indirectly) Capt. Laurence F. Safford. Dr. George Raynor Thompson, co-author of two basic books on the Signal Corps and former chief of its Historical Office, favored me with a couple of interviews. Mrs. Roberta Wohlstetter spent an afternoon with me, reviewing some of my problems and giving advice with her innate wisdom and exceptional erudition. On a special trip to Hawaii I was generously helped by Col. George W. and Dorothy Bicknell, Mr. Henry Mortara of RCA, Yoshio Hasegawa, Tadao Fuchikami, and Miss Janet E. Bell, curator of the Hawaii War Records Depository.

I am grateful to the Hon. L. Quincy Mumford, the Librarian of Congress, for facilitating and expediting my access to the invaluable collection of Japanese documents. On 2,166 reels of microfilm, the Library has custody of over two million pages of documents of the Japanese Ministry of Foreign Affairs. In them I found much of the information I needed to reconstruct the Japanese side of my story, on the basis of absolutely unimpeachable sources. More pertinent material came directly from Japan, some of it from the independent researches of Mr. Noboru Kojima. I was aided in the exploitation of this phenomenal source by Shumpei Okamoto of Columbia University, a young historian whose exceptional erudition is accompanied by a refreshingly objective attitude toward the Japanese personalities and events described in this book. Research in Japan was done for me by Mr. Kazunori Kato, my fellow member in the American Cryptogram Association. The German material was obtained through the help of Col. Rolf Göhring.

I am indebted to Arthur Neuhauser, Louis and Justine Smadbeck, Dr. Jerome A. Zane and Leonard J. Zakrzewsky for having read the manuscript and for the useful suggestions they offered.

At Random House, I received the encouragement and support I frequently badly needed from Bennett Cerf, Donald Klopfer and Charles Anthony Wimpfheimer. The Gargantuan job of final editing was done by Mrs. Barbara Willson, an exceptional lady who combines scholarship and meticulous attention to detail with an infinite store of patience.

No formal acknowledgment suffices to express my gratitude to Robert D. Loomis, senior editor at Random House. The book developed from a project he had conceived and for which he had chosen me as author. His involvement in my work was total. All through my difficulties and vicissitudes he helped me with indispensable guidance, giving me superb editorial help, wisely, firmly, with broad knowledge and great professional skill.

A final word of thanks to my wife and son, who had to endure all the sufferings that come from the stresses and strains of such a work, and who buoyed me with their unflagging good humor, compassionate understanding and devoted faith in me. Moreover, my wife typed and retyped innumerable pages of this manuscript (suggesting useful changes as she typed); and my son, in his junior year at prep school, helped me greatly in the preparation of the index.

To all of them, and to those mentioned in the notes that follow, my heartfelt thanks.

L.F.

Reference Notes

GENERAL REFERENCES

I. Bibliographies, Check Lists, Etc.

An Historical and Analytical Bibliography of the Literature of Cryptology, by Joseph S. Galland (Evanston, 1945).

A Catalog of Files and Microfilms of the German Foreign Ministry Archives, by George O. Kent (Stanford, 1962).

"Check List of Seized Japanese Records in the National Archives," by James W. Morley, *Far Eastern Quarterly,* Vol. 9 (May 1950), pp. 306–33.

"Pearl Harbor in Perspective: A Bibliographical Survey," by Louis Morton, USNIP (*q.v.*), Vol. 81 (Apr. 1955), pp. 462–69.

"Index of Translations [of Intercepted Messages] and Memoranda" [Prepared by Intelligence Branch, G-2, and Op-20-GZ], by Capt. Laurence F. Safford, in PHA (*q.v.*), Vol. 34, pp. 190–98.

Glossary of Cryptography, by David Schulman (N.Y., 1961).

Check List of Archives in the Japanese Ministry of Foreign Affairs, Tokyo, Japan, 1868–1945, by Cecil H. Uyehara (Washington, 1954).

Check List of Microfilm Reproductions of Selected Archives of the Japanese Army, Navy, and Other Government Agencies, by John Young (Washington, 1959).

II. Major Sources (recurrent references to them in the Notes are by abbreviated keys as listed in the column at left).

ALLEN   (a) *Hawaii's War Years, 1941–1945,* by Gwenfried Allen (Honolulu, 1949), Chapter 1, "December 7," and Chapter 9, "Internal Security"; (b) *Notes and References to Hawaii's War Years,* by Gwenfried Allen, Lloyd L. Lee, Aldyth V. Morris, and the Hawaii War Records Depository Staff (Honolulu, 1952).

AMFA   Archives of the [Japanese] Ministry of Foreign Affairs, Tokyo, Japan, 1868–1945, microfilmed for the Library of Congress, 1949–1951.

ATIS   Allied Translator and Interpreter Section, Supreme Commander, Pacific.

BUTOW   *Tojo and the Coming of the War*, by Robert J. C. Butow (Princeton, 1961).

DGFP   *Documents on German Foreign Policy, 1918–1945* (Washington, 1949–1964), Series C, Vol. 4; Series D, Vols. 11–13.

FEIS   *The Road to Pearl Harbor: The Coming of the War Between the United States and Japan*, by Herbert Feis (Princeton, 1950).

FEMT   *Documents* and *Exhibits, Transcripts* and *Judgment* of the International Military Tribunal for the Far East, Apr. 29, 1946, to Apr. 16, 1948, in Columbia University Law Library.

FRUS   *Foreign Relations of the United States: Diplomatic Papers*, issued annually in several volumes by the Department of State, Washington.

GREW   *Ten Years in Japan: A Contemporary Record Drawn from the Diaries and Private and Official Papers of Joseph C. Grew, United States Ambassador to Japan, 1932–1941* (New York, 1944).

GWYER   *Grand Strategy*, by J. M. A. Gwyer, Vol. 3 (June 1941–August 1942) in *History of the Second World War: United Kingdom Military Series* (London, 1964), Ch. 1, Sec. 3, pp. 16–20; Ch. 5, Sec. 4, pp. 130–37; Ch. 10, pp. 245–266; Ch. 11, pp. 267–90; Ch. 12, Sec. 1, pp. 291–92 and Sec. 2, 293–96.

HATTORI   *Dai-Toa Senso Zenshi* (A Complete History of the Greater East Asia War), by Col. Takushiro Hattori (Tokyo, 1953), 4 vols. English translation in the Office of the Chief of Military History; also see, one-volume edition in Japanese (Tokyo, 1965).

HILES   "Review of *Pearl Harbor: Warning and Decision* by Roberta Wohlstetter," by C. C. Hiles (Norfolk, 1962–1964, unpubl. MS.).

HOWETH   *History of Communications—Electronics in the United States Navy*, by Capt. L. S. Howeth (Washington, 1963).

HULL   *The Memoirs of Cordell Hull* (New York, 1948), 2 vols.

HWRD   Hawaii War Records Depository, a special collection of books, manuscripts, interviews, and official documents in the Sinclair Library of the University of Hawaii, under the direction of Miss Janet E. Bell.

INV. REP. Investigation Reports, District Intelligence Office, 14th Naval District, Hawaii.

JACOBSEN   *1939–1945: Der zweite Weltkrieg in Chronik und Dokumenten*, by Hans-Adolf Jacobsen (Darmstadt, 1961).

KIDO   Deposition of Marquis Koichi Kido, FEMT, Doc. 0002.

KIRBY   *The War Against Japan*, by S. Woodburn Kirby with C. T. Addis, J. F. Meiklejohn, G. T. Wards, and N. L. Desoer, Vol. 1 in *History of the Second World War: United Kingdom Military Series* (London, 1957), pp. 1–106.

KOJIMA   *Junigatsu 8* (December 7), a book about Pearl Harbor by Noboru Kojima (Tokyo, 1963).

LANGER-   *The Undeclared War: 1940–1941*, by William L. Langer
GLEASON   and S. Everett Gleason (New York, 1953).

LUPKE   *Japans Russlandpolitik von 1939 bis 1941*, by Hubertus Lupke (Frankfurt, 1962).

MORISON   *History of the United States Naval Operations in World War II,*
           Vol. 3: *The Rising Sun in the Pacific, 1931–April 1942*
           (Boston, 1947, rev. ed. 1953).

NA   National Archives:
           (a) Department of State Document File, Ser. No. 894; (b)
           Documents of the German Foreign Ministry, 1918–45; Film
           Serial Nos. 32, 82, 111, 154, 166, 174, 177, 184, 216, 1007,
           1068, 2316, 2931, 5703, 8886, 8887; (c) OKH (Oberkommando
           des Heeres), Attaché Department, Film Serial No. M341; (d)
           OKM (Oberkommando der Kriegsmarine), Archives, Film Se-
           rial Nos. P6, M179.

OCMH   Office of the Chief of Military History, Department of the Army,
           United States Army in World War II (Washington):
           (a) *Chief of Staff: Prewar Plans and Preparations,* by Mark
           Skinner Watson (1950); (b) *Washington Command Post: The
           Operations Division,* by Ray S. Cline (1951); (c) *Strategic
           Planning for Coalition Warfare, 1941–1942,* by Maurice
           Matloff and Edwin M. Snell (1953); (d) *The Fall of the
           Philippines,* by Louis Morton (1953); (e) *Strategy and Com-
           mand: The First Two Years,* by Louis Morton (1962), pp.
           3–130; (f) *The Signal Corps: The Emergency (to December
           1941),* by Dulany Terrett (1956); (g) *The Signal Corps: The
           Test (December 1941 to July 1943),* by George Raynor
           Thompson, Dixie R. Harris, Pauline M. Oakes and Dulany
           Terrett (1957); (h) *The Signal Corps: The Outcome (Mid-
           1943 through 1945),* by George Raynor Thompson and Dixie
           R. Harris (1966), Ch. 11, "Signal Security and Intelligence," pp.
           327–50. (i) *Command Decisions,* ed. Kent Roberts Greenfield
           (1960), "Japan's Decision for War," by Louis Morton, pp.
           99–124; (j) "Operational History of Naval Communications,
           December 1941–August 1945," Japanese Monograph No. 118
           (1953); (k) Miscellaneous monographs separately cited.

PHA   *Pearl Harbor Attack.* Hearings before the Joint Committee on
           the Investigation of the Pearl Harbor Attack, Congress of the
           United States, 79th Congress, in 39 vols.:
           Vols. 1–11: Transcript of Proceedings, Joint Congressional
           Committee, Nov. 15, 1945–May 31, 1946 (pp. 1–5560), Tran-
           script (pp. 1–14765);
           Vols. 12–21: Exhibits Nos. 1–183, and illustrations;
           Vols. 22–25: Proceedings of the Roberts Commission, Dec.
           18, 1941–Jan. 23, 1942;
           Vol. 26: Proceedings of the Inquiry conducted by Adm.
           Thomas C. Hart, Feb. 12–June 15, 1944;
           Vols. 27–31: Proceedings of the Army Pearl Harbor Board,
           July 20–Oct. 20, 1944;
           Vols. 32–33: Proceedings of the Navy Court of Inquiry,
           July 24–Oct. 29, 1944;
           Vol. 34: Proceedings of the Investigation conducted by Col.
           Carter W. Clarke, "pursuant to oral instructions of the Chief of
           Staff, United States Army," Sept. 14–16, 1944, July 13–Aug. 4,
           1945;

Vol. 35: Proceedings of the Investigation conducted by Maj. (later Lt. Col.) Henry C. Clausen, for the Judge Advocate General, U.S. Army, Nov. 23, 1944–Sept. 12, 1945; Vols. 36–38: Proceedings of the Inquiry conducted by Adm. H. Kent Hewitt, May 14–July 11, 1945; Vol. 39: Reports of the Roberts Commission, Army Pearl Harbor Board, Navy Court of Inquiry and Hewitt Inquiry, with endorsements.

Investigation of the Pearl Harbor Attack (Washington, 1946), majority and minority reports of the Joint Congressional Committee.

PLOETZ   Geschichte des zweiten Weltkrieges, a basic reference work in 2 vols., published by A. G. Ploetz (Würzburg, 1960). See Vol. II, Part E, Sec. C, "Geheimes Nachrichtenwesen: Japan," by Dr. Miriam Batts-Yoshida, pp. 828–32.

SHERWOOD   Roosevelt and Hopkins: An Intimate History, by Robert Emmett Sherwood (New York, 1948).

TOGO   The Cause of Japan, by Shigenori Togo, translated by Fumihiko Togo and Ben Bruce Blakeney (New York, 1956).

USNIP   United States Naval Institute Proceedings, published monthly in Annapolis, Md.

USNTM   United States Naval Technical Mission in Japan (1945–1946). Interrogations of Japanese officers and government officials.

USSBS   United States Strategic Bombing Survey (Washington): (a) Interrogations of Japanese Officials (1946) 2 vols.; (b) The Campaigns of the Pacific War (1946); (c) Japanese Military and Naval Intelligence Division (Japanese Intelligence Section, G-2), (1946).

WOHL-STETTER   Pearl Harbor: Warning and Decision (Stanford, 1962).

YARDLEY   The American Black Chamber, by Herbert O. Yardley (Indianapolis, 1931).

YOSHIKAWA   "Top Secret Assignment," by Ensign Takeo Yoshikawa, with Lt. Col. Norman Stanford, USMC, USNIP, Vol. 86 (Dec. 1960), pp. 27–39.

ZACHARIAS   (a) Interviews; (b) Secret Missions: The Story of an Intelligence Officer, by Rear Adm. Ellis M. Zacharias, in collaboration with Ladislas Farago (New York, 1946); (c) File: Notes, correspondence, and reports relating to Pearl Harbor and events leading up to it.

Prologue

The author was in Washington during the Pearl Harbor weekend, working as a consultant to the Secretary of the Navy. The Knox quotation is from his Annual Report, printed in the N.Y. Times, Dec. 7, 1941. For Roosevelt on Pearl Harbor eve, see SHERWOOD pp. 423–27; testimony of Comdr. R. L. Schulz, in

PHA, Vol. 10, pp. 4659–72. A pertinent letter from Capt. A. D. Kramer to Capt. L. F..Safford, reconstructing the delivery of the note to the White House from memory (while Kramer was serving in the Pacific) is inaccurate in details (cf. PHA, Vol. 8, pp. 3699–700).
For Wilkinson, Turner, etc., see *The Week Before Pearl Harbor*, by A. A. Hoehling (N.Y., 1963), pp. 129–30; also see testimonies of Turner, PHA, Vols. 32–33, pp. 988–1024; Wilkinson, PHA, Vol. 4, pp. 1723–1911; Beardall, PHA, Vol. 11, pp. 5269–91.
For a more detailed documentation of Washington on "the day before Pearl Harbor," see notes for Chapter 26.

1 Herbert O. Yardley and the "American Black Chamber"

Although Yardley himself wrote extensively about himself and his activities in cryptology—in *The American Black Chamber* (Indianapolis, 1931), *Education of a Poker Player* (N.Y., 1957) and, in thinly fictionalized form, in *Crows Are Black Everywhere*, with Carl Grabo (N.Y., 1945)—he often succeeded in obscuring rather than illuminating the story of his life. Practically nothing has been published about him and his work in the major works on cryptology—not a word in Fletcher Pratt's *Secret and Urgent* (New York, 1931), and only six lines in *Cloak and Cipher* by Don Tyler Moore and Martha Waller (Indianapolis, 1962), which lists him as "colonel" although he never rose beyond the rank of major in the Army Reserve.
This biographical sketch had to be reconstructed step by step, in a visit to Worthington, Ind.; in interviews elsewhere; from State Department records, newspaper references. Mr. W. I. Pryor, editor of the Worthington *Times* (who was Yardley's partner in the manufacture of a "secret writing" process) was helpful with information about the Yardley family and his boyhood in Indiana, and with glimpses of his later life.
Amb. Tracy Lay, who was Yardley's liaison with the State Dept., supplied some information about the inner workings of the "black chamber" in New York. Cols. George Waldo Bicknell and Joseph P. Kittner, who served with Yardley at his F Street headquarters in Washington in World War I, furnished substantive information about M.I.8. Some of the notes of Dr. John M. Manly, former head of the English department of the University of Chicago, who was one of Yardley's wartime associates and postwar consultants, provided additional insight into M.I.8 and the "black chamber."
The American Black Chamber was described by Joseph S. Galland, in *An Historical and Analytical Bibliography of the Literature of Cryptology* (Chicago, 1945) as "a romantically exaggerated, somewhat inaccurate, but very interesting book." Also see "Codes," *Saturday Evening Post*, Vol. 203 (Apr. 18, 1931), p. 16 et seq.; "Ciphers," *ibid.* (May 9, 1931), p. 35 et seq.; "Are We Giving Away Our State Secrets?," *Liberty* magazine, Vol. 8 (Dec. 19, 1931), pp. 8–13, all by Yardley. In the *Liberty* article he described his futile efforts to obtain copies of Japanese telegrams from the American cable companies.
Yardley's career in the State Department: from *State Department Register*, 1913–15 (Washington, 1915). The Signal Corps in World War I: from OCMH (f), pp. 16–69; *A History of the United States Signal Corps*, by ed. the *Army Times* (New York, 1961), pp. 112–142; and OCMH (h). Signal intelligence and security in the U.S. Navy during this period: from HOWETH, pp. 200, 201, 292–95.

There is no comprehensive and definitive history of cryptology, but those interested in these activities will benefit from "The Use of Codes and Ciphers in the [First] World War and Lessons to be Learned Therefrom" by W. F. Friedman, in *Signal Corps Bulletin* (July–Sep. 1938), mainly a translation of a work by the famous Swedish cryptologist Yves Gilden (whose "History of Decryptment," Eng. transl. by F. F. Flindt of an article in *Revue Internationale de Criminalistique*, Vol. 5 [1930], No. 2, is highly recommended). Also see "Codes and Ciphers (Cryptology)," by W. F. Friedman, in *Enc. Brit.* (1956), pp. 844–51. For other books, consult Galland, *op. cit.* Excellent brief descriptions of code-cracking as a tool of diplomacy is contained in *Formen und Stile der Diplomatie*, by Pietro Gerbore (Hamburg, 1964), pp. 140–68, and *Traité de cryptographie*, by André Langie and E.-A. Soudart (Paris, 1925).

For the State Department "code room," see *Outline of the Functions of the Offices of the Department of State*, by Natalia Summers (Washington, 1943), and *The Department of State: A History of Its Organization, Procedure and Personnel*, by G. H. Stuart (New York, 1949), pp. 3–4, 6–7, 27, 55, 79, 82, 145, 218, 252, 306–7, 363, 385–86. Also, *The Department of State Personnel and Organization, December 31, 1921* (Washington, 1922), and Congressional Hearings on the Foreign Service of the United States, *passim*, especially H. R. 12543, Committee on Foreign Affairs, 1920–21 (Washington, 1922); the N.Y. *Times*, Apr. 16, 1939, IV, p. 6.

For Doyle and Philander C. Knox: Stuart, *op. cit.*, p. 216; *Memoirs of an Ex-Diplomat*, by F. M. Huntington Wilson (Boston, 1945); *The South American Republics*, by T. C. Dawson, who was Doyle's associate in the Division of Latin American Affairs (N.Y., 1903), 2 vols.

For Japanese-American relations during this period: *American Diplomacy: A History*, by R. H. Ferrell (N.Y., 1959), *passim*; *The Far Eastern Policy of the United States*, by A. W. Griswold (N.Y., 1938); *Diplomatic Commentaries*, by Kikujiro Ishii (Baltimore, 1936). For the controversy over Yap, see *The International Aspects of Electrical Communications in the Pacific Area*, by L. B. Tribolet (Baltimore, 1929), pp. 130–34; Senate Doc. No. 106, 66 Cong. 1 Sess., p. 506; *Toward a New Order in Sea Power*, by Harold and Margaret Sprout (Princeton, 1940), pp. 91–93; *Japan in American Public Opinion* (N.Y., 1937), pp. 145–54.

During his "black chamber" period, Yardley was involved in an overt venture with a firm called Code Compiling Company, and in association with the famous cryptographer C. J. Mendelsohn, published a *Universal Trade Code* (N.Y., 1921 and 1928). An unpubl. MS. of his, written in 1933, was seized by federal agents and is in the custody of the Department of Justice. Entitled *Japan's Diplomatic Secrets*, it was planned as a sequel to *The American Black Chamber*.

The Japanese document expressing the belief that Yardley was behind the loss of several code books was written by Shin Sakuma, chief of the Cable Section, on Aug. 6, 1931.

For the controversy with the U.S. over cable rights on Yap: AMFA (3019 pp.), Reels 516–19; AMFA (collection of telegrams, Jan.–Nov. 1931), 533 pp., Reel UD 25; also AMFA (1916–23), Reel 522.

For the complexities of the Japanese language from the cryptological point of view, see Galland, *op. cit.*, p. 193; "A Cryptologist's Introduction to Japanese," in *The Cryptogram*, Vol. 33 (Mar.–Apr. 1966) pp. 77, 82, 82–83, 96; *Cryptography*, by L. D. Smith (N.Y., 1943); *Codes and Their Solution,* by D. Karashima (Tokyo, 1962); and "Japanese *Kana*," by "Fiddle" (Col. F. D. Lynch), *The Cryptogram* (June–July 1954), pp. 46–47. Sample of a "complete *kana* columnar transposition xenocrypt by "Oyoyo" (K. Kato of Tokyo) is in *The Cryptogram* (Mar.–Apr. 1966), p. 91.

2 Diplomatic Stud Poker

Background information was supplied by Dr. Stanley K. Hornbeck, Henry Suydam and Amb. Tracy Lay, who served as members of the American secretariat at the conference.

The best introductions to the conference is H. and M. Sprout, *op. cit.*, pp. 112–270, and *A Navy Second to None*, by G. T. Davis (N.Y., 1940). *A History of the United States Navy*, by Commodore Dudley W. Knox (N.Y., 1936) is a rueful account of the Navy's distress. Also see *Official Report of the American Delegation to the Washington Conference on Limitations of Naval Armaments* (Washington, 1922); and, for his part, see YARDLEY, pp. 283–317, incl. translations of the decrypted telegrams.

The Great Adventure at Washington, by Mark Sullivan (N.Y., 1922), special correspondent of the Baltimore *Sun* papers at the conference, is a fascinating journalistic account of the drama behind the scenes, even without reference to Yardley's backstage contribution.

Mr. Hughes himself explained his diplomatic strategy in the *American Journal of International Law*, Vol. 16 (July 1922), pp. 367 ff. a few weeks after the closing of the conference, and in *The Pathway to Peace* (N.Y., 1925), without, of course, even as much as hinting at the Yardley operation. The Japanese side was ably presented in *The Washington Conference and After*, by Ichihashi Yamato (Stanford, 1928) that appeared too early to reveal anything about the "American black chamber." Books like Stuart, *op. cit.* contain only the barest reference (p. 294) or none at all (as Ferrell, *op. cit.*) to Yardley's part.

On the other hand, massive documentation was obtained from the archives of the Japanese Foreign Ministry, which made a thorough investigation of the Yardley operation.

The incident in the geisha house in Tokyo: from ZACHARIAS (a); also see (b), pp. 12–13.

Merlo J. Pusey's Pulitzer Prize-winning biography of *Charles Evans Hughes* (N.Y., 1951) goes on through two monumental volumes without ever referring to the part of the "black chamber" in the Secretary's triumph at the Washington Conference.

Japanese documents in AMFA: (1) collection of telegrams (1921–23), Reels 48–49, 312–19, P46–47, UD52; (2) developments, Reel UD20; (3) limitations of naval armament, Reels 307–10; (4) public opinion in Japan, Reels 306–07.

3 The Secrets of Room 2646

Yardley's D.S.M.: from the *N.Y. Times*, Jan. 9, 1923; also see YARDLEY, pp. 321–24; the text of the citation from Department of the Army, OCMH, Hist. Serv. Div., Gen. Ref. Branch.

For the U.S. Navy's cryptological effort during World War I and after; HOWETH, p. xi, also "Communications Security," pp. 292–94, 295. The organization consisted of the Office of Naval Intelligence, the Director of Naval

Communications, and the Code and Signal Section of the Division of Operations. Also see *Report of the Chief Signal Officer to the Secretary of War* (Washington, 1919–22).

The abolition of ONI's cryptological efforts and secret-ink laboratory in 1918 was related by the officer (then a lieutenant j. g. in the Naval Reserve) whose unpleasant duty it was to break the news to the ONI cryptologists. For the evolution and functions of ONI, see PHA, Vol. 15, pp. 1864–66; "Office of Naval Intelligence," in *U.S. Naval Administration in World War II: Chief of Naval Operations*, Vol. 19, Pt. 3 (Washington, 1946), pp. 33, 123–24, 147; *Administration of the Navy Department in World War II*, by Rear Adm. J. A. Furer (Washington, 1959), pp. 17, 119–20; also *A Brief History of the Organization of the Navy Department*, by A. W. Johnson (Washington, 1940), pp. 180–84; "Theodorus Bailey Meyers Mason: Founder of the Office of Naval Intelligence," by Captain J. M. Ellicott, USNIP (Mar. 1952), pp. 265–67; "Command and the Intelligence Process," by Captain Rufus L. Taylor, *ibid.* (Aug. 1960), pp. 27–39. (Taylor is now a vice-admiral and deputy director of the CIA.)

More on Yap: "How Japan Fortified the Mandated Islands," by T. Wilds, USNIP, Vol. 81 (Apr. 1955), pp. 401–7.

The Hotel Benedick incidents, the acquisition of the Japanese fleet code, and the "inside story" of Room 2646: from ZACHARIAS (c); also see (b), pp. 75–98. Some additional historical material was furnished by Lt. Comdr. C. C. Hiles, USN (Ret.), who spent many years with the Asiatic Fleet and has made a study of cryptology.

Also, on Zacharias and Room 2646: Comments on ZACHARIAS (b), unpubl. MS. whose author wishes to remain unnamed.

The biographies of Zacharias, Capt. Watson, Adm. Long and Comdr. McCarran: from Dept. of the Navy, Bio. Branch.

Japanese military and naval attachés in the United States: (misc. attaché reports from U.S. 1920–22), AMFA, Reel 464; (1920–22), *ibid.*, Reel 608. Japanese wireless telegraphy in 1920–26: *ibid.*, Reels S639–43. Japanese observation of American naval maneuvers: (1088–pg. doc.), *ibid.*, Reels 429–30.

For Japanese-American naval policies of this period: *Statesmen and Admirals: Quest for a Far Eastern Naval Policy*, by T. V. Tuleja (N.Y., 1963), pp. 15–35; *The Influence of Force in Naval Relations*, by Capt. W. D. Puleston (N.Y., 1955); also his *Mahan: The Life and Work of Captain Alfred Thayer Mahan, U.S.N.*, (New Haven, 1939); "The U.S. Navy and the Open Door Policy," by L. C. Dunn, USNIP, Vol. 75 (Jan. 1949), pp. 53–65; "The Naval Arm of Diplomacy in the Pacific," by H. T. De Booy, *Pacific Affairs*, Vol. 8, No. 1 (1935), pp. 5–20; "Guam," by Rear Adm. G. J. Rowcliff, *Foreign Affairs*, Vol. 71 (July 1945), pp. 781–93.

4 The Mission of the Marblehead

I am indebted to Lt. Comdr. Charles C. Hiles, USN (Ret.), a lifelong friend and associate of Captain Safford, for some of the information used in this chapter. Safford's career has been reconstructed from his official Navy biographies and releases accompanying his awards; "Laurence F. Safford," Report No. 1473, U.S. Senate, Committee on the Judiciary; S. 1525, 85 Cong., 2 Sess., July 22, 1958; "Wider Horizons," by Comdr. L. F. Safford, USNIP, Vol. 63, No. 11 (1937), pp. 1537–52; "The Yangtze Patrol," by Dr. Esson M.

Gale, USNIP (Mar. 1955), pp. 307–15; references to his career in his testimonies, PHA, Vols. 8, 33, 36–38; records of the U.S. Asiatic Fleet in NA; also Hoehling, op. cit., p. 73; Yearbook of the U.S. Naval Academy (Annapolis, 1916); Register of Naval Academy Graduates (Annapolis, 1955). For the Finch, see Dictionary of American Fighting Ships, Vol. 2, Naval History Division (Washington, 1963), pp. 405–6. For the S-7: United States Submarines, by H. F. Morse, 3rd ed. (New Haven, 1946), pp. 11–14; also Ships' Data, U.S. Naval Vessels, (Washington, 1911–45).

Cryptological activities in the Office of Naval Communications: from HOWETH, pp. 200, 201, 293–95, 524, 525, 528. Adm. Bullard, ibid., pp. 197, 234, 353–54, 527, 531, and his official Navy biography; data from Archives of Reg. Publ. Section, Nav. Com. in a letter to Howeth, dated Dec. 29, 1957; papers of George H. Clark, in Engineering Library, MIT. "Codes" became the responsibility of DNC in Oct. 1917 (cf. "Communication Regulations of the U.S. Navy," 1918). For Room 1649, see Navy Dept. directories, 1920–28. The Division of Naval Communications was housed in the sixth wing of the "first deck" in the old Navy Building on Constitution Avenue, the Codes and Signal Section in Rooms 1647–49: Senior Clerk M. J. McGarn, the Section's permanent fixture, had his office in Room 1649; Codes and Ciphers was in Room 1647. The coding vault was upstairs, in Room 2621, near Communications Center in Room 2626 and the Telegraph Office in Room 2632. The DNC had his office in Room 1622.

For Capt. McLean: HOWETH, pp. 393, 409, 420, 536. For Research Desk: Safford biographies; ZACHARIAS (a); also (b) pp. 81–82. Ref. to Capt. Rochefort is based on ZACHARIAS (a), Rochefort's biography and his recapitulation of his career in PHA, Vols. 36–38 and Cong. Comm.; also testimony of Capt. Arthur H. McCollum, PHA, Vol. 8, pp. 3403–4. For the whole complex, see Chronological History of U.S. Naval Communications, in Navy Dept. Library, Nj3-U:N327c.

References to Japanese flag officers system: in PHA, Vol. 9, p. 4421 and Vol. 18, pp. 3335–36, also Safford's testimony, PHA, Vol. 36, pp. 61–62, and Rochefort, ibid., pp. 31–32. Circumstances of cracking of the code mainly from ZACHARIAS (a), (b), (c), and a source that desires to remain anonymous.

ONI activities: from ZACHARIAS (b); Hepburn and Galbraith: official Navy biographies, ZACHARIAS (a), and (b), p. 76; "Penetrate the screen," ibid., pp. 88–89. The missions of the McCormick and the Marblehead are described from information supplied during our collaboration on ZACHARIAS (b); also Ships' Data, U.S. Naval Vessels (loc. cit.) and the records of the U.S. Asiatic Fleet. Also see Communications in the Far East, by Frederick V. de Fellner (London, 1934). For "ambush by radio," see ZACHARIAS (b), pp. 88–98; Captain Craven's latter is quoted on p. 98.

For relations between U.S. and Japanese navies, see MORISON, pp. 29–31; for the Japanese navy during this period, ibid., pp. 19–27; U.S. naval attaché reports in ONI Files; and misc. docs. in AMFA, Sec. 2–4, Reels 408–9, and Reels 420–21. Visit of Japanese training squadrons, including explicit references to intelligence agents aboard, misc. docs., AMFA, Sec. 1–4, Reels 423–28.

Baron Sakamoto's article in Diplomatic Review (Tokyo, June 1927), reprinted in USNIP (Sep. 1927), pp. 1008–9.

Secret developments in the Japanese navy: La Revue Maritime (Apr. 1928), pp. 209, 305. For Agaki: Jane's Fighting Ships (London, 1927).

Japanese fleet problems and training exercises: MORISON, p. 25; also Japanese Navy Dept. pamphlet, attached to U.S. naval attaché report No. 187 (Tokyo, July 6, 1937).
Incident at Mihonoseki: USNIP (Aug. 1927).
Japanese maneuvers reported in the N.Y. Times (Oct. 25, 27, 31 and Nov. 27, 1927); USNIP, "Air Forces Used in Maneuvers" (Dec. 1927), pp. 1325-26. Suicide of Jintsu's captain: the N.Y. Times (Dec. 27, 1927).

5 "Gentlemen Do Not Read Each Other's Mail"

For Stimson's career and his diplomacy, see his diary and papers, in Yale University Library; On Active Service in Peace and War, by Henry L. Stimson and McGeorge Bundy (N.Y., 1947), pp. 139–62; The Far Eastern Crisis, by Henry L. Stimson (N.Y., 1936); Turmoil and Tradition: A Study of the Life and Times of Henry L. Stimson, by Elting Morison (Boston, 1960); Secretary Stimson: A Study in Statecraft, by Richard N. Current (New Brunswick, 1954), a critical survey of his major decisions; Henry L. Stimson and Japan, 1931–33, by Armin Rappaport (Chicago, 1963), pp. 2–44.

For background of international situation and pertinent docs.: FRUS, 1931–33 (Washington, 1946); The United States and Japan, 1931–1941 (Washington, 1942), 2 vols.; United States Diplomatic Correspondence, 1931–33, and NA (a); Memoirs, 1920–1933, by Herbert Hoover (N.Y., 1952); The United States and Japan, by Edwin Reischauer (Cambridge, 1950); War and Diplomacy in the Japanese Empire, by Takeuchi Tatsuji (N.Y., 1935); Survey of International Affairs, 1929–33 (Oxford, England, 1930–34).

Yardley's activities, see YARDLEY pp. 368–75.

The Tacna-Arica controversy arose over the treaty that ended the War of the Pacific (1879–84). Chile was given the southern provinces of Peru on the condition that a plebiscite within ten years would determine the eventual fate of this territory. No plebiscite was held, and in 1922 Chile and Peru agreed to arbitration by the President of the U.S., and in 1929 accepted the decision that Tacna be returned to Peru, with Chile retaining Arica and paying an indemnity (see FRUS, 1929).

Stimson's own account of the abolition of the "black chamber": in Stimson-Bundy, op. cit., p. 188; in YARDLEY, pp. 368–75.

The account of Yardley's arrangement with the Japanese, presented here for the first time, is entirely from the original Japanese docs., microfilm copies of which are in AMFA, Reels UD29–UD30. The War Department employee's contact with the acting Japanese ambassador in Washington is described in "Secret Document No. 48" in this series, dated Mar. 10, 1925.

The Yardley transaction was recapitulated in great detail on June 10, 1931, in a memorandum from the chief of the Cable Section, Shin Sakuma, to For. Min. Shidehara, Doc. No. 0157, a microfilm copy of which is in the author's possession. Another recapitulation of what Sakuma called "Yardley's treachery" was contained in a memo dated Apr. 6, 1933. Foreign Correspondent Takada's participation is described in documents dated Nov. 26, 1939, and Mar. 5, 1940.

The development of Japan's cryptological establishment is described on the basis of these original documents, including Sawada's and Sakuma's memoranda and reports, Doc. Nos. 0284–90.

For evolution of cipher machines, see Friedman's article in Enc. Brit. Vol.

215 (*loc. cit.*), pp. 4–5; "Modern Cryptology," by David Kahn, *Scientific American*, (July 1966), pp. 38–46; Moore and Waller, *op. cit.*, pp. 165–74. Jefferson's cryptodevice is described in his papers, Vol. 232, No. 41575 (Libr. Congr.); also see "Edgar Allan Poe, Cryptographer," by William F. Friedman, *Signal Corps Bulletin* (Oct.–Dec. 1937), pp. 54–75, which includes a picture of Jefferson's invention of the "cylindrical cipher device;" and Friedman's *Several Machine Ciphers and Methods for their Solution* (Geneva, Ill., 1918).

Compilation of patents: from *Chiffrieren mit Geräten und Maschinen*, by Dr. Siegfried Tuerkel (Graz, 1927), re Eng. transl., see notes for Ch. 6. More material on cryptodevices in *Tratado de Criptografía*, by Hercules Marthans Garro, Inspector General of the Policia de Investigaciones del Peru (Lima, Peru, 1965), which contains excellent descriptions of the German cipher machines.

For Ozeki's exploratory trip to Europe and the development of the Japanese cryptograph in 1930, see Sakuma's memorandum of Aug. 6, 1931; also "Opinions of the Navy Ministry concerning Codes," in AMFA, Reel S612; and *Teikoku Kaigun Kimitsushitsu*, by Adm. Toshiyuki Yokoi (Tokyo, 1953).

For Chiffriermaschinen A.G., see *Handbuch der deutschen Aktiengesellschaften* (Berlin, 1925–30). Also, for the whole complex: "Matematische und maschinelle Methoden beim Chiffrieren und Dechiffrieren," by Prof. Hans Rohrbach, written for Field Information Agency, U.S. Army, published in *FIAT Review of German Science, 1939–1946* (Wiesbaden, 1948); and his "Chiffrierverfahren der neuesten Zeit," *Arch. Elektr. Übertragung*, (Dec. 1948), pp. 362–69; *Hemlig Skrift Coder och Chiffermaskiner*, by H. Stalhane (Stockholm, 1925); and "Electrical Machine Can Make Eleven Million Codes," by H. H. Dunn, *Popular Mechanics* (Dec. 1922), pp. 849–50. I am indebted to Boris Hagelin, Jr., and Jerome Raymont for material and guidance in these and forthcoming references to mechanical cryptodevices.

For Cartier, see "Souvenirs du Général Cartier," by François Cartier, *Revue des Transmissions* (July–Aug. 1959), pp. 23–39, and (Nov.–Dec. 1959), pp. 13–51, and his writings on cipher machines (*q.v.*).

Withdrawal of ONI from cryptographic activities: ZACHARIAS (a). Capt. Baldridge: official Navy biography (he retired shortly afterward, in 1932, and died in Bethesda Naval Hospital on Jan. 9, 1952).

For William F. Friedman, see *Who's Who in America*, 1956–57, p. 730; official Army biography; H.R. 2068, 84 Cong., 2 Sess., May 10, 1956; H.R. No. 260, Senate Report No. 1815; "Cryptographer's Reward," *Newsweek* (May 14, 1956), p. 119; letter to the *N.Y. Times*, May 17, 1956; also scattered autobiographical references in *The Shakespearean Cipher Examined*, by William F. and Elizabeth S. Friedman (Cambridge, England, 1957) with photograph and data on the dust jacket; also Ch. 11 of OMCH (h), pp. 329–32, 336–37, 344.

For Friedman's writings, see annotated listing in Galland, *op. cit.*, pp. 67–71 (a total of 31 works are listed, including several marked as "restricted publication, not available to the public").

Col. Fabyan and Riverbank Laboratories: see collection of his papers and books in Libr. Congr.; biography in *Who Was Who in America, 1897–1942*; Wm. F. and E. S. Friedman, *op. cit.*, pp. 59, 205–07, 249–50.

U.S. Signal Intelligence in World War I and after: OCMH (h), Ch. 11/II; interview with Col. George W. Bicknell; and *Report of the Chief Signal Officer to the Secretary of War, 1919* (Washington, 1919); *Articles on*

Cryptography and Cryptanalysis, reprinted from *The Signal Corps Bulletin* (Washington, 1942), a microfilm copy of which is in the N.Y. Public Library.

6 Nothing Sacred, Nothing Secret

For the disavowal of Yardley's book and Mr. Stimson's categorical denial: the *N.Y. Times*, June 2, 7, 1931; denials of the President Wilson poison plot by Gen. March, W. H. Moran, chief of the Secret Service, and Rear Adm. Cary T. Grayson, the late President's physician, *ibid.*, June 1, 1931. Secretary Castle's statement in the N.Y. *Herald Tribune*, June 9, 1931.

Yardley's post-"black chamber" career was the subject of a rather lurid column: "Capitol Stuff," by John O'Donnell, in the N.Y. *Daily News*, Feb. 27, 1945, speculating that if Yardley's "secret bureau . . . had been re-established . . . there might never have been a Pearl Harbor." O'Donnell also revealed that "Yardley had been in China, setting up Chiang Kai-shek's code organization," helped Canada "set up a code bureau," and would have been hired by Col. William J. Donovan for the Office of Strategic Services but Mr. Stimson vetoed his employment. Yardley's mission to China was reported on Nov. 26, 1939, in a dispatch to the N.Y. *Herald Tribune* ("Herbert Yardley is now in Chungking, working for the Chiang Kai-shek government under a pseudonym"); and on Mar. 5, 1950, in a dispatch from Hong Kong to the Tokyo paper *Nichi-Nichi*, according to which he had gone to China with "the blessings of the State Department."

The American Black Chamber was reviewed in 1931 by W. S. Rogers in the *Saturday Review of Literature* (June 20, p. 908), by A. W. Porterfield in *Outlook* (July 1, p. 281), by Uffington Valentine in the N.Y. *Times Book Review* (June 14, p. 9), and by C. H. Grattan in *The Nation* (Aug. 19, p. 186).

See further: NA (a), No. 894.727; a memo about Yardley by Dr. Stanley K. Hornbeck, *ibid.*, No. 20; *Congressional Record*, Vol. 77, pp. 2698, 2699, 3125–39, 5218, 5333–34, 6198; Reports 18 and 206, House of Representatives, Report 21, Senate, 73 Congress; the N.Y. *Times*, Feb. 21, 1933.

For the discovery of the two messengers taking bets: the N.Y. *Times*, May 31, 1931.

The Japanese side of the Yardley crisis comes from interviews of Noboru Kojima with Ozeki, Ito, Inouye and Kameyama; deposition of Katsuji Kameyama, Def. Doc. No. 1079 (Aug. 13, 1947); the interrogation of Maj. Kusuo Matsuora, chief of the Cipher Section, Kwantung Army, by Capt. Sokolov of the Red Army at Khabarovsk, May 18, 1946; and the original documents in the Japanese Foreign Ministry's Yardley folders, as follows:

Collection of telegrams exchanged by For. Min. Shidehara and Amb. Debuchi, June 2, 3, 5, July 30, Aug. 10, Nov. 3, 1931;

"Draft of Answers to Hypothetical Questions in the Diet about Yardley's *Black Chamber* prepared by Chief of Cable Section" (handwritten by Shin Sakuma), July 25, 1931;

"Confidential—Concerning the Secrecy of Telegraphic Codes," Docs. Nos. 0284–90, Apr. 1, 1932;

"Circular Questionnaire sent to Missions Abroad for Suggestions for the Improvement of Code Security," Sep. 7, 1931;

"Memorandum No. 0157," by Sakuma, June 11, 1931;

"Reports of the Chief of Cable Section Concerning the Protection of Codes," Docs. Nos. 0291–97, Aug. 6, 1931; 0284 (n.d.).
"Top-Secret Report to the Foreign Minister on the Tightening of Telegraphic Security as a Result of the Yardley Matter," Docs. Nos. 036980, Aug. 15, 1931.
"Circular [discussing the Yardley case, signed by Shidehara]" to 28 Japanese diplomatic missions in Europe, 25 in South and North America, 4 in Africa, 16 in Asia, 9 in Russia, 31 in China, 21 in Manchuria and Mongolia, Sep. 18, 1931;
"Memorandum [by Sakuma for the Foreign Minister] concerning the Repercussions of the Yardley Matter," Aug. 22, 1931;
"Special Report on the Yardley Case," June 10, 1931.
"Concerning the Use of the Code Machine at the 1932 Disarmament Conference in Geneva," Doc. No. 0297, Aug. 6, 1931.
"Report on the Building and Distribution of Type-A Code Machine," Sakuma's report to the Foreign Minister on his conference with Capt. Ito, Aug. 9, 1931.
Sawada's memorandum on Ozeki's trip to Europe and the purchase of the Cryha machine, Oct. 17, 1929; also see, for cipher machines in general, *An Analysis of Cryptographers*, by Boris Hagelin, Sr., unpub. MS.; *Enciphering with Apparatus and Machines: An Introduction to Cryptography*, by Dr. Siegfried Türkel (Graz, 1927), transl. by Army War College, Fort Humphreys, D.C. (references to the Cryha machines are on pp. 31–49); "The Kryha Cipher Machine: A Mathematical Opinion," by Dr. Georg Hamel (Berlin, 1927); "Cryptographic Machines," by Lt. Col. Marcel Givièrge, *Le Génie Civil*, Sep. 2, 1922. For Japanese cryptotechniques, see PLOETZ, Vol. 2: *Die Kriegsmittel*, pp. 825–32.
For the *denshin-ka*: "The Japanese Foreign Office," by Prof. Kenneth Colegrove, *American Journal of International Law*; also see "Ordinance Regulating the Ministry of Foreign Affairs," No. 258 (1898), amended text published in *Yearbook of Foreign Ministry*, 1933, pp. 14–34; "The Diplomatic and Consular Services," in *Harai Kei Zenshu* (Complete Works of Kei Hara, Vol. 1, (Tokyo, 1929), pp. 978–1074. "The *denshin-ka*," wrote Prof. Colegrove (*op. cit.*, p. 600), "or Telegraph Service, receives and transmits the telegraphic messages. In order to secure secrecy, it is also charged with the coding of outgoing messages and with the decoding of incoming messages. According to general belief, the *denshin-ka* followed the usual European practice (and unhappily, the practice of the American government from 1917 to 1929) of purloining the telegraphic messages of foreign diplomats. There are ways known to the initiated for obtaining the contents of any message sent by a foreign government through Japanese telegraph and cable companies. Such messages, in the hands of the decoding experts of the Telegraph Service, are magically turned into Japanese words. Under French instructors, even before the [First] World War, Japanese officials made marked progress in the art of reconstructing secret codes and deciphering coded dispatches."
For Shidehara, see *Gaiko gojunen* (Fifty Years of Diplomacy), by Kijuro Shidehara (Tokyo, 1951), and his biography, by Heiwa Zaidan Shidehara (Tokyo, 1955).
For the biographies of Sawada and Sakuma: *Foreign Ministry Roster of Staff Members and Their Assignments*, 1929–30, 1931–32.
For the Manchurian Incident and Japanese politics of this period: *A History*

of Modern Japan, by Richard Storry (London, 1963), pp. 182–213; also his *The Double Patriots* (London, 1957); *Control of Japanese Foreign Policy*, by Y. C. Maxon (Berkeley, 1957).

Also deposition of Gen. Seiichi Kita, commanding general of First Army Group, Kwantung Army, dated Sep. 26, 1946, concerning Japanese army preparations to attack Manchuria and plans of war against the U.S.S.R.: in AMFA, Reel WT61. Also in AMFA: documents relating to Japanese policies toward Manchuria, Reels 155–56; the dispatch and withdrawal of Japanese army and navy forces during the Manchurian Incident, 1931–32, Reel S485; intelligence reports of the Kwantung Army, Reels WT9–10.

7 *The* RED *Machine*

For Safford's detour to sea, see his official Navy biography. For Dyer, Wright, Huckins, Holtwick: from Officer Biography Sheets, Dep. of the Navy, Bio. Branch; also *Registers of Graduates of the U.S. Naval Academy* (Annapolis, 1965) and *U.S. Navy Registers* (Washington, 1960). Idiosyncrasies of the group: from interviews.

Hagelin quotation from "Effect of Computers on the Security of Hagelin Cryptographer Type C-52," Crypto A.G. No. R 7002 e (Oct. 1962).

Yamaguchi incident: from ZACHARIAS (a), also see (b), pp. 160–64; Ohmai incident, *ibid.*, pp. 156–57; also PHA, vols. 34, p. 84; 33, p. 833; 12, p. 314; and Safford's references in his various testimonies. The Dulles quotations are from his *The Craft of Intelligence* (N.Y., 1963), pp. 51–52, 75–77.

For Japanese-American frictions: *America Encounters Japan*, by William L. Neumann (Baltimore, 1963), pp. 184–227, especially his shrewd assessment of Stimson's role in the deterioration of relations (pp. 190 ff.); *American Diplomacy in the Great Depression*, by R. H. Ferrell (New Haven, 1957); and Tuleja, *op. cit.*, pp. 36–83.

For Stimson's Non-Recognition Doctrine, see Stimson's diary entries of the period, especially Dec. 3, 1931, Jan. 3, 4, 6, 1932 (the doctrine was promulgated on Jan. 7); text in FRUS, 1931, Vol. 3. pp. 7–8; Stimson-Bundy, *op. cit.*; Rappaport, *op. cit.*, pp. 92–96; the N.Y. *Times*, Jan. 8, 1932, reporting Stimson's press conference; and "The Stimson Doctrine and the Hoover Doctrine," by Richard N. Current, *American Historical Review* Vol. 59 (Apr. 1954), pp. 513–42, showing the differences in the views and means of President Hoover and his Secretary of State.

For what Neumann called "the transition of the Stimson Doctrine from the Hoover to the Roosevelt Administrations," see Ferrell, *op. cit.*; "The Stimson Doctrine: F.D.R. versus Moley and Tugwell," by Bernard Sternsher, *Pacific Historical Review*, Vol. 31 (Aug. 1962), pp. 281–90; and Tuleja, *op. cit.*, pp. 62–69.

The Tuleja book also contains an excellent account of Roosevelt's "navalism," on pp. 84–115; for same, also see *American Foreign Policy in the Making*, by Charles A. Beard (New Haven, 1942), pp. 130–44; "F.D.R. and Naval Limitations," by George V. Fagan, USNIP, Vol. 81, No. 4 (Apr. 1955), pp. 414 ff.; scattered in *The Apprenticeship* and *The Ordeal*, by Frank Freidel (Boston, 1952 and 1954); "Franklin Delano Roosevelt: A Disciple of Admiral Mahan," by Wm. L. Neumann, USNIP, Vol. 78 (July 1952), pp. 712–19; his "Franklin D. Roosevelt and Japan," *Pac. Hist. Rev.*, vol. 22 (May 1953), pp. 143–53; and *The Future of Sea Power in the Pacific*, by Walter Millis (N.Y., 1935).

For the Japanese side of the story: Takeuchi, *op. cit.*; "The Movement for National Reconstruction and Its Concrete Plans," AMFA, Reel S26; misc. docs. relating to U.S. foreign policy, AMFA, Reel S15; and series captioned "Reprehensible Documents," AMFA, Reel US30. For the Japanese view as seen by an American: *With Japan's Leaders: An Intimate Record of Fourteen Years as Counsellor to the Japanese Government, Ending December 7, 1941*, by Frederick Moore (N.Y., 1942).

For the evolution of the Japanese secret services and the distribution of duties within them, see source references in notes for Ch. 12; also "Organization of the Japanese Intelligence Service," a memorandum prepared by Anthony ("Tony") Lovink, a Dutch diplomat who was head of the Netherlands East Indies intelligence service, dated Oct. 27, 1941, FEMT, Doc. No. 2613, Exh. No. 1325; and especially "General Mobilization, War Ministry: The Outline of Program Concerning the Execution of Intelligence and Propaganda Activities," Doc. Nos. H8751(4)–H8752(3), and SHI-KEI-H8760, dated May 20, 1936, FEMT, Doc. No. 7122, Exh. No. 151; also *Burn After Reading*, by Ladislas Farago (N.Y., 1961), pp. 175–87.

8 *The* Burakku Chiemba *and the Coming of* TYPE NO. 97

In the preparation of this chapter, ZACHARIAS (c) (incl. PHA, Vol. 18, pp. 3254–301) was extensively used, as were documents from AMFA, and FEMT. The "black chamber" in Mexico was actually so called in the secret order that set it up (*cf.* Adm. Yokoi, *op. cit.*); also see, for these activities, OCMH (j). The evolution of the "burakku chiemba" in Mexico: from *Interrogations of Japanese Officials in World War II*, Japanese Research Division, transl. of Japanese docs., Vol. 6 (Item 14); also BUTOW, p. 202. The Japanese in Mexico: AMFA, Reels S449, 702–3, 740, and Reel 28; *Secret Servants*, by Ronald Seth (N.Y., 1957), pp. 174–81.

For the Ribbentrop-Canaris-Oshima meeting: DGFP, Ser. C., Vol. 4; *The Case of Richard Sorge*, by F. W. Deakin and R. Storry, (N.Y., 1966), pp. 162, 182–84; Oshima interrogations, affidavits and testimony before FEMT, and Oshima correspondence; also BUTOW, pp. 136–37.

For Canaris, see his biography by K. H. Abshagen (Stuttgart, 1949); *Der geheime Nachrichtendienst der deutschen Wehrmacht im Kriege*, by Paul Leverkuehn (3rd ed., Frankfurt, 1960); and *Hitler's Spies and Saboteurs*, by Charles Wighton and Günther Peis (N.Y., 1958), based on the war diary of General Lahousen of *Abwehr II*. For German spy gadgets, see Leverkuehn, pp. 11, 2021; "Enemy's Masterpiece of Espionage," by J. Edgar Hoover, *Reader's Digest*, Vol. 46 (April 1946), pp. 1–6.

The German-Japanese espionage alliance was first revealed by this author, in *Ken* Magazine, August 1938; also see Leverkuehn, p. 41; Seth, *op. cit.*, *passim*. According to the latter, the budget of the Japanese secret service amounted to 13,814,000 yen ($4,000,000) at a time when Britain was spending $800,000 and the U.S. only $50,000 on this activity (*ibid.*, p. 149). More for the secret agreement of Germany with Japan: FEMT, Docs. 3191–92.

For Japanese espionage in Central America and along the American Pacific coast: *ibid.*, pp. 173–91; *Total Espionage*, by Curt Riess (N.Y., 1940), and his research material on the topic to which I had access; *Honorable Spy*, by J. L. Spivak (N.Y., 1939); *Betrayal from the East*, by Alan Hynd (N.Y., 1943). Also Japanese documents in FEMT and OCMH; in USNTM; and especially in AMFA, Reel S535 (investigations in Central America); Reels S291–294 (misc.

docs. relating to Japanese fishing activities along West Coasts of North, Central and South America 1923–43), in two sections, 4226 pp.; Reels S639–S643 (activities of Japanese military attachés, 1927–44), in four sections, 3862 pp. Date of spy alliance from PLOETZ, p. 828.

Report of "Jap watchers in Mexico," in ZACHARIAS (c). Safford's activities during this period: from his biography sheet in Dept. of the Navy, Bio. Branch.

For *zengen sakusen* and naval strategies: Tuleja, *op. cit.*, p. 88; ZACHARIAS (b), *passim*; CNO-SecNav File in NA; diary of Fleet Adm. William D. Leahy and papers of Adm. Harry E. Yarnell, in Libr. Congr., Fleet Problems: in *United States Fleet Problems*, Records, Naval Hist. Div. (SC)A16-3(5)F.P.; MORISON, p. 29; ZACHARIAS (b), pp. 118, 167–74; Klaus Mehnert in *Zeitschrift für Geopolitik*.

For Capt. Ingersoll: his biography sheet, and MORISON, Vol. 1, p. 206 n; Vol. 3, p. 49; functions of the CNO War Plans Division are described in "Organization of the Office of Naval Operations, Op-12 (War Plans)," in PHA, Vol. 16, pp. 1937 (excerpts). For the international situation and F.D.R., see "Roosevelt and the Aftermath of the Quarantine Speech, by John McV. Haight, *Review of Politics*, Vol. 24 (April 1962), pp. 233–59.

Development of Type No. 97 (B unit): from Sakuma memoranda (*q.v.*), also KOJIMA, Adm. Yokoi, *op. cit.*; "Nippon kaigun no kimitsushitsu" (The "Black Chamber" of the Imperial Navy), by Shiro Takago, *Shukan Asahi* (Dec. 8, 1961), pp. 24–26; and his "Nippon no black chamber," (The "Black Chamber" of Japan), *All Yomimono*, (Nov. 1952), pp. 157–75; correspondence with Rear Adm. Gonichiro Kakimoto and Comdr. Naosada Arisawa.

9 The PURPLE Code

The cracking of Japan's highest-grade diplomatic code was a well kept secret until the controversy developing over the Pearl Harbor disaster necessitated a gradual lifting of the veil. The first disclosure beyond the narrow line of the initiated was made by Gen. Marshall to "the General Officers comprising the voting members of [the Army Pearl Harbor Board] . . . in a closed session . . . on 7 August 1944." (Marshall affidavit, PHA, Vol. 35, p. 104.) At about the same time, witnesses before the Navy Court of Inquiry talked freely about the "Magic" operation, with the result that Marshall authorized "the Army officers concerned . . . to go into all the details regarding 'Magic' before the Army Pearl Harbor Board," meeting July 20–Oct. 20, 1944.

Simultaneously a small clique of Navy officers, determined to vindicate Adm. Kimmel by demonstrating that warnings at the disposal of Roosevelt and the State Dept. had not been made available to the commander-in-chief at Pearl Harbor, leaked information about "Magic"—much of it in expediently doctored versions—to Republican members of Congress who then wove the fragmentary data into tendentious speeches on the floor of the House. By May 4, 1945, when still another inquiry was staged under Adm. Hewitt, "Magic" was elaborately discussed by witnesses-in-the-know behind the closed doors of the inquiry. Then, on Nov. 15, 1945, during the testimony of Gen. Marshall before the Joint Congressional Committee in open session, the operation became publicly known.

References to "Magic," including its most intricate technical details, abound in the committee's 39-vol. transcript, especially in the testimony of Capt. Safford, who was most effusive and eloquent in reviewing the circumstances and techniques of the operation. Even so, WOHLSTETTER is the only

major book on the Pearl Harbor complex in which "Magic" figures prominently based on the transcripts of the various inquiries and Mrs. Wohlstetter's
interviews with some of the protagonists of the operation. However, her book
(which is politico-scientifically oriented) contains little if anything about the
technical aspects of "Magic," and nothing at all about developments at the Japanese end in the field of cryptology. While she was inclined to accept the
printed testimonies (marred by frequent memory lapses and occasional menda-
city) at face value, her scholarly, highly original and courageous book is
excellent and most useful for the better understanding of part of the intelligence factors in decision-making on the highest echelons.

This chapter is based on the author's independent researches conducted
over a period of twenty years (1946–66), much of it in association with Rear
Adm. Ellis M. Zacharias. Additional information came from Commander
HILES, and from monographs and interviews as listed below.

For the *Panay* incident, see GREW, pp. 232–40; HULL, pp. 559–63; Tuleja,
op. cit., pp. 171–73, 176, 178; the report of George Atcheson, Jr., then second
secretary at the American embassy in Chungking, who was aboard the gunboat
during the attack; entries for Dec. 12–16, 1937, in Adm. Leahy's diary in Libr.
Congr.; entries in *Asiatic Fleet, Diary of China-Japanese War*, 1937, in the
Naval Hist. Div.; Yarnell papers in Libr. Congr.; MORISON, pp. 16–18; the
N.Y. Times, Dec. 13–21, 1937.

Also, "The Yangtze Bombing," in *Japan Weekly Chronicle* (Dec. 23,
1937), pp. 816–17; "The Panay Incident, Dec. 12, 1937" (a comprehensive
official Japanese account prepared by the Research Bureau, Ministry of
Foreign Affairs in Jan. 1944), in AMFA, Reel NT54; and Monograph No. 144,
Japanese Research Div., OMH, SCAP.

For official Japanese "explanations" of the attack, see the *N.Y. Times*
(Dec. 15, 1937, p. 17, and Dec. 25, p. 1); also interview with Adm. Hasegawa
aboard flagship *Izumo* (*ibid.*, Dec. 20, p. 16) in the course of which he
"identified one flier in the third wave who had used machine guns against
Panay lifeboats." According to the Tokyo correspondent of the *N.Y. Times*
(Dec. 20), Adm. Nagano "had tears in his eyes" when discussing the *Panay*
incident; but four years later, this same Nagano became one of the two chief
architects of the Pearl Harbor attack, using similar tactics on a vastly greater
scale.

For the rape of Nanking, see FEMT, Pt. B, VIII, pp. 1011–19, 1023–24.
For Gen. Iwani Matsui: *ibid.*, 3509–13; *ibid.*, Pt. B, VIII, pp. 1016–17 and
Pt. C, X, pp. 1180–82; BUTOW, pp. 100–2; *The Knights of Bushido*, by Lord
Russell of Liverpool (N.Y., 1958), pp. 42, 45–47, 49, 243, 294–95. (In 1932
Matsui was the Japanese plenipotentiary delegate to the Disarmament Confer-
ence in Geneva. In 1946 he was sentenced to death and hanged.)

For anti-American incidents: BUTOW, p. 124; Grew affidavit, FEMT, pp.
10094–97, 10107–8, in which he said that he had personally filed "over 400
separate protests" by the end of 1938. For Japanese reaction to the *Panay*
incident: HULL, p. 561; GREW, p. 233. "That is indefinite," quoted by BUTOW,
p. 124 n. For list of incidents, see *N.Y. Times* (Dec. 14, 1937), p. 21.

U.S. Navy Court of Inquiry was held by Adm. Yarnell aboard the *Augusta*,
on Dec. 23, 1937 (see FRUS, *Japan*, 1931–1941, I, pp. 532–47; Yarnell papers
in Libr. Congr., incl. his letter to Adm. Hasegawa, Dec. 21, 1937; and *Asiatic
Fleet, Diary*, Naval Hist. Div.). The Court of Inquiry consisted of Capt.
H. V. McKitrick, Comdr. M. L. Deyo, Lt. A. C. J. Sabalot, and Lt. C. J.
Whiting as Judge Advocate. The unclassified portion of their findings was

printed in the N.Y. *Times* (Dec. 25, 1937, p. 4). Mitsunami was one of the few firebrands of the Imperial Navy. He had been made a rear admiral only a few days before the incident, which was his first active service command. See the N.Y. *Times* (Dec. 16, 1937, p. 1; Dec. 18, p. 8; and Dec. 25, p. 1).

For Saito: HULL, pp. 560–61, 629. For organizational changes in SIS: OCMH (h), Ch. 11, pp. 18–21, and Friedman testimony, PHA, Vol. 34, Pt. 2. The reconstruction of what became the "Purple" machine: PHA, Vols. 3, pp. 137, 1130, 1197; 8, pp. 3561, 3778; 9, pp. 4001, 4005; 10, p. 4773; 33, p. 833; 34, pp. 84–85; 36, pp. 68, 312, 347; 35, p. 673. Testimony of Friedman: *ibid.*, Vol. 37, 515–28; Safford testimonies, *passim*. Also, *The Final Secret of Pearl Harbor*, by Rear Adm. Robert A. Theobald (N.Y., 1954), pp. 32–41; Hoehling, *op. cit.*, pp. 71–81.

For Adm. Courtney: HOWETH, pp. 420, 539. For General Mauborgne: OCMH (f), *passim*. Japanese reluctance to believe cracking of the machine: letter of Noboru Kojima.

For secrecy: PHA, Vol. 2, pp. 792, 908; and testimonies of Safford, Bratton, and Kramer, *ibid.*, *passim*; Col. Dusenbury's affidavit, PHA, Vol. 35, pp. 25–26; also affidavits of Gen. R. C. Smith, Gen. Charles K. Gailey, Gen. W. B. Smith, Gen. L. T. Gerow, Gen. G. C. Marshall, *ibid.*; Gen. Marshall's letters to Gov. Thomas E. Dewey, PHA, Vol. 3, pp. 1128–39; WOHLSTETTER, p. 177; also, *ibid.*, general security arrangements, pp. 39–40, 64, 73, 168, 177–80, 397; disadvantages of excessive secrecy, pp. 129, 181 n, 186, 394.

The organizational structure, table of organization and operating procedures of "Magic" were reconstructed from testimonies and affidavits in PHA, especially those of Safford, Bratton, Kramer, Lt. Col. Frank B. Rowlett (Feb. 28 and Sep. 12, 1945); Col. Robert E. Schukraft (Vol. 10, pp. 4910–33 and affidavit, June 2, 1945); Gen. Sherman Miles (Vol. 27, 91–132f; Vol. 34, Pt. 1; Vol. 2, pp. 776–982; Vol. 3, pp. 1360–75, 1541–83; affidavit of Aug. 15, 1945); affidavits of Col. Rex W. Minckler (Aug. 21, 1945); Col. Harold Doud (Sept. 10, 1945); Sgt. (later Capt.) Howard W. Martin (Sept. 12, 1945); Mary J. Dunning, Col. Minckler's secretary in SIS; and Louise Prather, typist in SIS.

For Army monitoring stations, see PHA, Vol. 35, p. 35, and Vol. 37, pp. 1082–83. For Navy stations: PHA, Vol. 8, 3557, 3581, 3802; also HOWETH, App. L, pp. 587–88. For MS-5: testimony of Col. C. A. Powell, PHA, Vol. 22, pp. 352–65, 395–415, 428; Vol. 31, pp. 3885–3915; (his affidavit, in Vol. 35, pp. 179–81); also "MS-5 and MS-6," in unpubl. MS. (This station is nowhere mentioned in WOHLSTETTER, whose references to the other stations are on pp. 171, 174, 222).

Distribution procedures: Bratton's testimonies in PHA, *passim*; Kramer's testimonies, *passim*; PHA, Vols. 2, p. 788; 3, pp. 1100, 1147; 4, p. 1734; 8, pp. 3558–59, 3681, 3725, 3902; 9, pp. 4509, 4561; Jan. 23 agreement, Vol. 11, p. 5475; also interview with Dr. Stanley K. Hornbeck. For loss of flag officers code, see Safford letter to John R. Sonnett, May 17, 1945 (in PHA, Vol. 18, pp. 3335–36). For Rochefort *et al.* their biography sheets and affidavits of Holtwick and Holmes, PHA, Vol. 35, pp. 100–1, 182. For Indochina: FRUS, 1940, 1941.

10 *War on a Shoestring*

This chapter draws heavily on Col. Tsuji's books, articles and speeches. A "contradictious person," Tsuji is (or was, for it is not known whether he is alive or dead) a fighter, a fanatic, a bold adventurer—somewhat like Lytton Strachey's portrait of "Chinese" Gordon, "even a little off his head, perhaps though a hero." He fought hard and well in the war he helped to unleash, but only to "liberate" the people of East Asia from foreign rule. However, he took Japanese propaganda about the "co-prosperity sphere" literally, and was scandalized when the Japanese conquerors merely replaced the British and Dutch they had evicted. After the war he vanished in Asia, "wandering in disguise in China, Siam and Indochina," presumably fighting in Burma and the Philippines, to "secure Asia for the Asians." Then he returned to Japan, and early in the 1950's, was elected to the Upper House. In 1962 he disappeared again, and nothing has been heard of him since.

Though we are inclined to censure the Japanese for clandestine activities of the Hayashi-Tsuji group, KIRBY tells us (p. 78) that the British Singapore command also had its version of the *doro nawa* unit, its members reconnoitering Thailand in preparation for a "preventative attack" on that country (Operation Matador, *ibid.*, pp. 76–78, 170, 173–75, 180–86). The race was won by the Japanese, who had the advantages of timing and resolution.

Tsuji's famous book, *Shonan* (Tokyo, 1951), was translated into English by Margaret E. Lake, former lecturer at the University of Sydney, and was published, under the title *Singapore: The Japanese Version*, by St. Martin's Press (N.Y., 1960). I am indebted to H. V. Howe, who was Mil. Sec. to the Australian Sec. of the Army in 1940–46, for additional material from his own files, and to Miss Lake for clarification of certain obscure passages in Col. Tsuji's book.

The *doro nawa* unit was mentioned by HATTORI (Vol. 1, pp. 326–27, briefly and somewhat inaccurately), but was given great publicity at the time of Tsuji's return to Tokyo and the publication of his book. The organization of the Japanese secret service in the area is from the Lovink memorandum (*q.v.*); misc. docs. in AMFA; and PLOETZ, Vol. 2, pp. 828–32. Also see, "Secret Reconnaissance of Saigon and the Southern Part of French Indochina," by Lt. Comdr. Takeshi Fukuoka and Maj. Tokuji Sugaya, AMFA, Reel WT17.

The great debate in the War Ministry and Army General Staff: from HATTORI, *passim*; Gunbatsu koboshi (The Military Clique), by Masanori Ito (Tokyo, 1957–58), 3 vols.; *Taiheiyo senso zenshi* (The Historical Origins of the Pacific War), by Tokuzo Aoki (Tokyo, 1953), 3 vols.; and "Tosei-ha to kodo-ha" (The Imperial Way Clique and the Control Clique), by Sumihisa Ikeda, *Bungei shunju*, Vol. 34, (Nov. 1956), pp. 92–108. Also, affidavits of Gen. Shinichi Tanaka (FEMT, Def.Doc. 1661, Exh. 3029), Gen. Akira Muto (FEMT, Def.Doc. 2679, Exh. 3454), Col. Suzamu Nishiura (FEMT, Def. Doc. 1690, Exh. 3023); and from Gen. Ryukichi Tanaka's controversial and self-serving book, *Taisen totsunyu no shinso* (The Truth Behind the Plunge Into War), (Tokyo, 1955).

For the organization of the Japanese military establishment, see BUTOW, pp. 49–50, 53, 57, 61–74, 115–16 for the Army, and pp. 80, 82, 236 for the Navy; *Japan's Military Masters*, by Hillis Lory (N.Y., 1943), *passim*; *Japanese Militarism: Its Cause and Cure*, by John M. Maki (N.Y., 1945); *Control of Japanese Foreign Policy: A Study of Civil-Military Rivalry, 1930–45*, by Y. C. Maxon (Berkeley, 1957); and Capt. M. D. Kennedy's classics, *The Military Side of Japanese Life* (Boston, 1923) and *Some Aspects of Japan and Her Defence Forces* (London, 1928). For the plans of the U.S. General Staff: "War Plan Orange," by Louis Morton, *World Politics*, Vol. 11, (Jan. 1959), pp. 221–50, and OCMH (e), pp. 21–44, 67–91, 96–102; also *Strategic Plan-*

ning for Coalition Warfare, 1941–42, by Maurice Matloff and Edwin M. Snell (Washington, 1953), pp. 5–10, 13, 25, 43–48, 61, 80–81. The Nov. meeting of the General Staff: from HATTORI, and "Dai-toa senso wo maneita showa no doran," by Col. Kenryo Sato (who was present at the conference), *Kingu*, Vol. 32, (Oct. 1956), pp. 88–125. (Also see his article in the *Nichi-Nichi*, Mar. 11, 1941.) For the intelligence sources of the Tojo clique: Kameyama testimonies and affidavit, and deposition of Tateki Shirao, a copy of which is in my collection. The encroachment on the British code is acknowledged by KIRBY, p. 54. For the insecurity of the American codes, see FEIS; GREW, pp. 415, 417; FRUS, 1941, IV, p. 723 n; interview with Joseph W. Ballantine. Also see Kameyama affidavit.

11 *"Operation Z"—the Pearl Harbor Plan*

The evolution of Admiral Yamamoto's strategic thinking and his development of the Pearl Harbor plan is based on diverse sources, including interviews with Masanori Ito and Gen. Minami Genda; the postwar interrogation of the late Adm. Osami Nagano; interviews of M. Hanakata with Rear Adm. Tashido Nakaoka and Capt. Yasuji Watanabe of Yamamoto's staff; the depositions of Genda, Vice-Adm. Ryunosuke Kusaka, Capt. Mitsuo Fuchida, all for the defense in the Tokyo trial; and the following documents and books: "Pearl Harbor: The Planning Stage," *Weekly Intelligence*, Dec. 11, 1944, pp. 1–22; "Combined Fleet Top Secret Operation Order No. 1," *ibid.*; "Reply to Questionnaire Concerning the Pearl Harbor Attack," prepared by Liaison Committee of the Imperial Navy, Oct. 17–20, 1945, ATIS Hist. Inv. Sec., AGO 350.05, Nov. 1, 1945, No. 1032; "Pearl Harbor Questionnaire," *ibid.*, Nov. 8, 1945, No. 1038; USSBS (a).

Also, MORISON, pp. 3–79; Ito, *op. cit.*, pp. 7–34; OCMH (e), pp. 64, 96, 105–7, 122–25, 132, 204, 277–80, 284, 349–50; *I Led the Air Attack on Pearl Harbor*, by Mitsuo Fuchida (Annapolis, 1952); HATTORI; *Taiheyo senzo zenshi* (The Historical Background of the Pacific War), by Tokuzi Aoki, (Tokyo, 1953), 3 vols.; *Ichi gunjin no shogai* (The Life of Admiral Mitsumasa Yonai), (Tokyo, 1956); Sato, *op. cit.*; *Showa no doran* (The Showa Upheavals), by Mamoru Shigemitsu (Tokyo, 1952) 2 vols.; Tanaka, *op. cit.*; ZACHARIAS (b), pp. 189–198.

Also the following articles: "Admiral Yamamoto," by James A. Field, Jr., USNIP, Vol. 75, No. 10, (1949), pp. 1105–13; OCMH (i); "Pearl Harbor in Perspective," by Morton (see bibl. list); "Hawaii Operation," by Adm. Shigeru Fukudome, USNIP, Vol. 81, No. 12, (1955), pp. 1315–32; "Treachery' of Pearl Harbor," by Kiyoaki Murata, *ibid.*, Vol. 82, No. 8, (1956), pp. 904–6; "The Inside Story of the Pearl Harbor Plan," by Robert E. Ward, *ibid.*, Vol. 77, No. 12, (1951), pp. 1271–83.

For historical background, the following were consulted: "Documents relating to the Army and Navy Systems and Establishments," in AMFA (MT 5.1.1, 27, 29, 30); "Documents relating to the Training and Maneuvers of the Imperial Navy," *ibid.* (MT 5.1.3.32); "The Basic Tenets of National Defense and Proposals for its Strengthening," published by Shinbun-hon Rikugansho (Tokyo, 1934); *Japan's Pacific Mandates*, by Clyde H. Paul (N.Y., 1935); "Naval Preparedness in the Pacific," by Adm. Yates Sterling, Jr., USNIP, Vol. 60, No. 5, (1934), pp. 601–8; "Japan's Case for Sea Power," by Gumpei Sekine, *Current History*, Vol. 41, No. 11, (1934), pp. 129–35; "Japan and the London Pact," by Kiyoshi K. Kawakami, *The Nation*, Vol. 130 (June 25, 1930), pp. 727–29; "The Unsolved Naval Problems of the Pacific," by the same author, *Pacific Affairs*, Vol. 4, No. 4, (1931), pp. 863–79; "Japanese Naval Strategy," by Alexander Kiralfy, in *Makers of Modern Strategy*, eds. E. M. Earle, G. A. Craig and F. Gilbert (Princeton, 1943).

For the development of Pearl Harbor as a naval base, see "The American Navy in Hawaii," by Albert Pierce Taylor, USNIP, Vol. 54, No. 8, (1927), pp. 907–24.

For Adm. Togo and the battles of Port Arthur and Tsushima, see *The Maritime History of Russia, 1848–1948*, by Mairin Mitchell (London, 1949), pp. 33, 179, 322–29; *Togo*, by Georges Blonde (N.Y., 1963).

For Adm. Schofield's Fleet Problem XIV, see ZACHARIAS (b), pp. 116–23; "The Inside Story of Pearl Harbor," by Edwin Mueller, in *Secrets and Spies*, by eds. of *Reader's Digest* (Pleasantville, 1964), pp. 13–17; *U.S. Fleet Problems*, (SC) A16-3(5)/F. P., in Naval Hist. Div.

The article on the Port Arthur attack, considered a classic piece of war reporting, appeared in *Le Petit Journal* (Paris), on Feb. 22, 1904.

For the evolution of torpedo plane attacks, see *The Italian Navy in World War II*, by Comdr. Marc' Antonio Bragadin (Annapolis, 1957), pp. 44–49, 56; *A Sailor's Odyssey*, by Viscount Cunningham of Hyndhope (N.Y., 1951), pp. 283–87, 290, 428–29, mentioning that "the Japanese had based their tactics for the Pearl Harbour operation upon our attack upon the Italian fleet at Taranto;" and *Die verratene Flotte*, by Antonino Trizzino (Bonn, 1957), pp. 26–31. Secr. Knox's letter to Secr. Stimson, and Stimson's reply: in PHA, Vol. 14, pp. 1000–6. The correspondence was forwarded to Gen. Short (but not to Adm. Kimmel) on Feb. 7, 1941. The problem of Hawaii's air defenses was discussed during a special General Staff conference in Gen. Marshall's office, on Feb. 15, 1941. The minutes of the conference were reprinted in PHA, Vol. 15, pp. 1628–30.

12 Eyes on Hawaii

The Japanese still adamantly deny that they conducted any espionage in Hawaii prior to the Pearl Harbor attack. When Comdr. Itaru Tachibana, the only surviving member of the staff working in the *joho kyoku's* America Section in 1941, was asked during his postwar interrogation, "What role was played by agents in Hawaii?" he stated categorically, "None." (AG File 350.05 [8 Nov 1945] GB, SCAP.)

This chapter is based on the evidence presented by numerous Japanese and American documents; the testimony of the late Rear Adm. Irving H. Mayfield, the District Intelligence Officer of the 14th Naval District (PHA, Vols. 23, pp. 1039–68; Vol. 26, pp. 308–13; Vol. 37, pp. 558–75); interviews with Col. George W. Bicknell and Yoshio Hasegawa of the Honolulu Police, who was in charge of the surveillance of the Japanese consulate; on *Security Measures in Hawaii During World War II*, Col. Bicknell's unpubl. MS. on deposit in HWRD; *Wartime Security Controls in Hawaii: 1941–45. A General Historical Survey*—a 9-vol., 1500-pg. monograph prepared by the Office of Internal Security, U.S. Army Forces, Honolulu, T.H.

Col. Henry C. Clausen of the Office of JAG, with remarkable industry and investigative skill, has salvaged a great number of invaluable pertinent docu-

ments from the limbo of official files in Washington and Hawaii, including investigation reports of the DIO, 14th Naval District, and files of the FBI's Honolulu office (see Clausen's testimony, PHA, Vol. 9, pp. 4300–508, and the complete record of his investigations, PHA, Vol. 35).
For the background of Japanese interest in Hawaii, see *Hawaii: A History*, by R. S. Kuykendall and A. G. Day (Englewood Cliffs, 1961), pp. 110–11, 124, 129, 157, 165, 186–89, 190; *The Hawaiian Kingdom*, by Kuykendall. Vol. 2: *Twenty Critical Years* (Honolulu, 1956). The first Japanese, three sailors rescued from a shipwreck, arrived in Hawaii c. 1840. Diplomatic relations between Hawaii and Japan were established in 1871, after difficult negotiations lasting more than a decade, because the Japanese, forced open by Commodore Perry after centuries of isolation, "were not willing to enter into treaty relations with any more countries "(Kuykendall-Day, *op. cit.*, p. 111). However, by 1897 Japan was sufficiently involved in the Pacific power game to protest the U.S. annexation of Hawaii, "on the grounds that it would disturb the status quo in the Pacific and that it would endanger the rights of Japanese subjects in Hawaii" (*ibid.*, p. 188). Japanese immigration began in 1868 with the arrival of 148 laborers. It became a flood in 1886. The 1890 census showed that there were 12,000 Japanese (but only 2000 Americans) living in Hawaii, in a total population of about 90,000. By 1920 the Japanese comprised 42.7 percent of the population. On the eve of Pearl Harbor there were 160,000 Japanese in Hawaii, of whom 40,000 were aliens.
The structure, table of organization and functions of the *joho kyoku* (Naval Intelligence Bureau) were reconstructed from interrogation transcripts and reports of USNTM in Japan, 1945–46; the interrogation of Rear Adm. Nakamura and Comdr. Tachibana; "Japanese Naval Intelligence," *The ONI Review*, Vol. 1, (July 1946), pp. 36–40; USSBS (c); and the following original Japanese documents in AMFA:
Intelligence report on Koreans in Hawaii, Reel SP47; quasi-intelligence reports of Domei correspondents and informants at the branch offices of various Japanese commercial companies, Reel WT77; a paper outlining intelligence collection methods, Reel S572; misc. docs. on intelligence about the military establishments of various countries, Reel S620; Japanese intelligence bureaus abroad (1936–38), Reel S535; activities of Japanese military attachés, in three sections (1927–44), Reels S639–43; an intelligence report on the Honolulu Chamber of Commerce (1927), Reel 275; intelligence activities of Japanese steam-ship companies (1936–41), Reels S123–24; misc. docs. about docks and shipyards, Reel S121; the movements of foreign vessels (1939–44), in two sections, Reel S128; record of regulations governing the taking of photographs and making of motion pictures in foreign countries, Reel S322; interrogation of overseas Japanese nationals during their visits to the mother country, in two sections, Reels S467–68; the sale of docs. containing military secrets, Reel S32; intelligence reports on the military affairs, preparedness and military budgets of foreign countries: (1) general, Reel 411; (2) on the military preparedness of Hawaii, Reels 411–13; (3) naval intelligence reports, Reel 413; (4) weekly reports from the Army Intelligence Bureau on Hawaii, Reels 413–14; misc. intelligence reports on Manila, Reel 414; intelligence data about the U.S., in three sections, Reels 417–18; intelligence reports on the construction of warships in foreign countries, Reel 418; tables on Japanese residents abroad, Reel SP44; intelligence on various islands in the South Pacific, Reel SP42; same on North Pacific islands, Reels SP42–43.
For co-operation of *joho kyoku* with Foreign Ministry, see Interrogation No.

9 of Toshikazu Kase, Nov. 28, 1945, USNTM; Kameyama and Yamamoto depositions, FEMT.

For submarine surveillance of Hawaii, Adm. Kimmel's statement, Sep. 27, 1944, PHA, Vol. 32, pp. 15–16.

For the espionage activities of the Japanese consulate in Honolulu, see INV. REP., Feb. 9, 14, June 15, 1942, and Summary Report, Feb. 15, 1943; FBI-Honolulu Confidential Report File No. 65–414, Apr. 25, 1942; interrogation of Kimie Doue, Feb. 3, 1942; of Kotoshirodo, Mikami, Ichitaro Ozaki, Lawrence Nakatsuke, and others, Sept.-Oct., 1942; affidavits of Robert L. Shivers, FBI agent in charge, Col. G. W. Bicknell, Col. Edward W. Raley, Lt. Col. Byron M. Meurlott, Lt. Donald Woodrum, USN, Chief Ships Clerk Theodore Emanuel, USN, all in PHA, Vol. 35, pp. 29–32, 38–39, 43–44, 45, 48–49. For reorientation of consulate's clandestine activities from propaganda to intelligence: Ogawa telegram to Kita, Feb. 1, 1941.

The selection of Kita and Yoshikawa and their journey to Hawaii are best described in KOJIMA, pp. 113–19. For Kita, see *Yearbook of the [Japanese] Ministry of Foreign Affairs*, 1938–42; biographical data in *Foreign Ministry Registers*, 1938–1943; also *The Consulate General in Canton*, AMFA, Reel SP139, pp. 35300–25; *The FBI Story*, by Don Whitehead (N.Y., 1956, with a foreword by J. Edgar Hoover), pp. 190–92; WOHLSTETTER, pp. 373–77.

For Yoshikawa: INV. REP., Feb. 15, 1943, par. 71–95; KOJIMA; YOSHIKAWA, pp. 27–39; article in the *Ehime Shimbun*, reprinted in the *N.Y. Times*, Dec. 9, 1953; *But Not In Shame*, by John Toland (N.Y., 1964), pp. 8, 33; "The Man Who Spied on Pearl Harbor," TV script by Burton Benjamin (CBS broadcast, Dec. 3, 1961, contains filmed interviews with Yoshikawa and Comdr. Suguri Suzuki, *q.v.*); "Remember Pearl Harbor," *Time*, Dec. 12, 1960 (and two letters on the topic, *ibid.*, Jan. 2, 1961).

For the day-by-day activities of Kita and Yoshikawa, see desk pad and diary of the Japanese consulate in Honolulu, in PHA, Vol. 35, pp. 394–401; also interrogation of their personal maids, INV. REP., June 15, 1941, par. 47–56.

For the Rev. Hirayama, see File No. 65–492, FBI Report by Agent F. G. Tillman, Nov. 6, 1940, and FBI Report by Agent N.J. Alaga, Oct. 9, 1940; INV. REP., July 13, 1942. For "inside" and "outside" systems in Hawaii, and Okada's activities: Kotoshirodo interrogation, INV. REP., Feb. 15, 1943, par. 82–89. For Kotoshirodo: *ibid.*, *passim*; for Mikami: *ibid.*, Feb. 6, 1942.

For Kühn: Inv. Report, ONI, Feb. 13, 1939; INV. REP., Feb. 21, 1939, May 31, 1941, Feb. 9, 1942; Doue interrogation (*q.v.*); Suspect List, ONI, June 29, 1940; memo by J. A. Burns of G-2 Contact Office, Dec. 12, 1941; also *Secret Servants*, by Ronald Seth (N.Y., 1957), pp. 3–15; *Spies and Traitors in World War II*, by Kurt Singer (N.Y., 1945), pp. 89–97 (melodramatic but totally inaccurate); *History of the U.S. Army MIDPAC*, Vol. 14 (microfilm in HWRD), p. 3221; PHA, Vols. 23, pp. 655 ff; 26, p. 355; 27, p. 740; 29, pp. 1944 ff.; 30, pp. 3067–81; 35, pp. 320–23; 39, pp. 100, 429; Office of Civilian Defense Files, July 11, 1949, in State of Hawaii Public Archives (Maj. Carl R. Lauritzen to HWRD); statement of Joseph Savoretti, HWRD; statement of D. W. Brewster, Immigration Station, July 21, 1949; the Honolulu *Advertiser*, June 14, 15, 1943; *Star-Bulletin*, Apr. 15, 1943.

For Eto: INV. REP., Jan. 29 and June 15, 1942.

For codes and ciphers used by consulate and Samon Tatsekawa's functions, see collection of code logbooks, registers of messages, custodial and burning records, worksheets, and samples of coded telegrams, in PHA, Vol. 35, pp. 458–79.

For Tachibana and Okada: Inv. Rep., 13th Nav. Distr., May 1, 1941; 12th Nav. Distr., July 17, 1941; exchange of notes, in FRUS, 1941, IV, pp. 266–67, 272–74, 282, 283, 294–95, 507; HULL, Vol. 2, pp. 1011–12.

13 The Maze of "Magic"

Ind quotation from *A Short History of Espionage*, by Col. Allison Ind (N.Y., 1963), p. 239; ZACHARIAS (b), p. 81.

Hornbeck's view of "Magics": from interview. For collateral reports, see FRUS, 1941, IV: Dr. Stuart, pp. 29–30, 36–37, 117–18, 322–23, 389–90, 462–63 (though from Oct. 1941 on, they were less astute and reliable); Dr. Jones, pp. 306–10, 455–57, 459, 501–2, 555–58, 561–62, 641, 702–3; Mills and Bates, p. 256. For a typical Leahy report based on information from Chauvel, *ibid.*, pp. 45–47; also see *I Was There*, the memoirs of Fleet Adm. William D. Leahy (N.Y., 1950), pp. 44, 56–57, 463–68. For Williams, Peck and Krentz, see FRUS, *passim*.

For poor translations of "magics," see WOHLSTETTER, pp. 171–72, 174–75; Safford in PHA, Vol. 36, pp. 316–18; and especially the expert analysis of this serious problem in BUTOW, pp. 299, 334–35, 367–68, 377. Ben Bruce Blakeney, one of the defense counsels at the Tokyo trial of Japan's major war criminals, raised the issue when he charged that "the intercepted telegrams . . . were . . . so garbled, tendentiously phrased and so ineptly translated as to constitute very different documents from those dispatched by the Japanese Foreign Ministry." (FEMT, trscpt. pp. 43607–21.) For instance, BUTOW described the "Magic" version of cable No. 857 of Nov. 29, 1941, as "a strange hodgepodge of the correct and the incorrect." See FEMT, steno. rec., Section 111, p. 4, for the original, and PHA, Vol. 12, p. 199, for the translated form in which it reached the American officials.

For the interpretation of "magics," BUTOW, p. 335: "Such distortions as did occur through mistranslations are genuinely assailable as such, but the records of the liaison conferences . . . and the Japanese originals of the cables sent from Tokyo to Washington together reveal that the distortions did not essentially do violence to the reality of Japan's intentions." See Ballantine cross-examination, FEMT, trscpt. pp. 10901–39.

For Japanese codes and ciphers, see captured logbooks and catalogs of Japanese consulate in Honolulu, PHA, Vols. 35, pp. 403–9, 433, 439, 462–63, 676, 684; 12, p. 208; 36, pp. 64, 67, 85, 310 ff.; 37, p. 663. For codes of the Imperial Navy, see Combined Fleet Top-Secret Standing Order No. 52; Combined Fleet Top-Secret Order No. 169; Combined Fleet Top-Secret Order No. 171 ("Use of Codes"); "Joint Army-Navy Agreement Concerning Communications in Southern Operations"; and "Combined Fleet Wireless Communications Manual," all listed in "Communications," Sec. F, Combined Fleet Top-Secret Operation Order No. 1. Also see USNTM for interrogations of Adm. Kakimoto and Comdr. Arisawa; analysis of Japanese intercepts according to their "Magic" headings and classification.

For the Japanese army's cryptosystem, see FEMT, Doc. 2153, on interrogation and affidavit of Major Kusuo Matsuura, chief of Cipher Section, General Headquarters, Kwantung Army; and interrogation of Col. Tomokatsu Matsumura and Lt. Col. Morio Tomura, senior signal officers. For "S" codes, see note above, also (including their confiscation by U.S. Treasury agents) telegram of K. Muto to Foreign Minister, May 28, 1941; and Foreign Ministry Circular No. 1 to "All Merchant Vessels," May 30, 1941.

For the work of the U.S. Navy's cryptanalysts on Japanese naval codes, see Rochefort, PHA, Vol. 36, pp. 31–32; answers to questionnaire of the Judge Advocate: Vol. 32, trscpt. pp. 470–71; Vol. 10, pp. 4672–75, 4678, 4697–98; in Vol. 36: Wright, pp. 261–66; Woodward, pp. 319–25, 350–52; Dyer, pp. 418–23; Comdr. R. J. Fabian (of Cavite C/I Unit), pp. 68–79. Safford told Adm. Hewitt (ibid., pp. 61–62) that "Pearl Harbor's main mission was in attack on Japanese flag officers system"; and said that the best people he had, the Rochefort group, "was up at Pearl Harbor," while "90 percent of the personnel" he had in Washington working on 'Magic' "was inexperienced," in the service less than a year.

For U.S. Navy's fetish of secrecy, see MORISON, Vol. I, p. 107. For espionage dispatches sent in DIP, see message log of Japanese consulate in Honolulu, in PHA, Vol. 35, pp. 430–57; "Register of Messages Received," ibid., 458 ff.; PHA, Vol. 12, pp. 254–316. For reference to FBI: Whitehead, op. cit., pp. 190–92. For Kramer's evaluation of espionage dispatches, see PHA, Vol. 9, p. 4177; for McCollum's, Vol. 8, p. 3405; for Wilkinson's, Vol. 4, p. 1748.

For priorities, see Safford's index in which these priorities are listed as follows: Most Important; Very Important; Important; Unmarked—Normal; Supplementary; also see PHA, Vols. 8, p. 3395; 34, p. 83; 36, pp. 311, 313; Miles in Vol. 2, pp. 859–60.

14 "John Doe's" Secret Mission

I am indebted to Father Albert Novins of the Maryknoll Society Ossining, N.Y., for allowing me access to the papers of Bishop Walsh (who is now, at the age of seventy-six, held in a Red Chinese prison under sentence for espionage) and the late Father James Drought; to Dr. Stanley K. Hornbeck and Dr. Joseph W. Ballantine for illumination on the "John Doe" conversations; and to Rear Adm. Lewis L. Strauss, USNR, for invaluable material on the subject. See his Men and Decisions (Garden City, 1962), pp. 123–26, and his memorandum for Director, Office of Naval Intelligence, May 22, 1941.

Saito quotation: from his op. cit., p. 106. For Kido, see his deposition in FEMT, Def. Doc. 2502; also Tenno to Kido (The Emperor and Kido), by Kotaro Sakuda (Tokyo, 1948), passim; and BUTOW, pp. 163, 168, 175, 177–78, 181, 277. For Konoye's peace efforts: his Heiwa e no doryoku (My Effort for Peace), (Tokyo, 1946); Ushinawareshi seiji (Lost Politics), (Tokyo, 1946); "Memoirs of Prince Konoye, Dec. 1940–Oct. 1941," ed. T. Ushiba, in PHA, Vol. 20, pp. 3985–4010; Konoye Fumimaro, by Teiji Yabe (Tokyo, 1952).

For Matsuoka: "Yosuke Matsuoka and the Japanese-German Alliance," by John Huizenga, in The Diplomats, 1919–1939, eds. Gordon A. Craig and Felix Gilbert (Princeton, 1953); interrogation of Adm. Yonai, in USSBS (a); also Japanese Res. Div., OMH, U.S. Army Forces, Far East, No. 55773, p. 8; BUTOW, pp. 141–42, 208, 216–17; Matsuoka's anti-U.S. attitude, ibid., pp. 154, 162–63, 166–68, 228–32. For Matsuoka's role in "John Doe" negotiations: Konoye "Memoirs" (loc. cit.), pp. 5–8 (where the Foreign Minister's appraisal of the American attitude toward a rapprochement is described as "70% ill-will and 30% good-will"); Amb. Laurence Steinhardt's dispatches from Moscow to the State Dept.; FRUS, 1941, IV, pp. 921–23, 932–38, 940–41; Grew dispatches, ibid., pp. 188–90, 194–96, 198–200, 202–6, 234–38 (incl. his telegram of May 27 in which he characterized the "John Doe" episode as "a chapter in not quite orthodox diplomacy"). Matsuoka sabotaged an American-Japanese "understanding" by alerting the Germans to the secret negotiations, see BUTOW, 231–32; also AMFA, Reel WT9. Nomura on Konoye: his "Stepping-Stones to War," USNIP, Vol. 77, No. 9 (Sep. 1951), p. 929. HULL, II, pp. 982–83. For Nomura's appointment: AMFA, Reel WT72; an interesting interpretation of Nomura's choice in *The Time for Decision*, by Sumner Welles (N.Y., 1944), pp. 289–90; also Nomura's *Beikoku ni shishite* (My Mission to America), (Tokyo, 1951); "Secret Report of Ambassador Nomura to the Foreign Minister on his Mission to the U.S.," AMFA, Reel WT73.

For Kleiman and similar missions: FRUS, 1941, IV, *passim*; *Untold Story of Japanese-American Negotiations*, by Tetsuma Hashimoto (Tokyo, 1946); "Nine Years After," by Mitsu Kakehi, *Contempt. Japan*, Vol. 19 (July-Sept. 1950) pp. 389–402. For reference to Roy Howard: Nomura telegram No. 277, to Matsuoka, FEMT, Def. Doc. 1401–C–1, Exh. 2872 (also containing characterization of his relations with Postmaster General Walker and Sec. Hull).

For the Wikawa-Iwakuro efforts: Iwakuro deposition, FEMT, Def. Doc. 2589 (Nov. 4, 1947); Strauss, see above; Konoye "Memoirs," (*loc. cit.*), pp. 1, 34; FRUS, 1941, IV, pp. 51–53, 63, 69–70, 71, 73–75, 81, 95–97, 113–17, 119, 127–28, 161. (Wikawa was also called "Ikawa" by Prince Konoye and Bishop Walsh; Iwakuro's first name was variously given as Hideo and Takeo.) For the efforts of Walsh and Drought, see Walsh deposition, FEMT, Def. Doc. 2579, Exh. 3441; his "line-a-day diary," in files of Maryknoll Society; Konoye "Memoirs," pp. 1–12 (where the "Understanding" is represented as a "tentative plan presented by the American side"); HULL, II, pp. 984–85, 989, 991, 1003; Ballantine interview and his "Memoranda on Conversations [with Wikawa and Iwakuro]," in FRUS, *Japan: 1931–1941*, II, pp. 478–79, 483, 489–99; memo of Max W. Schmidt, *ibid.*, p. 495; Nomura's explanation of "Draft Understanding" in telegram No. 239 to Konoye, FEMT, Def. Doc. 1401–B–1, Exh. 2871; LANGER-GLEASON, pp. 314–15, 321, 465, 485; FEIS, p. 175; BUTOW, pp. 229, 230, 310–12, 313.

For the intervention of Postmaster General Walker, see *Who's Who in America*, 1952–53, p. 2512; LANGER-GLEASON, pp. 465, 476, 639; interview with Hon. Jesse Donaldson; "The Japanese Negotiations, 1941," in Walker papers (which incl. many of the original documents, especially important memoranda by Father Drought dated Mar. 11, 13, 17, 1941); FEIS, pp. 174, 176, 304, 308; and Moore, *op. cit.*; *The Secret Diary of Harold L. Ickes*, Vol. 3. *The Lowering Cloud* (N.Y., 1954). For Walker's reports to President Roosevelt and the State Dept.: FRUS, 1941, IV, 17–18, 21, 54, 55, 61, 63–64, 69–74, 95–107, 111–12, 119–22, 172–73, 179–80, 184–86, 263, 265, 266, 290, 316–17; also see PHA, Vol. 20, pp. 4284 ff., "Misc. docs. from the files of the late President F. D. Roosevelt."

State Dept. on "John Doe" episode: historical study by Harold F. Gosnell, in NA (a). For Donald W. Smith: his memo to the State Dept. from Vancouver, B. C., Feb. 25, 1941, in FRUS, 1941, IV, pp. 51–53; for Iwakuro's courtesy call on Grew, Feb. 27, 1941, *ibid.*, p. 53; also see unpubl. interview with Iwakuro by Joseph Newman, N.Y. *Herald Tribune* correspondent in Tokyo, Feb. 25, 1941.

For Hornbeck's objections: FRUS, 1941, IV, pp. 21–27, 55, ("the procedure which they propose is not adapted to the facts of the situation"), pp. 57–58, 142–46, 263–64. For Drought's prominent role, see Adm. Strauss's memo to

DNI, May 22, 1941 (stating that "the individual who had been responsible for the whole idea was a missionary, Reverend Father James Drought, of the Maryknoll Fathers"). For Mr. Roosevelt's "Dear Joe" letter to Amb. Grew (actually drafted by Alger Hiss, then assistant to Dr. Hornbeck, the adviser on political relations): FRUS, pp. 6–8; Grew's letter to F. D. R., ibid., p. 469. The Roosevelt-Hull-Nomura episode: from Konoye "Memoirs" (loc. cit), p. 33. For Mr. Hull's personality in connection with Japanese-American negotiations: Hornbeck and Ballantine interviews; Strauss, op. cit., 124–29; "The Hull-Nomura Conversations: A Fundamental Misconception," by R. J. C. Butow, Am. Hist. Rev., Vol. 65, No. 4 (July 1960), pp. 822–36; Stuart, op. cit., pp. 320, 337, 339, 397; Ferrell, op. cit., pp. 389–91; From the Marco Polo Bridge to Pearl Harbor, by David J. Lu (Washington, 1961), pp. 157–224; HULL, passim; Wm. L. Neumann, op. cit., pp. 200, 208, 270–73; Nomura in Beikoku ni shishite, passim, and his telegram to For. Min., see above. It may be interesting to note that Sumner Welles in The Time for Decision mentions Mr. Hull but once, and then only in connection with the trade-agreement policy of the Roosevelt Administration. Nowhere in Welles's references to the Japanese crisis is Mr. Hull brought into the picture, except to remark (p. 290) that "I took no part whatever in the conversations between the Secretary of State and Ambassador Nomura."

For Dr. Hornbeck, see Who's Who in America, 1966–67; p. 1002. Stuart, op. cit., 294, 304–5, 313, 330, 360, 395–96; FEIS, pp. 61, 98–99, 102, 123, 158, 173, 228, 229, 334; LANGER-GLEASON, pp. 326, 843 ff., 914 ff. For Hamilton, see Stuart, op. cit., pp. 295, 360; and personal recollections; for Ballantine, ibid., pp. 360, 384; HULL, pp. 988–89, 996, 1030–31, 1095–96, 1097. Hopkins quoted from SHERWOOD, p. 428–29.

For Iwakuro's career: his deposition, FEMT, Rev. Def. Doc. 2567; Exh. 3387; "The Guiding Principle of Manchukuo," ibid., Exh. 230; Diplomatic List, State Dept., 1941, May–Aug.; HULL, II, 1003–5, 1009–14. For Walker's usefulness to the Japanese: Normura's telegram Nov. 18, 1941; to For. Min. Togo about "a certain Cabinet officer"; LANGER-GLEASON, pp. 702–6, 873, 924; and FEIS, p. 307, where he wrote that at least one "idea which had been in both Roosevelt's and Hull's mind" had been "passed on to the Japanese by Postmaster General Walker." Also see Prince Konoye's references to Mr. Walker, in his "Memoirs" (loc. cit.), passim.

15 Moment of Crisis

For MS–5, see Col. Powell's testimony, PHA, Vols. 31, pp. 3885–3915, and 36, pp. 387–88; and his affidavit, Vol. 35, pp. 179–88; "MS–5 and MS–6," by C. C. Hiles. For Weizsäcker: NA (b), Film No. 177 (Apr.–June 1941); his Memoirs (London, 1951); record of his postwar trial, passim; correspondence with Dr. Erich Kordt.

The "Magic" version of the Japanese telegrams mentioned in this chapter, "indicating varying degrees of knowledge by the Japanese or suspicions by the Japanese that their codes were being read," printed in PHA, Vols. 4, pp. 1860–63, and 5, pp. 2069–70 (covering the period Jan. 23–May 30, 1941). For other documentation of this incident from a primary Japanese source, see AMFA, Reels UD17–19; also Reel S643. Correspondence with Gen. Hiroshi Oshima, Dr. Hans Thomsen and Dr. Heinrich Stahmer. Dr. Thomson's telegram in DGFP, D, Vol. 12, p. 661. Also see WOHLSTETTER, pp. 176–86; and statement by Maj. Gen. C. A. Willoughby, in PHA, Vol. 35, p. 87, complaining about U.S. Navy's handling of intercepts, apparently unaware that "Magic" was joint Army–Navy operation.

The reaction of Op-20-G and SIS to crisis, the "indiscretion" of Sumner Welles, and German coverage of Soviet embassy in Washington: based on interviews and correspondence with sources who wish to remain anonymous. For the Jan. 23, 1941, distribution agreement, see Kramer-Safford memorandum in PHA, Vol. 11, p. 5475, incl. listing of security violations and G-2-ONI controversy over distribution to White House; also see testimony of Rear Adm. John R. Beardall, in PHA, Vol. 11, pp. 5269–91; interview with member of White House secretariat.

The pertinent I.B. and GZ memoranda were: GZ-32, Apr. 30, 1941, "Early Intentions of Germany to Attack Russia"; GZ-1, "German Plans to Attack Russia"; GZ-9, "Crisis in German-Soviet Relations"; GZ-15, "German-Soviet Crisis," with a prediction of "German surprise attacks"; I.B. 1–155; all from Capt. Safford's index of translations and memoranda.

Stalin's refusal to accept this intelligence as reliable: from testimony of Col. Ismail Egge, quoted in *War of Wits*, by Ladislas Farago (N.Y., 1954), pp. 90–91. Togo quotation: see TOGO, p. 168. Additional information supplied by Col. Vladimir Rudolph and the late Boris Nikolaewsky.

16 *"Magic's" Finest Hour*

References to Col. Tsuji are from his book, *Singapore: The Japanese Version* (N.Y., 1960), pp. 15–17, and Col. Kumin's diary notes. Japanese reactions to the Russo-German war, see HATTORI, I, pp. 73–75, 116, 144–58. For the whole Russo-German-Japanese complex: "Relations of Japan with the Axis Powers and with the Soviet Union," FRUS, 1940, I; *ibid.*, 1941, IV, pp. 905–1030; Dept. of State. *Nazi-Soviet Relations: 1939–1941* (Washington, 1942), pp. 280–357; "Der Ausbruch des deutsch-sowjetischen Konflikts und des Krieges im Pazifik," in LUPKE, pp. 127–37; *German-Japanese Relations*, by Frank W. Iklé (N.Y., 1957). For inconclusiveness of China Incident, and its impact on Japanese decisions: an article by Gen. Iwane Matsui ("The Settlement of the China Incident and the Problem of the United States") in *Dai Ajia-shugi* (July 1941); for the Netherlands East Indies: FEMT, IPS 2631, 2748; AMFA, Reel WT32.

For Matsuoka during this period: "Mysterious Speeches of Mr. Matsuoka, July 1941," presumably from the papers of Prince Konoye (in FEMT, IPS 513) and Matsuoka's speech to members of the For. Min. staff, July 1941, in AMFA, Reel SP142.

The imperial conference: from "Resolutions, etc," FEMT, IPS 1652, pp. 1–2; "Cabinet Decisions, Liaison Conference Decisions and Imperial Conference Decisions . . . July 26, 1940 to Dec. 1, 1941," *ibid.*, IPS 2137; Tojo affidavit, *ibid.*, trscpt. pp. 36258–65, 36807–8; HATTORI, I, pp. 154–55, 158–59. The text of the resolution in Vol. 2 of "Chronological Tables and Major Documents pertaining to Japan's Foreign Relations" (Tokyo, 1955), pp. 531–32; FEMT, steno. rec., Sec. 77, p. 21. Also see affidavit of Adm. Keisuke Okada, FEMT, IPS 1749.

Preparations for war in the north: *Kogun: The Japanese Army in the Pacific War*, by Saburo Hayashi (Quantico, Va., 1959), pp. 19–23; affidavit of Gen. Seiichi Kita, of the Kwantung Army, FEMT, IPS 2467; LUPKE, pp. 134–35; statement of Col. Banzai, Japanese military attaché in Berlin, Aug. 5,

1941, DGFP, D, Vol. 13, pp. 282–83. Overall military implementation of the imperial conference resolution: BUTOW, pp. 218–48; HATTORI, I, pp. 177–82; Sato, *op. cit.*, p. 120; Tojo, FEMT, trscpt. pp. 3628o–83; "Monograph No. 45," Japanese Res. Div., OMH, U.S. Army Forces (Far East); also FEMT Case File No. 20, statements of Hattori and Sadatoshi Tomioka; Shimanouchi, *op. cit.*, pp. 120–23; Hayashi, *op. cit.*, pp. 22–25; misc. docs. regarding preparations for war, AMFA, Reel 585.

Indoor exercises: from Tsuji, *op. cit.*, pp. 21–22; "The First Table-Top Maneuvers for Total War," a document compiled by GHQ for Table Maneuvers, Aug. 1941, FEMT, IPS 1356; "Records of Progress of Theoretical Maneuvers for Total War," in AMFA, Reel 52; "Evaluation of the Results of Table Maneuvers in 1941," Total War Research Institute (Tokyo, 1941).

For German pressures on Japan: DGFP, D, Vol. 13, pp. 110–13, 375–79, 466, 760–62. For Red Army strength in Far East: LUPKE, p. 135, also Hayashi, p. 169. For Soviet coverage of Japan: Deakin-Storry, *op. cit.*, Ch. 13, "Siberia or the Pacific: Triumph of the Eleventh Hour," pp. 218–47; the documents which Ozaki procured for Sorge, in AMFA, Sec. 1, Reel S590. For military attaché reports: affidavit of Col. Alfred F. Kretschmar, FEMT, Exh. 2751; telegrams in DGFP, pp. 798–800, 805–6; Adm. Wenneker, *ibid.*, pp. 367–68; also see his affidavit, FEMT, Doc. 2734, and diary entry in *Nazi Conspiracy and Aggression* (transcript Nuremberg trials), A, p. 991.

Gen. Piggott: see his *Broken Thread: An Autobiography* (Aldershot, 1950), *passim*; *Behind the Japanese Mask*, by Sir Robert Craigie (London, 1945), pp. 84, 113, 127. For references to U.S. service attachés: see "Final Recommendations Far Eastern Intelligence Organization," a memo prepared for G-2 by Lt. Col. M. W. Pettigrew, on June 21, 1941, after an inspection trip to Thailand, Singapore, China and Japan (see his proposal that "we do what we can to increase [the] prestige" of the military attachés and military observers in the area); a summary presentation of 208 reports sent to G-2 by attachés and observers in the Far East, in PHA, Vol. 34, pp. 199–211, and Bratton's comments, *ibid.*, pp. 27–29. Also intelligence reports in ONI files. For Creswell and Smith-Hutton: their official biography sheets; CREW, pp. 237, 245, 294, 480, 494, 498–500, 505, 523. Their July 17 report, in FRUS, 1941, IV. Kroner's statement: PHA, Vol. 34, pp. 42–44; also see Bratton, *ibid.*, p. 24. President Rossevelt's statement: from Dennis McEvoy to whom it was made in the fall of 1941. Gen. Eisenhower: from his *Crusade in Europe* (Garden City, 1949), pp. 32–34. Also see WOHLSTETTER, pp. 337–38, 364, 369–70. Mr. Hull's telegram to Amb. Gauss, FRUS, 1941, IV, pp. 565–66. Grew's and Gauss's replies, *ibid.*, pp. 570–73.

Grew's telegram about imperial conference: *ibid.*, p. 287; Nomura's letter in Ballantine memorandum of July 5, 1941: *ibid.*, pp. 291–92. Kramer's reconstruction of proceedings traced from his GZ Memos, briefed in Safford's index. Hornbeck's praise: in his memo of July 5, 1941, FRUS, p. 290.

17 Games of War

For Prince Konoye's part in these events, and his character and personality, see Yabe, *op. cit.*; *Konoye Naikaku* (The Konoye Cabinet), by Akira Kazami (Tokyo, 1951); David J. Lu, *op. cit.*, pp. 156–208; character sketch by Tomohiko Ushiba, one of his private secretaries; KIDO, *passim*. His own writings include "Memoirs" (*loc. cit.*), *Heiwa e no doryoku* (*loc. cit.*), *Ushinawareshi seiji* (*loc. cit.*); collections of his speeches 1937–39, AMFA, Reel

SP142 (in two parts). The Nomura quotation is from "Stepping-Stones to War" in USNIP, loc. cit.
Proposed Konoye-Roosevelt meeting: "Memoirs," pp. 29–37. Text of his message to F. D. R.: FEMT, Doc. 3113, also FRUS, Japan: 1931–1941, II, p. 565; Grew's memo, ibid., p. 560: The President's reply: FRUS, 1941, IV, pp. 423–25, 470. State Dept. opposition to meeting: ibid., 403–5, 412–16, 419, 425–28, 449–50, 470–75, 478–80; FEIS, pp. 249–50, 252–54.
Konoye's resignation (six days after his fiftieth birthday): "Facts Pertaining to the Resignation of the Third Konoye Cabinet, 1941," FEMT, IPS 497; "Circumstances Surrounding the Resignation of the Third Konoye Cabinet," by KIDO, ibid., Exh. 2250; "Memoirs," pp. 49–53; also Ichi kozoku no senso nikki (The War Diary of a Member of the Imperial Family), by Prince Noruhiko Higashikuni (Tokyo, 1957), the man Konoye hoped would succeed him.
Konoye's audience with the Emperor, and the Sugiyama-Nagano confrontation, is described in "Memoirs," pp. 40–41, the only authentic extant source. Bishop Walsh's memo (which he left with Secretary Hull on Nov. 15, 1941) is printed in full in FRUS, 1941, IV, pp. 527–39; the original copy of Muto's laissez passer is among the Walsh papers at the Maryknoll Society, Ossining, N.Y. (Bishop Walsh's long "swan song" as a peace missionary has several derisive marginal notes by Dr. Hornbeck, who characterized the memo as "naïve.")
For some of the references to the background of Gen. Tojo's appointment as Premier, see KIDO and his special memorandum on the subject, FEMT, Doc. 3368; Sato, op. cit., pp. 19–24; and the brilliant reconstruction of the event, in BUTOW, pp. 90, 291–302, 308–9.
For naval planning and Yamamoto's indoor exercises: "Pearl Harbor: The Planning Stage," based on the interrogation of a PW who had been Yamamoto's confidential yeoman, U.S. Navy Weekly Intelligence Bulletin, Vol. 1, No. 22 (Dec. 8, 1944), pp. 1–22; replies to "Questionnaire Concerning the Pearl Harbor Attack," Liaison Committee for the Imperial Army and Navy (Oct. 17, 1945), especially answers by Adm. Osami Nagano, Capt. Sadatoshi Tomioka, Comdr. Tatsukichi Miyo, Capt. Kamito Kuroshima and Comdr. Yasuji Watanabe; "Reconstruction of Japanese Plans Leading Up to the Attack on Pearl Harbor," Navy Dept. memo (Oct. 1946); "Thoughts on Japan's Naval Defeat," by Rear Adm. Toshiyuki Yokoi, USNIP (Oct. 1960), pp. 68–75; an erudite historical study entitled "Hawaii Operation," by Vice-Adm. Shigeru Fukudome, ibid. (Dec. 1955), pp. 1318–21; "The Inside Story of the Pearl Harbor Plan," by Robert E. Ward, ibid. (Dec. 1951), pp. 1271–83; "The Japanese Decision for War," by Louis Morton, ibid. (Dec. 1954), pp. 1327–31. Also see PHA, Vol. 13 (Exh. 8, 8-A, 8-B, 8-C, 8-D), pp. 391–922, "Material Obtained by Army and Navy Primarily from Japanese Sources, Relating to Japanese Plans for Pearl Harbor Attack" (see table of contents attached to these exhibits).
For Army war games, see notes for Ch. 16. Col. Iwakuro's report to the Naval General Staff: in Konoye "Memoirs," p. 34. For footnote on recovery of Yamamoto's war plans: FEMT, Trscpt. pp. 11192–95, Doc. 17, Exh. 1252. Konoye's attempted assassination: FRUS, 1941, IV, pp. 464, 531 (Amb. Grew's informant was T. Uchiba, the Premier's private secretary); also FEIS, p. 282. For political murders in Japan: "Attempts by Extreme Nationalists to Assassinate Political Leaders, and Other Political Crimes," a secret survey and

report prepared jointly by the Ministry of Home Affairs and the Ministry of Justice, FEMT, Doc. 1125; also in AMFA, Reel WT32.

18 The Missed Clue

I am indebted to Mr. Hoshida and Miss Asakuru for some of the primary source material that went into the making of this chapter. For priority marking of confidential dispatches, see "Secret Instructions for Handling Urgent Telegrams," No. 209 (GO), Sep. 20, 1941. Text of telegram No. 83: in PHA, Vol. 12, Exh. 2, p. 261; Sep. 22 telegram: *ibid.*

Yoshikawa's activities during this period: from "File 336.92—Japanese Consulate and Consular Agents," U.S. Naval Intelligence Service, INV. REP. Feb. 15, 1943; also interrogations of Kotoshirodo and Mikami, *ibid.*; for Tsukikawa, PHA, Vol. 35, p. 363; and information from Takaichi Sakai and Ichitaro Ozaki. Yoshikawa's telegrams of Sep. 29: PHA, Vol. 12, Exh. 2, p. 262, and "Log of Outgoing Messages" in which they were excerpted.

For interception of Sep. 24 and 29 telegrams: Safford's index, and his notations on intercepts. MI-5: in Powell affidavit, *q.v.* (incl. functions and procedures). Clipper schedules in 1941: from *History of the Transpacific Air Services To and Through Hawaii*, by Pan American Airways, Inc. (Honolulu, 1944); and from Pan American Airways.

Konoye-Toyoda-Nomura controversy: from "Collection of Telegrams Exchanged between Amb. Nomura and Minister of Foreign Affairs Admiral Toyoda, Aug. 16–Oct. 13, 1941," AMFA, Reels WT54, WT75, WT80; and DGFP, Doc. 316, p. 503 (the information was given by Weizsäcker to Oshima on Sept. 14). Nomura-Hull conversations: in FRUS, 1941, IV. Memoranda of J. W. Ballantine, *ibid.*, pp. 470–75; Hull's telegram to Grew, *ibid.*, pp. 476, 494–97. For "leaks" in London, see State Dept. complaint, *ibid.*, p. 393. The information was given to Lord Halifax through Sir Ronald Campbell, the British minister in Washington, by Mr. Hamilton on Sept. 6 (FE Files, Lot 244, NA). For sequence of telegrams, see Safford's index with his notes.

Kramer's handling of Sep. 24 message and his general attitude to espionage messages (all in PHA): Vols. 9, pp. 4176–79; McCollum, in 37, p. 28; 8, pp. 3405–6; Kramer's interpretation of the telegram, 9, p. 4535; Wilkinson, 4, pp. 1746–48; Adm. Stark, 5, pp. 2174–75; Gen. Miles, 2, pp. 859–60; Bratton, 9, 4526, 4533–34, 4535. Failure to forward telegram to Adm. Kimmel, in 9, pp. 4193 ff., and Layton's comment quoted in WOHLSTETTER, p. 212.

19 The Pearl Harbor Spy

This chapter leans heavily on Col. Clausen's researches in Hawaii (the results of which were published in PHA, Vol. 35); on interviews and correspondence with Col. Clausen, Col. Bicknell, Mr. John F. Sonnett, counsel of the Hewitt Inquiry, and Yoshio Hasegawa, former lieutenant of the Honolulu Police Dept.; and on largely unpublished "internal security" material in the Hawaii War Records Depository. My thanks to Miss Janet Bell, custodian of HWRD, for giving me unrestricted access to the files of the Depository, and to Miss Gwenfried Allen (see ALLEN (a)), for sharing with me her consummate knowledge of the topic.

This aspect of the Pearl Harbor disaster was either overlooked or glossed over by those whose complacency or inefficiency enabled the Japanese to spy on the fleet at Pearl, up to the split second of the attack. However, Col. Bicknell called the significance of the espionage factor to Col. Clausen's attention, who then proceeded to search for pertinent documents and succeeded in unearthing the files of the FBI, of the Army's Contact office, and of the DIO, 14th Naval Distr., as well as other data without which the story of Japanese espionage in Hawaii could not be written. Unlike Mrs. Wohlstetter, who dismissed the Clausen Investigation and characterized its corrective affidavits as "notoriously unreliable" (WOHLSTETTER, p. 35 n), I wish to pay tribute to Col. Clausen, whose energy, curiosity and investigative skill has made a unique and crucial contribution to our understanding of the Pearl Harbor disaster.

In addition to Vol. 35 (Clausen Investigation) in PHA, the printed record of the various Pearl Harbor inquests include the following scattered source references: Vols. 7, p. 2997; 10, pp. 5091–5117; 13, 412 ff.; 15, p. 1867; 18, p. 3254 ff.; 22, p. 488; 23, p. 863 ff.; 26, pp. 337, 350–52, 359–61; 27, pp. 214, 738–41; 28, p. 1541 ff.; 29, p. 1687 ff.; 36, pp. 166, 223–24, 337, 523; 37, pp. 674, 911 ff.; 39, pp. 63, 101, 451; 40, pp. 137, 148. Also see the transcripts of HWRD staff interviews with Gov. Joseph B. Poindexter; Col. Bicknell; Robert L. Shivers; D. W. Brewster of the Immigration Station; Julian Behrstock of Foreign Broadcast Intelligence Service; Ray Coll, Sr., editor, Honolulu Advertiser; Richard K. Kimball; Daniel Liu, chief, Honolulu Police Dept.; Thomas C. Major; Lawrence Nakatsuka; and Willard Wilson, of the Hawaii branch of the Office of Censorship. Extensive use was made of Col. Bicknell's MS. (q.v.); two mimeographed monographs of the U.S. Army, in OCMH; and the following typescripts on file in HWRD:

Annual reports, bulletins and records of police departments, Honolulu (city and county), and Kauai and Maui counties; the radio broadcast log of the Honolulu Police Dept.; "The Hawaii Police Department in World War II"; a memorandum of Mr. Shivers, entitled "Cooperation of the Various Racial Groups [in Hawaii] with Each Other and the Constituted Authorities, before and after December 7, 1941"; and a Commerce Dept. publication, "Radio Intelligence Work Under Department of Commerce, Federal Radio Commission and Federal Communications Commission, 1910–1941."

Yoshikawa's double life was described in melodramatic detail by his colleagues at the consulate, especially Miss Doue, Takaichi Sakai, Richard Kotoshirodo (see his signed statement of Oct. 1, 1941), and John Mikami; his techniques of espionage, in INV. REP., Feb. 15, 1943, par. 71–95. For Seki, see ibid., par. 82–85, 88; for the trip to the "Big Island," ibid., par. 63–70.

For the American counterespionage establishment, see Bicknell, op. cit.; Mayfield testimonies; Wilkinson, PHA, Vol. 26, pp. 304–7 (incl. tapping of phones and illicit censorship of mail). For espionage suspects, see testimonies of Rear Adm. R. B. Inglis, PHA, Vol. 1, pp. 26–231, passim, and Wilkinson's answers to questionnaire of Hart Inqu., PHA, pp. 305–6. The surveillance of the Japanese consulate was undertaken by a special branch of the Honolulu Police Dept. under Lt. Hasegawa, who had at least two confidential informants on its premises. It was prompt intervention on the part of Hasegawa and Chief of Detectives Benjamin Van Kuren on the morning of Dec. 7, 1941, that secured most of the consulate's files (see "Japan Consul Raided," Honolulu Star-Bulletin, 2nd Extra, Dec. 7, 1941, p. 3), before the FBI moved in.

For the tapping of the consulate's telephones: affidavits of Emanuel, Woodrum, Shivers; testimony of Mayfield. Since Mr. Emanuel did the tapping at his home in Honolulu, the unusual number of telephone lines running into his house betrayed what was supposed to be a supersecret activity. For note on Yoshikawa's protracted obscurity, see Mayfield's letters No. 64A (June 15, 1941) and No. 54 (Feb. 15, 1943); USNIP, Vol. 86, No. 12 (1960), p. 27; and corr. with Col. Stanford. Yoshikawa's "fatalistic" view of his activities: from his article in USNIP, p. 39; and *Time* (Dec. 12, 1960), p. 23.

Yoshikawa's reports quoted in this chapter are all from "Logs of Outgoing Dispatches," seized by Lt. Hasegawa on Dec. 7, 1941; and, when quoted verbatim, from "Selection of Intercepted Messages Sent and Received by the Japanese Government and its Foreign Establishments . . . concerning Military Installations, Ship Movements, Espionage Reports," PHA, Vol. 12, Exh. 2, pp. 254–316.

The voyage of the *Tatsuta Maru:* from the consulate's log and Kita's telegrams. The mission of the late Comdr. Nakajima: from interrogation of Comdr. Tachibana, USNTM, and from KOJIMA. The Kühn assignment, *ibid.;* Kühn's interrogations and testimony of Eberhard Kühn (both in FBI Honolulu file); Kotoshirodo's interrogations; also see "Pre-War Honolulu Commercial Broadcasts Containing Coded Information for the Japanese Fleet," Report No. 234, by Lt. R. H. Peterson, USNR, DIO, 14th ND, Nov. 7, 1945.

For the voyage of the *Taiyo Maru:* CBS interview with Lt. Comdr. Sugari Suzuki (Dec. 3, 1963); Lord, *op. cit.,* pp. 16–18; YOSHIKAWA; Col. Bicknell's recollections and his report to G-2, in G-2 File No. 336.8, Oct. 7, 1941.

20 *"I May Make War"—A Secret Alliance*

Churchill on "Magics," see his *The Second World War,* Vol. 3: *The Grand Alliance* (Boston, 1950), p. 504; on Japan, *ibid.,* pp. 487–508. Roosevelt's statement ("I may make war"): from Churchill's letter to Field Marshal Smuts, dated Nov. 9, 1941, *ibid.,* p. 500. For developments at the Atlantic Conference: SHERWOOD, pp. 354–56; and messages from President Roosevelt to Secr. Hull, Nos. 121645 and 160115; memoranda by Sumner Welles on conversations with Prime Minister Churchill and Sir Alexander Cadogan, Aug. 10 and 11, 1941; record of Welles's report to the President, Aug. 11; and drafts of Anglo-American communications to Japan, Aug. 10, 15 and 16, 1941, all in PHA, Vol. 14, pp. 1252–99.

For British-Dutch-American strategic developments, see GWYER, Part 1, pp. 16–20, 118–24, 130–37, and especially 245–90; KIRBY, pp. 43–88 (A.B.C.1, p. 58; A.D.B.1, pp. 62–63; A.D.B.2, p. 76; U.S. objections, p. 86); PHA, Exh. 43, Vol. 14, pp. 1422–23; Exh. 49, Vol. 15, pp. 1485–50; Exh. 65, Vol. 15, pp. 1677–79; also Office of the Commander-in-Chief, China Station, "American-Dutch-British Conversations, Singapore, April, 1941, Report," dated Apr. 27, 1941, incl. Part IV, "Action Open to the Associated Powers," and Part VII, "Plan for Employment of Land and Air Forces."

Anglo-American exchange of technical information: OCMH (f), pp. 191–202; *Scientists Against Time,* by J. P. Baxter III (Boston, 1946), pp. 119–23, 142, 144–45, 202, 214, 216; *The Secret War,* by Gerald Pawle (N.Y., 1957), *passim.*

For G-2 and ONI objections: War Plans Division, WDGS, File 4340, "Exchange of Information with British Government," cited in OCMH (f), (p. 192). Material for the exchange of cryptological information was supplied by an unimpeachable private source. British possession of Enigma machines: from Boris Hagelin, Jr., and Garro, op. cit.; also correspondence with Gen. Marthans Garro.

Britain's ability to read American codes was long known to U.S. diplomats and cryptologists (see a report to the St. Paul (Minn.) Dispatch, May 8, 1916, "U.S. Secret Code Known in England") and to the Japanese as well (cf. "Misc. Docs. relating to British–U.S. Diplomatic Relations," 1929–41, AMFA, Reel S12).

For Sir William Stephenson's activities in the U.S. and his relations with President Roosevelt, see The Quiet Canadian, by H. Montgomery Hyde (London, 1962), passim; and interviews and correspondence with Capt. Hyde, Mr. Ernest Cuneo, Mr. Philip Horton, and the late Mr. Ian Fleming. On p. 213, Hyde states that James Roosevelt, the President's eldest son, had acted as special courier between F.D.R. and Stephenson to assure the absolute secrecy of these communications. My repeated efforts to corroborate this assertion brought no response from Amb. Roosevelt. Also according to Hyde, on Nov. 27, 1941, the President sent James Roosevelt to Stephenson in New York, "with a special message, the purport of which was not as yet known either to the British Foreign Office or to the British embassy in Washington," but which enabled Stephenson to cable to his own headquarters in London: "Japanese negotiations off. Services expect action within two weeks." When London, understandably stirred by the information, inquired about its source, Stephenson replied curtly: "The President of the U.S.A." See also FRUS, 1941, IV, pp. 685–87, "Memorandum of Conversation," dated Nov. 29, 1941, in which Secretary Hull recorded what he had told the British ambassador. "I expressed the view," he wrote, "that the diplomatic part of our relations with Japan was virtually over and that the matter will now go to the officials of the Army and the Navy with whom I have talked and to whom I have given my views for whatever they are worth." Lord Halifax's call on Mr. Hull was obviously upon instructions from London to obtain confirmation of Stephenson's report, the British government was forced to solicit information that President Roosevelt had given Stephenson two days before.

For British assaults on cryptographic secrets in the U.S. during this period, also see The Scarlet Thread: Adventures in Wartime Espionage, by D. Downes (London, 1953), pp. 57–62, 87–102. For activities of Sir Reginald Hall, see The Zimmermann Telegram, by Barbara W. Tuchman (N.Y., 1958), pp. 8–15, 113–14; The Eyes of the Navy, by Adm. Sir William James (London, 1956), passim; Life and Letters of Walter Hines Page, ed. by Burton J. Hendrick (3 vols., N.Y., 1923–26), Vol. 3, pp. 360–63.

For the Kurusu mission: Mr. Hamilton's memorandum of Nov. 4, 1941, in FRUS, 1941, IV, pp. 566–67; also ibid., pp. 570, 584, 599, 625. Foreign Minister Togo's telegram to Amb. Nomura, Nov. 4 (JD6251), Nov. 5 (JD6275), Nov. 6 (A6302): from Safford's index. For Kurusu's background, incl. his role in forging the Tripartite Pact while ambassador in Berlin: his own Nichi-Bei gaiko heiwa: waga gaiko-shi (The Secret Story of Japanese-American Relations: A History of Our Diplomacy), (Tokyo, 1952) and Nichi-Bei kosho hishi (Untold Stories of United States–Japanese Relations), (Tokyo, 1952), pp. 89–134; "Interview with Kurusu Saburo," in Shakai, Vol. 2, No. 2 (Feb. 1, 1947); "Report by Ambassador Kurusu Saburo on the Negotiations," in AMFA, Reel WT77; also information from Col. Bicknell, who met Kurusu in Honolulu for a long interview on Nov. 10, 1941; Lu, op. cit., pp. 217–37 (an excellent account of the mission).

Also see HULL, II, p. 1034 (where he recorded that For. Min. Toyoda had informed Amb. Grew *already on Oct.* 10 that "Nomura was very fatigued" and Toyoda "was considering sending a diplomat of wide experience to Washington to assist the ambassador . . . our first intimation of the sending to Washington of Ambassador Saburo Kurusu"); also *ibid.*, pp. 1056 and 1062–68. For Yuki, see his affidavit in FEMT, Def. Doc. 2064; and Hyde, *op. cit.*, pp. 212–13. (The "British scholar" in the "game" was Sir George Sansom, then serving as a minister-counsellor at the British embassy ·in Washington, D.C.)

21 How the Japanese Fleet Was "Lost"

For Grew's telegram about Cabinet change: FRUS, 1941, IV, pp. 541–43; his remonstrations with the State Dept.: paraphrase of the original telegram in GREW, pp. 467–70, and diary entry Nov. 4, 1941, p. 470; also Hornbeck interview. Langdon memos: FRUS, pp. 512–13, 519; Hamilton memo, "An Estimate of the Tojo Cabinet," *ibid.*, pp. 522–23; diametrically opposite interpretations by G-2 and ONI, *ibid.*, pp. 513, 519–20 (by Gen. Miles) and PHA, Exh. 80, dated Nov. 1, 1941, Vol. 15, p. 1815; also see SHERWOOD, p. 419, for a Navy report to Harry L. Hopkins in which Capt. R. E. Schuirmann of Adm. Stark's staff wrote on Oct. 17, 1941: "I believe we are inclined to overestimate the importance of changes in the Japanese Cabinet as indicative of great changes in Japanese political thought and action. . . . Present reports are that the new Cabinet to be formed will be no better and no worse than the one which has just fallen. Japan may attack Russia, or may move southward, but in the final analysis this will be determined by the military on the basis of opportunity, and what they can get away with, not by what Cabinet is in power." BUTOW, pp. 312–13, citing OSS Doc. No. 14601 in NA, prints the views of "an important American military officer in Tokyo (whose identity is known but cannot here be revealed)" that Konoye's resignation and Tojo's elevation to the premiership did not indicate "any radical change in Japanese policy" because Tojo was known to be "in sympathy with many of the ideas entertained by his predecessor." The "important American military officer" was Lt. Col. Harry I. T. Creswell, the military attaché in Tokyo. Many of the embassy's estimates were based on information supplied by T. Uchiba, Prince Konoye's private secretary, who professed to be pro-American, and a friend of Counselor Eugene Dooman. Actually the information he dispensed to Dooman was totally inaccurate if not deliberately misleading. In the wake of Konoye's downfall he assured his American friends that the Tojo Cabinet "would not be a military dictatorship bound to the most militaristic and drastic policy" (see FRUS, Japan: 1931–1941, II, pp. 689–92, and GREW, pp. 456–61). Dr. Stuart's estimate is in a Butrick telegram in FRUS, 1941, IV, pp. 562–63.

All Nomura-Togo telegrams quoted in this chapter are from "Collection of Telegrams between Ambassador Nomura Kichisaburo and Minister of Foreign Affairs Togo Shigenori," AMFA, Reel WT49; and "Telegrams from Minister of Foreign Affairs Togo Shigenori to Ambassador Nomura Kichisaburo," *ibid.*, Reels WT75, WT80, WT81. Duplicity of Kurusu's mission: HULL, II, pp. 1062–63, and Welles, *op. cit.*, pp. 289, 295. For the "campaign of deception," see FRUS, pp. 540–41 (Butrick); 544 (Col. Mayer); 555–58 (Dr. E. Stanley Jones); 562 (Butrick–Dr. Stuart); 574 (Grew); 584–85 (Butrick).

Adm. Yamamoto's final arrangements: "Principal Reasons for the Com-

mencement of Hostilities Against the U.S. and Great Britain," decisions of
the Liaison Conference, Nov. 11, 1941, in AMFA, Reel WT26; also
MORISON, pp. 85–91; interview with Lt. Comdr. Y. Shiga, PHA, Vol. 13, pp.
431–41, 484, 645; The Campaigns of the Pacific War (1946), pp. 12–23;
"Japan's Decision to Fight," ATIS, Research Rep. No. 131; "The Pearl
Harbor Operation," ibid., No. 132; interrogation of Adm. Nagano on Nov.
30, 1945 (in USSBS (a), 498) and Capt. Fuchida on Nov. 28, 1941 (USSBS
(a), 103), also Fuchida and Capt. Watanabe in USSBS (a); Japanese Destroyer Captain, by Capt. Tameichi Hara, with Fred Sato and Roger Pineau
(N.Y., 1961), pp. 43–50; Masanori Ito, op. cit., pp. 22–28.

Selection of date for the attack: HATTORI, I, p. 362; Ward, op. cit., p.
1279; Fukudome, op. cit., pp. 1321–22; Adm. Ugaki's speech, ATIS No. 131,
pp. 10–11; also see Hara's description of the briefing by Yamamoto and
Ugaki, and his "man-to-man" talk with Adm. Ugaki, op. cit., pp. 44–46. For
Yamamoto's doubts and letter to Adm. Hori: "Admiral Yamamoto," by James
A. Field, Jr., USNIP (Oct. 1949), p. 1112. Deployment of striking forces:
MORISON, pp. 88–90.

For security measures, see "Communications," Part F in Adm. Yamamoto's
Operations Order No. 1, pp. 41–62, especially sections 4a and b 1, 2, 3; PW
interrogation, in U.S. Navy Weekly Intelligence Bulletin Vol. 1, No. 2 (Dec.
8, 1944), p. 9; Par. in Annex, Adm. Yamamoto's Op. Ord.; MORISON, pp.
88–89; report of Comdr. Smith-Hutton in ONI Files; testimony of Rear Adm.
R. B. Inglis, PHA, Vols. 1, pp. 185, 238; 10, p. 4893; 11, 5356; 17, pp.
2635–36; 26, pp. 37, 128; 37, pp. 745, 756.

Call sign changes: PHA, Vols. 6, p. 2522; 10, p. 4680, 4903; 17, pp. 2601,
2636; 23, p. 664; 26, p. 866; 36, p. 16; 37, p. 754. U.S. surveillance of
Japanese fleet: PHA, Vols. 4, p. 1727–28 (Wilkinson); 36, pp. 13–15 (where
Capt. McCollum stated categorically that "our major dependence was per-
force based on radio intelligence without the benefit of check by visual
observations from time to time"). For radio intelligence and traffic analysis:
McCollum, in PHA, Vol. 36, pp. 17–18; also Vols. 6, p. 2523; 8, p. 3383; 10,
pp. 4829–42, 4892–94, 4903–4; also 14th Nav. Distr. "Communication
Intelligence Summaries," Nov. 1–Dec. 6, 1941; Pacific Fleet Intelligence
Officer "Reports," Oct. 27–Dec. 2, 1941; Pacific Fleet "Intelligence Memorandum," Dec. 1, 1941, all in PHA, Vol. 17, pp. 2601–71 (see table of
contents attached to Exh. 115,); "Pacific Fleet Intelligence Bulletin No.
45–41," Nov. 27, 1941, ibid., Exh. 115B, pp. 2677–79; also Layton, Vols. 36,
pp. 116–41 and, 10, pp. 4836–39, 4906.

For C/I Unit in Hawaii: PHA, Vols. 10, pp. 4673–74, 4697–98; 23, p. 675;
28, p. 863; in Cavite, testimony of Lt. Comdr. R. J. Fabian, Vol. 36, pp.
68–79. For Holmes: his affidavit in Vol. 34, pp. 100–101; and his official
Navy bio sheet of Mar. 10, 1950. (I wish to express my gratitude to Mrs.
Betty W. Shirley, Head, Biographies Branch, Office of Information, Department of the Navy, for prompt and generous help in gaining much of the
biographical data on the officers of the U.S. Navy mentioned in this book.)

Wilfred Jay Holmes (b. 1900 in Stockport, Mass., resident of Hawaii since
1935) was a remarkable and versatile officer, with an Annapolis diploma
(1922) and an M.S. degree in engineering from Columbia University. Originally a submariner, he branched out into communications and intelligence,
and wound up the war with the Legion of Merit and a Distinguished Service
Medal "for exceptionally meritorious services." He is also the author of widely
published popular stories, mostly about the Navy, under the pen name of Alec
Hudson.

For transmission of intel. reports through Foreign Ministry channels, see Kase interrogation in USNTM; Kameyama, affidavit, also FEMT, Trscpt. pp. 10570, 26204–6, 26190–91, 26193. The Ogawa-Yoshikawa exchange of telegrams: from PHA, Exh. 2, Vol. 12, pp. 254–316.

Mr. Hull's recognition of the utmost seriousness of the situation ("Intercepted messages from Tokyo were now proving beyond all doubt that the crisis was at hand") from HULL, II, pp. 1054–68, also FEIS, pp. 307–19. Roosevelt's access to intercepts, see McCollum ("The book, in whole or in part, went to the President, depending on what the aide to the President thought about it"), PHA, Vol. 36, p. 23; Beardall testimony (q.v.); and Kramer-Safford memorandum in Vol. 11, p. 5475.

22 Bratton's Last Stand

Col. Bratton testified five times before the various inquiries, signed a number of affidavits, participated in a round-table discussion—and told a different story each time. The deviations in his versions of events consisted not merely of such relatively minor matters as the approximate time sequence of certain deliveries, but of major claims and assertions which, on closer examination, proved to be totally at variance with the facts. It was, indeed, one of the bizarre features of the testimonies of men like Bratton and Kramer—mere extras on the stage but fated to play a major part during a brief personal involvement in historic events—that they could not recall with anything approaching absolute accuracy what they had done during the fortnight preceding the Pearl Harbor attack.

In the reconstruction of Bratton's role and activities during the crucial period described in this chapter, I relied on his *final* testimonies before Col. Clark and the Joint Congressional Committee, and on the corrective investigations of Gen. Cramer and Col. Clausen, including a number of affidavits the latter elicited from eyewitnesses (see PHA, Exh. B, Vol. 35, pp. 20–108, especially the affidavits of Col. Dusenbury, Gen. Ralph C. Smith, Miss Mary L. Ross, Brig. Gen. Thomas J. Betts, Lt. Gen. Walter Bedell Smith, Lt. Gen. Leonard T. Gerow, Maj. Gen. John R. Deane, Maj. Gen. Sherman Miles; and Bratton's own affidavit of July 27, 1945, in which he stated: "Any prior statements or testimony of mine which may be contrary to my statements here, including among other things as to the processing and delivery of material, and to whom and when, should be modified and considered changed in accordance with my statements herein. This affidavit now represents my best recollection of the matters and events set forth, and a better recollection than when I previously testified before the Army Pearl Harbor Board, and is made after having my memory refreshed in several ways and respects.") I am satisfied that Col. Bratton's final testimony before the Joint Committee, covering 456 pages of typewritten transcript, represents and may be properly accepted as the definitive recapitulation of his activities during this period. I am, moreover, indebted to Mr. A. A. Hoehling, who conducted extensive interviews with the late Col. Bratton for additional information.

For Bratton's biography, see Army biographical file; and PHA, Vol. 9, pp. 4508–09; for his career in G-2 Far Eastern Section, *ibid.*, pp. 4560–61; also Hoehling (*op. cit.*, pp. 68–70, 81, 158, 161, 171, 177, 202, 205) for a warm and intimate pen-picture of the man; and WOHLSTETTER (pp. 172, 176–77, 217, 281, 285, 287, 307–12, 395) for a shrewd analysis of his effectiveness in G-2. His part in these events and activities during this period, from his testimonies before PHA, Vols. 9, pp. 4508–628; 34, pp. 10–30 (in four parts) and 69–74 (round-table discussion); Cramer, in Vol. 3, pp. 1443–97, *passim*. For his relations with McCollum: PHA, Vols. 36, pp. 10–42 and 8, pp. 3381–448. For his friendship with Gen. Isoda, see Gen. Miles memorandum of Sep. 2, 1941; for his custodianship of "magics": his affidavit, FEMT, Def. Doc. 2094, Aug. 18, 1947.

Nov. 26 "Ten-Point Note:" see Bratton, PHA, Vol. 9, pp. 4556–48; HULL, II, pp. 1077–82; FRUS, *Japan:* 1931–1941, II, pp. 764–70; *ibid.*, 1941, IV, pp. 623–25, 626, 627–30, 633–40, 642–46, 661–65 (final draft), 665–66 (Hull's report to the President and brief memo recording delivery of the note); three telegrams from Hull to Grew, incl. text of note, PHA, Exh. 75, Vol. 15; docs. relating to proposed "Modus Vivendi," *ibid.*, Exh. 18, and Vol. 14, pp. 1084–1200; PHA, Exh. 168, Vol. 19, pp. 3666–95; State Dept. file copy of the document; State Dept. statement to the press announcing the delivery of the note; State Dept. Press release No. 585, Dec. 7, 1941; President Roosevelt's remarks at press conference, Dec. 2, 1941; Army comments, FRUS, 1941, IV, pp. 630–31; Navy comments, *ibid.*, pp. 631–32.

For Japanese reactions to the "Ten-Point Note": Amb. Grew's dispatch of Dec. 1, 1941; also see GREW, pp. 482–86 (" 'Washington Has Delivered an Ultimatum to Us' "); three intercepted messages from Amb. Nomura to Tokyo, in PHA, Exh. 94, Vol. 16, pp. 1975–86; *Journey to the Missouri*, by Toshikazu Kase (New Haven, 1950), pp. 60–64, based entirely on American revisionist histories; and TOGO.

For Sec. Stimson: Stimson-Bundy, *op. cit.*, pp. 364–94; Stimson diary (*loc. cit.*), and excerpts in PHA, Vol. 11, pp. 5431–40; Stimson's chronological statement, *ibid.*, pp. 5416–28 (his editing of Gen. Marshall's warning message to Gen. Short is on pp. 5123–25); his testimony before PHA, Vols. 27–31, pp. 4037–94; his answers to questionnaire of J.C., pp. 5441–63; "Summary of My Views as to the Responsibility of Members of the Army," *ibid.*, pp. 5428–31; affidavit, June 7, 1946, FEMT, Doc. 2216; also see Cramer, *op. cit., passim;* "How Stimson Meant to 'Maneuver' the Japanese," by Richard N. Current, in *Mississippi Valley Hist. Rev.*, Vol. 40 (June 1953), pp. 67–74.

For President Roosevelt's "dilemma": SHERWOOD, pp. 429–30; LANGER-GLEASON, pp. 324, 690; *President Roosevelt and the Coming of the War, 1941*, by Charles A. Beard (New Haven, 1948) presenting the revisionist concept of history, refuted by S. F. Beamis in *Journal of Mod. Hist.*, Vol. 19 (Mar. 1948), pp. 55–59 ("The First Gun of a Revisionist Historiography for the Second World War"); S. E. Morison in *Atlantic Monthly*, Vol. 82 (Aug. 1948), pp. 91–97 ("Did Roosevelt Start the War?"); and Stimson-Bundy, *op. cit.*, pp. 392–93: "The disaster at Pearl Harbor raised questions of responsibility," they wrote, "and even of guilt, which occupied the attention of a half-dozen boards and committees during and after the war. . . . He [Stimson] was satisfied that the major responsibility for the catastrophe rested on the two officers commanding on the spot—Admiral Kimmel and General Short. It was true that the War and Navy departments were not fully efficient in evaluating the information available to them, and of course it was also true that no one in Washington had correctly assessed Japanese intentions and capabilities. . . . The men in Washington did not foresee this attack; and they did not take the additional actions suggested by the retrospective view. . . . Much of the discussion of Pearl Harbor was confused by a preposterous effort to demonstrate that President Roosevelt and his advisers had for some unfathomable but nefarious reason 'planned it that way.' " For a reasoned discussion of the controversy, with a position somewhere between the two points of

views, see *The Genesis of Pearl Harbor*, by William L. Neumann (Philadelphia, 1945); and especially his *America Encounters Japan* (*loc. cit.*) Ch. 12
and 13, pp. 218–89. This author's own conclusions coincide with those of Dr.
Neuman. For an interesting foreign appraisal: "Pearl Harbor und der Eintritt
der Vereinigten Staaten in dem zweiten Weltkrieg," by Josef Engel, in
Historische Forschungen und Probleme (Wiesbaden, 1961), pp. 358–73,
where Dr. Engel concluded: "It is not the task of the historian to pronounce a
verdict. There was but one person who should have borne the responsibility.
He was Roosevelt, who needed a provoked incident to enter the war and was
prepared, in the interest of his higher aim, namely, the defeat of world-enemy
Hitler, to demand this sacrifice from the Americans. However, responsibility is
not synonymous with guilt. Roosevelt never accepted responsibility for Pearl
Harbor in public. As President of a nation at war, he could not possibly do so.
If he possessed true greatness and had lived, he would have certainly assumed
this responsibility after the war."

For letting Japan "fire the first shot," see OCMH (b), p. 75: "In a certain
sense," Dr. Cline wrote, "the Army, in view of the overwhelming evidence
long available that the Japanese might open hostilities by launching such an
assault against American positions in the Pacific, including Hawaii, and in
view of the virtual certainty that they would gain some initial success, was
prepared to be fatalistic about the initial onslaught." Also see *Strategic
Planning for Coalition Warfare, 1941–1942*, by Maurice Matloff and Edwin
M. Snell (Washington, 1953), pp. 1–10, 32–77, for American war plans
developed along defensive lines.

For Dr. Hornbeck's part in these events, see FEIS, pp. 228, 229, 241, 334;
LANGER-GLEASON, pp. 696, 704, 839, 843 ff., 849, 907, 914 ff.; his memo of
Nov. 27, 1941, is reprinted in FRUS, 1941, IV, pp. 672–75; also Adolf A. Berle
diary entry, quoted in WOHLSTETTER, p. 264.

For the "winds message" complex, by far the best analysis of this murky and
controversial topic is in WOHLSTETTER, pp. 52, 62 f., 186, 204, 214 ff., 226,
307–8, 388; texts, *ibid.*, 214 ff. The complete compilation of pertinent mate-
rial is in PHA, Vol. 18, pp. 3303–31 (see table of contents attached to Exh.
142). For interception of "winds code" in the Netherlands East Indies, see
Safford's "handwritten note given to Adm. Hewitt or Lt. Comdr. Sonnett,"
May 30, 1945, reporting on his conversation with Walter Foote, who was
American "Consul General at Batavia, Java, from 1927 until the capture of
Java by the Japanese in 1942" (in PHA, Exh. 151, Vol. 18, pp. 3343–44); for
Foote's own pertinent telegram to the State Dept., FRUS, 1941, IV, p. 713,
dated Dec. 4, 1941, 10 A.M., and ending with the comment: "I attach little
or no importance to it and view it with some suspicion. Such have been
common since 1936." Bratton's views of the "winds code" were expressed
repeatedly during his testimonies, most forcefully in PHA, Vol. 9, pp. 4515–16,
where he said that "undue emphasis" had been placed on this complex in
testimonies (mostly by Safford) before the various investigation bodies.

Original documents used in this chapter include the draft of Gen. Marshall's warning message of Nov. 27, 1941; "Memorandum for the President,"
by Gen. Marshall and Adm. Stark, Nov. 27, 1941; a message of Gen. Adams,
the Adjutant General, to Gen. Short, dated Nov. 26, 1941, advising him of
the flight of two B-24 aircraft "for special photo mission . . . to Truk Island
in the Caroline Group and Jaluit in the Marshall Group"; and Gen. Gerow's
memorandum for Gen. Marshall about the Nov. 27 meeting in Sec. Stimson's
office.

23 Japan Deploys for War

For the imperial conference of Dec. 1, 1941, see BUTOW, pp. 258–63; HATTORI, I, pp. 229–37; Togo, *op. cit.*, pp. 240–43, 234–55; affidavits of Gen. Tojo (FEMT, Exh. Nos. 2954 and 2955), Shimada (pp. 34664–67), Kaya (pp. 30655–58), Suzuki (pp. 35224–25); Tojo's interrogation, Feb. 6, 8, 11, Mar. 1, 1946; depositions of Kumaichi Yamamoto, FEMT, Def. Doc. 2014, Exh. 2915, pp. 11–12, Def. Doc. 2686, Exh. 3444; Kido's affidavit. The full text of Togo's explanation in FEMT, Def. Doc. 1892, Exh. 2955. Resolution from "Record of Imp. Conferences" in FEMT, Doc. 1652, Exh. 588, p. 7. For sequence of events: "Time Chart for Dec. 6, 7, and 8, 1941," FEMT, Doc. 2665; *Taiheiyo senso zenshi* (The Historical Background of the Pacific War), by Tokuzo Aoki (Tokyo, 1953), 3 vols.

The crash of Maj. Sugisaka's plane is related on the basis of HATTORI, I, pp. 364–67; for background, see BUTOW, pp. 369–70; KIRBY, pp. 127–29. Sugiyama-Nagano audience: from HATTORI, p. 365. War messages, *ibid.*, pp. 363–64. The progress of the striking forces is from data in MORISON, "Outward Passage of the Striking Force," pp. 88–94, "The Advance Expeditionary Force," pp. 95–98; also Fuchida, *op. cit.*, Fukudome, *op. cit.*; depositions of Adm. Kusaka (FEMT, Def. Doc. 1974, Exh. 3010, pp. 4–5); Capt. Fuchida (*ibid.*, Def. Doc. 1982, Exh. 3008); Capt. Genda (*ibid.*, Def. Doc. 1974, Exh. 3009); also Lord, *op. cit.*, pp. 8–27. *Tatsuta Maru* episode: from HATTORI, I, p. 235.

For activities of Kumaichi Yamamoto, see his depositions, and draft of documents, in FEMT, Doc. 3134B, Exh. 2975B; activities of Japanese consulate general in Hawaii, see notes to previous chapters; cook's telephone call, from Shivers affidavit, PHA, Vol. 35, p. 43. The work of the Cable Section is described on the basis of Kameyama's affidavit and testimonies (*q.v.*), and Takagi, *op. cit.*, and Toshiyuki Yokoi, *op. cit.*; also interrogation of Code Room personnel by USNTM. Telegrams in PHA, pp. 208–48.

Movements of Japanese forces in East Asia: from HATTORI, KIRBY; and Tsuji, *op. cit.*, pp. 67–79. Incident in Batavia: PHA, Vol. 18, pp. 3343–44.

Controversy concerning declaration of war and timing of delivery: Togo, *op. cit.*; Kase affidavit, FEMT, Def. Doc. 2063, Exh. 2960; Ward, *op. cit.*, p. 1279; HATTORI, I, pp. 312, 355; statement by Rear Adm. Tomioka, quoted by Morton, *op. cit.*, p. 121; *Japan and Her Destiny*, by Mamoru Shigemitsu (London, 1958), pp. 266, 268; "On the Declaration of War Against the United States and Great Britain," by the chief of the Treaty Bureau, Min. For. Aff., in PHA, Vol. 18, p. 2944–45; "Investigation of the Problem of Initial Hostile Action at the Outset of War," conducted by a group of international lawyers for Min. For. Aff., AMFA, Reel WT54; "Draft of a Public Statement to be Made by the Ministry of Foreign Affairs Concerning the Termination of Negotiations Between Japan and the U.S.," *ibid.*, Reel WT39; memorandum by Torao Ogata, chief secretary to the Higashikuni Cabinet (1945), concerning the circumstances surrounding the opening of hostilities, *ibid.*, Reel WT82; transcript of Prince Higashikuni's press conference on same subject, Sep. 18, 1945; "Declaration of War Against the U.S. and Great Britain," draft of the Imperial Rescript, from the files of the Privy Council, AMFA, Reel WT51.

The Tsuji quote is from his *op. cit.*, p. 74; Hattori's intelligence estimate, from HATTORI, I, p. 357. Transmission of Japanese telegrams: from Kameyama affidavit; also schedule in PHA, Vol. 14, pp. 1413–16; and Kase interrogation by USNTM. Also, *Sunk: The Story of the Japanese Submarine Fleet*, by Mochitsura Hashimoto (N.Y., 1954); and Lord, *op. cit.*

24 A Week of Indecision

The crisis in traffic intelligence, see Layton testimony in PHA, Vol. 36, pp. 116–41; also Vol. 10, pp. 4836–39, 4906 (where he ventured the startling opinion that "contrary to the testimony of the Japanese, the ships that attacked Pearl Harbor were never addressed after Nov. 16," and that "the code signal for attack, 'Climb Mount Niitaka,' had never been sent"). A critical analysis of the ordeal of radio intelligence on the eve of Pearl Harbor was prepared in 1945–46 by this author and is included in ZACHARIAS (b), "The Lessons of Pearl Harbor—I. The Test of Intelligence," pp. 225–36; also see McCollum and Rochefort, as noted above.

For the controversy over the tapping of the Japanese consulate's phone, see Capt. Mayfield in PHA, Vol. 36, and Lt. Woodrum, *ibid.*, and Shivers affidavit in Vol. 35; additional information from Col. Bicknell; Shivers testimonies, PHA, Vols. 23, pp. 1401–47, and 31, pp. 3201–25. For U.S. Navy's refusal to co-operate with British Admiralty on communications: FRUS, 1941, IV, p. 711. For the tentative character of the Hull note, see FEIS, p. 320. The note, as handed to Nomura and Kurusu, carried the notation: "Strictly Confidential, Tentative and Without Commitment." In a postwar letter to Zacharias, Adm. Nomura described his failure to transmit the notation with the note as his "worst blunder."

For events at Warm Springs, Ga., in connection with Tojo's speech: *Roosevelt and the Warm Springs Story*, by Turnley Walker (N.Y., 1953), pp. 263–66; interview with Comdr. Fox; also HULL, II, 1089–90; Grew's telegram, FRUS, p. 707. For text of Tojo's speech: AP dispatch in the *N.Y. Times*, Nov. 30, 1941, also FRUS, *Japan: 1931–1941*, II, pp. 148–49; for Japanese "apology": *ibid.*, p. 778; Togo, *ibid.*, p. 149; LANGER-GLEASON, p. 909.

Intercepts awaiting F.D.R.: Kramer on Terasaki as "head of Japanese espionage in Western Hemisphere," PHA, Vol. 9, p. 4201 (Intercept File No. 7140, Vol. 12, pp. 234–35); Kameyama's telegrams, *ibid.*, pp. 208–12; Togo's telegram to Oshima in Berlin, *ibid.*, 204, 205–6; also "File of Japanese Embassy in Berlin," AMFA, Reels UD17–19, and *Nazi Conspiracy and Aggression* (Nuremberg trials), I, pp. 866–68, and V, 566 ff.; FEMT, Exh. 802; FEIS, pp. 329–30, 336. For OPNAV signals Dec. 2, 1941, to Adm. Hart, and Dec. 3 to Hart and Adm. Kimmel, Commandant 14th and 16th Naval Distr., see PHA, Vol. 13, "Basic Exhibit of [Navy Department] Dispatches," pp. 1407–8. The supersecret code word "Purple" was mentioned in the Dec. 3 signal to Hart.

For the loss of the Japanese naval code: testimonies of Safford and Rochefort. For arrangements with cable companies in Honolulu: PHA, Vols. 10, p. 4676, and 35, p. 836; Wilkinson, 26, p. 307; Mayfield, 36, pp. 331–32; Woodrum, 36, pp. 224–25; George Street, 36, pp. 243–44. For efforts to read intercepts received from RCA: testimony of Lt. Woodward, 36, pp. 350–52; Rochefort, 10, pp. 4677, 4686; Dyer 36, pp. 247–49.

For F.D.R.-Quezon controversy: PHA, Vol. 21, pp. 4491–511, with enclosures. References to Churchill: from his *op. cit.*, p. 505, 599; also FEIS, pp. 334–35. For Yamamoto's communications with Nomura, see PHA, Vol. 12, p. 178; phone conversation using "hidden words" code, *ibid.*, pp. 179, 188–91. Typical examples of U.S. "bureaucratic diplomacy" during these days: FRUS,

1941, IV, pp. 661–65, 671, 672–75, 709–11; for contradictory view of diplomats, *ibid.*, p. 715.

For publication of secret U.S. war plans: Chicago *Tribune*, Dec. 4, 5, 1941; "A Military Danger: The Revelation of Secret Strategic Plans," by Capt. Tracy Barrett Kittridge, in USNIP, Vol. 81 (July 1955), pp. 731–43; *The Chief of Staff: Pre-War Plans and Preparations*, by Mark S. Watson (Washington, 1951), p. 359; LANGER-GLEASON, pp. 735–41, 923–24; Sec. Stimson's press conference, Washington *Post*, Dec. 6, 1941; SHERWOOD, pp. 410–18; for text of the compromised plans, see "Copies of Defense Plans," PHA, Vol. 15, pp. 1423–70.

For Yoshikawa's and other intelligence reports: "Analysis of Espionage Messages Sent by Ensign Yoshikawa to Chief, Section 5, Third Bureau, Naval General Staff," based on reprint of intercepts, PHA, Vol. 12, pp. 254–316. Bratton's activities on Dec. 3: see notes for Ch. 22; his dispatch to Col. Fielder, PHA, Vols. 34, pp. 21–22; 9, pp. 4594–96; also affidavits by Fielder (Vol. 35, pp. 87–89), Rochefort (*ibid.*, pp. 22–23, 26–27); Margaret McKinney (*ibid.*, pp. 28–29); Mary L. Ross (*ibid.*, pp. 36–37).

For "winds code," see Safford's testimony (that spark-plugged the controversy) before PHA, Vol. 27, pp. 109–91, also in Army Board's "Report," PHA, Vol. 3, pp. 1445–47, and Cramer's critical comments, *ibid.*, pp. 1463–66; Safford's more detailed testimony, Vol. 8, pp. 3579–95, and Vol. 36, *passim*. Also testimony of Col. Sadtler, Vol. 34, pp. 64–69, and his affidavit in Vol. 35, pp. 98–100; Col. Friedman, *ibid.*, pp. 35–36, also in Vol. 36, pp. 305–8; Adm. Noyes, Vols. 32–33, pp. 1026–51; memo from Comdr. John Ford Baecher to Seth Richardson, May 22, 1946, Vol. 11, p. 5477, listing all "references to and all messages quoted concerning the winds code in the compilation of so-called 'History'" written in 1942 of the activity of the Communication [Security] Unit," presumably compiled by Safford. Controversy over erroneous or misleading translation of winds code, see Friedman's testimony, PHA, Vols. 36–38, pp. 307–8; also WOHLSTETTER, pp. 224–25, apparently based on interview with Friedman; Brotherhood, PHA, Vols. 32–33, pp. 919A–30; Vol. 36, pp. 143–47.

25 "Magic" on the Eve

For Safford's schedule on Dec. 6, 1941, see PHA, Vol. 8, pp. 3558, 3562–63, 3574–75, 3577; for Kramer's, *ibid.*, pp. 4157–221. For documentation of the incident involving Mrs. Edgers, see her testimony, in PHA, Vols. 36, pp. 303–18; Kramer, 9, pp. 4167–74; Safford, 36, p. 317. The crucial telegram with Kühn's "simplified signal system" is in PHA, Vol. 12, pp. 267–68. The analysis of espionage messages is based on data from:

(a) "Log of Outgoing Messages [of the Japanese consulate general in Honolulu]," to Foreign Ministry, Seattle, Los Angeles, San Francisco; (b) "Matching of Telegrams" to Washington, New York, and other Japanese diplomatic outposts; (c) "Japanese Messages concerning Milit. Installations, Ship Movements, etc."; (d) "Index of Translations and Memoranda Re: Pearl Harbor," PHA, Vols. 11 and 35. Mrs. Edgers died in Tokyo in 1957.

Translation of Yoshikawa's telegram of Dec. 6, 1941: from testimony of Col. A. B. Laswell and Lt. Woodward, PHA, Vol. 36, pp. 319–23; and Capt. Joseph Finnegan, *ibid.*, pp. 251–52. Gen. Cramer's assessment of intelligence: from Vol. 3, pp. 1466, 1475–76; also see memorandum of Col. Clausen to Special Assistant in the Office of Secretary of War, "Pearl Harbor as Attack

Target," Vol. 35, p. 120; and his Exh. Nos. 5 a, b, c, d; 7 a, b.
Functions and activities of SIS on Dec. 6 are described on the basis of data
in testimonies and affidavits of Col. Minckler, PHA, Vol. 35, pp. 217–18; Col.
Doud, ibid., pp. B223–24; Col. Schukraft, ibid., p. 201; Lt. Col. Rowlett,
ibid., pp. 67, 225–26; Miss Louise Prather, ibid., p. 232; Miss Mary J.
dunning, ibid., pp. B229–31; Capt. Martin, ibid., pp. 227–28.
  For "Pilot Message," see log printed in PHA, Vol. 14, p. 1413; references to
this intercept abound in the various transcripts; for its text, see ibid., p. 238.
For delay in forwarding this intercept: Kramer, PHA, Vol. 9, 4188, 4199, 4207;
Bratton, ibid., pp. 4536–37, 4574.
  For Bratton's mounting apprehensions, see ibid., pp. 4530, 4534, 4557–58,
4563; and his conversations with McCollum, ibid., pp. 4580–81; McCollum's
analysis, PHA, Vol. 36, pp. 29–30. Delay in delivering Winant cables to G-2:
PHA, Vol. 9, p. 4570. Interception of 14-part note: Safford, PHA, Vol. 4, pp.
3562–63; Bratton, ibid., pp. 4512–13, 4523, 4527, and Vols. 1–11, passim.
Also see PHA, Vol. 35, pp. 206–8; affidavit of Col. Dusenbury, ibid., pp.
49–51. For Kramer's nocturnal deliveries, see Hoehling, op. cit., pp. 152–56;
and Kramer's own testimonies.

26 F.D.R.—December 6, 1941

Roosevelt's "day before Pearl Harbor" had to be reconstructed bit by bit from
widely scattered sources, including the President's appointment book (in the
Library at Hyde Park, tantalizingly incomplete); the White House telephone
log (compiled post festa from whatever notes the switchboard operators kept):
see PHA, Vol. 15, p. 1633; and such books as F.D.R., My Boss, by Grace Tully
(N.Y., 1949); This Is Pearl, by Walter Millis (N.Y., 1947); Franklin D.
Roosevelt, by Alden Hatch (N.Y., 1949); SHERWOOD, pp. 423–27; How War
Came, by Forrest Davis and Ernest K. Lindley (N.Y., 1942); White House
Physician, by Vice-Admiral Ross T. McIntire (N.Y., 1946); In Brief Author-
ity, by Francis Biddle (N.Y., 1956); LANGER-GLEASON, pp. 927–33; FEIS, pp.
337–39; The Secret Diary of Harold L. Ickes, Vol. 3: The Lowering Clouds
(N.Y., 1954); PHA, Report, pp. 429–31; also dispatches in the N.Y. Times
and Washington Post, Dec. 6, 7, 1941. The reference to Budget Director
Harold Smith is from Hoehling (op. cit., pp. 115–16), who had access to Mr.
Smith's diary. Additional information from Mrs. Jack Lewis who was White
House correspondent of Newsweek at this time and permitted me to draw
upon her diary and files.
  For scrambler phone at the White House: the N.Y. Times, Oct. 8, 1939;
and ibid., Magazine, Sep. 22, 1941, p. 5. For Amb. Winant's telegrams, see
PHA, Vol. 2, pp. 493–95; ibid., Vols. 14, pp. 1246–47, and 19, pp. 3648–51;
also Letter from Grosvenor Square, by John Gilbert Winant (Boston, 1947).
The Grew quotation is from GREW, p. 469; F.D.R.'s statement about intelligence: from Burn After Reading, by Ladislas Farago (loc. cit.), p. 205; also
see ibid., pp. 188–204, a description of the U.S. intelligence community on
the eve of the Pearl Harbor attack.
  For the intelligence aspects of the disaster, see WOHLSTETTER, which is
primarily an analysis of the failure of the American intelligence system to warn
of the impending attack and enable the policy makers to make the appropriate
decisions and arrangements to meet the onslaught. Also see her "Cuba and
Pearl Harbor: Hindsight and Foresight," in Foreign Affairs (July 1965), pp.

691–707; and "The Failure of Intelligence Predictions," by Benno Wasserman, *Pol. Studies*, Vol. 8 (June 1960), pp. 156–69. Intelligence available on Dec. 6 (in PHA): from "Documents concerning Intelligence Information relating to Japanese Military and Naval Units in the Far East," Exh. 21; "Compilation of the Location of U.S. and Japanese Naval Forces, as of Dec. 7, 1941," Vols. 20, pp. 4121–31; ONI reports in 15, pp. 1768–73; ONI "Fortnightly Summary," Dec. 1, 1941, in 15, pp. 1837–63; "Selection of ONI Memoranda Reporting Japanese Fleet Locations, Nov. 4–Dec. 3, 1941," *ibid.*, pp. 1870–1900; symbols and maps, Vol. 16, p. 2444; "Estimates of Japanese Forces in Indo-China," 20, pp. 4115–20.

Also KIRBY, pp. 116–17, 179–82; "Japanese Naval Air Operations in the Philippines Invasion," by Brig. Gen. Koichi Shimada, with Clarke H. Kawakami and Roger Pineau, USNIP, Vol. 81 (Jan. 1955), pp. 1–17; MORISON, pp. 187–88. Failure to detect Japanese approach to Pearl Harbor: *ibid.*, pp. 127–29. For Adm. Hart's report, with Capt. Schuirmann's memo, see PHA, Vols. 2, pp. 493–94, and 15, pp. 1680–81. Hart's "scouting forces" did not include the "defense information patrol" of picket ships the President had ordered him to assemble and send into the waters around Indochina—hostilities commenced before the patrol could be organized. In this connection Dr. Neumann wrote in *America Encounters Japan* (p. 277): "Since Admiral Hart was already conducting what the Navy Department considered adequate reconnaissance by planes and submarines, this unusual request for picket ships suggested to one of their commanders that they were being sent out to provide an inexpensive casus belli." Also see "The Strange Assignment of U.S.S. *Lanikai*," by Rear Adm. Kemp Tolley (who was in command of one of the picket ships), in USNIP, Vol. 88 (Sep. 1962), pp. 71–83.

The shooting down of the British reconnaissance plane: from HATTORI, I, p. 367, and KIRBY, p. 181. For schedule of deliveries to F.D.R., see FEMT, Def. Doc. 1500-J-6, Exh. 2969; also PHA, Vol. 11, pp. 5480–81.

The Casey mission to F.D.R. continues to remain one of the mysteries of the pre-Pearl Harbor diplomacy. LANGER-GLEASON (pp. 915 and 918) bemoaned the "absence of any record of these conversations." Describing whatever little documentation there is as "mere scraps of evidence," they wrote (p. 920): "This phase of the pre-Pearl Harbor crisis is so poorly documented that it has invited very compromising interpretations." For these "compromising interpretations," see Beard, *op. cit.*; *Pearl Harbor: The Story of the Secret War* by George Morgenstern (N.Y., 1947); *The Final Secret of Pearl Harbor*, by Rear Adm. Robert A. Theobald (N.Y., 1954); *The Truth About Pearl Harbor*, by John T. Flynn (N.Y., 1944); and a number of critical articles Dr. Harry Elmer Barnes published in *Perpetual War for Perpetual Peace* (Caldwell, 1953). These books stimulated what Kenneth S. Davis, in *Experience in War* (N.Y., 1956), called the "conspiracy theory of history," according to which Roosevelt had "plotted" the attack on Pearl Harbor. The conspiracy theory was met head on by Adm. S. E. Morison and discredited in MORISON, pp. 127–42. Also see his review of the Beard book ("History Through a Beard") in *Atlantic Monthly*; an editorial in the N.Y. *Times*, Dec. 12, 1945; and *Roosevelt in Retrospect: A Profile in History*, by John Gunther (N.Y., 1950), pp. 318, 321.

In the present book, the Casey mission was reconstructed from data in LANGER-GLEASON, p. 928; FEIS, 308, 312, 335, 337; PHA, Vol. 11, pp. 5165–66, and *Report*, pp. 429–31; testimony of Adm. Stark, *ibid.*, pp. 5215–19. Also see *Parliamentary Debates*, House of Rep., Canberra, Australia, V. 169. Miss

Tully's letter to S. W. Richardson was reprinted in PHA, Vol. 11, p. 5510; other pertinent correspondence and memoranda, *ibid.*, pp. 5508–9. The incident in Australia: from testimony of Lt. O'Dell, PHA, Vol. 34, pp. 59–66; also in PHA, Vol. 9, pp. 4504–14; Bratton, *ibid.*, pp. 4564–70. For the repercussions of the Casey mission, see testimony of Capt. Creighton, PHA, Vol. 10, pp. 5080–89, claiming that he could not remember the source of his information and thought that what he had reported was "really nothing more than rumor." The testimony elicited this comment from LANGER-GLEASON (p. 921): "If so, it remains inexplicable that a message of such gravity should have been transmitted by a responsible officer on the basis of mere talk. The truth or falsity of this telegram is among the important problems relating to Pearl Harbor which have yet to be verified." Also see testimony of Sumner Welles in PHA, Vol. 2, p. 493, and other relevant material in PHA, Vol. 10, p. 4803; "Interrogatories and Replies of Brigadier General Francis G. Brink," (the American military attaché in Singapore), PHA, Vol. 11, 5514–16.

For Hart-Phillips conversations and accord, see MORISON, p. 157; PHA, Vol. 14, p. 1412 and pp. 1933–34. From the voluminous documentation of F.D.R.'s message to the Emperor: FRUS, 1941, IV, pp. 697–98, 721–25, 726–27; and PHA, Vol. 15, pp. 1727–34. Mr. Hull's opposition was forcefully stated on Nov. 29 in a memo to F.D.R. (FRUS, 1941, IV, p. 688) that contained the remark: "My personal view continues . . . to be that its sending will be of doubtful efficacy, except for the purpose of making a record." FEIS (pp. 335–36) found "no convincing record or account" that would have justified the Secretary's opposition; also see HULL, II, 1093–94.

The message was held up in Tokyo on orders of Gen. Tojo. It got to Amb. Grew for delivery to the Emperor via the Foreign Ministry only shortly before the attack. See affidavit of Kase, FEMT, Def. Doc. 2063, also pp. 26175–79; affidavit of Yasumasa Matsudaira, *ibid.*, pp. 26179–81. News of the arrival of the telegram with the President's appeal was withheld even from For. Min. Togo, who learned about it from a UP dispatch from Washington and sent a frantic query to Nomura for clarification. The telegram was finally delivered to Grew in the evening, and was submitted to Togo at 12:15 A.M., Dec. 8 (Tokyo time). Togo presented it to the Emperor at around 3 A.M., twenty minutes before the attack on Pearl Harbor was mounted. For details, see Grew affidavit, FEMT, trscpt. pp. 10967–79, 10986–89, his *Ten Years in Japan*, pp. 486–93, and his *The Turbulent Years*, pp. 1249–53. Text of the President's message in FRUS, *Japan: 1931–1941*, II, pp. 784–86. For a brilliant account of this incident, see BUTOW, pp. 387–93.

Lt. Schulz's mission to F.D.R.: from his testimony in PHA, Vol. 10, pp. 4659–71; also testimony of Beardall, PHA, Vol. 11, pp. 5271–73; FEIS, p. 339; Hoehling, *op. cit.*, pp. 135, 150–52, 158; testimony of Capt. Harold D. Krick, USN, the last witness before the Joint Committee, see PHA Vol. 11, pp. 5555–60; LANGER-GLEASON, pp. 932–34; and especially SHERWOOD, pp. 426–27.

27 The Creeping Hours

The few Marshall biographies offered little help in the preparation of the Chief of Staff's activities on Dec. 7, 1941, nor were the general's own testimonies of much use. There is virtually nothing on this topic in *Marshall: Citizen Soldier*, by William Frye (Indianapolis, 1947); and the account of the day presented in *The Marshall Story: A Biography of General George C. Marshall*, by Robert Payne (N.Y., 1951) is impressionistic and superficial. (However, it contains this interesting observation on p. 155: "For a brief while the destiny of America had been in Colonel Bratton's hands. If he had come to the office a little earlier, if he had read the message a little more quickly, if he had telephoned to Marshall even a few seconds before he actually telephoned, if it had occurred to him to order an airplane up to find Marshall as he went riding alone on that sunlit morning, if any of these things had happened, the message which should have been sent to Hawaii might have been received in time.") Even *George C. Marshall*, by Forrest C. Pogue, Vol. 2 (N.Y., 1966), supposedly the definitive biography based on the general's papers, added little new to what was already amply known from the published records.

However, excellent background data was found in *Together: Annals of an Army Wife*, by Katherine Tupper Marshall (N.Y., 1946); and in Mark Watson's *Chief of Staff* (*q.v.*), a penetrating study of this remarkable institution by the late military editor of the Baltimore *Sun*. Invaluable original material was generously supplied by Brig. Gen. Frank McCarthy, wartime secretary of the War Department General Staff, and Mr. John Speakman of Harrisburg, Pa., one of the general's orderlies.

For Marshall's innate aloofness, see Mrs. Marshall, pp. 78, 89–90; for the routine of life in Quarters No. 1, pp. 56–58. The McIntire reference is from his *op. cit.* For opinions on Capitol Hill, see the N.Y. *Times*, Dec. 7, 1941. Schedules of Miles and Gerow: from their testimonies, affidavits and memoranda, in PHA, *passim*.

For Safford's absence during the day: his testimony in PHA, Vol. 8, pp. 3574–75. Work in Op-20-G is described on the basis of Safford's account (*ibid.*, pp. 3572, 3574–75, 3577); and the testimonies in PHA of Lynn (Vols. 32, pp. 734–40, and 36, pp. 140–42); Brotherhood (*ibid.*, pp. 919A–30 and 143–47, respectively); Pering (Vol. 33, pp. 812–15); Lt. Comdr. Allan A. Murray (Vol. 36, pp. 433–41). The sequence of interceptions: from PHA, Vol. 14, pp. 1413–16; and from Safford's index of intercepts (Vol. 34, pp. 190–98), which also contains many illuminating "briefs" and remarks. For the receipt of intercepts Nos. 902, 907 and 910, see Pering testimony; Kramer, PHA, Vols. 8, pp. 3893–4221, *passim*; 36, pp. 128–39, 576–96; 37, pp. 950–87; also WOHLSTETTER, "Late Signals," pp. 40–70, and "Last-minute Magic," pp. 219–27; Hoehling, *op. cit.*, pp. 150, 152–53, 155–56, 158, 161, 163, 171–72. (My request for an interview with Capt. Kramer elicited no response.)

For Safford's contention and the repudiation by Kramer, see PHA, Vol. 8, pp. 4179–83; as Kramer himself put it (p. 4182): "I swear to it, Senator, and have always sworn that I never intended in the least to imply that those remarks I made indicated an attack on Pearl Harbor or, in fact, any overt intention on the part of the Japanese directed toward the U.S." No amount of coaxing by the Republican members of the Joint Committee could make him change his stand.

For Pearl Harbor before the attack: MORISON, pp. 98–100; *Hawaii, A History*, by Kuykendall and Day (*q.v.*), pp. 253–55; and ALLEN (a), pp. 1–3; also see *History of the U.S. Army MIDPAC*, microfilm in HWRD, Vol. 1, pp. 34–62; interviews with Col. Bicknell, Chief of Police Liu and Naoji Yamagata, as well as those conducted by Dr. Steele F. Stewart, in HWRD; Hoehling, *op. cit.*, pp. 181–85; *But Not in Shame*, by John Toland (N.Y.), pp. 7–10,

15–17, 20–28. About the rumors: MORISON, p. 142; Rochefort, PHA, Vol. 37, p. 552; and rumor studies in HWRD.

Condor-Ward incident: from testimonies in PHA of Comdr. Hubell (Vol. 36, pp. 253–55); Capt. Outerbridge (ibid., pp. 55–60); Lt. Underkofler (ibid., pp. 275–78); Radioman 3/C Richard W. Humphrey (ibid., pp. 245–46): Lt. Comdr. Harold Kaminsky (Vol. 23, pp. 1035–41); Comdr. V. R. Murphy (Vol. 26, pp. 209–10). The action is summarized in MORISON, pp. 96–97. For the operation of the gate, see ibid., p. 97; Hubell's testimony; and Adm. Stark's correspondence with Adm. Kimmel, in PHA, Vol. 17, pp. 2700–7. For Hawaii's defenses in general, standing plan and standard operating procedures: PHA, Vols. 15, pp. 1645–76; 16, pp. 1937–40; 17, pp. 2707–12.

Secr. Knox tried to persuade Congress to appropriate funds for "the protection of the Navy's Shore Establishments," including those at Hawaii. When he failed to get the money, he wrote to the chairman of the House Appropriations Committee that he had done all in his powers to meet his "grave responsibility," and now felt that further responsibility "for any catastrophe which might occur in a Shore Establishment of the Navy" no longer rested with him. (See SHERWOOD, p. 435: cf. Knox's letter to Stimson, mentioned in Ch. 11).

Bratton's activities, see notes for Ch. 22. His specific references to Gen. Marshall, and reconstruction of the events of the morning: PHA, Vol. 9, pp. 4517–19, 4525–26, 4529, 4546–49, 4552–55; and Vol. 34, pp. 10–30, 69–74. Miles memorandum: PHA, Vol. 9, p. 4551. Also see "Memoranda for the Record on Events of Dec. 7, 1941," in PHA, Vol. 14, pp. 140912; also testimonies of Gerow and Miles, and Gerow's memo to Marshall, dated Dec. 15, 1941; General Marshall's pertinent testimonies in PHA: Vols. 27–31; 22–25; 32–33; 3, 11.

For activities of Stark and his aides in the Navy Department, see their testimonies, and especially "Log of the Watch Officer, Office of the Chief of Naval Operations, from 1145, Dec. 6, 1941, to 2000, Dec. 7, 1941," in PHA, Vol. 19, pp. 3508–33. Kramer in State Dept.: affidavits by Maxwell Hamilton, PHA, Vol. 16, p. 2015; Stone, Vol. 35, pp. 203–4; George W. Renchard, ibid., p. 202; testimony of Dr. Hornbeck, Vol. 33, pp. 763–72. For Adm. Stark, PHA, Vol. 32, pp. 2–194, 320–24, 774–810; Hoehling (based on "prolonged interviews" with Stark), op. cit., pp. 154–55, 160–67. For Stark's characterization as "lacking ruthlessness, etc.," from SHERWOOD.

Kalbfus quote: from 1942 ed. of his book, p. 140; Stimson quote, from PHA, Vol. 11, p. 5248, and his On Active Service loc. cit., p. 392; for Adm. Kimmel and his functions, see PHA, Vol. 17, pp. 2832–66; training program and schedules in Pearl Harbor, Exh. 113-A, 113-B, 113-C, 114; and Kimmel memo, Dec. 5, 1941 (on "Steps to Be Taken in Case of War with Japan Within the Next 24 Hours"), PHA, Vol. 17, pp. 2714–15.

Sign on Marshall's door was put there by McCarthy; also see, Mrs. Marshall, op. cit., p. 59. Narrative of Gen. Marshall's message to Gen. Short: from PHA, Vol. 34, pp. 6–7; testimony of Col. French, ibid., pp. 31–34, and his affidavit in Vol. 35, pp. B81–82; testimonies in Vol. 25, pp. 1842–47, and Vol. 31, pp. 186–206. Processing of message in San Francisco and Honolulu: from Mr. Henry Mortara, District Manager, RCA Communications, Inc., Honolulu; I am also grateful to Messrs. Arthur T. Murray, Plant Manager, ITT World Communications, Inc., and Ira F. Stinson, Government Relations, ITT, both in Washington, for useful information and demonstrations regarding the transmission and delivery of messages.

Timetable of Japanese moves: FEMT, Doc. 2665. Final preparations for the attack: Fuchida, *op. cit.*, p. 945. For President Roosevelt's day, see McIntire, *op. cit.*; and especially *The Time Between the Wars*, by Jonathan Daniels (Garden City, 1966), pp. 336–46.

28 "This Is Pearl!"

Last-minute activities at the Japanese embassy: from Yuki's affidavit; *The Lost War*, by Masuo Kato (N.Y., 1946), a journalist who was present at the embassy; Kurusu, *op. cit.*; Nomura, *op. cit.*; and recollections of Code Clerks Takeshi Kajiwara, Masana Horiuchi, Hiroshi Hori. The best account of the receipt of the news of the attack in Washington: in Daniels, *op. cit.*, pp. 341–42; also see MORISON, pp. 100–1; Hoehling, *op. cit.*, pp. 186–87; and the testimonies of Adms. Stark and Noyes.

For final Hull-Nomura-Kurusu meeting: HULL, II, pp. 1095–97; FRUS, *Japan: 1931–1941*, II, pp. 786, 793. In the morning of Dec. 7, Mr. Ballantine prepared a memo for Mr. Hull with suggestions for what to tell Amb. Nomura, but it was still predicated on the negotiations that the State Dept. expected would continue (see FRUS, 1941, IV, pp. 728–29). Delay of notes: see "'Treachery' of Pearl Harbor," by Kiyoaki Murata, from the *Nippon Times*, June 8, 1956, reprinted in USNP (Aug. 1956), pp. 904–6. Mr. Murata based his article on "revelations" by Itsuro Hayashi, a defense attorney at FEMT, which in turn were based on Yuki's affidavit. Reports on damage by Col. Smith: from War Department, Office of the Chief of Staff file.

Activities in the Honolulu consulate, see "The Consulate Prepares for War," based on statements by Takaichi Sakai, Kimie Doue, Ichitaro Ozaki and Richard Kotoshirodo, in "Espionage Activities, Japanese Consulate Honolulu," INV. REP., Feb. 15, 1943; also *ibid.*, Feb. 14, 1942, for Yoshikawa's last-minute espionage activities and the accuracy of his reports; YOSHIKAWA, p. 38; Hasegawa and Bicknell interviews; and documents in HWRD.

Delivery of Gen. Marshall's message to Ft. Shafter: interviews with Edward Klein, Fuchikama and Henry Mortara; also see PHA, Vols. 7, pp. 3163–64, and 11, p. 5297; Lord, *op. cit.*

For eyewitness stories of the attack, see compositions of Mercedes Correa, Charles Harkins, Paul Withington; diary of Charles Hite, Secretary of Hawaii; memorandum by James B. Mann; copies of KGMB broadcasts, all in HWRD; also *Good Evening*, by William Ewing (Honolulu, 1943); ALLEN (a), 4–8; and "Honolulu and the 7th of December 1941," *Western City*, Vol. 18 (Jan. 1942); also "Record of the Activities of the Military Department (Hawaii National Guard and Hawaii Territorial Guard), Dec. 7, 1941 to June 30, 1944"; and National Guard (Hawaii), *Annual Report of the Adjutant General*, 1941, in HWRD.

The final Japanese message is from Safford's index. Also see "Log of Radio News Broadcasts Given on Dec. 8 (Japanese Time), Japan Broadcasting System," by "Announcer Umino," FEMT, Doc. 1657-A and transcript of recorded broadcasts, Dec. 8, 1941 (from 6 A.M. to 9 P.M.), *ibid.*, Doc. 1633-A.

Index